# Growing Up in Twentieth-Century America

# Growing Up in Twentieth-Century America

## A History and Reference Guide

ELLIOTT WEST

**Greenwood Press**
Westport, Connecticut • London

Library of Congress Cataloging-in-Publication Data

West, Elliott.
    Growing up in twentieth-century America : a history and
reference guide / Elliott West.
        p.    cm.
    Includes bibliographical references and index.
    ISBN 0–313–28801–1 (alk. paper)
    1. Children—United States—History—20th century.  2. Children—
United States—History—20th century—Bibliography.  3. United
States—Social life and customs—20th century.  4. United States—
Social life and customs—20th century—Bibliography.    I. Title.
HQ792.U5W423    1996
305.23'0973—dc20        95–38652

British Library Cataloguing in Publication Data is available.

Library of Congress Catalog Card Number: 95–38652
ISBN: 0–313–28801–1

First published in 1996

Greenwood Press, 88 Post Road West, Westport, CT 06881
An imprint of Greenwood Publishing Group, Inc.

Printed in the United States of America

The paper used in this book complies with the
Permanent Paper Standard issued by the National
Information Standards Organization (Z39.48–1984).

10 9 8 7 6 5 4 3

Copyright Acknowledgments

The author and publisher gratefully acknowledge permission for use of the following
material:

Illustration of *Mad Magazine's* Alfred E. Neuman. MAD Magazine is trademark and
copyright © E.C. Publications, Inc. All rights reserved. Used with permission.

For Richard,
brother and friend

# Contents

# —— Acknowledgments ——

The research and writing of this book were done with generous support from Fulbright College of the University of Arkansas, Fayetteville, and with the encouragement of its dean, Bernard Madison. My thanks go to him and to my departmental chair, Daniel Sutherland, who also helped in any way he could. I am grateful to friends and colleagues up and down the hall—Randall Woods, Tom Kennedy, David Chappell, Jeannie Whayne, Elizabeth Payne, David Edwards, David Sloan and others—who gave good advice and kept me laughing through low points. With their ideas, questions, and generally outrageous behavior, my cyberpals on the Bobwahr helped more than they can know. Suzanne Smith, Mary Kirkpatrick, and Miriam Twyford all did their part with the many details needed to turn a rough manuscript into a book. Special appreciation goes to my graduate research assistant, Brian Miller, who did heroic legwork in chasing down leads and filling in the gaps.

Barbara Rader of Greenwood Publishing Group first approached me about this project. I blithely agreed to sign on, little realizing the size of the job. Barbara's guidance and advice have been enormously helpful along the way, and her patience and friendliness have made the task far more enjoyable than it might have been. Nita Romer has been equally supportive in the latter stages. Both are the most pleasant of taskmasters.

As usual my family has carried much of this load. My children up and away—Elizabeth, Bill, and Richard—and those still at home—Garth and Anne—have had to put up with their father's distraction. All have grown up knowing what a friend calls the historian's "hundred-year stare." I thank them for their forbearance. All along they have also given me countless insights into the complex business of being young and growing out of it. Indirectly they have let me into the equally complicated world of living and working as a parent. For all that, they have my deepest appreciation. My mother, Betsy West, has given her usual boundless encouragement and confidence. I am grateful, too, for the friendship of my brother George. From Suzanne Stoner, my wife and finest friend, I have received more than I can measure, much less repay.

I have dedicated this book to my older brother, Richard. When I try to recall my own childhood, he is always there. He still is, and my life is much the better for it.

# Introduction

How can we describe a "typical" American family during the early years of the 20th century? Such a family lived on an isolated farm, in a gloomy and crowded tenement, or in a quiet neighborhood of tree-lined streets. That family scraped by on the labor of the father, mother and seven children, who picked cotton, gathered rags, or washed and pressed shirts twelve hours a day; they passed their days in tidy schoolrooms and offices; they moved around the country looking for work. Come evening, they fell exhausted into bed or relaxed around a parlor organ, singing "I Want to Go Back to Michigan." They told how their ancestors had climbed a pine tree out of the earth and into their world; they read news from the old country and felt homesick for the forests of Lithuania, for the farm they remembered in southern China, or for the Mexican highlands. They complained about the dirt sifting from the roof of their sod house or about the taxes on their thousand-acre estate. They thanked God for the chance to come and work in America's packing yards or because no black folk or strange, garlic-smelling immigrants lived in their neighborhood of modest bungalows.

Ruiz, Larson, Williams, Limp, Johnson, and Blue Jacket; Chin, Green, Erickson, Goldstein, Chappell, and Gump; Payne, Finlay, Westermeier, Szasz, Lone Wolf, Smith, Marcos, Lewis, and Kim: they were as diverse and scattered in their ways and appearances and means of living as in any society in the history of the world. Nobody can describe the typical American family in 1900, because there wasn't one. There still isn't.

Telling *the* history of American children is impossible. Any statement made about young people—their homes, play, work, attitudes, fears, problems, and pleasures—can never be adequate. No matter how true it might be about some, it will almost surely be completely, laughably false about others. Nonetheless, it still is possible to find some general points to make about American girls and boys, something that tells us about the lives of many of them at a particular time during the past hundred years, and how those lives were changing.

In *Growing Up in Twentieth-Century America,* I have tried to bring together some generalizations that can teach us something both about children and about the society around them. But readers are warned: I have not tried to tell the whole story of children in this century. I have chosen to write about some topics and to leave others out. Rather than touching briefly on hundreds of subjects, my strategy has been to choose certain ones that I think hold important clues to understanding what it has been like to grow up in the United States since 1900. I have tried to look at each of these topics closely enough to suggest its significance. That has meant devoting several pages to Barbie dolls, child migrant workers, and IQ tests, for instance, while slighting or ignoring subjects that another historian might think are essential. It has been a selective process, but one that still has left room to tell a good deal about young America.

Readers will probably notice certain themes that run throughout the book. One is the diversity of children and their experiences. How a child has grown up has varied enormously, depending on many factors, including what part of the country we are looking at, the family's ethnic and cultural background, and whether that child lives in a city, suburb, small town, or farm. One of the most significant differences—and another theme—has been a family's wealth, or lack of it. Persistent poverty has set the experiences of millions of children apart from those of others and has made the history of our young people one full of ironies and contradictions. Yet another theme has been the crucial transforming role of technology in the lives of all Americans, but especially the youngest ones. Technology has contributed to another vital part of the story—the continuous efforts by young people to shape their own lives and futures, even as adults were trying to direct their children's days according to how they thought things ought to be. This pull-and-tug shows up in everything from schoolrooms to toy stores.

The most pervasive theme in these pages can be stated simply. Children and society cannot be understood apart from one another. Girls and boys are formed partly by their physical, cultural, and emotional surroundings; those surroundings in turn are continually changed and shaped by children's choices and evolving desires. This has been true everywhere and at all times, but in America during the 20th century, as will be shown, young people have had an unprecedented influence on the society around them. I have tried to suggest something of that interaction between children and American life—in public health and entertainments, foodways and law, housing and employment.

To give some structure to this sprawling subject, I have divided the 20th century into four periods, each with its own chapter. Each chapter in turn is divided into a brief introduction and six sections. The first section in each chapter, entitled "At Home," is devoted to a wide range of topics, including housing, eating habits, attitudes and values, and other aspects of daily life. The section "At Play" concerns children's amusements, toys, and leisure activities. "At Work" discusses young America's role in the economic life of the family and the nation, as well as the influence of work on children's lives. The next section, "At School," is about education, both schoolroom experiences and the broader connections between schooling and national life. Topics under the section entitled "Health" include some of the physical threats to children, medical developments that have reduced those threats, and public policies that have affected young people's well being. The final section in each chapter, "Children and the Law," takes up part of the complicated story of children's place in our legal system and what that story tells us about the way adult society has perceived its youth.

These divisions are artificial, of course. We cannot look at education without taking the law into account. Housing and health are bound together, and so are work and play. Still, I hope this arrangement is useful. A reader can stay with a single broad area, such as play and amusements, and move through the century, getting some sense of how some things have changed and others persisted. Or he or she can keep to one part of the century—the first years or the last, for instance—and look into different aspects of children's lives in those years. My goal has been a flexible organization for both browsing and research.

For each chapter I have also provided a bibliographical essay in which I mention books I found most useful in my research. Each essay is arranged to correspond roughly with the chapters' sections, and a reader in search of resources on a specific topic should be able to find something helpful without too much trouble. Together, these essays comprise an extended, elaborate invitation: they are a call to further study. The subject of American children in the 20th century is far, far too large for any one book. My best hope is to send readers off in search of more about this significant and revealing part of the story of America.

# Growing Up in Twentieth-Century America

# Chapter 1

# 1900–1920

## INTRODUCTION

The century that now is drawing to a close has been called "the century of the child." That phrase has little to do with numbers: boys and girls made up a much larger proportion of American society in 1800 than in 1900 or 1950. Rather, it refers to the ways adults have thought about children and the roles played by young people in their families and in society.

Much earlier in our nation's history children were considered something like imperfect adults. They came into the world like seeds of mature individuals, it was thought; and the job of parents and society was to provide good soil for their growth and to prune and trim them so they would grow up straight and well shaped. Children were also thought to be naturally wild and immoral. It was essential for adults to break that rebelliousness and to control them through strict discipline beginning in infancy. Only then would girls and boys grow to become good citizens and morally upright women and men.

A new view of children emerged in the 19th century and came into its full flowering in the 20th. In this perspective, childhood was seen as a unique and distinctive time of life. A boy or girl was not merely an adult in the making; he or she had ways of thinking and seeing the world utterly different from those of grownups. Children had their own emotional and psychological needs that responsible parents had to meet. To the extent that children had inherent qualities, they were considered innocent, almost angelic creatures who should be protected from a sinful world. But beyond that, a child's character and nature were largely formed by his or her surroundings and treatment. An infant was not inherently *anything*: the lessons and environment provided by the parents shaped the growing child.

Late in the 19th century this view of children was extended into the years of "adolescence"—a term coined and popularized during this period. Young people from about thirteen to twenty, later called "teenagers," also had their own emotional traits and demands, their distinctive crises and needs. These years were now seen as especially dangerous and trouble-filled. Young Americans were being introduced to adult responsibilities and work and encountering a world of temptations, even as they were experiencing the turbulent emotional storms of that stage of development. Once again, just as with infants and children, parents had to keep close and sensitive watch over their daughters and sons, providing counsel and guidance and carefully monitoring their adolescents' exposure to the world beyond the family.

With this new view of young America, parents carried a heavy load of responsibility. It was up to them to provide the right sort of environment for their children for at least the first twenty years of life. They had to pay close attention to their youngsters' evolving characters and their peculiar needs that changed year by year. The stakes were high. A new adult sent into the future was largely a product of the skills and care shown by his or her parents during the previous two decades.

This new view of childhood and adolescence moved young people more and more toward the center of the family's life. The complicated, challenging job of child rearing demanded of parents a new spirit of dedication. Closely related to this change was a new vision of the family itself. An older ideal—one dominated by a strong father exercising power firmly, but fairly—gave way to what historians call the "companionate family." The father was to share power with the mother and rely less on authority and more on love and affection. He was to be more like an equal companion, both to his wife and to his children. Feelings of sympathy and friendship were to bind the family together and furnish the ideal atmosphere for rearing children, which, after all, was now the family's main purpose.

So "the century of the child" refers to the time in our history when young Americans seemed to become, for many people, the center of their attention and concerns. This change, of course, was not universal. The new attitudes were more common among some groups than others, and even those who expressed the new values often fell far short of living up to them. The companionate family and the modern view of childhood were ideals. They told of broad and general changes in popular values.

Those changes, well underway during the years between 1900 and 1920, have continued to build and evolve through the rest of the century. (And adults have continued to violate and ignore those ideals, too.) As will be shown, the results have been all around us, not only in how parents and children have treated one another inside their homes, but also in public life: from our movies, songs, and advertising jingles to our eating habits, work, and laws.

In many other ways the first two decades of the 20th century were a fitting introduction to the America we have come to know. The United States was growing in population, in power, in influence among other nations, and in wealth, although millions still lived in terrible poverty. A transformation into a modern industrial economy, the second most rapid of any nation in history, had begun during the generation before the Civil War. Gathering momentum in the late 19th century, this great change culminated in the years after 1900. Both cities and farms were being made over by revolutions in technology, transportation, and communications, part of a broader shift in the lives of Americans of all ages.

During 1900–1920, a period historians call the "progressive era," our governments—local, state, and national—took on unprecedented powers and responsibilities, including part of the job of looking after the nation's children. For the first time we sent our men to die in a war that had begun outside our own part of the world, a conflict called the Great War at the time but later labelled World War I. This was a kind of terrible coming-out party, a bloody recognition that the United States had emerged as a muscular force on the world scene and a global economic power. These years witnessed technological innovations that, at the time, seemed truly miraculous. By 1920, millions of us were working, playing, dressing, feeding, and amusing ourselves in ways rare or unknown when the century opened.

Due in large part to immigration, the nation's population grew by about 30 million during these twenty years, or nearly 40 percent, from 76 million to 106 million people. The pace of growth had slowed considerably from that of a few generations earlier, but, although the birth rate was falling, children still made up a large part of American society. Just about one-third of all Americans during those years were under fourteen years old.

Those Americans were on the move, as their relatives had been since the birth of the republic and would continue to be through the century. Tens of thousands continued to move west, just as in the 19th century, but many more followed a different pattern, leaving farms and small towns for the cities. As the century opened, about 37 percent of Americans lived in towns and cities (up from 24 percent only twenty years earlier). During the next twenty years the trend continued. The census of 1920 reported that for the first time in our history more people lived in towns and cities (about 51 percent) than in the countryside. We became officially an urban nation.

And another population trend was at work. Nearly 15 million persons immigrated to the United States between 1900 and 1920. Most of these newcomers differed from those who had come to American shores a few decades earlier. In the "old" immigration before the mid–1870s, most immigrants had come from the British Isles and northern and western Europe. (Another important source of newcomers in the mid-19th century, Asians, particularly Chinese, had been essentially banned by laws in the 1880s. Only in the 1960s would they again be admitted in significant numbers.) The "old" immigration was soon overwhelmed by "new" immigrants from nations of southern and eastern Europe—Italy and Sicily, Poland, Russia, the Balkans and the Baltic countries. In one of the heaviest years of this foreign influx, 1914, nearly three-quarters of all immigrants came from southern and eastern Europe. These new arrivals carried with them customs very different from the ones that had been familiar to past generations, and American children growing up in these years were exposed to a wide range of traditions imported with the fresh arrivals. Many who had been born in this country, however, found these new Americans strange and in some ways threatening. New immigrants were changing America, and a lot of older residents didn't like it.

Immigration was only one source of stress and tension in American life. As in all times when change comes rapidly and runs deep, many worried about the implications for the future. And as always when people have concerns about the years ahead, their doubts frequently settled on the embodiment of tomorrow—the many children they saw around them.


### AT HOME

Nothing showed more clearly the great differences among American children than their immediate surroundings—their homes. Family houses ranged from mansions of almost unbelievable luxury to the most squalid and crowded hovels. Housing reflected regional and cultural variations, from Navajo hogans in the Southwest to log houses in the northern woods. Increasingly, however, common housing styles began to appear throughout the nation, the result of important, powerful forces that would make the styles of living more similar throughout the United States.

A few examples will clarify the diversity of homes in which children grew up. Some of the worst were the tenements built by the thousands in the rapidly growing cities. A tenement was the result of a basic dilemma of the city. The poorest workers found most of their work near the center of the city, where the cost of land was the highest. Families with the least money, then, had to find housing where living space was most expensive. The answer was obvious: crowd as many people as possible into the fewest possible square feet. A tenement neighborhood was lined with stone, brick, or wooden buildings, each three to six stories high. Each floor of each building housed two, three, or even four families. A typical apartment had two tiny "bedrooms," sometimes as small as seven-by-eight feet, and one larger room, perhaps twelve-by-ten, which served as a living area and kitchen. Here might live a family with two parents and five or more children and often an older relative, friend, or boarder as well. Each floor had a common toilet and sink in the dark central hall. The few windows let in little light, as the closely crowded buildings mostly blocked out the sun.

Stuffing so many people into so little space made parts of American cities the most crowded acreage in the world. The prime example was New York City's Lower East Side. This area, east of Broadway from the Battery to Houston Street, was the favored destination of many immigrants, especially the "new" immigrants from southern and eastern Europe. In 1910 the Lower East Side held nearly 400,000 persons, more than the population of the entire state of Montana. The population density was greater than in Calcutta, Tokyo, or any city on the planet. In many other urban areas, from Boston to Chicago, more than fifty thousand persons lived in every square mile. If you could walk those streets, you would notice right away the many children living in those crowded neighborhoods, for large families were common among the immigrant working classes. The New York journalist Jacob Riis told of a typical block where 180 children lived in only two buildings.

Many poorer families moved around frequently—floated, really—to find shelter wherever they could, staying with different family and friends or with whoever would have them. Ethel Waters, who would grow up to be one of the country's most respected African-American blues and gospel singers as well as a successful actress, spent her childhood in the Philadelphia slums. Only very rarely did she live in one place for more than a cou-

The most crowded place on earth. On New York City's lower east side, tens of thousands of children, many of them new arrivals from eastern Europe, worked and played and helped define what it meant to be "American." *Courtesy of Seaver Center for Western History Research, Natural History Museum of Los Angeles County.*

ple of weeks. One of her longer stays was in the heart of the city's prostitution district, where she shared a three-room hovel with her mother, grandmother, uncle, and two aunts. Ethel and her friends ran errands for prostitutes and used what they earned to buy food from street vendors:

> A bunch of us would often sleep all night on the street, over the warm
> iron gratings of bakeries or laundries. Our families didn't care where

we were, and these nesting places when you put your coat under you, were no more uncomfortable than the broken-down beds with treacherous springs or the bedbug-infested pallets we had at home.[1]

The wide–open countryside of rural Nevada or Idaho might seem the opposite extreme from the teeming streets of New York City or Chicago, but, in fact, the families and their homes in those places had a lot in common. In both cases people were trying to begin new lives with few resources, and they could not afford much living room. Houses were usually built with the minimum materials and at the least possible cost. Materials for a sod house on the Great Plains, briefly described in this chapter's section on children's work, might cost as little as twenty dollars. Where trees were available, families built log houses that took plenty of muscle power but little cash. Western settlers used every device imaginable to make shelter for themselves. They dug makeshift caves out of the sides of hills, converted their wagons into homes, and set up house in abandoned boxcars. Some in the Pacific Northwest hollowed out the huge stumps of recently felled trees, then moved in. For all their variety, most of these new western homes had a few points in common. They were usually simple rectangles, from twelve to twenty feet on a side. The interior might be a single room or might be divided into two or three small rooms. As in the city tenements, much of a boy's or girl's family life—eating and sleeping, arguing and playing—took place within these cramped quarters of two or three hundred square feet.

Elsewhere in the country, wherever poorer families could be found, children were growing up in crowded conditions. Throughout the South tenants and other small farmers lived in "shotgun" houses, introduced long before from West Africa. Here three or four rooms were strung straight together, with all doors lined up; supposedly a gun could be shot into the front door and out the back without hitting anything. Another common style was the "dogtrot," in which two rooms were connected by an unwalled, covered walkway; a kitchen, often only a lean-to, was attached to one side. This arrangement allowed the easy, free flow of breezes in that hot, sticky climate; and even more prosperous families found it sensible. Shirley Abbott remembered her grandmother's large dogtrot in central Arkansas:

The house Grandma lived in was as wide as a mansion, unpainted pine, with a porch that ran along the front, where we children ran clattering up and down, for the planks were not tightly nailed.

Through the middle of the house was a breezeway where Ranger spent his air-conditioned afternoons. Grandma always had a dog named Ranger, long after the original hound was gone. On one side of the breezeway were the kitchen and the "front room;" on the other, two vast bedrooms, each with four feather beds made up with rough linen and no counterpanes. On the front porch were a shallow enamel basin and a bucket and a dipper and a bar of Cashmere Bouquet, which had recently replaced the homemade lye soap. We were forbidden to waste water—what we didn't drink out the dipper we emptied into the basin for wash-ups.[2]

In other parts of rural America, poorer families lived packed close together in ramshackle houses. In an impoverished New England farming region, a reporter at the turn of the century wrote of small "gray, moss-grown, . . . dilapidated" farmhouses with leaning chimneys, yards "overgrown with rank weeds and overrun with pigs and poultry" and barnyards "littered, miry, and foul-smelling."[3]

Although some working-class families had quarters considerably better, their houses were still cramped compared to equivalents today. Most lived in apartments. A typical example had four rooms, one of them a kitchen. Beds and minimal furniture (simple chairs, a chest of drawers) were crowded in. No space could be wasted on closets; pegs on the wall and a couple of trunks held coats and a few items to be stored. The kitchen was the main area of social life. Often there was no money or room for an icebox, so food was bought daily, usually from nearby street vendors or a small corner grocery. Alfred Kazin, who would go on to become one of America's finest literary and social critics, recalled the apartment he knew as the son of Russian immigrants in Brooklyn, New York:

The kitchen held our lives together. My mother worked in it all day long, we ate in it almost all meals except the Passover *seder*, I did my homework and first writing at the kitchen table, and in winter I often had a bed made up for me on three kitchen chairs near the stove. On the wall just over the table hung a long horizontal mirror that sloped to a ship's prow at each end and was lined in cherry wood. It took up the whole wall, and drew every object in the kitchen to itself. . . . A large electric bulb hung down the center of the kitchen at the end of a chain that had been hooked into the ceiling; the old gas ring and key still jutted out of the wall like antlers. In the corner next to the toilet was the sink at which we washed, and the square tub in which my mother did our clothes.[4]

These quarters were pretty tight for a normal-sized household. Life was even closer for the many families who took in boarders. Boarding—paying for both living and eating in a particular place—served a dual purpose for both parties. A family got precious income and often a chance to maintain connection with distant relations, as renters often were newly arrived kin or friends; boarders found reasonably good living facilities, an introduction to a larger community, and some sense of family in a bewildering new world. A typical setting around 1913 might be a family of eight, plus one boarder, living in a four-room flat. All slept in one room, with three or four children to a bed. When families made boarding a business, things really got crowded. A study of Polish and Lithuanian working-class families in Chicago about 1915 found that each had an average of four boarders. A Pennsylvania family in the same period stuffed as many as three boarders in each bed every night. The mother did all their laundry (for a fee), while a daughter shined their shoes every Saturday night at twenty-five cents per pair.

Boarding remained a familiar part of family life among the working class throughout the first half of the century, and in some cases well after that. For children in these households, there was a continually changing cast of characters in their kitchens and bedrooms. Family life was intimate and personal in many ways, but boarders kept it also connected to the community beyond and even to countries and towns an ocean away.

Besides these other styles of housing—tenements, dogtrots, soddies and the rest—a new type, the bungalow, was becoming increasingly common in American cities. These homes were the favorites of the nation's large and growing middle class. While middle-class Victorian houses of the late 19th century had been ornate and formal, the bungalow was simple, informal, and efficient. It usually had one story, three or four bedrooms, and a spacious front porch, which suggested the connection between the family and the natural world beyond the home. Ideally such a house would be set on a large lot with trees, flowers, and a well-kept lawn. Popular magazines of the day, such as Ladies' Home Journal, Good Housekeeping, and Woman's Home Companion, championed the bungalow as the ideal setting for growing children.

During these early years of the century, a fairly substantial bungalow could be bought for two or three thousand dollars. (The equivalent in 1990 would be $27,000 to $40,000.) For considerably less money, tens of thousands of families bought their houses through the mail, disassembled, then put them together themselves. The spread of an efficient national railroad network allowed the movement of heavy loads to most towns of even modest size. Late in the 19th century mail order companies had appeared, the largest being Sears, Roebuck and Company, which offered to sell and deliver virtually any sort of product virtually anywhere in the nation. From Arizona to Maine, Idaho to Florida, customers could look through huge catalogues and send in orders for clothes, carriages, toys, bathtubs, phonograph players, carpets, libraries—and, by 1900, houses.

Sears was the largest of many suppliers of houses-by-mail. Excited families could choose from among dozens of designs—the Sears house catalogue of 1918 had nearly 150 pages—illustrated with photographs and drawings of the finished products. Some had as many as twelve rooms, though most were of modest size. The prefabricated house arrived in a boxcar, disassembled, with an average of about 30,000 parts (not including nails and screws). With instructions and blueprints already in hand, builders went to work. Promoters claimed the smallest cottage could be completed in a single work day, the others within a few weeks. The Aladdin Company advertised a comfortable bungalow for $885 (or about $11,000 in 1990) and a "warm, strong winter home" with five rooms for under $300 (about $4,000 in 1990), "shipped anywhere in 24 hours."

Mail order houses, along with the simpler and generally inexpensive housing styles, for the first time made homeowning possible for hundreds of thousands of American families. More than a hundred thousand prefabricated houses were sold by Sears alone. The majority of the nation's families still could not afford a house of their own, but as later chapters will show, the number that could would continue to grow in succeeding decades.

Inside these houses, where so many children would grow up, things were changing too. Many of the basic "conveniences" taken for granted by most children today were rare at the century's start. Home lighting, for instance, was a matter of kerosene lamps, candles, or wicks floating in bowls of oil. Such light did encourage a kind of family togetherness—children and parents huddled together around the inadequate flame—but it also required frequent refilling of lamps and cleaning of chimneys. The lights could also be hazardous, with many thousands of oil lamps burning every evening in crowded urban neighborhoods. The great change came with development of the incandescent bulb, or "light bulb," and dependable electrical power in American cities. Less than 10 percent of American homes were wired for electricity in 1907; by 1920, nearly 35 percent were.

Central heat was another major breakgthrough in home technology. Before, home stoves left parts of a house unheated, especially during the long winter nights. Girls and boys shivered under piles of covers, sometimes aided by heated soapstones or "bed bricks." By 1900 the luckier youngsters were enjoying steam radiators and floor furnaces that produced and distributed heat evenly throughout the house.

Probably most welcome of all was the appearance of plumbing systems that piped relatively clean water into the home and took away raw sewage. A system that collected fouled water, treated it, and returned drinkable water was an enormous and expensive undertaking for a city, but it also became one of the most necessary, once medical specialists began to understand how diseases could be spread through contaminated water. As will be discussed elsewhere in this chapter and in others, better sanitation was a major factor in improving children's health and reducing their death rate. And just as important, running water in the house made an enormous difference in the day-to-day lives of young America.

Take, for instance, bathrooms. Until the 20th century, a separate room for baths and toiletries had been practically unknown except in the homes of the wealthiest. A bathtub, usually made of tin or copper, was stashed away until bath time (usually once a week, traditionally on Saturday night in time for church the next morning). Then it would be hauled out, usually set up in the kitchen, and one-by-one the children would be plopped into heated water and scrubbed down. For human waste, there was the "privy," or "outhouse," or "necessary house," placed well away from the home. A chamberpot, or "thunderjug," might be kept in a bedroom to be used at night and emptied in the morning.

Outhouses were so much a part of American life and folklore that some persons opposed replacing them with indoor facilities, but many more were happy to be rid of the privy's inconvenience. Outhouses, of course, also added to sanitation problems. Before sewers were provided, a major city had tens of thousands of them, all collecting waste that in time percolated into the public's common water system, contaminating it. Indoor plumbing was not just a convenience; it was a medical necessity. Toilets, or "stools," at first were placed in closets. Soon, however, the triple hygienic functions of the ridding of bodily waste, bathing, and cleaning of hands and face were brought together in one room.

After 1900 bathrooms were increasingly common among the rapidly expanding number of middle-class houses. This separate space, typically near the bedrooms, included a permanent tub, toilet, and sink. As implied in the name of the nation's major manufacturer of these fixtures, American Standard, they usually had uniform fittings so builders could readily install them and they could fit into mail order homes. To emphasize cleanliness, they were dazzlingly white. Other features of the American bathroom soon appeared. Toilet paper had been available in sheets that were large and unwieldy, although certainly better than the older alternatives of newspapers, outdated catalogues, tree leaves, and corn cobs. In 1899, Edward and Clarence Scott began marketing softer toilet "tissue" that came in rolls of small sheets perforated for easy tearing. Like all the fixtures around it, toilet paper rolls were stark white.

Bungalows were laid out with plenty of space for relaxed living. The Victorian "parlor" was out of favor; instead, there were "living rooms" as well as bedrooms large enough for intimate lounging. These houses were also reflections of the gathering attention to children and the ideal of a close and loving relationship among parents, sons, and daughters. Larger Victorian homes often had nurseries set apart from the main areas of the parents' lives, especially from the master bedroom, but the new arrangement was different. If there were a nursery, it ought to be "within eyeshot and earshot of the mother." Stairs, balconies, and every other feature of a house should be constructed with children's safety in mind. Finally, young people needed to have part of the house for their own. An article in *Good Housekeeping* argued that "every house which shelters children should have, if possible, its children's room . . . [where they] should be allowed perfect liberty. There should be an opportunity to do anything, from making mud pies to painting in water colors."[5]

All these developments marked something vitally important: the appearance and spread of a style of housing that would become the norm of the American middle class. These houses would continue to evolve throughout the century, but the basics were established in these early years. Homes like these—distinctively designed and furnished—were expressions of prevailing values about the ways parents and children ought to behave and live with one another. They would be the setting in which millions of young Americans would grow up, learning about themselves and the world outside, enjoying the pleasures and suffering through the trials of family life.

For many thousands of American children, however, any of the homes described above, from the most spacious and comfortable to the most cramped, remained a distant dream. At the opening of the century, the economic distance between the richest and poorest Americans probably was greater than at any other time in our history—although, as will be seen, poverty has remained a terrible problem in our society until the present day. The practical buying power of the nation's wealthiest families in 1900 almost defied description, but at the other end of the economic scale were others living literally on the edge of starvation. Poverty was particularly appalling in the cities. In the countryside the poor at least might gather food through hunting or gardening a stray plot of land, but in urban America there were few options.

In these cities, homeless Americans lived by the tens of thousands. Because the gathering of such information from these times was primitive, we have nothing close to precise estimates, but all authorities agree that the numbers were enormous. And the most disturbing sights of all were the many children sleeping in doorways and alleys in every major city in the country. The problem was not new. Especially at earlier times of vigorous immigration, cities along the Atlantic coast had seen crowds of homeless young on their streets. During the Civil War, by one contemporary estimate, New York City alone held as many as thirty thousand vagrant girls and boys, mostly children of Irish and German immigrants who had flooded the nation's largest city during the previous twenty years. Some were orphans, some abandoned, others runaways, and still others had simply been separated from their parents during their journeys into and around America. The influx into cities from the countryside and from other countries coming at the turn of the century worsened this problem.

Over the years different solutions had been tried to deal with the problem of these parentless or dependent young. As an early answer, they had been sent to poorhouses (also called almshouses), sometimes with their impoverished parents and sometimes alone. Here they were housed with persons of all ages who were unable to support or care for themselves. Investigations showed some children born in these places and others brought as young as two years, sometimes because of birth defects or diseases such as epilepsy. Once admitted, they frequently remained for years, sometimes all their lives—which typically were short.

An increasingly common solution, seen as a great step upward from the almshouse, was the orphanage, or orphan asylum. Orphanages appeared to be an efficient and economical means of dealing with a complicated situation that potentially was enormously expensive. In roomy buildings a staff could oversee large numbers of children according to well-established rules and a common discipline. Food could be bought in bulk and prepared in large kitchens, and the inmates themselves could handle much of the upkeep. Squads of orphans might be trained as a work force to produce

This young girl was one of more than 150,000 children living in American orphanages around 1910. The care of children without parents would remain a major concern throughout the century. *Courtesy of George Eastman House/Lewis W. Hine.*

goods to help finance the entire operation. Some orphanages were funded by private charities or religious groups, others by state and county governments.

The census bureau reported that in 1910 there were 1,151 institutions for dependent children in the United States, most of them orphan asylums. New York had 154; Wyoming had none. The Pacific coast and New England had the largest numbers of institutions relative to their populations, each with about one for every 55,000 persons; the South had the least, with roughly one per 150,000 persons. These institutions held a total of about 150,000 children. (Nearly 2,500 children still were confined to almshouses in 1910.) Conditions varied. Especially in some early orphanages the food was scarce and poor, facilities primitive, and discipline harsh, even brutal. After the turn of the century, living standards and treatment improved. Children were worked hard by later standards, but probably no harder than most young people of the time. The superintendent of a New York orphanage asked the young people in his institution to write short essays on how they had spent the previous Saturday. Most told of a day that blended a lot of labor with some playtime. A twelve-year-old wrote:

Saturday before breakfast I swept the basement and scoured the sink. Then I washed, cleaned my teeth well and went into the dining room where I ate my breakfast. After breakfast I made my bed, after which I went down stairs and emptied the dirt barrel and burned the rubbish. When I had put my barrel away and had finished my work in the cottage I put up a bird house in the bushes next to our cottage. I softened up and made level the dirt on our lawn. After dinner I went out into the pantry and helped wash dishes. When the dishes were finished I had to go out and work again on the lawn with my pickax and shovel . . . then I was allowed to go out and play ball. When the game was finished I went into the cottage and read until the bell rang for supper. After supper I went out and played tag until the curfew rang when I came in and went to bed.[6]

There were complaints. Besides the unhealthy and abusive conditions in some orphanages, critics argued that the system was too cold and aloof, denying children the warmth and affection they might have gotten from parents. A man who grew up in an orphanage and went on to have a successful career recalled that orphanage life "meant essentially shelter, the actual necessities in the way of clothes, and food which primarily served the purpose of preventing starvation, rather than . . . common sense nourishment. The attitude of those responsible . . . was that the boys and girls were unfortunate objects of charity, and therefore should be content with whatever was done for them."[7] Concern over such emotional coolness partly reflected the clash with the ideal of the companionate family. A healthy upbringing was thought to depend on a close, affectionate home with parents and children living and working together in happy union.

An alternative to orphanages, one closer to the family ideal, was the foster home. Homeless children might live with temporary parents, who would be paid for the extra costs and responsibilities. As will be discussed in the next chapter, authorities turned increasingly to this solution in the years ahead, although it, too, had its difficulties. Another possibility, of course, was to find permanent homes with parents willing to adopt these children as their own. Charitable and religious organizations, and, increasingly, state agencies, tried to place orphans and other displaced youngsters with families who would rear them to adulthood.

One of the most ambitious adoption experiments was that of the "orphan trains," the inspiration of Charles Loring Brace, founder of the Children's Aid Society. Brace was shocked by the thousands of homeless and impoverished young and the conditions they lived in, especially in eastern cities, during the 19th century. His answer was to devise a system of gathering these children and sending them to towns and farms farther west where they would be matched up with adults eager to take them in. In Illinois or Iowa, he believed, a street urchin from Boston or New York City would find a healthier life, both physically and spiritually. The idea caught on. Between 1854 and 1929 an estimated two hundred thousand orphaned, abandoned, and neglected children were transported by rail out of eastern cities to the countryside, mostly in the West. Before the trains arrived notices like this one were posted: "Wanted, Homes for Children, a company of homeless children from the East will arrive at Troy, Mo., on Friday, Feb. 25th, 1910. . . . Come and see the children. . . . Distribution will take place at the Opera House."[8] When the trains pulled in, crowds were waiting to choose the new additions to their households.

Some boys and girls were eventually adopted, but many were kept essentially as foster children. Older children, especially, were terribly homesick—and often hard to control. New parents had their complaints. If the Society wouldn't take back the boy he had taken into his home, one farmer wrote, he would put him in a reformatory: "He stole my wife's wedding ring."[9] Some children ran away. Many headed back east within a few years. Younger children of three or four years naturally adapted more easily to their new environment. In the end no simple conclusions can be made about such a large undertaking lasting seventy-five years. Many adoptive parents acted out of compassion; their children later would look back on them with deep love and gratitude. Western families also were looking for extra help because, as will be discussed below in the section on work, children's labor was a valuable asset on a western farm. Motives were complex, a mixture of self-interest and generosity, sympathy and exploitation.

Something else was going on here as well. When Brace concentrated on the problems of eastern cities and looked for answers to western towns and farms, he was expressing a common worry and hostility toward the new urban America. Like so many of his generation and ethnic background, he was deeply troubled by the waves of immigrants washing into the country and crowding the cities of the Atlantic coast. In fact, despite the term "orphan train," many children were not parentless but were given up by mothers and fathers who were having difficulty caring for their young. Brace and the Children's Aid Society were expressing the anxiety that, in a changing America, especially in its teeming urban centers, children were being lost to a new world with ideals and values very different from their own.

Most disturbing of all, in the new America, children seemed to be moving farther from the influence of their parents and other authorities. In the cities young people spent much of their time away from the household, playing and working in a world most adults did not really understand. Out there, mothers and fathers feared, their youngsters faced all sorts of dangers, physical and moral. How would all this affect their sons and daughters?

Many parents dealt with these fears by trying to reassert more influence over their children. They hoped to keep their children closer to them even when they were away. They wanted their sons and daughters to choose the values that they themselves believed were proper and right, values that were expressed most clearly within the family household. They were striving to keep their children morally "at home" when they left the house and went off to play and work in the larger world. Fathers and mothers expressed this hope in many different ways—through education, building "family centered" houses, passing laws about everything from movies to child labor, even through buying certain kinds of toys.

These efforts are discussed in this chapter and the ones following. One example might be mentioned here: During the 20th century adults have created and promoted many different kinds of organizations for children meant to help children have fun, learn about the world, and get to know other young people. Through these organizations, adults have tried to cultivate and encourage certain values and to discourage others, intending to exert a kind of loving control over the young.

One of the most successful and familiar of these organizations appeared in the United States early in this century, the Boy Scouts. Scouting originated in Great Britain, the inspiration of Robert S. S. Baden-Powell. A general and military hero, Baden-Powell founded the organization to encourage physical fitness, knowledge of the natural world, and, most important, the development of proper morals and character. This, he believed, would offset the growing materialism and the conflict between rich and poor that he feared in modern Britain.

The idea caught on in the United States—scouting was established here around 1911–1912—and for much the same reasons. Earlier movements— the Sons of Daniel Boone and the Woodcraft Indians—had tried to inspire boys to spend more time camping and hiking and studying nature. The first looked back to hardy pioneers as its model, the second to Native Americans. Boy Scouting, however, proved far more successful than either. Scouts emphasized an efficient organization, overseen by adults, that would continue indefinitely, bringing more young people in as others grew out of it. A "troop" was organized into smaller "patrols," while regional and national councils set policy and guidelines for the whole system. There would be common uniforms and equipment. Soon the *Handbook for Boys* appeared, part of every scout's training, full of instructions, regulations, and lore. Its purpose, according to an early edition, was to make scouting "throughout America . . . uniform and intelligent." In 1912 the national organization began publication of a magazine, *Boy's Life,* sending it to each scout.

The reason the Boy Scouts appealed to young males was simple: it gave them the chance to have lots of fun. Meeting together, taking weekend trips into the countryside, learning "woodcraft," and playing at pioneers and Indians—there was plenty to amuse a boy. The structure of scouting, with its step-by-step series of accomplishments from "tenderfoot" to the lofty perch of "eagle," offered a sense of accomplishment and self-confidence. As has always been the case in activities organized by adults, from schools to soccer leagues, boys also used scouts occasionally to make their own kind of fun. Sitting around campfires and sleeping in tents, scouts snuck cigarettes, gambled, and told stories that would never show up in *Boy's Life.*

Nevertheless, the men and women who organized the American scouting movement had other purposes. The Boy Scouts can be seen as a response to two fears about children in a changing America. First, worries about the city: Most parents had grown up in small towns or on farms, and, while cities attracted them, they also were frightening. Parents feared their children would be corrupted there. Scouts would get their sons out of the cities, if only briefly, and bring them close to the natural world that so many parents thought was a purifying influence on growing adolescents. Second, parents worried that modern America generally held all sorts of new moral dangers for young men and women. The Boy Scouts would be part of a campaign to instill traditional virtues in their youngsters.

The first thing scouts learned—the key to entering at the lowest level— was the Boy Scout Pledge: "On my honor I will do my best, to do my duty to God and my country, and to obey the scout law, to help other people at all times, to keep myself physically strong, mentally awake, and morally straight." The pledge was adopted closely from the British version, with a few changes; the American pledge, for instance, deleted the English promise that "a scout smiles and whistles under all circumstances." The Pledge would be worn into the memory of millions of American boys over the next many decades. It was an unwavering commitment to respect religion and government and a prevailing moral code. (The scout motto, "Be Prepared," was both an encouragement of character and a play on Baden-Powell's initials.)

Once in scouting, a boy worked through the ranks by earning a series of "merit badges." Requirements for these stressed not only the learning of certain skills, from cooking and woodworking to swimming and various athletics, but also citizenship and upright behavior. Meetings often featured talks on the dangers of various sins.

Scouting was an early and continuing example of many programs and institutions that would appear throughout the century, arising from a genuine concern for the well-being of young people. It offered them chances to enjoy themselves and learn something. It also expressed some common anxieties among grownups, and it was part of an effort to control and direct children's lives outside the home and shape their characters according to certain standards. Whatever its purposes, one thing was clear: it was popular. By 1914 there were more than 100,000 Boy Scouts in the United States, and eight years later, about 430,000. It would prove to be one of the most persistent youth movements in American history.

## AT PLAY

Playing is a serious business. As children play they sometimes express deeply-rooted emotions and fears. Sometimes they show their creativity or act out and learn about the actions they observe in parents and other adults. Play can also be an example of young people preserving and carrying into a new generation traditions that other children have known for generations, sometimes for centuries.

Then and now, playtime has usually been the part of life in which boys and girls have found their greatest independence, when they have been most on their own. On a school playground, a vacant lot in a city, or in a country field, boys and girls playing on their own have been largely free to express themselves. That does not mean, however, that adults have not been involved. Parents and other grownups always have tried to influence their youngsters' world of games and toys and other amusements, but they have been only partly successful. At the beginning of the 20th century—and now, as we approach its close—play has been an area of contest, a kind of playground itself, where older and younger Americans have pushed against one another as they have pursued what they have wanted and needed.

Among other things, play can teach us about the diversity of children's lives at any particular time in our history. It also demonstrates how American boys and girls, regardless of where they live, have much in common. In some ways children in small towns and on farms play differently from those living in the city; yet playtime in the countryside also has many similarities with urban amusements.

Over the decades differences in play have reflected the peculiarities of life in rural and urban America. Farm and ranch children usually had access to horses, mules, and other domesticated animals, and often they built their play lives around those animals. Roaming on horseback held a special fondness. The writer Hamlin Garland recalled of the youths of his early years in Iowa that "they lived in the saddle when no other duties called them, . . . and the world seemed a very good place for a boy."[10] Riding or not, boys and girls felt a remarkable freedom in exploring the woods, fields, hills, and creeks. Fiorello La Guardia, who would become one of New York City's most famous mayors, grew up in Prescott, Arizona. He wrote later that the desert and mountains around the town were a "paradise," a perfect playground "not measured in acres, or in city blocks, but in miles and miles."[11] Youngsters living in more isolated areas made pets out of wild creatures—raccoons, owls, squirrels, prairie dogs, coyotes, fawns, and pigeons—that they caught or found when young. Conversely, they enjoyed hunting and killing animals, especially snakes. Students on the plains of eastern Colorado killed sixteen rattlesnakes outside their schoolhouse during one day's lunch recess.

Despite the differences between amusements in cities and in the country, there has always been a common culture of play throughout the United States. During the early decades of the 20th century, children could be seen playing many of the same games in vacant lots in Brooklyn and in schoolyards in Arizona and Alabama. These organized games had certain common characteristics. Most were highly physical and usually required a good bit of room. Elaborate equipment was unnecessary, and usually the players needed nothing but themselves. Many games stressed agility, strength, and a degree of shrewdness. Typically games were brief, so several could be played in a short span of time.

Perhaps most important, these games had simple rules that were easily and quickly learned. For the most part, their patterns and appeal had been tried and tested for generations, passed from older girls and boys to younger siblings and friends. One of the most familiar and enduring games among young children, "Ring a Ring a Rosy" (or "Ring Round Rosy"), had its roots in the scourge of the bubonic plague in mid-fourteenth century Europe. "How Many Miles to Miley Bright," which the historian Edward Dale remembered playing on the Texas plains, originated in medieval England.[12] In other words, childhood games were among the most deeply rooted and widely spread features of national life.

Here are a few examples:

*Fox and Geese.* A large design in the shape of a wheel with a hub and four or six spokes was drawn on the dirt (or tramped down in the snow). One person, chosen as the "fox," stood at the hub while the others, the "geese," lined up along the wheel's spokes and rim, which were called "rivers." At a signal, the game began. It was a variation of tag, except that the "geese" had to stay on the "rivers" and each point where the lines intersected was a safe base. A tagged "goose" was immediately transformed into the new "fox," who then began a new stalking.

*Ante Over.* Also called "Anti-I-Over," "Annie Over the Shanty," or some variation of those sounds, this game required some sort of barrier, perhaps a relatively low building, a very large rock, or even a substantial wagon. Two teams placed themselves on either side of the barrier. One called out "Ante Over!" (or the variation) just before throwing a ball (or rock or tightly knotted rags). If those on the other side failed to catch whatever was thrown, they then threw it back with the same call. If they caught it, however, they raced around to the other side, and the catcher tried to hit an opponent with the object. Anyone struck joined the attacking team. One team won when it annihilated the opposition or if it outnumbered the enemy when the game was called.

*Run, Sheep, Run.* Players divided into two teams, each with a captain. One team hid, with its captain (who did not hide) helping them find the best spots. The second team, directed by its captain, then began searching while the captain of the hiding team called out warnings and encouragement. When any hidden player was spotted, the captain of the searching team called out "Run, Sheep, Run," and all players instantly bolted for the safe base, or goal. Any hiding player tagged was eliminated. If the captain of the hiding team saw a good strategic opportunity, he, too, could call out "Run, Sheep, Run," triggering a rush for the base.

These games served some obvious purposes. They offered vigorous exercise for young people, and, with that, the chance to express aggression. Although all involved teams, they also gave individuals a chance to display their physical skills and sometimes their cleverness and intelligence. All players had a chance to introduce themselves, establish a reputation, and raise themselves in the estimation of others. Finally, because these games worked by easy rules and were nearly universally known, they were marvelous mechanisms for creating and keeping bonds among groups of children, even if those children were strangers to one another. These amusements served as a kind of generic language with which young people forged and maintained their own communities.

Some games had another purpose. Children played to act out—to "rehearse"—the roles they realized they would be expected to play as adults. A simple example popular among younger children was "Oats, Peas, and Beans." As a boy stood in the center, a ring of others joined hands and moved around, singing a refrain, then pausing while the child in the center called out verses going through a farmer's round of work ("Now the farmer sows his seed . . .") and in time choosing a girl as "wife." As the pair knelt, the others sang:

> Now you're married, you must obey,
> You must be true to all you say,
> You must be kind, you must be good,
> And keep your wife in kindling wood.[13]

Millions of children passed their spare time mimicking the adult world in other ways, "playing out" roles and domestic dramas with one another and reconstructing adult worlds in miniature, making tiny farms with wagons made from spools of thread and barns from tin cans.

Children in the growing cities amused themselves with many of the same games played in farmyards and in hamlets from Happy Corner, Vermont, to Dusty, Washington. They also found all sorts of new ways to have fun. Some of these urban amusements reflected the remarkable technological changes of the day. Among the favorite children's entertainments, for instance, were motion pictures, which first began to be shown in larger cities shortly before the turn of the century. For five cents a boy or girl could enter an arcade to watch films with titles like *The Car Man's Danger, An Attack on an Agent,* and *The Adventures of an American Cowboy.* They especially enjoyed comedies and films with plenty of action and adventure, from Indian battles out West to struggles between criminals and detectives. Mixed in were a few shortened versions of literary classics, such as Charles Dickens's *A Tale of Two Cities* and Lew Wallace's *Ben Hur.* To children of that day these were terribly exciting. Motion picture producers quickly recognized the large potential market and began producing dozens of films to appeal to young people. Surveys revealed just how popular these movies had become. In Portland, Oregon, nine out of ten young people patronized cheap movie theaters, and nearly one out of three said they went to two or more every week. In New York City in 1911, according to one poll, about one child out of eight paid to watch at least one feature every day.

Some young people attended movies with their parents, and some theaters had adults in attendance to watch over the behavior of the audiences. But in most cases the young customers were left to watch the films on their own. Often the showings were in makeshift theaters with a screen hung in back and chairs set randomly around the floor. These movie houses became something like clubhouses. The famous reformer Jane Addams, referring to arcades in her neighborhood, observed that "young people attend the five cent theaters in groups, with something of the 'gang' instinct, boasting of the films in 'our theater.' "[14] As much as the films themselves, the appeal seems to have been the chance to get together, romp, and flirt beyond the gaze and control of adults.

That was exactly what alarmed many reformers, moralists, and social critics of the day. Movies are a good example of how young people's play became an area of contest between the older and younger generations. Ministers, school administrators, and others were disturbed by what they believed was a decline in the moral character of city children. They thought that these films were at best no help at all in dealing with this social problem. At worst, they said, arcades were a major threat to the proper upbringing of American children. Critics objected, first, to the content of motion pictures. Far from uplifting, they said, the stories too often stressed excitement for its own sake. Some glamorized criminals and shadier characters, they warned. In any case, they did not emphasize for young people the virtues of good citizenship and moral uprightness; nor did they educate boys and girls in the literary and artistic heritage necessary for a proper citizenry.

Second, critics argued that all sorts of unsavory things were happening in these theaters. Children learned foul language and took on dangerous habits. Perhaps worst of all were sexual temptations of young people at a vulnerable age. In the dim theaters, reported the Chicago Vice Commission, boys were able to "slyly embrace the girls near them and offer certain indignities." The Society for the Prevention of Cruelty to Children agreed wholeheartedly. The " 'moving picture' abomination" could hardly be more threatening, the SPCC claimed in its report for 1909: "Boys and girls are darkened in the room together while the pictures are on, and, . . . indecent assaults upon the girls follow, often with their acquiescence. De praved adults with candies and pennies beguile children with the inev result. . . . GOD alone knows how many are leading dissolute lives          ι at the 'moving pictures.' "[15]

Besides movies, urban children were drawn to other businesses ιι    reformers found highly worrisome. "Penny arcades" offered a wide array of amusements. Some, such as shooting galleries, ringtoss games, and machines measuring the power of a person's grip, assessed some skill or strength, and so they provided a chance for a young man to show off to friends. By their nature, these games also tempted players to gamble. There were also mutoscopes, or "peep shows," in which, for a penny or so, a customer would look through an eyepiece to see a short presentation of flickering images, a kind of minimovie. The scene might be of racing fire engines, a bit of crude comedy, or an exciting boxing exhibition. For young male customers, among the most alluring mutoscope were those that claimed to reveal women disrobing or dancing suggestively. The actual performance very rarely lived up to expectations; there were, after all, rigorous laws against public obscenity and indecent displays. Nonetheless, reformers and other community leaders who worried about the characters of youngsters found the peep shows and other arcade amusements as threatening and objectionable as the moving-picture theaters.

Reformers lashed out against these new forms of public entertainment that the growing population of urban young people found so exciting. Such protests became part of a movement for new laws and regulations to bring under greater control the private lives, including the play, of children living in an urban environment. As will be seen elsewhere in this chapter, the result was a growing body of laws and regulations that expanded the responsibilities of local and state governments. Reformers *were* able to exert at least some influence on the lives of children at play.

Nevertheless, their success was limited. At bottom, they were alarmed over changes that would be difficult, if not impossible, to stop. Urban children enjoyed a great deal of independence, and they were becoming important figures in the rapidly changing economic order of American cities. They comprised a vast market of hundreds of thousands of consumers willing to pay for certain kinds of entertainment. Aggressive businessmen were bound to exploit that market. Motion pictures were an unstoppable, irresistible force. Because these enormously popular films were quite brief—rarely more than half an hour each—theater owners could also "turn over" the audience many times each day, crowding children into the rooms, showing the movies, and then herding them out to make way for the next group of paying customers. So even as the motion pictures were becoming an important part of the national economy and a familiar aspect of leisure life, children were becoming a crucial element in the success of this industry.

Apart from any commercial enterprise, city boys and girls amused themselves on their own. Much of this activity took place in public spaces that were their most accessible playgrounds, the streets. In the summer of 1913, social workers in Cleveland, Ohio, tried to discover what young people did with their private time during the day. Interviewing nearly fifteen thousand boys and girls, they found that more than half spent their spare time on the streets. Some played at what the adults thought were acceptable pastimes—baseball and other ball games, kite flying, and jacks, for instance; but most, the interviewers reported, were not doing anything. What "doing nothing" really meant, however, was playing in ways of which the social workers disapproved. These children were gambling with dice and pitching pennies, gossiping and taunting one another, stealing from fruit stands, and writing on the walls of buildings.

Young people, especially boys, also fought a lot. Although it is difficult to measure such things, some authorities believe that the level of violence and violent play was increasing around the opening of the 20th century, perhaps because so many people were being crowded together so rapidly. An immigrant boy on New York City's Lower East Side recalled defending a vacant lot he and his friends considered their personal play area. "Some of our boys stole tops of wash-boilers at home, and used them as shields," he wrote. "Others had tin swords, sticks, blackjacks. The two armies slaughtered each other in the street. Bottles were thrown, heads were cut open."[16]

As the Ohio survey also showed, however, not all play was so openly belligerent or dangerous. Of all organized urban play, probably the most common was baseball and its street variation, stickball. The youngsters' passion reflected the phenomenal popularity of baseball among adults. By the late 19th century, this game had become something close to a national obsession, played in western mining camps and on isolated ranches as well as in small southern and midwestern towns and, of course, in large cities. Adult amateur teams drew as many fans as professional teams. In 1914 the Cleveland, Ohio, city championship (between the Telling Strollers and the Hanna Street Cleaners) was watched and cheered by an estimated eighty thousand persons. The first professional baseball league was founded in 1876, but only in the 1890s did professional play become a major business. Soon team owners were building stadiums that fans could reach easily on the new trolley lines; the Brooklyn Dodgers, in fact, earned the nickname "trolley dodgers" in reference to the dozens of trolley cars around the stadium that customers had to avoid on game days. Attendance at major league games doubled between 1903 and 1908, and by 1910 baseball could rightfully be called America's "national pastime."

Young people enjoyed riding the trolleys to the stadium to cheer on their favorite professional teams, but, predictably, they also emulated their favorites and played games of their own, on formal playing fields when they were available, but more often on vacant lots and on the streets. For a bat they used any sturdy stick, from a shovel handle to a reasonably straight tree limb, and for a ball, a great variety of homemade spheres, even rocks. This naturally led to other difficulties, especially broken windows and further crowding on streets already clogged with carts, buggies, street vendors, and animals. Still, the games were irrepressible. Children "will play . . . in spite of all travel and obstruction," a journalist wrote not long after the Civil War. By the early 20th century, these determined games of baseball and stickball had become a standard part of urban life.

In movies, children were using an adult business to pursue their own fantasies and fun, often to the alarm of older Americans. In street games like baseball, boys and girls were both mimicking the adult world and creating play that was entirely their own. That play was a kind of middle ground between the lives of younger and older Americans. In still other amusements, adults tried to use play to encourage in children certain attitudes and behavior.

The best examples were manufactured toys. Designed and produced by adults, then usually bought by other adults and given as gifts to boys and girls, toys often told at least as much about adults as about the youngsters who played with them. More will be discussed about toys in the next chapter, but a few examples from early in the century are worthy of mention here.

One of the most popular toys at the turn of the century was the cast-iron mechanical bank. A bank might not come to mind when one thinks of toys, but these items, which first appeared in the 1870s, were not just places where money was stored. Such banks were cast in the shape of a familiar figure or scene—from organ grinders and circus performers to Humpty Dumpty and policemen. When a coin was placed in the place provided and a lever pushed, the coin was flung through an opening, to be saved for the future. The possibilities activated by the coin seemed almost endless. William Tell shot a coin from his crossbow, over his son's head and into a tree-bank. Football players pounced on coins; baseball pitchers threw them past batters. Sleazy politicians slipped money into their pockets. More than three hundred types of mechanical banks were manufactured over a couple of generations. They remained popular for more than half a century, through the 1920s (and valued collectables later).

A parent who gave a child a bank to play with was trying to reinforce one obvious kind of behavior—saving money. Few lessons were stressed more in Victorian America than the value of planning ahead and setting aside something for difficult times that might lie ahead, and a girl or boy who laughed at a penny shot into a dog's mouth might associate saving with life's enjoyments. There was also a darker side to the values represented in the banks. Some of them reflected the racial and ethnic prejudices that ran deep in American society. The Reclining Chinaman bank showed a Chinese man lying on a log with a rat running by, while the Paddy and the Pig bank displayed another often ridiculed figure, an Irishman, with a whiskey jug in his pocket. Several examples portrayed African Americans through insulting stereotypes, such as the Boys Stealing Watermelons bank. Through these savings toys, then, parents were communicating both admirable virtues and prevailing prejudices to young people.

Many other kinds of cast-iron toys could be bought early in the century—fire engines, carriages with horses in harness, and other figures from children's daily life. Early cap guns had a small gunpowder cap exploded by a pistol's hammer. A few of these, like the banks, involved an extra action, and these too could reflect prominent attitudes. In the Chinese Must Go pistol, a cap was put in the mouth of a Chinese man. When the trigger was pulled the mouth slammed shut and the cap went off, and simultaneously the man was kicked in the pants by a white American wearing a derby.

Some of the best examples of toys meant to instill values and messages in children were dolls. As a small model of a human being, a doll is naturally used to act out and practice the lessons of living and dealing with other people. Some form of dolls can be found among children in virtually every culture on earth. Both girls and boys have always made their own, out of socks and pieces of fruit, whittled wood and molded clay, and, from very early in our history, dolls have also been manufactured and sold.

Dolls generally—and especially those bought in stores and given as presents—have always been a tool used by grownups to inspire certain behavior in children. Most obviously, parents give them to daughters to encourage them into traditional domestic roles: as mothers, homemakers, and caretakers of the sick. Through their look and dress, dolls can also become standards of appearance, beauty, and fashion. None of this means, of course, that children necessarily receive or accept the messages given to them through dolls. A student of childhood in the late 19th century found many young girls much preferred sledding, ball games, wrestling, and tag to spending time with their dolls. "Wouldn't you rather play with dolls?" an adult asked two girls playing horse and rider. "We'd rather run," they answered. And rather than cuddling and healing their doll-children, many girls instead lashed out violently, spanking and beating them, force-feeding them with dirt, even hammering nails into their bodies.[17] These children were finding their own meanings and acting out their own dramas, sometimes disturbing and often starkly different from the ones their elders were teaching.

Whether absorbing lessons from adults or expressing their own, young America in the 20th century has been infatuated with dolls. One of the earliest, most popular, and most enduring dolls originated in a family tragedy. In 1915, Marcella Gruelle, the young daughter of Indiana political cartoonist Johnny Gruelle, lay ill with tuberculosis. To amuse her, her father gave Marcella a rag doll found in his attic. He named the doll Raggedy Ann and invented a series of stories about it. The next year Marcella died. Gruelle published a book of Raggedy Ann stories, which was sold with dolls as a promotional lure. The book did well, but the doll, with its male counterpart Raggedy Andy, became an American classic. They are still popular today, survivors of the tradition of simple dolls lovingly stuffed and hand-sewn by parents unable to afford more expensive versions.

Raggedy Ann appeared on the market at virtually the same time as another famous American doll. A magazine illustrator, Rose O'Neill, created a child cartoon character for the magazine *Woman's Home Companion* around 1910. So popular was this figure—named "Kewpie," a play on "Cupid," the childlike god of love—that O'Neill commissioned a sculptor to create a doll version she could offer for sale. The result was a doll with chubby cheeks, dimpled knees, a bright smile and a distinctive curl of hair on the forehead. Kewpie Dolls eventually sold in the millions, and O'Neill became one of the few females to play a prominent role in the toy industry (or in any large business in the early 20th century). Just what it was about these dolls that appealed to parents and children is difficult to say. Something in their appearance aroused affection and the impulse to protect and nurture.

Dolls could reflect other concerns of adults, including politics. A prominent political figure, in fact, inspired one of modern America's most enduring playthings. In the fall of 1902, President Theodore Roosevelt traveled south to settle a dispute between Louisiana and Mississippi. While there, Roosevelt, an avid sportsman, went on a bear hunt. When newspapers reported that the president had spared the life of a captured bear, the owner of a Brooklyn toy shop began selling a fluffy brown bear with button eyes made by his wife. He called it "Teddy's Bear." After a few years the teddy bear had become one of the most popular items in the nation's toy stores. It still is.

On a grander scale of entertainment were the amusement parks that reached their heyday between World War I and the early 1920s. Amusement parks can trace their origins to traveling carnivals and county fairs, but they took their modern, recognizable shape late in the 19th century. The most famous was at Coney Island, just south of Brooklyn, New York, and nine miles from Manhattan. At first this beach had been a resort and lounging area for well-to-do Victorians, but by the turn of the century something very different had appeared. Coney Island first gained broad popularity as a bathing resort for customers of modest means—working-class New Yorkers who took to the waters, played on the beach, and strolled along the famous "iron pier." After 1900, however, a series of increasingly large and ambitious "parks" were opened at Coney Island—Steeplechase Park, Luna Park, and Dreamland—that offered exciting rides and other amusements, including the Shoot the Chutes, Mountain Torrent,

Tickler, and Helter Skelter. On its opening day in 1903, Luna Park drew more than 45,000 persons, and for years more than a million persons flocked to Coney Island every summer.

The centerpiece of most large amusement parks was the thrilling roller coaster ride. Its origins reach back as early as an elaborate sledding course in St. Petersburg, Russia, in the mid-1600s and French prototypes in the early 1800s. The modern "scream machine" took form in the late 19th century. The first one on Coney Island, the Switchback Railway, soon inspired many others that ran ever faster along more twisting, curving courses. By the mid-1920s, more than 1,200 were in operation.

Coney Island's success made it a model for amusement parks that sprang up in cities throughout the country. An estimated two thousand parks were attracting millions of patrons annually in the early 1920s. Many were small operations; others, such as Kennywood near Pittsburgh, Riverview Park in Chicago, Elitch Gardens in Denver, and Cedar Point in Sandusky, Ohio, were much more ambitious, bedazzled with lights at night and offering thrilling rides and exotic sights.

Persons of all ages came to these parks, of course, but, from the start, they were special favorites of the young. The rides and other enticements were especially designed to attract teenagers and young adults. Other characteristics made these parks particularly appealing to customers of those ages. They were either in or close to cities, easily accessible by trolley lines—in fact, they often were built or bought by railway companies. For a dime or so an adolescent could hop on a streetcar and, after a short ride, be at the gates of one of these places. Many featured strange, even bizarre, entertainments. Promoters at one Coney Island park sold thousands of tickets to watch the electrocution of an elephant. There were "freak shows" like Jolly Trixie, Queen of Fatland ("It Takes Seven Men to Hug Her") as well as otherwise forbidden sights, like "exotic dancers" and "The Original Turkish Harem." Rapid, frantic rides tossed and pressed male and female customers close to one another. "Will She Throw Her Arms around Your Neck and Yell?" asked an ad for the Cannon Coaster. "Well, I Guess, Yes!" Slower rides through dark tunnels gave a chance for physical affection otherwise unacceptable in public. The whole atmosphere allowed and encouraged spontaneous mingling, flirting, and brief friendships on young people's own terms, far from prying eyes of adults.

Amusement parks in those years were a form of escape for many young adults. Alarming to parents, they provided an opportunity for daughters and sons to move beyond the family's reach. They were also spectacular demonstrations of the new buying power of young people and their influence on the changing American marketplace.

## AT WORK

As the 20th century opened, America's children were doing a huge portion of the nation's work. From North Dakota homesteads to the wharves of San Francisco to mills and factories of North Carolina and Ohio, girls and boys labored to pay for meals on their families' tables. They ran errands and peddled goods on the streets, shucked oysters and herded cattle. They helped produce the clothes Americans wore, the food they ate, the bottles from which they drank, the fuel that kept them warm, and the chairs and beds where they sat and slept.

Measuring the extent of child labor was then—and is now—a difficult and slippery job. The census of 1900 was very precise in telling us how many children, ages ten to fifteen, were "gainfully employed" in that year: 1,750,178, or nearly one child out of every five. That represented an astounding increase of more than a million working children since 1870. And the number was still growing. The census figure for 1910 was just under two million. Then, for reasons noted later in this chapter, the number dropped dramatically. By 1920, the census reported, just over a million American children were employed, roughly one out of every twelve.

|      |           |          |
|------|-----------|----------|
| 1900 | 1,750,178 | 18.2%    |
| 1910 | 1,990,225 | 18.4%    |
| 1920 | 1,060,858 | 8.5%[18] |

But these figures only tell part of the story. What about children under ten years old? Tens of thousands of them worked on the streets, in their homes, on the farms, and even in factories. Investigators found boys as young as eight working ten hours a day in Georgia textile mills. And what did "gainfully employed" mean? Did those numbers count boys and girls who sold pencils or newspapers for a few hours after school? Probably not. More than a million of the "working children" in 1900, furthermore, were agricultural laborers, but this figure apparently only included more or less full-time farm workers, not the hundreds of thousands of young people who worked several hours a day on their family farms.

The census tally, then, barely begins to measure how much children were working and contributing to the American economy, and it only hints at the difficulties and tragedies that laboring children experienced early in this century.

Despite the abundance of working children, the sons and daughters of the growing middle class—professionals, middling businessmen, and other fairly affluent Americans—were working less and contributing less to family income. There were two basic reasons. First, as discussed elsewhere in this chapter, attitudes toward children were changing. Increasingly, they were considered as living through a time of life with unique traits and special needs, including a prolonged formal education and protection from the pressures and temptations of the adult world. That meant young people should stay out of the workplace until they had passed through their adolescence. Second, with rising income, middle-class families had less reason to put their children to work. Office managers, doctors, factory foremen, high-level clerks, merchants, and others in similar occupations often earned enough to provide for all their families' economic needs. Even if more income was needed, children could have given little help in those kinds of jobs, unlike work on a farm. The essential employment that bought the food and paid the rent or the mortgage was increasingly separated from the home; fathers bid their wives and children good-bye in the morning and returned at day's end.

Middle-class children did not necessarily stop working altogether. They usually had household chores and might take on extra jobs to make money for themselves. Housework was no small matter. Properly cleaning and maintaining a middle-class home, according to a book published in 1908, required about fourteen hundred hours a year, or about twenty-seven hours a week. Sons and daughters were expected to pitch in at these tasks— sweeping and mopping, cleaning windows, beating rugs, scrubbing walls and washing curtains dirtied by soot from lamps and dust from the street, and more. But if middle-class children helped out quite a bit, they were not providing income to help their families get by. Parents could afford to keep them out of work. This trend would continue throughout the 20th century. As time passed, more sons and daughters of the middle class would spend less time working, and parents would rely less on their labor.

Elsewhere in America, however, the situation was quite different. As the economy expanded and changed, families chased new opportunities, faced new stresses and demands, and frequently found themselves in new economic dilemmas. Some parents had to rely more on their youngsters, not less.

Such was the case with the oldest type of child labor—that on the farm.

The growth of American agriculture during the last part of the 19th century was nothing short of astounding. Between 1870 and 1900, European-American farmers claimed more than 430 million acres of additional farmland. Amazingly, that was more than had been settled during the previous 263 years, since the first permanent English colony had been established at Jamestown in 1607. (It is worth emphasizing that most of what was called "new" land had been "settled" and worked for centuries by other families—those of American Indians—before the expanding European-American society took over these millions of acres for their own uses.) Most of that land, but not all, was west of the Missouri River, on the Great Plains, in the Southwest, and in the country between the Rocky Mountains and the Pacific coast. That expansion of the farmer's frontier, furthermore, continued after the turn of the century. The famous Homestead Law, passed in 1862, was amended in 1909 to give an individual or family more acres under certain circumstances to begin a farm. As transportation improved and prices for wheat, corn, and other farm products rose during several years after 1900, farmers moved into areas they had ignored in the past. Millions of more acres were homesteaded, much of it in the states of the northern Great Plains, such as Montana and North and South Dakota.

For the tens of thousands of families beginning new lives as farmers in the West, the work of children was critically important. There was so much to be done—a house to build; land to plow, prepare, plant, and harvest; a garden to tend; livestock to care for; and fields to fence. And somehow the settlers had to feed themselves during the many long months before the land gave up its first produce.

Children had a hand in all this work. A sod house represented an investment of little cash—most were built with less than thirty dollars in materials, and some cost less than three dollars—but they demanded considerable labor. Pieces of sod, held together with mattings of roots, were sliced from the prairie, usually in bricks two or three feet long, a foot or so wide, and several inches thick. These were stacked into walls, then laid over a wooden framework for a roof. Older sons could help with this job. The first breaking of the fields also was heavy work usually done by men and larger boys. After this stage, however, younger children could help. Before planting, the clods of dirt had to be broken up. This "harrowing" might be done by a boy or girl on a horse or mule pulling a simple machine, or sometimes a log; or children and adults might work the ground by hand, using hoes or even knives to break up the clotted soil. Then came planting. Corn seed could easily be laid down by children, sometimes after punching a hole in the soil with a stick. The father of a large North Carolina family was asked by a farm machinery salesman why he had not bought a corn planter. "I already have eight," he answered.

Once the crops were up, youngsters were expected to keep the fields free of weeds. They worked as human scarecrows, running around and flapping their arms to frighten away the flocks of birds hungry for the seed and the livestock hoping to graze the green shoots. At harvest time, adults once again did the heaviest work in bringing in some crops, such as wheat, although younger girls and boys were relied upon in harvesting corn, cotton and others. Timing now was crucial. Crops had to mature properly, but as autumn approached, so did the chances of an early frost or a storm that could destroy the whole year's effort. That meant everyone—young and old—had to work the fields from first light to last. The pace and load of labor were brutal. On hot August and September mornings, remembered a woman who had worked the fields of east Texas as a child, the rows of cotton faced her "like a monster." She worked more than twelve hours a day in the stifling heat for weeks: "Sometimes I would lie down on my sack and want to die. Sometimes they would pour water over my head to relieve me."[19]

Not only on the western frontier but everywhere in rural America, from Indiana to Alabama to Vermont, work was an inescapable part of a child's life. What would a typical day have been like for a farm girl? She would rise well before dawn to milk cows, gather eggs, bring in wood, and help prepare breakfast. During the day, when not in school, she might help in the fields. Both girls and boys were accomplished herders, often by the age of six or seven, taking cattle to pasture and watching over them on horseback. A girl would be expected to help with the dozens of jobs that made up her mother's work in and around the house: cooking, cleaning, mending, sewing, and caring for the garden, making butter and preparing eggs for sale in town, shelling corn and canning and pickling food for winter eating.

Perhaps with the help of her brothers, she would take part in the grueling tasks of washday, usually once each week—soaking and scrubbing each piece of clothing, sheets, tablecloths, and other linens, sometimes beating the dirt out with a "battling stick," wringing and hanging it all out to dry. For clothes washing and bathing, she would help make soap. Wood ashes from weeks of cooking fires were gathered in a "hopper." Water was poured through the ashes and strained to produce lye, which was combined with lard and fats kept from slaughtered animals, then formed into bars and cakes and left to harden. The result was a harsh but effective soap. (Like many jobs around the farm, this one was potentially dangerous. Lye was powerfully corrosive. Mothers and children sometimes were horribly scarred when it fell onto their skin or blinded if it splashed into their eyes. Young children occasionally mistook the "lye bucket" for drinking water. When swallowed, lye destroyed their throats and digestive tracts, and little could be done to save them.) Late in the day, a girl would turn to more milking and chicken-feeding and more help in preparation of a meal. It made for a long day, fourteen hours or so of hard work, and probably she would be in bed not long after dark.

This farm girl and her brothers and sisters also provided much of the day-to-day food for their families. They fished and hunted squirrels, rabbits, deer, grouse, quail, and other birds. They spent hours gathering wild plants. Many weeds were delicious when served raw as salads or boiled as greens. A man who grew up on the Nebraska plains remembered that his family had a motto about the weeds in their yard: "If you can't beat 'em, eat 'em."[20] Along the creeks were berries and fruits that could be eaten fresh or canned as preserves. Especially during the early years of a farm, there was little cash coming in for purchasing sugar, coffee, matches, and other items a family could not make for itself. Children helped earn cash, too. They sold the tanned skins of animals they had shot or trapped. They hired out as herders to neighbors with no working children of their own.

Life for children was changing quickly and dramatically in the farmlands, as it was everywhere in America. Within a generation, as will be seen in later chapters, parents would be relying less on the help of their young people in making their farms work and pay. But during these first years of the century, children were what they had been since the earliest days of European settlement—essential laborers on scores of thousands of family farms.

Children played vital roles in supporting their families elsewhere in turn-of-the-century America. Interestingly, the closest parallel to the children's importance in the rural economy was in that part of the nation that would seem most different from the isolated farms of Montana and Mississippi—the teeming, congested cities. As was the case on the frontier, urban America was experiencing a great flood of newcomers pushed out of their old homes by difficulties and drawn by the hope of new opportunities. And just as on frontier homesteads and in sharecropper country, immigrants to the city faced an array of unanticipated troubles. They needed the help of all family members to get by, children included.

For all the vigorous economic activities in American cities, fathers, the usual breadwinners of the home, often could not earn enough to support their families. In 1900 a factory worker on the average made less than $450 a year, or not much more than eight dollars a week. Unskilled or semiskilled workers brought home barely five dollars a week—when they were able to find work. Only rarely could men count on regular employment. Even manufacturing workers, according to one study, were typically out of work about sixty days a year. Most unskilled laborers would set off to look for work every day, sometimes finding it but often not. For millions of fathers, then, income from work was skimpy and uncertain.

And it was rarely enough. At the turn of the century, a family of five needed about five hundred dollars a year to pay for essentials, more than the average earnings of a factory worker. The budget of a factory worker's family in 1904 showed food and rent taking more than six out of every ten dollars he brought home. Additionally, there were bills for coal and gas for fuel, clothing, payment on loans, and some extras, including seven dollars for the year's recreation.[21] If such a father found work every day (which was highly unlikely), he probably could not earn enough to cover even such a bare-bones budget.

Somebody had to come up with the difference. Wives and mothers were needed for essential work around the house; moreover, relatively few jobs were open to women. That left the younger family members. Among the working class of the cities, it was the children who most commonly provided the second incomes so crucial to their families' survival. As you might expect, young people played this role more often among immigrant families struggling to establish themselves in the new country. In Philadelphia of 1880, for instance, children born in America contributed up to about thirty percent of their families' income, while Irish children contributed from thirty-eight to forty-six percent.

Boys and girls, some as young as five or six, labored at a remarkable variety of jobs, but most urban child labor fell into three broad categories. First was "home work," sometimes called the "tenement trades." Children labored, usually with their families, in rooms of the crowded buildings that housed some of the cities' poorest residents, helping to produce a large variety of items. They sewed cheap clothing out of pre-cut pieces. They fashioned artificial flowers and lace, strung beads, and made bedding and powder puffs. Although cigarettes were manufactured in factories, cigars still were produced by hand. After adult tenement workers rolled together tobacco leaves of various grades, a child often took the final step: licking the cigar so the spittle would help hold it together. In a full day's work a girl or boy might perform this process on a thousand cigars.

It is very difficult to estimate how many young people were involved in tenement labor. The number surely runs into the scores of thousands. The census of 1910 reported that in New York City alone such commercial work was done in more than thirteen thousand tenements. At least half of these young workers, and perhaps as many as three-fourths, were girls. Some worked full time with their parents; others put in hours after school. In all cases the work was monotonous, difficult, physically taxing, and outright dangerous, as these buildings were breeding grounds for disease. "Few other kinds of labor sapped the strength and spirits of children quite so pervasively," one historian has written. "The factory child at least went home to a different environment after work; the young tenement worker had no place to go but the street."[22]

Those streets were the sites of a second category of jobs. In the "street trades" children peddled a variety of goods and services. Newsboys sold the newspapers that were becoming an essential part of urban life. (Daily circulation of these publications rose from 2.4 million in 1879 to 24 million in 1909.) Besides the "newsies," there were bootblacks and youngsters selling chewing gum, cigars, candy, magazines, and artificial flowers. These young salesmen often were described as "independent" merchants; and in a sense they were, as they usually bought their goods from a manufacturer or wholesaler, then kept whatever income they received over what they had paid. In another sense, however, they were vulnerable and dependent on their suppliers. And if poor weather or bad luck left them with an armload of papers or boxes of unsold gum, the losses came out of profits that were already pitifully small. These youngsters learned to be aggressive and imaginative. They shouted out variations of the most sensational headlines about bloody murders, scandals, and horrendous disasters, and they clustered around the most likely spots, such as train depots: "Every passenger who alights is immediately besieged, and the boys tumble over each other in order to make the first sale."[23]

Nearly as common as peddling was "junking," picking through trash heaps and dumps. Some children met their family needs directly by scavenging fuel coal from railway yards and wood from vacant lots. Others gathered rags and other castoff items to sell to junk dealers. This was big business: the Department of Commerce estimated in 1916 that $265 million dollars in scrap metal and ten million pounds of wastepaper were picked up that year by junkers, many of them children. Boys also worked as messengers, carrying packages and relaying information at a time when urban communication was primitive and inefficient. Nearly every downtown block had its office, with uniformed youngsters from twelve to eighteen and older ready to answer a call. During the day messenger boys worked for businessmen, but in the evening, after offices had closed for the day, they found their customers in less legitimate enterprises, including houses of prostitution. Many street children, in fact, picked up extra money recruiting clients for prostitutes, and the men and women in bordellos sent them out to buy alcohol and narcotics. As Ethel Waters remembered of her early years in Philadelphia, girls and boys would serve the prostitutes in other ways, weaving their job as lookout into their playtime:

> Any of us slum children could smell out a cop even though he was a John, a plain-clothes man. These brilliant sleuths never suspicioned that we were tipsters for the whole whoring industry. Usually we'd be playing some singing game on the street when we spotted a cop, a game like Here Comes Two Dudes Riding . . . [W]e boys and girls in the know would start to shout the songs, accenting certain phrases . . . The other kids, even those who weren't lookouts, would innocently imitate us, and in no time at all the whole neighborhood was alerted. The street women would disappear, the lights would go out, and the doors would be locked in the sporting houses.[24]

The street trades were dominated by boys. One study found only 168 girls among 17,669 children selling newspapers in several cities. Incomes varied. Newsboys who hawked their papers full time on a busy corner, often after paying for control of such a strategic location, might make four or five dollars a day—excellent pay. Beginners, on the other hand, might work several hours for fifty cents, or twenty-five, or even ten cents. Most who worked consistently for most of the day probably made between five and eight dollars a week. Many boys, however, worked the streets only sporatically, hawking and junking for a few hours after school and only when their families were in special need of extra funds. All told, hundreds of thousands of young people made money at these trades at some point in their lives. Among those who worked as "newsies" in their youth were the composers and musicians Irving Berlin and Louis Armstrong, the diplomat Ralph Bunche, comedians Joe E. Brown and all the Marx brothers, film director Frank Capra, and two U.S. Supreme Court justices, William O. Douglas and Earl Warren.

The third category employing urban children was industrial labor. By 1900 the United States had emerged as the leading industrial nation in the world. One result was an extraordinary demand for workers in American factories, as by 1900 more than two-thirds of all industrial workers labored in large-scale plants. Owners found that children, from eight through adolescence, could perform many essential tasks. Some businessmen argued that youngsters were better than adults because of their "nimble fingers" and great energy—not to mention that children were paid far less. In a sense this was nothing new. From the earliest twitchings of American manufacturing, children had labored alongside their elders. In 1820, for instance, nearly half the workers in New England textile mills were youngsters. What was new was the scale—and in many cases the nature and the dangers—of child industrial labor.

An example was the glassmaking industry. Here was a case of an ancient craft producing at a far greater pace in new industrial workplaces, most of them in New Jersey, Pennsylvania, Indiana, and West Virginia. At least 7,500 boys under sixteen worked in glass factories in 1900. A "mold boy" crouched and steadied an iron mold, blistering hot, as a glassblower blew a bottle into shape through his long tube. A "snapping-up" boy then took the bottle to the "glory hole," where its neck was melted and shaped, as a "cleaning-off boy" knocked pieces of glass off the blower's tube. Finally, a "carrying-in boy" took the bottle rapidly to an oven set at a lower temperature where it cooled slowly. Furnace rooms were terribly hot—between 100 and 130 degrees Fahrenheit—and filled with fumes and silica dust that inflamed the workers' air passages. A "carrying-in" boy might cover twenty miles a day as he moved around in this atmosphere. Much of the work was done during the slightly cooler hours of the night, leaving teams of exhausted boys to find their way home at dawn. Most of these young workers came from outside the families of the older employees. "I would rather send my boys straight to hell than send them by way of the glass house," an older worker explained.

Glass factories were not the only places where children worked under appalling conditions. Another dramatic example of a very old industry expanding rapidly to meet society's new needs was coal mining. Coal, after all, was the fuel that powered much of the rest of industry as well as the heating source of millions of homes. New technologies were applied as demand soared. What always had been a risky business became one of the country's most dangerous occupations. Boys under sixteen or so were usually too small for the heavy work underground, but they labored in other ways. Some were put in charge of the mules that pulled the carts, directing the animals with whips or shouted orders and feeding and watering them in company stables, some of them deep in the earth. Many worked as "breaker boys." After coal was blasted and dug from below, it was lifted to the top of a tall structure and dumped down a series of chutes. As conveyors carried the coal toward storage bins, breaker boys sat alongside the chutes, leaning over and picking out the slate and other refuse. Shifts typically were ten hours long with few breaks to rest and eat. It was back-breaking—or rather, back-bending—work that left many children with curved spines, sunken chests, and sloping shoulders. The coal dust they breathed was so thick they needed miners' lamps on their heads to see. The sharp rock cut and bruised their hands and led to nagging infections and blood poisoning. The buildings were sweltering in summer, drafty and frigid in winter.

In another major industry, textiles, manufacturers were not just producing more, they were expanding into different parts of the country. One of the country's earliest industries, textile production had always been concentrated in New England; then, during the late 19th century, it shifted rapidly into the southern states where the main raw material, cotton, was grown. In 1880 less than five percent of the textile spindles in the country were in the South; the share had grown to forty percent by 1915. The number of southern mills grew from 180 to more than 900 during the twenty-five years after 1880. By 1915 the South had more mills than in all the rest of the country.

To work in those mills, owners called on families, almost entirely white, who in the past had barely scratched out a living as farmers. Instead of producing cotton in the field, they would help turn it into cloth and clothing in the mill. These families often welcomed the chance to make what was, to them, a good wage. And just as on the farm, they expected their young sons and daughters to work with them in the mill. Nonetheless, wages were deplorable even by the standards of that day. In 1900 men in the Carolinas were paid an average of three cents an hour. And children, as always, made less than adults. Younger boys and girls were paid as little as a dime a day, and even after working for several years, they might receive as little as sixty or seventy-five cents. Many worked as much as seventy hours a week, sometimes in back-to-back shifts. An investigator in North Carolina found a ten-year-old girl who had just finished working more than twenty hours with only short breaks for two meals.

Mill children most commonly worked as "spinners" and "doffers." As the combed cotton was made into thread, it was spun rapidly onto spindles aligned in long rows. When a thread broke, the "spinner" re-tied it and started the spindle turning again. One child was responsible for as many as eight hundred spindles. Once the spindle was filled, the "doffer" removed and replaced it. Adolescents worked as "threaders," laboriously putting thousands of threads into small holes in the looms that would weave it into finished cloth. All of them worked in poorly ventilated mills,

Paid pennies per hour, these boys worked all night in a Georgia textile mill. Their smiles to the contrary, many suffered from exhaustion and a variety of diseases that flourished in the mills. *Courtesy of Photography Collections, University of Maryland Baltimore County.*

breathing air filled with lint, or "fly," which left many young people with lung damage before their twentieth birthdays. Most worked barefoot. Smaller children working as "spinners" had to climb and reach high on the rows of twirling spindles. By some accounts, accidents in the cotton mills, usually cuts, mangling, and amputation of fingers, were twice as common as among young workers in other industries.

## AT SCHOOL

In their education, as in everything else, the experiences of American children varied enormously at the beginning of the 20th century. Some went to school in drafty shacks and brought books from home, often the Bible, as texts; others were taught in up-to-date buildings with libraries and modern equipment. Teaching techniques in one school could be dramatically different from those used nearby, and so could the quality and training of the teachers.

A few trends, however, were fairly obvious. Three in particular brought dramatic changes to American education at the opening of the century. First, more young people were attending schools. Second, the bureaucratic structure of the nation's schools was expanding and becoming more specialized. And third, as enrollments soared and schools were reorganized, educators were debating more than ever the goals and methods of teaching. American education was changing profoundly, reflecting the great transformations of the nation itself.

As the century opened, more young people—far more, in fact—were attending school than had ever before in the nation's history. In 1900 there were about 21.4 million persons between the ages of five and seventeen living in the United States; of these, about 15.5 million, or roughly 72 percent, were enrolled in schools. That represented a huge increase over the previous generation. In 1870 only 6.8 million persons, or about 57 percent of the comparable population of youngsters, had attended school. The number of schoolhouses more than doubled between 1870 and 1900, and the value of school property increased more than four times. Schooling, in other words, was rapidly becoming one of the most common, unifying experiences for American youth.

But it would be easy to make too much of those statistics. For one thing, most children left school after only a few years. Going to high school still was a rare experience in 1900; only about eight out of every hundred persons between fourteen and seventeen were enrolled in that year. Though this situation would soon change substantially, throughout the first decades of the 20th century most students did not pursue public education beyond elementary school.

Moreover, many students did not attend classes regularly. Of all those enrolled in all schools, only about 68 percent could be found at their desks on a typical day. Schools were in session on the average for 144 days a year, but a typical student was in class only 99 days, or about twenty school weeks. School attendance also differed greatly from place to place. Children were far more likely to go to school in some parts of the country, such as New England, the Ohio Valley, and some of the West, than in others, like the South and Southwest. In Cleveland, Boston, or other typical cities, young people of the middle and upper classes were much more likely to be found in class than those from the working class. In general, attendance was considerably higher in urban than in rural areas and in some rural areas more than others. For the academic year of 1909–1910, for example, the average term for urban schools across the country was 184 days, compared to 138 days for schools in the countryside. In thinly settled Arizona, however, rural school terms averaged barely a hundred days that year. In some of its districts, schools were open only three months out of twelve.

The reasons for this spotty attendance had to do with the makeup of American society, the children's varied circumstances, and the different challenges and limitations of their lives. Hundreds of thousands of children were from families that had recently emigrated from countries, such as those in eastern Europe, with little tradition of public education, especially for girls. Parents in these families sometimes resisted sending sons and daughters to school, especially when those youngsters could be put to other uses. And, as discussed elsewhere in this chapter, there were plenty of things for children to do. Urban working-class fathers and mothers, scrambling to find enough money for rent and food, were tempted to send their children out to work rather than off to classes.

Simply getting to and from school could be difficult and time-consuming. This was especially true in much of the far West, where European-Americans had just started to settle and where the land could sustain only a few families within a large area. On the Montana plains, for instance, a school district with only one schoolhouse and only ten or so children might cover a thousand square miles, and some of its students might ride thirty or more miles a day to attend class. These farm and ranch children, like their urban counterparts and rural children in more settled areas, were also responsible for much of the work their families needed done for survival. Parents were almost sure to keep them home for weeks at a time, especially when it was the season to plant, care for, and harvest crops. Many school officials admitted that, whatever the laws, it was useless to expect children, especially boys, to show up during those weeks. That left winter as the most likely time for education, but during those months the weather was bound to keep many youngsters at home. Starting off on the long trip to school with a blizzard on the way was foolish, even potentially fatal.

So in very different parts of American society, similar circumstances kept children away from school. South Dakota farmboys, "newsies" and "junkers" just arrived in Philadelphia from Poland and Sicily, and ranch daughters in New Mexico—all were pressured by circumstances to spend their time in other ways than by attending classes. If many children stayed away from schools, usually in violation of the law, it was partly because they were so important and valuable to their families and immediate communities.

Other children were discouraged by discrimination and poor support. The most obvious—and appalling—example was that of African Americans in southern states. The South, the nation's poorest region, spent far less on its schools generally. In 1900, for instance, northeastern states spent about four dollars per capita (that is, based on total population) annually on public education. The West, trying to create and maintain schools from scratch, spent more. But in the deep South, the per capita expenditure was barely over one dollar. That was for all schools, white and black; support for African American education was far, far less. In the southern states (and, it ought to be emphasized, in most of the rest of the United States), education was rigorously segregated by race. The justification for this division, as accepted by the U.S. Supreme Court until much later, was that schools, as well as transportation, lodging, restaurants, entertainment houses, hospitals, cemeteries, and virtually all public accommodations, were "separate but equal." Black and white children might go to different schools, the argument went, but one school was as good as another.

But that was simply not the case, as the funding for those classrooms showed. For example, white schools in South Carolina in 1914–1915 received $10.70 per capita; black schools, $1.09. Louisiana provided $16.44 per capita for its white students, $1.81 for its blacks. The disparity was less on the edges of the South—the corresponding figures for Kentucky were $10.30 and $8.91—but the general pattern prevailed. The salaries of African American teachers, in general, were about half those of their white contemporaries, but in some places the gap was much greater. Additionally, black teachers were expected to teach many more children. In Wilcox County, Alabama, in 1907–1908, teachers in white schools earned $12.30 per student; their counterparts in black schools were paid $.37 per child.[25]

Not surprisingly, black children spent much less time in schools than whites. The average school terms for whites in Alabama, Louisiana, Mississippi, and South Carolina were 131, 156, 123, and 125 days, respectively. Black schools in those states were open 90, 93, 101, and 74 days. The reasons for this grim record, however, went well beyond state funding. Most black families lived as tenants and sharecroppers and faced enormous pressure to produce as much as possible from their small plots of land if they were to provide for their own basic needs and keep their debts to a minimum. That required just about everyone, from children of five or six to the elderly, to work in the fields much of the year. These youngsters, in other words, lived by their own variation of the situation that was keeping other boys and girls, from New York City to Utah, on the job and out of school. The tighter the grip of farm tenancy in the South, the less time students spent at the schoolhouse. This situation would persist. Even in 1930, 86 percent of black families in Arkansas were farm tenants or share-croppers; their children spent an average of 81 days per year in school. In Virginia, on the other hand, where only 38 percent of African American families were tenants, a black child was in class an average of 128 days.[26]

So some children were spending a good bit more time in school than others, and education was much less a part of some students' lives than others. Nevertheless, the trend during these years was very clear: Between 1900 and 1920, the percentage of young people attending schools crept gradually upward, and youngsters were staying in school longer. By 1920 nearly eight out of ten children between five and seventeen were enrolled in school, and, of those, about three out of four were actually in a class-room on any given school day. On average, a schoolchild attended school 121 days a year, which was quite a jump from 99 at the turn of the century. Education was becoming more and more a part of growing up American.

With more students filling the nation's classrooms, the need to restructure and reorganize schools became evident. The pressure naturally was the strongest where the growth was the greatest, most of all in the cities. The system of graded schools, with students moving year-by-year through classes with other children of roughly the same age and level of ability, was well established in 1900; and, increasingly, it became the sole method of organ-izing schools in more populated areas. One of the most dramatic devel-opments was the tendency of students to stay in school into the upper grades—that is, into high school. As already mentioned, only about 8 percent of persons between fourteen and seventeen were attending high schools in 1900, but the percentage had nearly doubled by 1910, to 15 percent; then it more than doubled again, up to 32 percent in 1920.

One reason was that laws were changing, requiring students to stay in school longer; but there were also practical reasons. Many parents, espe-cially those of the middle class, believed that a longer education and greater skills were necessary to prepare their sons and daughters for adult lives. As another part of this chapter will show, states were also passing child labor laws that kept young people from the working classes out of certain kinds of jobs, especially in factories; and some new industries had fewer jobs for young people anyway, especially for young females. With fewer chances to move into the workplace, adolescents were more likely to stay in school. High schools, furthermore, typically offered training in vocational skills, from mechanics and agriculture to clerical and domestic work. For many adolescents, staying in school, at least until the ninth or tenth grade, was a sensible response to the changing rules and opportunities of their world.

As more students stayed on through more and more grades, the job of running schools became more complicated. That, in turn, led to the appearance of two educational figures—the principal and the superintendent. In the past schools with several classes had relied on one of the teachers, sometimes called a "principal teacher," to oversee the operation. Now the principal became exclusively an administrator, with the sole responsibility of running things. A superintendent, in turn, was needed to run rapidly growing districts that were turning into elaborate bureaucracies, with many schools of different levels, dozens of specialized teachers, expanding curricula, and many buildings and other facilities.

All this, of course, was very expensive. During the first two decades of the 20th century, taxpayers were running up an ever larger bill to pay for expanding school systems. In 1920, for the first time, the American people could boast (or complain) that they had a billion-dollar school system. Nationwide, the total expenditure that year for public education ($1,036,151,209) was nearly five times what it had been in 1900 ($214,867,718).

With so much else changing in American education, it was not surprising that educators and others in public life were also asking fundamental questions about the purposes of schooling and how they could best be achieved. The United States was emerging as a major world power; its people were experiencing transformations in virtually every aspect of their lives. Every year seemed to bring bewildering problems and astounding opportunities hardly imagined in an earlier generation. The future, in short, was both exciting and profoundly troubling. How were we to meet this challenge? Education seemed to be the most valuable means of reaching toward our potential, or at least of avoiding some national calamity. The children, those who would preside over future homes, businesses, and governments, would have to be ready. And that meant taking a hard look at the schools.

Critics found plenty to complain about. Probably the most common criticism was that the subjects taught and the methods used had little to do with children's lives outside the classroom. Mathematics was taught abstractly, history and geography through memorization of facts with no discussion of their implications or results. Instruction in chemistry, biology, and other sciences consisted of laws, equations, and experiments seemingly unconnected to the world beyond the laboratory. In other words, said many critics, the schools were failing at their most basic duty. Education, although supposedly preparing students for useful and fulfilling futures, in fact was mostly divorced from "real life."

The person most associated with educational reform was John Dewey, philosopher and professor first at the University of Chicago and then at Columbia University. Schools, he argued, should be training grounds for a democratic society. Therefore, they had to stimulate children's natural curiosity and sharpen their skills of inquiry that could be applied to the world beyond the school grounds. Classrooms also should be places where students practiced dealing with others in society, including those in authority (in this case, their teachers). So, Dewey wrote, the schoolroom and society should reflect one another. Classes ought to be "embryonic communities." Education should pay less attention to traditional approaches and more to the concerns and potentials of students. In *The School and Society* (1900), Dewey used a striking image to make his point. In most schools at that time, he wrote,

> the center of gravity is outside the child. It is in the teacher, the textbook, anywhere and everywhere you please except in the immediate instincts and activities of the child himself. . . . Now the change which is coming into our education is the shifting of the center of gravity. It is a change, a revolution, not unlike that introduced by Copernicus when the astronomical center shifted from the earth to the sun. In this case the child becomes the sun about which the appliances of education revolve; he is the center about which they are organized.[27]

Other critics agreed that schools should make more of an effort to reflect students' realistic needs, but particular proposals varied. Some, such as David Snedden, professor of education at Columbia University, emphasized vocational training to prepare young people for the sort of employment that likely awaited many of them. As noted above, high schools increasingly introduced classes in mechanical and domestic trades. In some programs, students were "tracked"—evaluated early in their school years to determine their interests and abilities—and then channeled mainly into vocational classes or into more traditional academic courses. This was done in the name of social efficiency and for the good of the students. Education, it was argued, had to become more specialized, and for those young people most suited for such labor, vocational classes were ultimately more valuable than lectures in English literature and physics.

But who would decide which students were suited for what kind of training? Some reformers thought "tracking" and stress on vocational skills were potentially unjust and posed a threat to a truly democratic society. Putting students into manual training, after all, was almost certainly a way of setting the future course of their lives. In making those decisions, judging the girls and boys who stood before them and determining how they would spend their adult years, teachers and administrators could be guided by personal assumptions and biases about gender, ethnicity, economic background, even dress, appearance, and demeanor. Females, many assumed, belonged in domestic life, not in the professions, so they should specialize in home economics; while a son of a Lithuanian dock worker presumably was naturally suited for factory work and thus ought to spend his days in mechanical training. A boy growing up in a family of doctors or businessmen, on the other hand, should be "tracked" toward a career as a lawyer or executive. In the name of efficiency and service to the students, some said, this kind of education was really narrowing the horizons of American youth. Among them was John Dewey, who argued that the result would be to limit opportunity and to build even higher walls among classes of Americans.

Critics of education disagreed about what needed to be done, and others, in turn, disagreed with the critics. Concentrating on the student's social needs and catering to demands of the day—making the child, as Dewey put it, the sun around which education revolved—could produce a society ignorant of its cultural fundamentals. Instead, those on that side of the argument felt that teachers should focus on the basics of mathematics and science, literary "classics," and the outlines of American and European history. All students ought to study these subjects, which were the common heritage of the American nation.

What would it have been like to go to school in 1900? The answer varies enormously, as was true of everything about American children. Students were taught different sorts of subjects by many kinds of teachers of varying quality and training. They sat in drafty, poorly lit buildings and in comfortable, well-equipped classrooms. They studied antiquated textbooks and used the most up-to-date equipment and educational aids. As they left their classes for the last time, some young people were well prepared and others wretchedly educated. Most would look back on their classrooms with mixed feelings.

In all sections of the country, hundreds of thousands of children were educated in what had been a familiar feature of American life for generations, the one-room schoolhouse. This institution was the result of a prob-

In one-room schoolhouses like this one in Kansas, with plenty of flags and moral sayings on the walls, students were taught patriotism along with history, mathematics, and literature. *Courtesy of Kansas Collection, University of Kansas Libraries.*

lem that had nagged at rural Americans since the earliest public schools were established. When only a few families without much money were spread out over a large area, how could they educate their children? The obvious and practical answer was to send all sons and daughters to a single, centrally located school with one teacher. In 1913 there were about 212,000 one-room schools operating in the United States; and half of the nation's public school students attended classes in them.

Some were substantial buildings in long-settled rural country, but in areas recently settled by European-Americans, children and teachers met in abandoned sod houses, cowboy bunkhouses, miners' cabins, and the backrooms of saloons. A survey in 1918 of country schools in South Dakota found that more than ninety percent still relied on outhouses and twenty percent had no drinking water. In half of them, children drank from a common dipper rather than from individual cups. A typical school in this region, wrote a spokesman for the U.S. Department of Education, was little different from one in the 1840s. Southern schoolchildren, especially African Americans, often sat in cramped shacks, poorly heated in winter, stifling and plagued by swarms of mosquitoes in warmer months.

Regardless of its condition and whatever its many practical advantages, the one-room schoolhouse had one serious drawback: it put an enormous burden on the teacher. Somehow he or she had to accommodate the needs of a roomful of children of different ages, abilities, and levels of learning. Looking over her class on the first day of a term, a schoolmistress might see frightened five-year-olds, a bright boy or girl of eight or nine experienced at algebra, a sixteen-year-old barely able to write his name, and immigrant students from Sweden or Russia fluent in their own language but unable to write English.

The first step, often taking up to a couple of weeks, was to determine which students belonged at which grade level. Then they were arranged accordingly within the single room, sometimes at desks and often on benches. A veteran of a Colorado schoolhouse described the scene there:

> I was on a long seat that looked like it held three or four kids. I was the only one in the first grade. In the next row, a boy and a girl sat on another long seat. They were in the second grade. Ray was in the third row with another boy that was in the third grade. Fred was the only one in the fifth grade. He was in the fourth row. One girl sat in the next to the last row, alone. She was in the ninth grade. Last but not least, there were a boy and a girl who sat in the back of the room. They were in the twelfth grade.[28]

Once students were sorted, the teacher had to work with each group to lift them into the next level by term's end. Students naturally had to work much of the time on their own, reading and practicing mathematics and writing skills, but they also were absorbing what they overheard from their teacher testing others in higher grades.

The quality of education depended above all on the instructors and their dedication. Some students complained of incompetence and abuse, but many who grew up through this system testified that the close, individual attention worked remarkably well. As the years passed these schoolhouses, and the experience of learning within them, would become increasingly rare, but they helped shape the minds and characters of millions of people.

For better or worse, the one-room schoolhouse was the educational cornerstone in much of America during the earliest years of the century.

Education elsewhere was moving in quite a different direction. As the overall population grew and more Americans were concentrated in towns and cities, districts turned increasingly to a system with students organized by grades. Such a system had to have larger schools to hold the growing congregations of students. The result were institutions that could hardly have been more different from one-room schoolhouses—sprawling buildings, many of them multistoried, with long halls flanked by rows of rooms filled with hundreds of young people. Educational specialists held up an ideal that they hoped would serve as a model for school officials across the country. A book published in 1919 urged that a schoolhouse be built on a hill in "a moral neighborhood" away from traffic. It ought to face east or south and have some shade trees and lilacs planted around it. The building must be well lit and ventilated and "honestly built." A classroom should have movable furniture and five rows of desks, with six to eight in a row, and windows that admitted light over the students' left shoulders. On the walls should be slate blackboards and cork for pinning pictures. In decoration dull colors were recommended, such as sage and cream, because bright tones "weary the eye and fatigue the brain."[29]

Few districts could live up to those standards. In some middle-class urban neighborhoods and in more affluent small towns, students did meet in spacious well-constructed buildings. They studied from recent textbooks, well-designed maps and globes, and books chosen from well-stocked libraries. But such cases were the exception. Urban districts typically faced major obstacles to accommodating floods of new students. Most were pitifully underfunded. Some held classes in converted office buildings and warehouses, their classrooms stuffy, windowless, and dreary. Some were newer and more impressive. Harry Gold's, where he attended classes with the future actor Edward G. Robinson and with Jacob Javits, who would grow up to be a prominent U.S. senator, was like "a bastion, . . . surrounded by a steel picket fence," with huge front doors, spacious classrooms with large windows, and steel staircases with wooden banisters that Harry and his friends slid down sidesaddle.[30]

Even buildings like those, however, typically were filled to bursting with students and were chronically short of teachers. So crowded were New York City's elementary schools in 1905 that nearly two-thirds, all of them in immigrant districts, had to operate on part-time schedules: students went to class half a day to allow others to take their places during the other half.

Regardless of where a boy or girl went to school, the teacher more than likely was a woman. That had not always been the case. Early in the history of the United States, nearly all teachers were men, but by the opening of the 20th century, nearly ninety percent of all schoolteachers were female. There were at least a couple of reasons for this change. By the standards of the Victorian age, women were thought to be especially well-suited to caring for children, preserving moral standards, and providing emotional warmth and affection. Those traits were considered helpful, even essential, to education in its fullest sense, and so women were favored as school-teachers. Teaching, then, provided an opening for ambitious young women at a time when most professions, such as medicine, law, and the ministry, were almost completely closed to females. Education offered young women respectable work, enough salary to survive, and, just as important, the chance to live independently. For a young woman not interested in mar-rying and rearing a family, at least not right away, teaching school was about her only professional choice.

Female or male, by the early 20th century the teacher was more likely to have had some formal training, as compared with teachers of a gener-ation earlier. The number of "normal schools," institutions designed to produce professional educators, was increasing rapidly, and the enrollment in these schools more than doubled between 1890 and 1900. Though not equally distributed across the country—there were far more in the North-east and Midwest than in the South and West—the normal schools rep-resented a national trend to professionalize and standardize public education. Students in normal schools were taught recent theories of learn-ing and were trained in what were considered the most effective curricula and techniques of instruction.

Still, the training and quality of teachers varied tremendously from place to place. In most cases, it was up to local officials to decide whether a person was or was not fit to teach; and in those parts of the country where there were many schools but few instructors, it was always tempting to accept inadequately prepared applicants—and in some cases just about anybody—to take charge of a classroom. In isolated parts of the country-side, for instance, it was not so unusual for students showing up on the first day of school to find as their teacher a girl or boy of fifteen or sixteen, who had been a student in the same schoolhouse the previous term. In other cases, school officials hired men and women looking for temporary work, who were often ill-educated and rarely dedicated to doing the best job possible.

An important cause of shoddy teaching was the abysmally low pay in most districts. A study of thirty-four states in 1914 revealed the appalling situation in rural schools. Men received an average of forty dollars a month; women, thirty-three dollars. (Here was another important reason more and more women were hired: they were cheaper.) In the buying power of 1990, such salaries were not much more than five hundred dollars a month. To compound the problem, teachers could normally find work for only six or eight months a year. To cut expenses many lived with families of their students, often sharing beds with children they taught during the day. When they had their own rooms, the facilities were not always comfortable. A Nebraska teacher recalled that on winter nights in her room the "door hung with icicles and heavy frost. . . . [She lay] shivering under blankets and dressed in a flannel robe and pajamas, a coat and socks, her breath made a thin sheet of ice around the pillow and covers as she kept her head under the covers and tried to sleep."[31]

The nature of students also differed considerably according to where one was attending school. In one-room schoolhouses, the range of ages could be considerable. Boys from farms and ranches spent a good part of their time at work and out of school, sometimes taking off a year or two from classes to help out the family; so they moved slowly through their lessons, year after year. A similar situation could be found in the cities, where many young people also had to split their time between school and work, and where immigrant children, fighting to adjust to a new culture and language, often could not work at the levels of native-born children of their age. In a schoolhouse on the Colorado plains or in a classroom in the immigrant district of Boston or Chicago, a girl of seven or eight might find herself sitting next to a young man of sixteen, twenty, or even older. Those students, regardless of their ages, likely came from an array of backgrounds and traditions, Hungarians and Irish, Italians and Poles, and others reared in villages and crowded city neighborhoods in many parts of the United States. Classes mirrored the diversity of American life.

How teachers treated their students, and how students felt about it, naturally varied as well. Even the most determined teachers were often harried, overworked, and exhausted by the demands of the job. Often they resorted to corporal punishment to enforce discipline and express displeasure at poor performance. In his class in New York City, one man remembered, the teacher "seldom used the ruler to measure anything except the distance between a long overhead swing and the student's hand." Another teacher, perhaps to save energy, encouraged other students to strike a child who had not done assigned work. Besides physical punishment, students often remembered their instructors as cold and aloof, demanding, giving out plenty of criticism but few compliments. Others, however, recalled their time in school much more fondly. Their teachers were warm, affectionate, and full of praise for work well done. Some children found emotional rewards in school that they missed at home. An immigrant daughter remembered her sixth-grade teacher, who "would help me, hug me and nurture me. My mother was not a nurturer."[32]

These remembrances were as mixed and contradictory as everything else in American education as the nation began a new century. Veterans of country schoolhouses looked back on sadistic teachers who beat them, locked them in closets, and, according to some stories, fired pistols in the air to emphasize their authority. A survey of Slavic children in Chicago in 1913 found that eight out of ten would have preferred working in a factory to going to school even if economic need had not forced them to work. Yet a man who grew up on New York's Lower East Side recalled his teacher as "a grand lady . . . a beautiful woman [who] smelled of heaven" and treated him with gentle concern, and a woman from the same area looked back almost worshipfully on her fifth-grade instructor: "She changed the course of my life. She gave me everything she had and more. Because of her I was introduced to everything that is good in the United States."[33]

## HEALTH

In 1900 life was chancy for American children, especially the youngest ones. It is difficult to estimate how many children died annually at the start of the century, mainly because deaths (and births) often went unrecorded. This was especially true outside the cities, but the lack of vital statistics was a problem virtually everywhere. Census takers relied on what they called the "death registration area," where records were kept reasonably well. In 1910 that area included twenty-one states and forty-three cities in other states, plus Washington, D.C.

The sketchy figures that came out of these places were dreadful. According to one authority, in 1900 about one out of every four babies died before he or she reached the age of five. That estimate may well be high, but another study concluded that in 1915 the rate of death among children during their first five years was *at least* 10 percent. Everyone agrees, furthermore, that African American and Native American boys and girls were in far more danger than white children. The 1900 mortality rate for non-white infants under five has been estimated at 35 percent, compared to 15 percent for whites. Statistically, that is, black parents on a Mississippi farm or a Navajo mother and father living on a reservation in Arizona would have been lucky if they did not watch one child out of every three die before it was old enough to go to school.

The United States was emerging as one of the wealthiest and most powerful nations in history. Why, then, were so many of its children dying? Seen in context, infant mortality was all too common everywhere in the world, even in such "advanced" nations as England. Throughout history, until quite recently, the first few years of life have always been the most precarious. As an early folk saying put it, the miracle is not that we live to be fifty, but that we live to be five. The threat to the very young, as the new century opened, was considerable, and the reasons behind it are revealing.

Children were in danger, first of all, because medical authorities were remarkably ignorant about the causes, nature, and treatment of diseases. Many advances in medical knowledge had been made during the previous half century, but far more still lay ahead. Breakthroughs in prevention and treatment, furthermore, usually made their way only slowly down to the grassroots practice of medicine. Millions of Americans, for that matter, had no access whatsoever to licensed doctors. Finally, by studying children's illnesses and deaths, we can learn a good deal about the social conditions of Americans of all ages, their bewildering problems, and the wide gaps that separated the rich and poor, the white and nonwhite, the lucky and the less fortunate.

A broadening understanding of the nature of diseases was helping in the battle to save the children. One of the most fundamental developments in the history of science had come during the late 19th century with the "germ theory." Scientists previously had believed that diseases could be traced to such causes as "impure blood" and deadly mists and vapors. The origins of illnesses were thought to be essentially chemical. But by the 1860s, specialists were increasingly convinced that many diseases were biological in origin. They were caused, wrote one authority, by tiny organisms living in the human body. In the 1870s and 1880s, researchers developed techniques to cultivate bacteria so they might be studied. By 1890, scientists had identified the microorganisms—the "germs"—that caused cholera, pneumonia, diphtheria, tuberculosis, typhoid, and several other maladies. This was a discovery of immeasurable value. With the cause clearly identified, researchers could turn to the means of preventing and treating diseases that had been virtually invincible for centuries.

A particularly dramatic success was the case of diphtheria. Diphtheria was one of the most prominent killers of children; it was also one of the

most terrifying. Two or three days after a child was exposed to the diphtheria bacillus, the first symptoms set in. A slight sore throat turned gradually more painful; but worse than that was the rapid swelling of the throat
(victims were said to have "bullneck") and the appearance of a thick
membrane along the breathing passage. It was this development ("diphtheria" is Greek for "membrane" or "shield") that brought the greatest
danger. The disease can eventually damage the heart and nervous system
and produce paralysis, but before that the yellowish or green membrane
can fill the throat, slowly suffocating the young victim. Parents, brothers,
and sisters sat by helplessly as they watched a child fighting desperately to
breathe and, too often, losing the battle. Sometimes adding to the horrifying
course of the illness were hallucinations, probably caused by fever and the
reduced supply of oxygen to the brain. A young girl who survived her bout
remembered "dreams of animals and snakes that filled all space, writhing,
in constant motion, coming closer to me but never quite in on me. . . . The
horror of it all was very real and for months those dreams returned, causing
me to wake in a cold sweat."[34]

Diphtheria was extraordinarily contagious. The bacillus was easily
passed through the air or by the touch of a victim. Children caught the
disease by playing with friends' toys or handling a pencil at school. The
bacillus could pass from the hands of an exposed child to the udders of a
cow he milked, next to the milk itself, then to his brothers and sisters at
the dinner table. The dust around a sick child's bed could be dangerous
for weeks. The result, predictably, was the rapid spread of the disease
through families and communities. When it struck in especially virulent
forms, between 30 to 50 percent of infected children died. It was not un-
common for a family to lose two, three, or even more children in a week
during an epidemic. Doctors and parents could do little to help except keep
the victims quiet. Some tried to scrape the membranes or even to cut open
the children's throats to ease their breathing.

The breakthrough in combatting this child-killer came in Germany,
where Emil Behring and Shibasaburo Kitasato developed a serum in 1890
from patients surviving the disease. Behring then pioneered a process for
producing a serum from infected horses that could provide immunity in
inoculated children. Another important step was the development of the
"Schick test." A tiny amount of diphtheria toxin was injected under a
child's skin. A reaction showed that the patient had never been exposed to
the disease and so should be inoculated.

These discoveries were doubly important. Not only did they provide an
effective and reliable means of preventing and curing one of the most vi-

cious diseases in history, they also clearly and dramatically demonstrated the validity of the new germ theory and showed how valuable serum and inoculation could be in the warfare against a previously deadly malady. The consequences of inoculation were shown in the diphtheria mortality statistics for three American cities:

### Deaths from Diphtheria per 100,000 Persons

|          | New York | Chicago | Boston |
|----------|----------|---------|--------|
| 1890–94  | 134.4    | 117.3   | 112.2  |
| 1900–04  | 58.0     | 33.9    | 53.7   |
| 1910–14  | 28.0     | 37.9    | 20.0   |
| 1920–24  | 14.0     | 17.5    | 20.2   |
| 1940–44  | 00.1     | 00.8    | 00.4[35] |

Not all diseases would prove so easily beaten, but the same essential approach was used in the assault on many contagions that had savaged Americans, young and old. Families also gradually gained a better understanding of how illnesses happen, and with that came a greater appreciation of hygiene and fundamental changes in personal habits. Out of the medical breakthroughs early in this century have come two of the most familiar refrains of childhood, the parent's command to "put that down, it's dirty!" and "wash it before you eat it, it's got germs on it!"

In the end, however, a better medical understanding of the threats to children's health could not be separated from other aspects of their lives: what their home life was like, how their families lived day-to-day, and how and where they worked and played. The social aspects of childhood diseases were just as important as the physical.

These years witnessed the growing realization of just how closely a child's chances of living a healthy life were linked to his or her economic condition. Poor young people were far more likely to suffer ill health than those of the middle classes and more affluent families. Reformers and social critics lashed out against what they charged was a national scandal. In *The Bitter Cry of the Children,* John Spargo wrote:

> I think it can safely be said that in this country, the richest and greatest country in the world's history, poverty is responsible for at least 80,000 infant lives every year—more than two hundred every day of the year, more than eight lives each hour, day by day, night by night throughout the year. It is impossible for us to realize fully the immensity of this annual sacrifice of baby lives.[36]

These youthful sacrifices took place throughout the nation, on farmsteads and in slums, in mining camps, fishing villages, and sheep ranches. Some of the worst conditions were among impoverished southern farmers, especially African Americans, who had limited, inadequate diets and worked under the harshest conditions. Few had access to medical advice and services, as shown in a study in one part of rural Mississippi in 1918. Of forty-three babies who died during their first year, a physician was present at the death of only fifteen; among the twenty-eight black infants, only six had a doctor at hand when they died. Isolated from towns and plagued by poor roads, unaccustomed to seeking out doctors, many families relied on folk remedies. As her baby was dying, one mother bound the child's feet and hands with red onions to try to cure the "griping in the stomach and the stretches."[37]

Similar situations could be found in every region. Among homesteaders on the Montana plains, fewer than a third of the mothers in one survey lived within ten miles of a physician. In the area studied, more than 5,500 square miles, there was no hospital. More than two-thirds of the mothers had delivered their children without the help of a doctor or midwife. Another study in Rhode Island found midwives using snuff to dress the freshly cut umbilical cords and feeding newborns mixtures of molasses and urine.[38]

Some of the clearest illustrations of the connection of poverty and child health occurred in the expanding cities. Working-class families lived packed closely together, frequently in highly unsanitary conditions. Tenement apartments rarely had adequate ventilation and sunlight. Scores of persons might share the same water sources and toilet facilities. Garbage disposal was sporadic at best. Illnesses, once established, spread quickly and efficiently among these dense populations, and such highly contagious "childhood diseases" as measles, whooping cough, and diphtheria could sweep through tenement blocks with astonishing speed.

Poor neighborhoods, in other words, were perfect breeding grounds for contagious illnesses, but children were threatened by more than their physical surroundings. Just as significant were the social conditions of their lives. When a family moved to New York City or Baltimore from a farm or village in the American countryside or in Europe, its daily patterns of life changed profoundly. Often, for instance, the mother had to work outside the home at least part of the day. Typically, moving to the city also meant that the family would leave behind relatives and close friends who had helped with domestic work. One result was that the familiar methods of caring for young children were no longer possible. A mother could not always stay close to home to watch over and breastfeed her infant; neither

A New York City street scene in the 1890s. Overcrowding and poor sanitation, not to mention rotting horses that had dropped dead during summer heat waves, bred and spread diseases fatal to thousands of children living in urban slums. *Courtesy of Library of Congress.*

could she turn it over to a grandmother, aunt, or close friend. Instead, babies were left to the care of others with little experience, often children only slightly older. The reformer John Spargo reported case studies he found in a New York mill town:

> A forty-three year old Irish immigrant mother who worked for seven dollars a week had borne five children. All had died under eighteen months of age, three of convulsions and the others of diarrhea. All had been cared for by other children while the mother worked.
>
> A single mother, thirty-four, had two surviving children out of six.

One, age eighteen months, was cared for by the other, age nine years. One child had died of convulsions, two of bronchitis, and one had been accidentally scalded to death while the mother was at work.[39]

As in these cases, a leading cause of death of poor urban infants often was some variation on digestive disorders. "Convulsions" were typically a symptom or reaction to difficulties that began with the child's diet. The danger might be contaminated food or simply a meal that an infant was not old enough to digest. Investigators in one city found a baby of three weeks fed on stewed cabbage and others slightly older eating sausage and pickles, sardines, vinegar-soaked bread, and strips of raw bacon. Two of these infants died of gastritis, as did thousands of others treated similarly. The more basic cause, however, was the family's inability to care for its youngest members in the usual ways.

The most treacherous time of all was the earliest stage of life, when the infant was most vulnerable and dependent on a mother who often could not afford to be at hand. The census of 1910 for the first time included a table showing the number of deaths among children by age during their first year. The results were stunning. Of all who failed to reach their first birthday, a third died during their first month and a fourth during their first week of life. One out of ten did not survive their first day. Many of these, especially those who survived the first month, succumbed to dysentery, enteritis and other intestinal difficulties; many others, in particular the very youngest, died from congenital defects, malformation, and, above all, from premature delivery.

Such causes suggested a fundamental reason behind many infant deaths: poor prenatal care and the ill health of mothers. Most pregnant women had no access to medical help or advice; most had inadequate diets and worked far too hard. A study in Johnstown, Pennsylvania, in 1913 included this summary of a Polish immigrant woman's delivery of her baby:

At 5 o'clock Monday evening went to sister's to return washboard, having just finished day's washing. Baby born while there; sister too young to assist in any way; woman not accustomed to midwife anyway, so she cut cord herself; washed baby at sister's house; walked home, cooked supper for boarders, and was in bed by 8 o'clock. Got up and ironed next day and day following; it tired her, so she then stayed in bed two days. She milked cows and sold milk day after baby's birth.

This woman keeps cows, chickens, and lodgers; also earns money doing laundry and char work. Husband deserts her at times; he makes $1.70 a day. A 15-year-old son makes $1.10 a day in coal mine. Mother thin and wiry; looks tired and worn.[40]

A baby born under those conditions was likely to be physically weakened and lack adequate sustaining help during its first crucial weeks. Such short-comings, in turn, were directly linked to poverty. Mothers gave their new-borns so little because they, themselves, were so desperately pressed to survive. The Johnstown study found that infants whose fathers made less than $520 per year were twice as likely to die than those with fathers making more than $1,200.

Other diseases threatened all young people, from newborns to teenagers. Among the most common were respiratory illnesses. One baby out of six who died during its first year was a victim of bronchitis or pneumonia. These diseases, too, were especially common among the poor, both because of the dank, ill-heated housing and the crowded conditions that allowed easy passage of the guilty germs from person to person.

Of all diseases of the lungs, the most terrible was tuberculosis. Some authorities, in fact, consider tuberculosis the most deadly illness of all time, as well as one of the oldest. By some estimates, it has killed a billion persons during its long history. Tuberculosis has been such an efficient killer be-cause it is superbly adapted to human beings. Its active agent often allows its human host to live with few effects. Even when it cripples and kills, it typically permits its victim to survive for years, even decades, while that person continues to move around, work, play, and come into contact with many thousands of other people. The tuberculosis bacilli can easily move from one human host to another; thus, tuberculosis can spread and persist among enormous numbers of people, killing some and debilitating others as it roots itself deeply in a community for generation after generation, a familiar part of human society and its suffering.

The tuberculosis bacilli typically settles in the lungs, although it sometimes is found in other organs, bones, and joints. It can gradually destroy lung tissue, cause hemorrhaging, and starve its host of oxygen, bringing death by slow suffocation. As the damage progresses, the victim suffers fits of coughing, often bringing up blood from the lungs. This is the main means of the disease's transmission, as the bacilli is spread through the air in tiny droplets of water and fluid expelled during these coughing bouts. Because its encroachment on the patient's health was slow, tuber-culosis was responsible for the deaths mainly of older children (and, of course, adults), not infants. But its impact on youths and adolescents could be horrendous, and many of those not killed carried the seeds of catastrophe into later life.

Tuberculosis was by no means an affliction of poorer Americans; wealthy and socially prominent persons died of it as well. And yet, just as obviously, families crowded into tenements were especially vulnerable. Bacilli can survive outside the body for relatively long periods of time if left undisturbed in cool, dark places. The close interiors of urban housing—as well as the shops, saloons, and factories—became reservoirs of the disease. Overwork and inadequate diet also left residents of these areas particularly susceptible. Infection rates in some neighborhoods, known as "lung blocks," were as much as ten times the national average. One investigator traced the history of a single one-room apartment in New York City. During one stretch of seven years, four families lived there, each probably leaving behind germs to be picked up by the next. Five members of those families died during that time. On one city block, 265 cases were reported over a nine-year period; many more certainly went unreported.

The deaths of children, of course, measured only the ultimate price of poor health and degraded living conditions. For every fatality, there were many more children who suffered debilitating diseases, some of which left them physically or mentally impaired for the rest of their lives. Among the most common long-term illnesses of the poor was rachitis, or rickets. Caused by poor diet, both of the children themselves and of their mothers during breastfeeding, rickets left its characteristic mark on boys and girls: malformed skulls, flat chests, and twisted legs and spine. Measles, chicken pox, whooping cough, mumps, and other diseases familiar to childhood moved more easily through crowded neighborhoods of the poor. With inadequate access to medical help, these youngsters were more likely to suffer such permanent disabilities as blindness, lung disorders, or brain damage caused by unchecked fever.

Campaigns for better children's health proceeded on several fronts. In the training of physicians, the study and teaching of pediatrics was increasingly stressed during the first generation of the 20th century. This was a remarkably late development; the American Pediatric Society was founded only in the 1880s, and the first English-language journal on children's medicine was begun in 1884. Yet, by 1905, a nationally prominent pediatrician could report "stupendous" progress in his field, especially in the application of new antitoxins and the expanding study of childhood maladies. Diphtheria, he went so far to say (with considerable exaggeration), was now "viewed with serenity."[41] Another approach to detecting and treating childhood diseases was through public education. As seen elsewhere in this chapter, schooling was becoming one of the few experiences that most American young people had in common. It made sense, then, to use the school as a means to assess and improve the state of child health. In the late 19th century, a few cities began systematic health inspection of students, then appointed school nurses to oversee programs for detecting disases and improving hygiene.

Obviously, however, these approaches could only begin to confront the massive problems at hand. More had to be done to reach the causes of ill health—and as early as possible in children's lives. In a few cities, mostly in the Northeast, medical authorities and social welfare agencies began programs to instruct pregnant women in fundamental prenatal care. In a particularly ambitious experiment in 1911, the poorer sections of New York City were divided into small districts and each assigned an obstetrical nurse, who tried to locate all pregnant women, partly through door-to-door canvassing. Those women who agreed to participate were visited every ten days, examined, urged to find a midwife or doctor for delivery, and given advice on diet, daily habits, and work to avoid. In these areas, stillbirths and deaths among very young infants suddenly dropped well below the average for the city as a whole.

Basic to prenatal advice was the issue of milk, and, in a way, the "milk question" was a focal point of much of what was being learned about children's health. Investigators came to realize that working mothers had to rely on others—often other children only slightly older—to care for their infants. Obviously, these mothers could not breastfeed their babies; instead, they had to rely on cow's milk sold in cities. Such milk, however, often was an ideal breeding place for the contagions that doctors were learning were so harmful, especially to the digestive systems of the very young. Milk brought in from the countryside had plenty of time to spoil, and many city dairies were exceptionally unsanitary. A few, following the pattern of an earlier generation, were located next to breweries and distilleries; cows were fed the watery slops left from the fermentation of beer and whiskey. These animals produced bluish "swill milk," which was thin and frequently diseased. One study found that even some of the most modern dairies had cows infected by tuberculosis. An important part of the solution was pasteurization, the heating of milk to destroy bacteria and the sealing and cooling of its containers to prevent new contamination. Pressed by social reformers and health organizations, many cities began requiring pasteurization of commercial milk. By 1916, 80 percent of the milk supply in Boston and Chicago was pasteurized, as was 88 percent of New York's and 95 percent of Pittsburgh's. The results were startling. In these cities, infant mortality rates dropped much more rapidly than elsewhere. Declines were especially sharp in diarrheal disorders and steepest of all in infant deaths during the summer—the time when milk spoilage was the most dangerous.

Such reforms, arising from the increased awareness of the causes of disease and the special dangers among the poor, brought heartening changes during the first years of the 20th century. The infant mortality rate declined by a startling 20 percent between 1915–1919 and 1920–1924. The drop was most impressive in the cities (where, of course, the greatest improvement was needed). New York's rate, measured as the number of children dying during their first year for every thousand births, dipped from 247 in 1885 to 183 in 1900, then even more dramatically during the next twenty years, from 183 to 80.

Still, the conditions of children's health were deplorable in many parts of American society, and staggering dangers and difficulties remained. Perhaps the most important advancement was no single discovery or program but, rather, the widespread acknowledgment that a child's physical well-being was ultimately inseparable from the general quality of her or his life.

## CHILDREN AND THE LAW

The status of children under American law changed dramatically during the late 19th and early 20th century, reflecting two ways of thinking about young people that were expressed in other aspects of national life considered in this chapter, such as education and concern for health.

First, there was the idea that children and adolescents were fundamentally different from adults: boys and girls were not simply underdeveloped and imperfect adults. Childhood, rather, was a distinctive stage in the development of every individual. Children had their own mental and emotional makeup. At their early stage of life, young people enjoyed their own special opportunities and faced their own problems and dangers. It followed that society should have its special obligations to children, and government ought to provide children special protection.

That seemed an especially good idea because, second, it was emphasized that children were the nation's most important resource. As the United States emerged as one of the world's most powerful countries, and as we began to realize the enormous potential of our industry and of such abundant nonhuman resources as coal, iron, timber, and fertile soil, more attention was given also to the youngest members of society, those who would be responsible for fulfilling the national potential and directing the nation's course in generations ahead.

Under English and American law, children had traditionally been treated somewhat differently from adults. Below the "age of reason," they could not be held responsible for criminal acts; and, for a few years after that, they were presumed to be incapable of fully understanding the nature of their offenses. But at the turn of the century the "age of reason" was set as low as eight or ten years in most states. Young persons were assumed to be able to understand their crimes by fourteen or so; and if authorities could prove that they comprehended their offenses earlier, still younger boys and girls could be prosecuted as adults. As for confinement and punishment, in many states persons as young as eleven or twelve were put into jails and prisons with adults. Pardons granted by the governor of Georgia in 1895 suggest the extent of the practice:

William Whitlock.—Convicted of misdemeanor . . . sentence, twelve months in chain gang. Pardoned in consideration of the fact that the defendant is quite a youth, about thirteen years of age . . . and that he is a simple, weak-minded boy.

Wade Hampton.—Convicted of burglary . . . sentence, five years. At time of his conviction was a mere child, and since confinement has lost a leg. Pardoned after serving one half of his sentence.[42]

By the turn of the century several states had reformatories where youths were segregated from adult convicts, but virtually all were what one historian has called "junior prisons," poorly funded and characterized not by programs of rehabilitation but by harsh punishment, overcrowding, boredom, difficult work, wretched food, and various other abuses. An employee of New York's House of Refuge, the first such institution, founded in 1825, remembered in 1871 that "I have seen boys punished for not completing their tasks, so that blood ran down into their boots."[43]

A fundamental change in this system began almost precisely at the start of the 20th century with the founding of a juvenile court system. Although Massachusetts courts had held separate hearings for children as early as the 1870s, the first juvenile court was established in Chicago in 1899; it would become a model for many others during the next two decades.

The driving force behind a separate juvenile justice system, however, came not from Illinois, but from Colorado. Benjamin Barr Lindsey, the son of a telegraph operator, took office as a municipal judge in Denver in January 1901. Soon afterwards police brought in a boy for stealing coal from the railroad yards. His guilt was clear, and, without much thought, Lindsey sentenced the boy to the reformatory. Suddenly from the back of the court-room came what Lindsey recalled as "the most soul-piercing scream of agony that I had ever heard," coming from the boy's mother as she learned her son was to be taken from her. Badly rattled, Lindsey adjourned his court. Looking into the case, he found that the boy lived with his mother and ill father in a small shack. Like many poor urban children, he took coal to sell and to use for home heating. This was "not a criminal," Lindsey decided, and "not a bad boy, just a boy." Investigating further, he found that many young people brought up on charges lived under similar circum-stances. Further, children were sometimes held in jails with hardened adult criminals for weeks or even months before trial. It was not, he concluded, a system well suited either for the children or for society.[44]

Initially, Lindsey worked through a school truancy law that gave him broad authority over "juvenile disorderly persons" and allowed him either to send young offenders to reformatories or to suspend their sentences as long as they attended school and "conducted themselves properly." With the cooperation of Denver officials, Lindsey began hearing all juvenile cases separately from adult cases. He also recruited probation agents, mostly from among truant officers, to oversee the children's lives outside the court-room. In effect, he was creating an unofficial juvenile court system. In 1903, Colorado formalized this process with passage of the Colorado Juvenile Court law, patterned on the Illinois statute but also expanding on it.

Lindsey became not just a pioneer but also an evangelist for juvenile courts. He wrote and spoke tirelessly to promote this new relationship between young people and the law, and in the process he developed an international reputation as the "kid's judge." Within two years of passage of the Colorado law, ten states had juvenile courts, and by 1909 the num-ber had risen to twenty-two. In 1915, some variation of the system was operating in virtually the entire country—forty-six states plus Washington, D.C., and three territories. Rarely has such a fundamental change come so quickly to the American legal system.

Juvenile courts represented much more than a different way of processing young people within a body of laws. Their justification rested on the as-sumption, first, that youthful offenders often were victims of circum-stances—poverty, lack of supervision, exposure to corrupting influences, and products of families that were failing in their duty to raise respectful citizens. The same, of course, might have been said of older lawbreakers, but advocates of juvenile courts stressed that the young, unlike adult criminals, were still in the process of character formation. The values and behaviors of their adult lives would be determined during their childhoods and adolescence. These attitudes reflected a new way of thinking about young offenders, the concept of juvenile delinquency. The term "juvenile delinquent" had been around for a long time, but earlier it had meant merely a lawbreaker who happened to be a child. Now it came to suggest a young person who was breaking society's rules because he or she was responding to a dangerous and corrupting environment and because vital institutions, the family and the school most of all, were not passing on proper values and a respect for society.

The implications of such thinking were wide-reaching. If a girl or boy broke the law, it was not because of an innately criminal personality, a "bad seed" that was bearing fruit. Rather, as a child moved through the early stages of growth and formation of character, she or he was being diverted off the proper, socially acceptable course. But it was not too late: if helped in time, the delinquent child could be set back on a constructive course of development. Juvenile delinquency, in other words, was not a regrettable but unavoidable part of life. It was, instead, a problem that could be analyzed and corrected. Society—and justice—would be best served by rehabilitating young people, not by punishing them and imprisoning them with men and women bound to corrupt them further.

The law establishing Colorado's juvenile courts specifically stated that the court's custody and discipline of the child ought to resemble as closely as possible that of good and responsible parents. As far as possible, the law went on, "any delinquent child shall be treated, not as a criminal, but as misdirected and misguided, and needing aid, encouragement, help and assistance."[45] By taking on the roles of parents, however, courts naturally began trying to regulate the children's lives far more extensively. Taking care of them, guiding them toward respectable adulthood, had to mean more than stopping outright criminal activities. Juvenile delinquents, according to the Colorado statute, included not only young thieves and vandals but any boy or girl under sixteen who hung around pool halls or saloons, who walked around the streets at night without a legitimate purpose, or who had a habit of using "vile, obscene, vulgar, profane, or indecent language." Potentially, then, the juvenile court system, in the name of serving and protecting children and society, was extending its reach much more broadly into the private lives of young people.[46]

In fact, other laws, based on the same assumptions, were meant to control what children could and could not do and what could be done with them. Some, for instance, imposed heavy fines and jail terms on adults who encouraged or contributed to the delinquency of children. Others tried to regulate the behavior and habits of young people. A good example had to do with the popular city entertainments discussed elsewhere in this chapter. Especially objectionable to reformers were the new motion pictures watched by tens of thousands of young people every day. After looking at 250 features, spokesmen for the Ohio Humane Society concluded, in 1910, that four out of ten were "unfit" for children, mainly because they depicted such crimes as murder and burglary. In another survey, an Ohio teacher reported that a movie too often "teaches boys to become bandits, murderers, teaches arson. Shows how to get money without work."[47] Municipal and state laws launched a dual attack on the situation: film producers were censored and forbidden to portray certain kinds of activities, and operators of movie houses were required to regulate or prohibit attendance by children unaccompanied by adults.

The campaign to "clean up" the films and theaters also suggests the frustrations of regulating children and their personal habits. Censorship and attendance laws had limited effects because children had become such a powerful influence in the urban marketplace. Simply put, there were many more children than reformers. Producers and owners could not afford to deny entirely what the boys and girls wanted. If they had, according to an official in the Moving Pictures Exhibiting Association, three-quarters of them would go out of business. Many things, to be sure, were kept off the screen: nudity, "gruesome" scenes, abortion, adultery, drunkenness, counterfeiting, "sensual kissing," and women smoking, among others. Yet, that left plenty of room for topics and scenes that bothered the critics but thrilled the children. A particular favorite, crime, remained a common subject, although details of how criminals actually operated were forbidden. Regulations against unaccompanied youngsters in theaters proved so difficult to enforce that police and officials more or less ignored them. A survey in Cleveland, Ohio, in 1913, revealed that children without adult supervision comprised two-thirds of the evening audiences in the city theaters.

New child labor laws also were designed to protect American youngsters from special dangers and abuses that accompanied the transition of the United States into a modern, industrial society. America's economy had changed, bringing new opportunities but also many risks for young people. In particular, children were being pressed into work that threatened their physical and moral well-being. Tens of thousands of vulnerable girls and boys, the hope of the country's future, were put in danger so a few might profit. That, reformers said, had to stop.

In a sense, the term "child labor reform" is misleading, for reformers were not opposed to children laboring. Virtually everyone seemed to agree that work was a good and healthy part of growing up. No one, for instance, questioned the value of sons and daughters working on family farms or helping out with household labor. Such work, it was agreed, strengthened young people's characters and encouraged self-discipline and respect. Rural labor, in fact, could be just as exploitive as that of the cities and factories, as will be discussed in later chapters, but in the opening years of the 20th century, child labor in the countryside was largely ignored by reformers and critics.

Reformers, instead, concentrated on particular kinds of child labor, especially that in the factories and, to a lesser extent, on the streets and in the tenement trades. They appealed in part to their listeners' consciences. Putting boys and girls of ten years or even younger to work in coal mines and cotton mills, filling their lungs with coal dust and lint, and exploiting their labor for pennies a day—that was simply wrong, the reformers argued. Realizing that to succeed they had to appeal to the large and growing middle class, reformers also spoke to the self-interest and patriotism of that group. They argued, first, that many young children in the street trades turned to crime, so taking shoe-shine boys and flower-sellers off the streets and putting them in school would reduce the threat of thieves and other crooks. Second, they pointed out that youthful workers in textile mills, glass factories, and other industries often ended up in hospitals or in poorhouses by the time they should have been entering their most productive years of work. Like the young criminals, these people, worn out early for the profit of a few, would end up costing middle-class taxpayers a sizable bundle. Just as important, the full potential of these young Americans was being wasted, reformers said; and, in the long run, that robbed the nation of its true capacity for wealth and greatness. If the United States was going to compete with other nations in the 20th century—if it was going to find its rightful place in the world—then it should protect its greatest resource: its children. Reformers, then, were appealing to the optimism and nationalism of the middle class as well as to their pocketbooks and their sense of right and wrong.

The most important and effective force behind this reform was the National Child Labor Committee (NCLC), founded in 1904. Led by activists like Florence Kelley, Felix Adler, and Edgar Murphy, NCLC set out to publicize some of the horrendous conditions among working children. In this, they were helped especially by the powerful work of two men who now are considered pioneers in documentary photography, Jacob Riis and Lewis Hine. Riis, a Danish immigrant and journalist, concentrated on conditions in urban slums, especially those in New York City. Hine documented conditions in the nation's factories and mines, especially the textile mills and coal mines of the South. The visual and written exposé of working conditions began to strike a nerve. The NCLC sought passage first of state laws regulating child labor. They had some modest success, but in states where the conditions were the most deplorable, the opposition from businessmen and industrialists often was the greatest. After great pressure, for instance, Georgia passed a law prohibiting factory labor by girls and boys under twelve unless they had dependent parents. Once such laws were passed, though, they were often very difficult to enforce, largely because states did not provide adequate money or manpower. New York, for example, had a law regulating child labor in its 42,000 factories but hired only two agents to investigate the factories.

Many reformers felt that federal legislation was needed to deal with this national problem. The NCLC began pushing for a national law well before 1910, but it was opposed not only by powerful economic interests but also by those who believed that the Constitution did not grant Congress power to pass such laws. Finally, in 1916, President Woodrow Wilson, who had previously opposed a child labor law, supported the effort, hoping to win support during that year's bitterly fought presidential race. With Wilson's support, the Keating-Owen Act was passed. This law attempted to regulate child labor on the basis of the power of Congress to control interstate commerce—that is, the movement of products between two or more states. It outlawed the interstate shipment of goods that children under fourteen had helped produce. Further, it forbade shipment of goods from mines or quarries that employed young people under sixteen or any goods produced by companies that employed children under fourteen for more than eight hours a day. The Keating-Owen Act was the first federal child labor law, and reformers believed they had won a crucial victory.

Their celebration was brief, however. Two years later the Supreme Court struck down the Keating-Owen Act. By a five-to-four vote, the Court ruled that Congress's argument that it could limit child labor under its power to regulate interstate commerce was faulty, and so the law was unconstitutional. Lasting federal legislation regulating child labor would come only in the 1930s, as will be discussed in the next chapter.

Obviously, the success of child labor reformers was mixed. They played important roles in passage of state legislation—by 1920 every state had *some* kind of child labor law—and they at least had established a precedent for federal legislation. As stated earlier in this chapter, the number of "gainfully employed" children reported in the census declined dramatically between 1910 and 1920. That decline was partly the result of regulation of industries, like coal mining and the mills, that were exposed by crusaders against child abuse in the workplace. (The number was also shrinking, however, because industrial work was becoming more complex and, therefore, less suited for children.)

Reformers also gained valuable experience in organizing nationally and in working with politicians. Their greatest accomplishment was opening the eyes of the middle-class American public to conditions facing hundreds of thousands of working children; beyond that, they exposed some aspects of life among the very poorest Americans to millions of other Americans. In so doing, they were paving the way for later victories.

Nonetheless, after nearly two decades of this crusade, most child labor, including some of the most abusive, remained unregulated. Even the best state laws had serious problems; and, in many parts of the country, employers could hire young boys and girls to do just about any sort of job. Reformers, furthermore, might be criticized on other grounds. By concentrating on certain kinds of labor, especially that in factories and mines, they ignored some of the worst conditions; and they paid virtually no attention to child labor in the countryside.

It might also be argued that these reformers were missing the real problem behind the grim scenes of youngsters of eight and ten working long hours as bobbin boys and runners for the glass ovens. Those children usually were working because their families needed the money they brought home. By taking girls and boys off the job, child labor laws were making poor families even poorer. Reformers were dealing more with symptoms than with causes. The basic problem was grinding poverty and the low pay of adult breadwinners.

Changes in children's law showed the same themes found in other topics of this chapter. As in education, American governments—national, state, and local—were involving themselves more and more in the lives of young people, trying to shape their upbringing for the children's good and that of society. Labor laws tried to protect young people from economic exploitation. As in new programs for children's health, juvenile delinquency was considered not an inherent flaw but a kind of social illness that called for sympathy, careful diagnosis, intelligent treatment, and programs of prevention. All grew from the notion that a girl or boy was both a valuable individual and an irreplaceable resource that had to be protected and nurtured for the nation's future.

## BIBLIOGRAPHICAL ESSAY

For the general history of the years covered in this first chapter, 1900–1920, students can turn to several informative books for a good general picture: John M. Cooper, Jr., *The Pivotal Decades: The United States, 1900–1920* (New York: Norton, 1990), Robert Wiebe, *The Search for Order, 1877–1920* (New York: Hill and Wang, 1967), David M. Kennedy, *Over Here: The First World War and American Society* (New York: Oxford University Press, 1980), Edward M. Coffman, *The War to End All Wars* (New York: Oxford University Press, 1968), and Neil A. Wynn, *From Progressivism to Prosperity: World War I and American Society* (New York: Holmes and Meier, 1986).

### At Home

General readers and scholars alike can benefit greatly from reading the volumes in The Everyday Life in America Series. These books cover many aspects of social history from the colonial period to the recent 20th century. The two pertinent ones for this chapter are Thomas J. Schlereth's *Victorian America: Transformations in Everyday Life, 1876–1915* (New York: HarperCollins, 1991) and Harvey Green's *The Uncertainties of Everyday Life, 1915–1945* (New York: HarperCollins, 1992). Both are exceptionally well written and provide fascinating looks at the ways Americans were living day-to-day—their housing and playtimes, family life and work, health and habits, and much more. For the history of the American family, the best recent work is Steven Mintz and Susan Kellogg's *Domestic Revolutions: A Social History of American Family Life* (New York: The Free Press, 1988), which traces the American family from the prerevolutionary era to the 1980s, with emphasis on the 20th century. Bringing together the best literature on this sprawling subject, Mintz and Kellogg treat families with intelligent, commonsensical analysis. The dwellings of American families is the subject of Clifford Edward Clark, Jr.'s *The American Family Home, 1800–1860* (Chapel Hill: University of North Carolina Press, 1986), which describes the broad changes in housing styles and relates this to larger developments in American society. For the years considered, Clark offers a look at evolution of Victorian styles, the emergence of suburban residential architectures, and the modernization of living space within homes. An insightful look at how dwellings express the values of those who build and live in them is the subject of Gwendolyn Wright's *Building the Dream: A Social History of Housing in America* (New York: Pantheon, 1981). For a good general history of child rearing, see Mary Cable's *The Little Darlings: A History of Child Rearing in America* (New York: Scribner, 1975).

Much research still needs to be done regarding poverty's hold on children during these years, but there are some good beginnings. Still very useful is Robert Bremner's *From the Depths: The Discovery of Poverty in the United States* (New York: New York University Press, 1956), which stresses the moral concern and sense of justice of reformers. A more recent work, Susan Tiffin's *In Whose Best Interest? Child Welfare Reform in the Progressive Era* (Westport, Conn.: Greenwood Press, 1982), demonstrates that reformers also were trying to bring a measure of control to their society. LeRoy Ashby's *Saving the Waifs: Reformers and Dependent Children, 1890–1917* (Philadelphia: Temple University Press, 1984) is another useful look at poverty and some of the ways reformers tried to deal with its effects, as is Peter Holloran's *Boston's Wayward Children: Social Services for Homeless Children, 1830–1930* (Rutherford, N.J.: Fairleigh Dickinson University Press, 1989).

Geraldine Youcha's *Minding the Children: Child Care in America from Colonial Times to the Present* (New York: Scribner, 1995) is especially useful on the subject of programs directed at alleviating the difficulties of the poor, though covers a much broader subject. One of the few books on the history of public policy on the care of dependent children is Winifred Bell's *Aid to Dependent Children* (New York: Columbia University Press, 1965). Marilyn Irvin Holt's *The Orphan Trains: Placing Out in America* (Lincoln: University of Nebraska Press, 1992) is an excellent study of the famous scheme to transport children who had no parents or who were especially mired in poverty to the countryside. Of the several examples of organizations from the period that were meant to mold the moral natures of boys and girls, such as the YMCA and YWCA, I have focussed on the Boy Scouts of America. An insightful book on the origins of scouting and the YMCA, their predecessors, and the social climate that produced them is David I. Macleod's *Building Character in the American Boy: The Boy Scouts, YMCA and Their Forerunners, 1870–1920* (Madison: University of Wisconsin Press, 1983).

Any consideration of poverty early in the 20th century and its effects on children should also take into account the considerable literature from investigators and reformers of the time. To them, the plight of the child in many ways summed up what they considered the scandalous conditions in American life. Moreover, the reformers knew that emphasizing children's suffering was a particularly effective means of appealing to the middle-class voting public. Among the most influential of these books were: Jacob Riis, *How the Other Half Lives* (New York: Charles Scribner's Sons, 1892) and his *The Children of the Poor* (New York: Charles Scribner's Sons, 1892), Robert Hunter, *Poverty* (The Macmillan Company, 1904), John Spargo, *The Bitter Cry of the Children* (New York: The Macmillan Company, 1907), William T. Stead, *If Christ Came to Chicago* (Chicago: Laird and Lee, 1894), Edward Clopper, *Child Labor on City Streets* (New York: The Macmillan Company, 1911), and Mary White Ovington, *Half a Man: The Status of the Negro in New York* (New York: Longmans, Green and Company, 1911).

## At Play

The Everyday Life in America Series, mentioned above, includes much interesting and amusing material on play among both children and adults. A particularly good and nicely illustrated book of essays on different aspects of play and entertainment during the 19th and 20th centuries is *Hard at Play: Leisure in America, 1840–1940*, edited by Kathryn Grover (Amherst: University of Massachusetts Press, 1992); included are two chapters on children's play and an appendix on games. Anthropologists and sociologists have treated play very seriously and have written several books on the deeper meanings of play and games within society. Those interested in this subject might begin with three books by Brian Sutton-Smith: *The Folkgames of Children* (Austin: University of Texas Press, 1972), *Play and Learning* (New York: Gardner Press, 1979), and *Toys as Culture* (New York: Gardner Press, 1986).

In the bibliographical essays ending each chapter, I will refer to two books on the history of American toys. They are about the only works available on the subject, but, fortunately, each does its job well and both serve up plenty of information and delicious trivia. The first, Richard O'Brien's *The Story of American Toys: From the Puritans to the Present* (New York: Abbeville Press, 1990), is organized chronologically; the other, Gil Asakawa and Leland Rucker's *The Toy Book* (New York: Alfred A. Knopf, 1992), is organized topically according to the kind of toy under consideration. A recent study considers dolls as historical evidence of attitudes toward and of young girls, at least until the eve of the Great Depression: Miriam Formanek-Brunell's *Made to Play House: Dolls and the Commercialization of American Girlhood, 1830–1930* (New Haven: Yale University Press, 1993).

Several other works seek, generally successfully, to examine different aspects of children's play and games as revelations of their times and places. Two good examples are Cary Goodman's *Choosing Sides: Playground and Street Life on the Lower East Side* (New York: Schocken Books, 1979) and Dominick Cavallo's *Muscles and Morals: Organized Playgrounds and Urban Reform, 1880–1920* (Philadelphia: Temple University Press, 1981). For research on children and early films, the place to start is David Nasaw's *Children of the City: At Work and at Play* (Garden City, N.Y.: Anchor Press/Doubleday, 1985) and his *Going Out: The Rise and Fall of Public Amusements* (New York: Basic Books, 1993).

For a brief, but analytical, look at the century's first great amusement park, with some fine photographs, see John F. Kasson's *Amusing the Millions: Coney Island at the Turn of the Century* (New York: Hill and Wang, 1978).

## At Work

The best single volume on child labor reform remains Walter I. Trattner's *Crusade for the Children: A History of the National Child Labor Committee and Child*

*Labor Reform in America* (Chicago: Quadrangle Books, 1970). Its emphasis—as is true of most of the literature—is on labor in industrialized America, not in rural regions. For a look at children's work on the frontier, see Elliott West's *Growing Up with the Country: Childhood on the Far Western Frontier* (Albuquerque: University of New Mexico Press, 1989), which also discusses the effects of that work on children's values and perceptions of themselves. Some of the general books on the history of childhood consider laboring children. Of these, Robert Bremner's three two-volume sets, *Children and Youth in America,* is especially helpful, including revealing documents on working conditions and on reform movements that responded to that situation. An excellent, provocative book that places child labor in the complicated context of children's emotional value to adults is Viviana A. Zelizer's *Pricing the Priceless Child: The Changing Social Value of Children* (New York: Basic Books, 1985). The best recent treatment of children's work on the streets, one that provides a balance of the benefits and dangers of such work, is the previously mentioned *Children of the City: At Work and at Play* by David Nasaw. Finally, Jeremy P. Felt's *Hostages of Fortune: Child Labor Reform in New York State* (Syracuse: Syracuse University Press, 1965) presents a case study of the issues, the reforms, and their limitations in one state.

## At School

American education has attracted more attention from writers than just about anything else connected to childhood. The essential starting place is the work of Lawrence Cremin, a leading historian of education. On the period studied here, see his *The Transformation of the School: Progressivism in American Education, 1876–1951* (New York: Alfred A. Knopf, 1961), and, as background, refer to his *American Education, The National Experience, 1783–1876* (New York: Harper and Row, 1980). The early decades of the 20th century comprised one of the most influential periods in the history of public schooling. Several books give that time close scrutiny or consider it as part of a longer survey, among them: David B. Tyack, *The One Best System: A History of American Urban Education* (Cambridge: Harvard University Press, 1974), Edward Krug, *The Shaping of the American High School, 1880–1920* (New York: Harper and Row, 1964), Daniel Calhoun, ed., *The Educating of Americans: A Documentary History* (Boston: Houghton Mifflin Co., 1969), and Edward J. Power, *Main Currents in the History of Education* (New York: McGraw-Hill, 1970). On the kindergarten movement and some of its early results, see Michael S. Shapiro's *Child's Garden: The Kindergarten Movement from Froebel to Dewey* (University Park: University of Pennsylvania Press, 1983).

Several books relate progressive education to political and social currents of the day, sometimes taking a critical point of view. One of the most thoughtful critics of American education is Michael B. Katz, whose *Class, Bureaucracy, and Schools: The Illusion of Education Change in America* (New York: Praeger, 1971) and *Reconstructing American Education* (Cambridge: Harvard University Press, 1987) express this view. Another useful book putting schooling in the context of the day is Ronald D. Cohen and Raymond A. Mohl's *The Paradox of Progressive Education: The Gary Plan and Urban Schooling* (Port Washington: Kennikat Press, 1979).

The quality of education any child received depended on his or her background, situation, and resources. The most obvious example was the far poorer schooling offered to African American children both in the South and elsewhere. The essential work on education for black children in the South is Louis R. Harlan's *Separate and Unequal: Public School Campaigns and Racism in the Southern Seaboard States, 1901–1915* (Chapel Hill: University of North Carolina Press, 1958). For excellent discussions of education within the larger historical scheme of things, see C. Vann Woodward's superb *Origins of the New South, 1877–1913* (Baton Rouge: Louisiana State University Press, 1951) and Rayford W. Logan's *The Negro in American Life and Thought: The Nadir, 1877–1901* (New York: The Macmillan Co., 1954). On black education outside the South, see Judy Jolley Mohraz, *The Separate Problem: Case Studies of Black Education in the North, 1900–1930* (Westport, Conn.: Greenwood Press, 1979). For Native American education during this period, see Evelyn C. Adams's *American Indian Education: Governmental Schools and Economic Progress* (New York: Arno Press, 1971); and on schooling for immigrant children, especially those on the Atlantic coast, see *American Education and the European Immigrant,* edited by Bernard Weiss (Urbana: University of Illinois Press, 1982) and Selma Berrol's *Immigrants at School: New York City, 1898–1914* (New York: Arno Press, 1978).

## Health

While education and schools have attracted a lot of scholars, the history of children's health is a strangely neglected topic. In fact, there are few good social histories of disease, medicine, and public health in the United States. A welcome exception is Richard A. Meckel's *Save the Babies: American Public Health Reform and the Prevention of Infant Mortality, 1850–1929* (Baltimore: Johns Hopkins University Press, 1990). A basic reference work, *The Cambridge World History of Human Disease,* Kenneth F. Kiple, general ed. (Cambridge and New York: Cambridge University Press, 1993) is fairly technical but still a superb browsing ground for anyone interested in medical history. Also useful are John P. Dolan and William N. Adams-Smith's *Health and Society: A Documentary History of Medicine* (New York: Seabury Press, 1978) and Otto Bettmann's *A Pictorial History of Medicine: A Brief, Nontechnical Survey of the Healing Arts* (Springfield, Ill.: C. C. Thomas, 1956). Most of the contemporary works on the children of poverty noted above reveal something about the sanitary and health conditions affecting the young, although often this is overly sensational. Each of the volumes of Bremner's documentary history *Children and Youth in America,* mentioned above, has lengthy sections on children's health and health issues, presenting revealing, well-selected documents and contemporary articles. Some basic grim measurements are to be found in *Historical Statistics of the United States: Colonial Times to 1970,* two volumes (Washington, D.C.: U.S. Bureau of the Census, 1975).

Possibly difficult to locate are two books containing basic facts and figures on children's health (and lack of it) during 1900–1920 and after: Sam Shapiro, et al., *Infant, Perinatal, Maternal, and Childhood Mortality in the United States* (Cambridge: Harvard University Press, 1968) and Carl L. Erhardt and Joyce E. Berlin, eds., *Mortality and Morbidity in the United States* (Cambridge: Harvard University Press, 1974). A fine recent exception to the lack of good, readable histories of disease—and one concerning what was probably the greatest killer of the early 20th century—is Frank Ryan's *The Forgotten Plague: How the Battle against Tuberculosis Was Won—and Lost* (Boston: Little Brown, 1993). A difficult kind of health problem is the subject of Leo Kanner's *A History of the Care and Study of the Mentally Retarded* (Springfield, Ill.: C. C. Thomas, 1964). The public health issue that attracted the most attention during the early 20th century was milk, its quality and its dangers. Older works on this topic, published at the time when the issue was the hottest, include M. J. Rosenau's *The Milk Question* (Boston: Houghton Mifflin Co., 1912) and Lina G. Straus's *Disease in Milk, the Remedy Pasteurization* (New York: E. P. Dutton and Co., 1917), but a more accessible source is a discussion in Harvey Levenstein's *Revolution at the Table: The Transformation of the American Diet* (New York: Oxford University Press, 1988). Oddly, some of the best written and most entertaining history of medicine has concerned those who have abused their patients' trust. For two examples by James Harvey Young, see *The Medical Messiahs: A Social History of Health Quackery in Twentieth-Century America* (Princeton: Princeton University Press, 1967) and *The Toadstool Millionaires: A Social History of Patent Medicines in America before Federal Regulation* (Princeton: Princeton University Press, 1961).

## Children and the Law

Two essential starting points for anyone interested in children's law, delinquency, and public attitudes toward "wayward" young are by Joseph M. Hawes: *Children in Urban Society: Juvenile Delinquency in Nineteenth-Century America* (New York: Oxford University Press, 1971) and *The Children's Rights Movement: A History of Advocacy and Protection* (Boston: Twayne Publishers, 1991). The second, which is especially useful to the beginning student, is a brief, readable survey of the child's place in the law from the colonial period to the present; the chapters on the period 1900–1920 are among its best. An equally important source concentrates on movements to cope with what many saw as a crisis in both society and the family: Anthony Platt's *The Child Savers: The Invention of Delinquency* (Chicago: University of Chicago Press, 1969). Yet another important work, Steven Schlossman's *Love and the American Delinquent: The Theory and Practice of "Progressive" Juvenile Justice, 1825–1920* (Chicago: University of Chicago Press, 1977), recounts what actually happened in the courts of the day, analyzing how some of the assumptions and biases of social workers and judges were expressed in treatment of young people considered delinquents.

The best single book on juvenile courts is Ellen Ryerson's *The Best Laid Plans: America's Juvenile Court Experiment* (New York: Hill and Wang, 1978). It follows the story of the development of the juvenile court, the ideals behind it and personalities involved, and some of the system's weaknesses. The person most associated with development of the juvenile court system, Benjamin B. Lindsey, wrote books important both for what they tell about him and his motives and as influential appeals to the public's sensibilities: *The Beast,* written with H. J. O'Higgins (New York: Doubleday, 1975), and, with Rube Borough, *The Dangerous Life* (New York: Arno Press, 1974). These books provide a deep understanding of the beginnings of this important part of the history of childhood and treatment of children by our legal system.

## Personal Recollections

Finally, no look at children and their lifestyles during any time in history is complete without listening to the children themselves. In fact, their words should be our starting place. As is true for all parts of the 20th century, there are several excellent memoirs that shed light on the experience of growing up at the turn of the century and during the years immediately following. Bruce Catton, who would become one of our great historians of the Civil War, told of his youth in Michigan in *Waiting for the Morning Train: An American Boyhood* (Garden City, N.Y.: Doubleday, 1972), and another famous American, B. F. Skinner, a pioneer in behavioral psychology and educational theory, wrote of his boyhood in *Particulars of My Life* (New York: Knopf, 1979). For three excellent memoirs of life on the frontier of the Great Plains, see Marquis James's *The Cherokee Strip: A Tale of an Oklahoma Boyhood* (New York: Viking Press, 1960), Edward E. Dale's *The Cross Timbers: Memories of a North Texas Boyhood* (Austin: University of Texas Press, 1966), and Sanora Babb's *An Owl on Every Post* (New York: McCall, 1970, and later editions). The first two authors became prominent historians; the third, a successful novelist.

Ethel Waters, born in 1900, lived in poverty on the streets of Philadelphia on her way to becoming a renowned African-American actress and singer. About her childhood, read *His Eye Is on the Sparrow,* written with Charles Samuels (Garden City, N.Y.: Doubleday, 1950). Waters's autobiography is excerpted in a fine collection of several from African Americans in the 19th and 20th centuries: Jay David, ed., *Growing Up Black* (New York: William Morrow and Co., 1968). Another childhood account from black America, also excerpted in *Growing Up Black,* is Richard Wright, *Black Boy* (New York: Harper and Brothers, 1945, and later editions). For an excellent account of a Native American girlhood, see Polingaysi Qoyawayma, *No Turning Back* (Albuquerque: University of New Mexico Press, 1964). The large body of writing on childhoods of European immigrants, most of them set in cities of the Atlantic coast, includes: Mary Antin, *The Promised Land* (Boston: Houghton Mifflin Co., 1969), Mike Gold, *Jews Without Money* (New York: Avon, 1972), Edward Bok, *The Americanization of Edward Bok* (New York: Pocket Books, 1965), and Richard Gambino, *Blood of My Blood* (Garden City, N.Y.: Doubleday, 1974).

## NOTES

1. Excerpt from Ethel Waters's autobiography, *His Eye Is on the Sparrow,* in Jay David, ed., *Growing Up Black* (New York: William Morrow and Co., 1968), 158–59.

2. Shirley Abbott, *Womenfolks: Growing Up Down South* (New Haven: Tichnor and Fields, 1983), 159–60.

3. Robert H. Bremner, ed., *Children and Youth in America: A Documentary History,* Vol. II (Cambridge: Harvard University Press, 1971), 6–7.

4. Alfred Kazin, *A Walker in the City* (New York: Harcourt, Brace, 1951), 65–66.

5. Clifford Edward Clark, Jr., *The American Family Home, 1800–1960* (Chapel Hill: University of North Carolina Press, 1986), 153.

6. Bremner, *Children and Youth in America,* Vol. II, 288–89.

7. Ibid., 285.

8. Geraldine Youcha, *Minding the Children: Child Care in America from Colonial Times to the Present* (New York: Scribner, 1995), 199.

9. Ibid., 200.

10. Hamlin Garland, *Boy Life on the Prairie* (Boston: Allyn and Bacon, 1926), 95.

11. Fiorello La Guardia, *The Making of an Insurgent: An Autobiography: 1882–1919* (New York: Capricorn Books, 1948), 19.

12. Edward Everett Dale, *The Cross Timbers: Memories of a North Texas Boyhood* (Austin: University of Texas, 1966), 90.

13. Kathryn Grover, ed., *Hard at Play: Leisure in America, 1840–1940* (Amherst: University of Massachusetts Press, 1992), 241.

14. David Nasaw, *Children of the City: At Work and at Play* (New York: Basic Books, 1993), 124.

15. David Nasaw, "Children and Commercial Culture: Moving Pictures in the Early Twentieth Century," in Elliott West and Paula Petrik, eds., *Small Worlds: Children and Adolescents in America, 1850–1950* (Lawrence: University Press of Kansas, 1992), 15.

16. Bernard Mergen, "Made, Bought and Stolen: Toys and the Culture of Childhood," in ibid., 98.

17. Miriam Formanek-Brunell, "The Politics of Doll Play in Nineteenth-Century America," in ibid., 121–22.

18. Bremner, *Children and Youth in America,* Vol. II, 605–607.

19. Elliott West, *Growing Up with the Country: Childhood on the Far Western Frontier* (Albuquerque: University of New Mexico Press, 1989), 73.

20. Charles O'Kieffe, *Western Story: The Recollections of Charley O'Kieffe, 1884–1898* (Lincoln: University of Nebraska Press, 1960), 36–37.

21. Thomas J. Schlereth, *Victorian America: Transformations in Everyday Life* (New York: HarperCollins, 1991), 80.

22. Walter I. Trattner, *Crusade for the Children: A History of the National Child Labor Committee and Child Labor Reform in America* (Chicago: Quadrangle Books, 1970), 146.

23. Nasaw, *Children of the City,* 75.

24. Waters, quoted in David, *Growing Up Black,* 159.

25. Rayford W. Logan, *The Betrayal of the Negro: From Rutherford B. Hayes to Woodrow Wilson* (New York: Collier Books, 1965), 287.

26. Henry Allen Bullock, *A History of Negro Education in the South: From 1619 to the Present* (Cambridge: Harvard University Press, 1967).

27. Dewey, quoted in Bremner, *Children and Youth in America,* Vol. II, 1119.

28. Robert H. Rodgers, *The Money Domino: A Childhood Adventure across the Texas Plains to Colorado* (Lubbock: West Texas Museum Association, 1990), 69.

29. E. C. Earl, *The Schoolhouse* (Washington, D.C.: 1919).

30. Harry Golden, *The Right Time: An Autobiography* (New York: G.P. Putnam's Sons, 1969, 43.

31. Andrew Gulliford, *America's Country Schools* (Washington, D.C.: Preservation Press, 1984), 68–69.

32. Selma Berrol, "Immigrant Children at School," in West and Petrik, *Small Worlds,* 49, 50.

33. Ibid., 42–60.

34. West, *Growing Up with the Country,* 234.

35. Kenneth F. Kiple, ed., *The Cambridge World History of Human Disease* (Cambridge and New York: Cambridge University Press, 1993), 683.

36. John Spargo, *The Bitter Cry of the Children* (New York: Quadrangle Books, 1968), 20.

37. Bremner, *Children and Youth in America,* Vol. II, 973–74.

38. Ibid., vol. II, 989, 998.

39. Spargo, *Bitter Cry of the Children,* 40–41.

40. Bremner, *Children and Youth in America,* Vol. II, 970–71.

41. Ibid., 819–20.

42. Ibid., 444.

43. Ibid., 439.

44. Joseph M. Hawes, *Children in Urban Society: Juvenile Delinquency in Nineteenth-Century America* (New York: Oxford University Press, 1971), 224.

45. Ibid., 239.

46. Ibid.

47. Nasaw, "Children and Commercial Culture," in West and Petrik, *Small Worlds,* 15.

# Chapter 2

## 1921–1940

### INTRODUCTION

The first ten years following the Allied victory in World War I appeared to be the most prosperous in U.S. history. The ten years after that, however, witnessed our nation's worst economic disaster, the Great Depression. Children growing up through these years experienced, in the most dramatic way imaginable, both the glittering promises of American life and the frightening possibility that such wondrous expectations might disappear almost overnight.

World War I was fought as an idealistic crusade to "make the world safe for democracy," in the words of President Woodrow Wilson. In the war's aftermath the American people seemed to turn away from idealism and from a concern for problems beyond our borders; instead, they pursued some of the pleasures brought by the changes of the last few generations. When they think of the "Twenties," many Americans picture people indulging themselves by dancing frantically to jazz, drinking bootleg liquor in illegal bars called "speakeasies," and driving through prosperous cities in flashy automobiles. This was also one of our greatest decades for sports fans. College football for the first time became a popular national entertainment. Many followers of baseball believe that the 1920s was a golden age never approached since. Movies, as will be shown below, became a weekly ritual for millions of parents and children. A booming electrical industry offered all sorts of devices and expensive toys to be enjoyed inside the family home.

And yet, just beneath the surface were troubling tensions and problems. As discussed in the previous chapter, many Americans distrusted the societal changes of these years. In particular, they worried about the effects of the "new" immigration from eastern and southern Europe. They were alarmed at much of what they saw in cities, including the many opportunities for young people to get into trouble. Some were shocked by what they thought was a loosening of moral attitudes during the pleasure-seeking years of postwar America. These fears found their most extreme voice early in the decade of the 1920s with the rise of the second Ku Klux Klan, which condemned everything from Catholics and Jews to movies and modern novels. Of much more lasting effect were two laws regulating immigration: the Immigrant Act of 1921 and the Johnson-Reed Act of 1924 severely limited the number of persons allowed into the country annually and established a quota system that heavily favored "old" immigrants from Great Britain and western and northern Europe. Most hopeful immigrants from eastern and southern Europe found the golden door to America slammed and locked, and American society began to lose some of its diverse flavor. The percentage of foreign-born persons in the United States steadily declined until the 1960s, from 8.2 in 1910, to 6.2 in 1930, 3.4 in 1950, and 2.6 in 1960.

The prosperity of the 1920s, furthermore, was not all that it seemed. American farmers suffered throughout the decade from falling prices and large debts. The "real" income of middle-class families—their ability, that is, to buy things—grew much more slowly after 1925. The nation's wealth was spread very unevenly among its people. At the bottom of the order, the poorest 20 percent of Americans in 1929 earned about 5 percent of the nation's income and owned virtually no property. At the top, the richest 1 percent possessed an astounding 45 percent of all stocks and bonds, real estate, and other such assets.

These conditions contributed to the disastrous economic collapse that began in late 1929 and continued for the next three years. The Gross National Product (the total value of everything produced in the country) declined by nearly half, from $103 billion to $55.6 billion, while Americans' personal income shrank from $85.9 billion to $40.5 billion. The prices of everything from fur coats to hamburgers dropped dramatically, but this was little help to consumers who had little money to spend. Billions of dollars in savings evaporated as more than five thousand banks failed between 1929 and the spring of 1933. The most painful symptom of the Great Depression came as millions of American workers lost their jobs. Between the fall of 1929 and the spring of 1933, an average of 100,000 persons every week found themselves suddenly unemployed. The number of persons out of work during that period rose from a little over a million to more than 13 million. Areas that depended most on industry were hit the hardest. Toledo, Ohio, reported a 70 percent unemployment rate, and in the steel town of Donora, Pennsylvania, only 277 out of 13,900 workers held full-time jobs.

The Great Depression lasted until the United States edged toward its second world war at the end of the 1930s. The low point, however, came in 1933. A new political administration under President Franklin D. Roosevelt instituted a series of federally funded programs that eased the unemployment crisis, although the number of persons unable to find work continued to hover around 8 million. Roosevelt's New Deal also reshaped the relationship between the national government and its citizens, including some of the government's responsibilities toward American families and children.

Population continued to grow, and people continued to move. The census reported an increase from 106.4 million to 132.1 million persons between 1920 and 1940. Urban migration continued as well. In 1920, for the first time in our history, a majority of Americans were living in larger towns and cities, and by 1940 urban dwellers made up nearly 60 percent of the population. Part of that shift resulted from the ongoing exodus of blacks from the rural South to northern cities. The coming of the depression set still more Americans in motion. Wretched conditions in poorer areas sent families off in search of something—anything—better. Out of the South and the southern plains came scores of thousands of migrants, collectively called "Okies," who headed mainly toward the Pacific coast looking for work; thousands more went in the same direction from the Midwest and northern plains. "They roll westward like a parade," wrote a man who watched the tide from his Idaho home.[1] Not all movement was voluntary. In a little-known episode in our history, government agents rounded up more than 400,000 naturalized Mexican-Americans, some of them born in the United States, and deported these *repatriados* south into Mexico to help relieve the pressure on the new federal welfare system.

The Great Depression had another obvious effect on our population. If we continued to grow, we did not do so as rapidly as in the past. The depression put a temporary brake on reproduction. As times got tougher, couples postponed marriages, and many who did marry put off having babies. The birth rate, measured as the number of babies born for every thousand women between fifteen and forty-four years, dropped to its lowest point in our history.

There were changes, too, within American families. As discussed in the first chapter, new attitudes and values were taking root at the opening of the century, and as the years passed, fathers and mothers, daughters and sons continued to remake this fundamental part of our society. Some of the most important changes concerned fathers and the roles they played. The ideal of the "companionate family" emphasized a close and affectionate bond among all family members. The father was still expected to make money and provide for the family's needs, but he was no longer seen as the main source of authority and maker of all important decisions. The new ideal put forth a more democratic family led by tolerant parents who were friends and guides to their children. A main responsibility of the father was to help both sons and daughters in their emotional and psychological development. A good father was to be understanding and sympathetic, and he was expected to spend considerable time playing with and listening to his children on terms that were close to equality. "We are a gang," as one father wrote in a magazine article in 1927. "And I don't insist on being the leader of the gang more than my share of the time. . . . We don't have any heavy father and subservient son stuff. No sirree, not in *our* family."[2]

But this more democratic family and the new roles of fathers also raised some difficult questions. How, in practical terms, were fathers supposed to fulfill their various responsibilities? Working men usually spent their days away from home, so even if both parents hoped to be loving companions to their children, mothers usually had much more opportunity for this role. As a result, survey after survey showed what one researcher called an "overwhelming mother-preference" among both boys and girls.[3] In fact, both mothers and fathers found it increasingly difficult to act out the role of nurturing friend because, as demonstrated throughout this book, children's play, schooling, and social lives took place mostly outside the house and away from both parents. As families demanded more and more goods in the American marketplace, a father's main job became providing the money to buy them. Trying to keep up with the demand kept fathers away from home even more, leaving less time to spend with children. Then, in an especially cruel blow, the depression threw millions of breadwinners out of work. Unemployed fathers then could take no pride even in the limited role of moneymaker. At a time when men were supposed to be coming closer to their sons and daughters, many felt they were being pushed to the edges of their children's lives.

Changes in the family and attitudes toward the family were hardly universal. New values and ideals were more common among the middle classes than among working classes and recent immigrants. These values, nonetheless, were an increasingly familiar part of American life, as were the frustrations that came with them.

## AT HOME

As Americans entered the third decade of the 20th century, the nation was as contradictory as ever. It remained among the most diverse societies on earth, and yet it was being transformed by powerful unifying forces. The many regions of the country were being knit together by increasingly efficient systems of transportation, so the same kinds of goods made by the same companies could be distributed and sold and used by families from coast to coast. New technologies allowed the instantaneous radio broadcast of information and entertainment throughout the continent. In one of the most sweeping developments in the history of the American people, many families suddenly could buy an automobile, which allowed them to move from place to place—even across the entire country if they wished—quickly and with unprecedented freedom. Improved transportation and communication brought Americans more than ever into contact with one another, and encouraged among them a similar style of life.

The pull and tug between these two aspects of national life—diversity and the making of a common American culture—continues today. Then and now, this American drama is acted out in the homes of the nation's families. And, always, much can be learned about American culture by observing where children lived, what they ate, and how they passed the hours inside their houses.

New laws in the 1920s closed the American door almost entirely to immigrants from many countries, but the millions who had arrived during the previous two generations had made the United States an extraordinarily diverse society. Public and private life was woven through with rituals and customs carried from Europe, Asia, and Latin America. Clothing styles seen on the streets, food sold by vendors and in small groceries, accents and expressions heard in public places—all reflected the ethnic and cultural complexity of the nation. This variety was found in many parts of the nation, not just in the cities of the Northeast. In parts of Minnesota, German was spoken more often than English; Czechs dominated whole counties of central Texas; shop signs in North Dakota towns showed Norwegian and Swedish names almost exclusively; Iberian Basques sang in their native tongue to the sheep they herded in Idaho and Nevada. Large portions of the Southwest were cultural extensions of Mexican settlements south of the border.

As at the start of the 20th century, this cultural patchwork was on display in the many types of homes American children knew growing up. Daughters and sons of Kentucky coal miners lived in "company towns," inside two-room clapboard houses, each like the others along the dusty streets. On the wide lots in residential neighborhoods of Kansas plains towns like Abilene, where the future president Dwight Eisenhower grew up, boys like him knew large and drafty Victorian houses with broad wrap-around porches and surrounded by towering elms and oaks transplanted from the East. Children in northern New Mexico, living in villages founded before the Pilgrims arrived in Massachusetts, slept inside adobe houses filled with the sharp scent of pinyon wood burning in corner fireplaces. More recent arrivals from Mexico worked for the railroads and lived in boxcars converted into houses. From the Southwest, these immigrants fanned out across much of the country, with some children growing from infancy to adulthood knowing nothing but such rolling homes. As late as 1928, a "boxcar camp" in Chicago housed 372 children. Some homes continued centuries-old traditions. Seminole and Miccosukee Indian children of southern Florida lived in *chickees,* which traced their origins to tribes of the Gulf coast, including some there before the first Spanish settlers arrived. Framed by cypress and palmetto logs and thatched by palmetto fronds, these small dwellings featured a raised platform where family members sat, visited, and slept, protected from rising swamp water.

This mingling of old and new was typically American. With this diversity naturally came tensions, not only between immigrants and long-time residents, but also within immigrant families. As described in the previous chapter, children of immigrants were soaking in the ways of the new country, taking on habits and values that often clashed with the attitudes and customs of parents who had grown up in very different places. At the same time, the older customs held on, adding to the mix of lifeways that always has been one of the nation's basic traits.

An incident recalled by Monica Sone, a Japanese-American girl living in Seattle in the 1920s and 1930s, suggested the stresses of the generations that were pulled between those two worlds. As a young girl, Sone attended

Despite laws limiting immigration, children from other cultures, like this Japanese-American boy in Los Angeles, have negotiated the difficult path of growing up in a society very different from those of their parents. *Courtesy of Security Pacific Collection/Los Angeles Public Library.*

public schools, then went to Japanese school in the afternoon. With her friends she celebrated all the usual holidays, from Christmas and Independence Day to Lincoln's Birthday and Memorial Day, but every spring she and the other students in the Japanese school also attended a ceremony at Nippon Kan Hall in observance of Tenchosetsu, the birthday of the Japanese emperor. In this solemn ritual, the audience sat in utter silence while a prominent community leader opened an ornate cabinet to reveal, for the only time during the year, the emperor's photograph. Next, another man read from a scroll the emperor's instructions to all Japanese subjects (although few understood the message, which was written in highly formal language). Finally, the audience was led in three shouts of "Banzai!"—a traditional salute meaning "May you live ten thousand years!"

Most young students did not especially look forward to the occasion. One year, Sone recalled, the school principal rose to lead the final shouting, but stopped and pointed to the back of the hall:

> Then, splitting the air with his tongue, he thundered out, "You, down there, the girls, I mean . . . take off your hats this instant. It is an insult to the Emperor . . ."
>
> In the rear of the room sat a group of high school girls. As young women of impeccable taste in Western style, they had worn their best hats to an important afternoon affair. They stared defiantly back at Mr. Ohashi, but he roared at them again. "Take them off!"
>
> Mr. Ohashi was in the finest fit of purple pique. He kept his accusing finger leveled at them and they wilted, one by one. Flushed and embarrassed, they unpinned their veils and untied their bows with trembling fingers and removed their pretty spring bonnets.[4]

This confrontation summed up the conflict between old and new habits that was an essential part of growing up for millions of young Americans with immigrant parents.

Such conflicts worked themselves out in less dramatic ways in tens of thousands of families. Young Latino children of the Southwest listened to grandparents' stories of village life in Mexico, tales of crafts and conflicts, fiestas, scandals, ghosts, and heroism. The storytellers meant to maintain a cultural link with the country and people left behind, but their tales were always competing with the popular culture bombarding the youngsters: "Grandmother Perez's stories about the witches and ghosts of Los Conejos get scant audience, in competition with Dick Tracy and Buck Rogers."[5]

Conflict often surfaced over fashion and appearance. Girls of the 1920s wanted to adopt the styles of the day—lipstick, short dresses, and bobbed hair. Their elders resisted, and some teenagers dressed in one outfit in the morning, changing at school into another they secretly carried from the house. A *corrida,* or ballad, of the day expressed the adults' attitudes. It was called "Las Pelonas," or "The Bobbed-Haired Girls":

> Red Bandannas
> I detest,
> And now the flappers
> Use them for their dress.

The girls of San Antonio
Are lazy at the *metate* [a stone used for grinding corn].
They want to walk out bobbed-haired,
With straw hats on.
The harvesting is finished,
So is the cotton;
The flappers stroll out now
For a good time.[6]

That *corrida,* from San Antonio, tells us that young Americans throughout the country, regardless of their cultural heritage, were embracing many
of the same new customs and fashions. Children and teenagers usually are
most eager to pick up and practice such new ways of life, and technological
advances were speeding the process.

Some of the most powerful forces encouraging cultural change and promoting common ways of living among young people throughout America
have been new forms of communication. One of the most dramatic examples swept over the nation during the years following World War I: the
radio. Americans have enthusiastically embraced many technological wonders over the years, but few infatuated them more than the radio. Experiments with "wireless communication" were made late in the 19th century,
but the first previously announced broadcast took place in 1906.

A series of technical breakthroughs during the next decade opened the
way for commercial broadcasting. The earliest radio program—if it could
be called that—came only in 1920, when an amateur operator and official
for the giant electrical company Westinghouse, Dr. Frank Conrad, began
broadcasting phonograph recordings from his Pittsburgh, Pennsylvania, garage as part of experiments in new transmission equipment. When he discovered that other operators were listening in, he announced regular
broadcasts twice a week and borrowed recordings from a local dealer,
whose sales suddenly rose dramatically. A local department store began
selling radio receivers so others could hear "Dr. Conrad's popular broadcasts." A large transmitter constructed atop Westinghouse's tallest building
became the nation's first commercial station, KDKA. On election night in
November 1920, listeners in the area heard bulletins on returns from across
the country. America's radio age had begun.

Only four years later, 5 million homes had radio sets. By the end of the
decade a third of all homes had them; by 1934, ownership had risen to 60
percent, and by 1939, to 86 percent; additionally, there were more than 6
million radios in automobiles. Programs were broadcast by hundreds of

stations scattered across the nation, many of them knit together by 1930 into two radio networks, the National Broadcasting Corporation (NBC) and the Columbia Broadcasting System (CBS). As would be true of cars and televisions, Americans pursued this product more enthusiastically than anybody else. In the mid-1930s, more than four out of ten radios in the world were in the United States.

This new passion naturally competed with other kinds of technological amusements that, in their own day, had won the public's heart. Americans in 1940 passed a total of a billion hours every week listening to their radios, more than seven times the hours spent watching movies. With music coming over the airwaves, consumers had less reason to buy another bit of earlier wizardry, phonograph records. Spending on recordings and phonograph equipment dropped 95 percent between 1920 and 1930.

Radios could be quite cheap—one of the chief reasons people had bought so many of them—but some of the best were housed in elegant, heavy cabinets of wood or veneer. By one estimate, in fact, radios in the mid-1920s accounted for a third of the value of all furniture in the country. Still, it was possible to build a radio receiver with only a simple headset, a coil of wire, and a germanium crystal available at a drug store for a couple of dollars. All but the poorest families could afford radios, and, because radio waves were broadcast instantly over vast distances, this new entertainment was quickly accessible to people living in some of the country's most isolated regions. Electrical outlets were unnecessary; sets could be rigged up to batteries, including those in cars or trucks. Children on farms and ranches in the Dakotas, on the Oregon desert, deep in the West Virginia hills and in the Maine woods—boys and girls who had no hope of seeing a movie or speaking over a telephone—all could tune in to baseball games, musical programs, and comedy shows, just as their city cousins could in St. Louis or Baltimore.

So accessible were radios, in fact, that a boy or girl could buy the makings of his or her own by saving from an allowance or the pay for odd jobs. Never before had such a marvel of technology, such a window onto distant places and an enthralling source of amusement, been so easily within the reach of the individual child. Even a nickel film in a city theater was a collective experience that was over in an hour or so. A radio was a child's own possession, and he or she could wander over the dial at will, pausing to listen and to reach out into the world. Nothing in the history of childhood amusement had come close to matching the radio's mix of variety, independence, and power.

Radio was also a family entertainment. Just as it could pull a son or daughter away, allowing remarkable freedom and escape, it also could draw children and parents together. As a popular program began, the family sat around the set, all ears turned in common to the speaker. The antics and crises of radio characters were discussed around the dinner table by mothers, sons, daughters, aunts, grandparents, and fathers. The medium's unifying power went even farther. Surveys showed that listeners in the inner cities, the suburbs, in small towns and on far-flung farms all preferred more or less the same broadcasts. The stories, people, and events projected out and through American radios became a kind of national folklore, a rare common ground for young and old, immigrant and native-born, city and country dwellers.

Within limits, that is. By far the most popular radio program of the 1930s was "Amos 'n' Andy," broadcast over NBC and sponsored by Pepsodent toothpaste. Freeman Gosden and Charles Correll, both white, spoke in crude dialect as the two title characters, fictional Chicago black men who engaged in a variety of hairbrained schemes and got into frequent trouble with authorities, friends, and wives. African Americans generally were deeply offended by its degrading stereotypes; more than 750,000 signed a petition protesting the show. Among whites, however, "Amos 'n' Andy" enjoyed a staggering popularity. It was broadcast publicly in department stores and restaurants and even in movie theaters, which stopped their projectors for the fifteen-minute episodes. Children seemed as addicted as their parents. When NBC initially scheduled the program at 11:00 P.M., eastern time, thousands of frustrated parents wrote that their sons and daughters refused to go to bed until the program was over. Alerted to the problem (and no doubt hoping to keep the younger audience hooked) the network moved "Amos 'n' Andy" to 7:00 P.M., then rebroadcast it at 11:30 so fans on the Pacific coast, too, could hear it at the dinner hour.

Boys and girls listened faithfully to other programs pitched mainly at adults, such as "Fibber McGee and Molly," a comedy about a middle-class married couple. Most children were at school when their mothers tuned into daytime serial dramas that focused on women's romances and personal tribulations. Because they were usually sponsored by prominent brands of laundry detergents, these programs quickly were dubbed "soap operas." Three of them already could be heard in 1931, and by the end of the decade the airwaves were flooded by sixty-one soap operas.

Other forces were having a similar effect, pulling together Americans, young and old, into common experiences. An increasingly efficient rail transportation system allowed goods and people to move around the country more easily and quickly. That meant that throughout the nation girls and boys were buying the same products (or having them bought for them). Students in Wisconsin dressed for school in the same kinds of clothes that were seen the same morning in Los Angeles and Boston. More and more American children read the same magazines and, as will be discussed, played with the same toys.

They also began to eat alike. Early in the century, and increasingly as the years passed, Americans began to adopt the same foodways. What and how they were eating provides evidence of what was happening to change American society.

Take, for instance, a product that is still a familiar part of most children's lives—breakfast cereals. Breakfast in the 19th century had been a prodigious meal, at least among those who could afford it. Farm families and those of the urban middle class sat down to tables groaning with beefsteak, ham, bacon, eggs, fried potatoes, pancakes, and coffee, all of it prepared by hard-worked servants or mothers and eaten at a leisurely pace. Such fare was considered necessary for a full day of work ahead, especially for those doing heavy labor outdoors.

By the turn of the century those attitudes and practices were changing. One result was the marketing of ready-to-eat breakfast foods bought at a local grocery. The earliest packaged breakfast food was Kellogg's Corn Flakes, created by William R. and John H. Kellogg, brothers who ran a popular health resort in Battle Creek, Michigan. One of their clients, Charles W. Post, a real estate speculator and former Texas cowboy, devised his own products, Grape-Nuts and Toasties. A Denver restaurateur, Henry Perky, entered the field with Shredded Wheat. All were introduced to the public by the mid-1890s. By the early 20th century they had several other competitors.

The rapid appearance and acceptance of breakfast cereals reflected several important developments. They were one of the earliest foods to be marketed nationwide via the national web of railroads. Easily stored and safe from spoilage, they paved the way for the tens of thousands of other food products that in time would crisscross the country to family dinner tables. Cereals also told of a growing concern over the connection between diet and health. Sold sealed in boxes, they all appeared to be hygienic and free from the contamination that parents feared in many of the foods they bought. Not only that, they were said to be full of nutrients that promoted strong and healthy bodies. Grape-Nuts, according to Post, even built up the brain and helped cure malaria and loose teeth.

Finally, breakfast cereals said a lot about changing patterns of life among many Americans. Cereals were especially suited to life in the city. Unlike on the farms, where long hours were spent at heavy labors in the fields, city children and their working fathers passed their days in more sedentary ways, sitting at desks in schools and in offices. They could get by on a much smaller intake of fuel. These ready-made foods, furthermore, could be prepared almost instantly—an important advantage. City folks had to hold to a much tighter time schedule than their relatives in the countryside. Fathers increasingly worked not for themselves but for large businesses and factories, where they were expected to come and go right on time. More children were going to school, and they had to be in their seats when classes began. Family members, that is, had to leave the house quickly, and breakfast cereals, ready to eat with a pouring of milk, got them out the door on time. Cereals also made the morning easier for middle-class mothers, who were increasingly responsible for making their families' breakfasts, as reliable and inexpensive servants were becoming harder and harder to find.

The phenomenal popularity of these early breakfast foods quickly encouraged others. Kellogg and Post expanded their offerings. Buying out several competitors, Post formed General Mills, a corporate giant that would produce dozens of cereals in the decades ahead. Some complained that these did not give children, or anyone else who ate them, an adequate start for the day. And unlike later sugared and flavored concoctions, early cereals were also bland, almost tasteless. Critics called them "shredded doormats." Nonetheless, during the 1920s and 1930s, these breakfasts-in-boxes became a standard item in millions of homes—and a familiar part of growing up in America.

What about the other meals? What young people found waiting for them at lunchtime and dinner also was changing. The boom in breakfast cereals was only one part of a much larger phenomenon, the expansion of the food-processing industry. Here again, plenty can be learned about changes in the lives of children and parents by looking at what was on their plates.

For much of American history rural families had grown, raised, and hunted most of their own food. Those living in the cities bought what was carried in from the country. Farmers and city-dwellers alike prepared food for themselves, or hired servants to do the work—baking bread, slicing meat and blending it into stews and soups, washing and trimming vegetables, making pies and other desserts. Meal preparation added up to a large part of the domestic workday and kept women and their helpers close to their kitchens.

Early in the 20th century, this familiar part of the workday routine began to change. Women who were responsible for their family meals increasingly relied on food that not only had been produced but, more important, had been largely prepared elsewhere. By the time these foods reached the household, they were almost ready for the table. "Processed" foods had alluring advantages. As the years passed, more women were either unable or unwilling to spend most of their days in their kitchens. Working-class mothers often had jobs away from home; those in the middle classes found it increasingly difficult to hire domestic help. Industrially prepared foods saved them all time and effort.

Moreover, as families moved to the cities, the lives of children and parents shifted away from the home and toward institutions and entertainments beyond—to schools and movie houses, department stores, street games, and work in factories and offices. Quickly prepared meals fit this trend nicely. On top of everything else, processed foods usually were cheaper, as mass manufacturing techniques and mass marketing gradually drove down their prices.

Take, for instance, bread. Making this most basic American food had taken anywhere from four to six hours of kitchen labor. By the time of World War I, huge commercial bakeries were turning out millions of loaves, already sliced and ready to be buttered and eaten. This, in turn, nudged popular taste in a particular direction, as would so many other technological developments in daily life. Mass baking produced a white "pan bread" that was much lighter and airier than the coarse types favored by many Americans, especially new immigrants. So convenient and appealing was commercial bread, however, that preferences gradually shifted: sliced white bread became the American norm. At the end of the 1930s, when the annual value of mass-produced bread was estimated at more than twenty-five times that of bread baked at home ($514 million vs. $20 million), more than 7 billion pounds of white bread was sold, far surpassing the 1.7 billion pounds of all rye, whole wheat, and hearth breads combined.

On the dinner table also might be found a variety of vegetables "fresh" from the can, as well as a growing selection of canned soups. The most popular brand of soup, Campbell's, sold at eight cans for a dollar on the eve of the depression. About 1925, Charles Birdseye devised a method of "quick-freezing" foods that allowed the contents to be thawed without becoming an unappetizing glob. It took a few years for frozen foods to catch on—among other things, some sort of home freezer was needed—but then their popularity grew at a phenomenal clip. In 1934 sales totalled an impressive 39 million pounds, and a decade later an astounding 600 million pounds were sold. Technology also altered family tastes by making available products that in the past had seemed bizarre and exotic. Early in the 1920s, for instance, the Del Monte company launched a strenuous marketing campaign to introduce the American public to pineapple. Soon millions of children were happily eating slices from the can.

Though most obvious in the cities, these dinner-table transformations extended into the countryside as well. Among relatively well-to-do farmers, mealtime was changing and improving during the 1920s and 1930s. An improved understanding of nutrition gradually made its way into kitchens in the countryside and small towns as well as the cities and suburbs. New ideas about the value of diverse, balanced diets were spread through home economics courses in high schools and through 4-H Clubs, which had more than 750,000 young members by 1930. Strangely enough, the move toward better nutrition was encouraged by the farmers' economic troubles. In the past, when the market offered high prices for a few products such as wheat, corn, and cotton, farmers had been tempted to use their land to grow only such crops. But with the collapse of the agricultural boom after World War I, farm families were more likely to turn to raising many different crops, including some they could eat themselves.

Part of that diversification brought a rise in consumption of milk. It is commonly thought that all farm children always have drunk plenty of cow's milk, but that has not been the case. Especially outside the Midwest, many farms had no cattle. During the 1920s, however, hard-pressed southern farmers bought some milk cows to fatten their incomes—and also because they had heard the opinions that milk was the one most healthful food for children and adults alike, a wonder food brimming with vitamins and other bodily necessities. Taking on a cow or two was another way of promoting their children's vigorous growth. Nine out of ten farmers in the Mississippi cotton country in 1927 owned their own milk cows, and among New Hampshire families owning cows a few years later, three out of four consumed a quart of milk per person per day. So it was, oddly, city-dwellers and large businesses that had taught many farm families the value of drinking milk.

Part of this same change encouraged the eating of fresh fruits, especially citrus. Improved rail and road transportation brought these previously exotic foods within the reach (and the budget) of both urban and rural Americans. By the early 1920s, farm families surveyed in Missouri, Ohio, Kentucky, and Kansas ate an average of a hundred pounds of grapefruits, bananas, oranges, and lemons every year.

In the cities, suburbs and countryside, food processing and the continuing revolution in the national transportation system opened up all sorts of eating experiences unimaginable for young people of an earlier day. In that sense, the horizons of young people were vastly expanded. Changes in American life were extending the reach of young people's minds and all their senses, including their taste buds.

Yet, paradoxically, this dietary revolution narrowed perspectives as well. For most American children by 1940, especially those in the cities, mealtime was becoming an increasingly disconnected event. A few generations earlier young girls and boys knew, more or less, where their food had come from. Usually they had helped plant it, care for it, harvest it, slaughter it, and process it. But girls and boys at mid-century saw and knew little about the origins and history of what they were eating. Where had those syrupy peaches come from, and the peas, the tuna in the casserole, the sliced bananas, the stack of bread, and the glass of milk? Why, from the can, the box, the carton, the refrigerator, the freezer, and, before all those, from the grocery store. And before that? Before that was a mystery.

Another product of the technology of these years, however, has had a far greater impact than all others on the lives of American children and their families: the automobile. At the opening of the 20th century, the automobile was considered a kind of expensive, interesting, but sometimes troubling toy. The machines had been around for years, but they had never caught on, partly because their cost, more than a thousand dollars each, was far beyond the reach of most Americans. In the entire country there were only about eight thousand autos. Only half had been made in the United States. The world leader in auto manufacturing was France; many basic terms still in use today come from French: "garage," "chassis," "chauffeur," and "automobile" itself.

Most Americans in the early 20th century seemed to think of cars as noisy nuisances; laws in some states decreed that an auto could not go faster than four miles per hour and had to be preceded on the road by a man waving a red flag. There was not much reason to think that automobiles would ever be a significant part of everyday life. An editor in 1899 wrote that the "horseless carriage" was a plaything of the well-to-do that "will never, of course, come into as common use as the bicycle."[7]

This might have been the least correct prediction in American history. Arguably, no force in this century, not even television or computers, has transformed American life and customs more than the automobile. By 1920 autos already were unavoidable in many parts of the country, but the big push in production lay just ahead. During the next twenty years, and especially during the 1920s, the number of cars increased enormously—as did their influence on Americans of all ages.

The car culture swept quickly through most of American life, including its children's playtime. Here a daughter of the middle class takes her dolls for a ride inside her Denver home. *Photo by Harry Rhoads, courtesy of The Denver Public Library, Western History Department.*

Part of the reason for this explosion in autos was an expanding knowledge of how to make them. Better technology and workmanship in car bodies and engines naturally made them more appealing. Furthermore, cars exploded on the marketplace because the national landscape was changed to prepare for them. Cars, after all, are not much good if there are no roads and streets for them. City streets were made over to allow easier movement of auto traffic, and cars began to crowd horses and buggies out of the way. As for the areas outside the cities, gradually, and then more aggressively after 1920, dirt roads were replaced by paved ones that were also better marked for long-distance travel. The discovery in 1906 of huge deposits of oil in east Texas provided more and cheaper fuel.

The most important innovation, however, came in the method of putting cars together. Earlier, one or a few workers labored on one car until it was assembled; then they began another. Just about every manufactured product was made in much the same way. Starting in 1914, however, that process changed. In a factory in the Detroit suburb of Highland Park, Michigan, Henry Ford introduced a moving "assembly line" for putting together automobiles he had been selling for several years. In this system, each auto was assembled step-by-step as it passed along a moving track. Workers stood at each step of the process, repeating their one task as car after car came to them. The auto then passed on to the next stages, where other workers would also do only their one part of the assembly, time after time, as each new car arrived in front of them.

Assembly lines, many employees complained, made their work horribly boring, but Ford found that this system produced cars much more quickly and efficiently; and, as a result, he could sell them much more cheaply. His basic product was the Model T, or "tin lizzie," or "flivver." Its engineering was simple, it was easily repaired, and it ran very efficiently; after 1914 its streamlined assembly made it steadily cheaper. In 1910 Ford sold the Model T for $950. During the next fifteen years, while prices of almost everything else were rising, Ford's cars sold for less every year, and in 1925 "tin lizzies" cost less than $300 each, or roughly three-months' wages of the average American worker. By that time, Ford's plants were turning out one car every ten seconds, or about nine thousand a day. At the end of the 1920s, half of all automobiles in the world were Fords. The stunning expansion of the number of cars is shown in this table of registered American automobiles:

**Automobiles Registered in U.S.**

| | |
|---|---|
| 1905 | 8,000 |
| 1915 | 2,332,426 |
| 1925 | 17,481,001 |
| 1935 | 22,567,827[8] |

The automobile revolution eventually changed just about everything in American life. For children, cars (and trucks) would help determine what they played with, how they spent their summers and other time away from school, how they entered adolescence, and how they used and abused the new freedom of those years. Cars drove through their dreams. Teenagers would sing about them and make them into their own works of art. Young men and women courted and had their earliest sexual experiences in Fords, Chevrolets, Dodges, Buicks, and Chryslers. And, in increasing numbers, they died in them.

Nothing was affected more by autos than the family. After Americans began piling into cars by the millions, parents and children would live together differently—in some ways very differently—from those who had never seen a Ford or Oldsmobile. The car's effects will be mentioned now and again in the chapters to come, but some of the most immediate results for families and children came in the years between 1920 and 1940.

The coming of the car, for instance, affected children's health. In the long run, Americans discovered that auto exhaust polluted the air, and eventually auto accidents would be the leading cause of death among Americans of all ages; but in the short run, cars helped eliminate the threats to good health posed by horses. The tens of thousands of horses used for transportation in a large city like Boston or Chicago produced staggering amounts of manure every day. An enterprising journalist in Rochester, New York, calculated that his city's twenty-five thousand horses produced enough waste in a year to pile one acre 175 feet deep in manure. Sixteen billion flies would find a home there, he figured. Here was one of the reasons that the journalist H. L. Mencken recalled the Baltimore of his youth as smelling "like a billion polecats." It doesn't take much imagination to picture some of the ways that production of horse dung influenced the health of those living around it. Furthermore, when horses died, they were left where they lay until city workers got rid of them; and unlike abandoned automobiles, these carcasses were more than just eyesores. Cars rust; horses rot.

Even before 1920, the number of animals living in cities was dropping, partly because of autos and partly because of electric trolleys. Horses in New York City declined from 128,000 to 56,000 between 1910 and 1920; and in Chicago, from 68,000 to 30,000. After 1920, those numbers plummeted.

In the countryside, horses were certainly not vanishing, but autos still were having quite an influence. Early on, in fact, sales of cars to farm families were proportionately greater than those in the cities. Automobiles gave rural Americans a way to ease the isolation and loneliness of living far from stores and neighbors. Suddenly boys and girls on farms in Iowa or Oregon had a chance to meet new friends and get to know places they could see only rarely without the sputtering car that took them lurching along rutted country roads. A government agent asked a farm wife in the

1920s why she and her husband had bought a car, even though they had not yet installed indoor plumbing. She answered: "You can't go to town in a bathtub."[9]

Here was the greatest appeal of the automobile—a freedom and independence of movement. In towns and cities as well as in the country, a family with its own motorized wheels gained overnight all sorts of options previously unthinkable. They could go where they wished when they wished (assuming roads were available), and unlike riding on the trolley or subway, the cost was no greater for a mother, father, and four or five youngsters than for an adult traveling alone. A government report in the early 1930s summed up the auto's allure:

> Close at hand and ready for instant use, it carried its owner from door to destination by routes he himself selected, and on schedules of his own making; baggage inconveniences were minimized and perhaps most important of all, the automobile made possible the movement of an entire family at costs that were relatively small.[10]

That freedom had many implications for future Americans, including, ironically, new ways they would become restricted and confined. Among the most important and immediate changes had to do with the places that many families made their homes, especially in the nation's cities. Until now, urban children usually lived near where their parents worked. Most homes were close to central parts of cities or to factories that typically were near railroad lines. Trolleys had begun to change that pattern. Electric railways allowed parents to move their families farther away from the congested cores of cities, out to suburbs from which fathers could still ride to and from work. These suburban families were mostly middle and upper middle class, with fathers working as merchants, professionals, or factory foremen.

The new neighborhoods had broad streets with wide lots and large houses of two and three stories. It was in those suburbs, especially, that the new styles of housing described in the last chapter, such as the bungalows, sprouted up in great numbers. This movement out of the city core was a very important development in the history of family life, the start of a trend that still continues. Increasingly, more and more young Americans have grown up farther and farther from the centers of cities where most had lived in earlier times—although, as will be noted below, living away from the inner city has always been much more difficult for poorer families.

Early suburbs had to be built close to the few trolley lines that radiated out from the city center, but automobiles changed that. With a car, a family could travel to and from the city from anywhere that had access to roads and streets. Huge areas on the outskirts of Cleveland, Houston, St. Louis, and other cities suddenly could be transformed from fields and pastures into neighborhoods swarming with children. Because that land also cost much less than property closer in, houses could be built and sold more cheaply, and because most families enjoyed higher incomes during the decade following World War I, every year tens of thousands of parents who had never owned a home were able to buy one for themselves and their children. The trend mentioned in the first chapter—city families with modest incomes suddenly able to buy their first house—speeded up.

The result was a gigantic housing boom in the 1920s, much of it in the new suburbs opened by the boom in automobiles. At the start of the decade, a little less than half of American families lived in their own homes. During the next several years, those with the money to build and buy started to do so at an unprecedented pace. An average of nearly 900,000 new houses were begun every year between 1922 and 1929, which was more than twice as many as in any comparable period in the past. Overwhelmingly, these houses were in the new neighborhoods on the outskirts of the cities. As car sales skyrocketed, suburbs were growing twice as fast as the central parts of the hundred largest cities in the United States.

Not every American family could take part in these major changes. It still took a good bit of money to buy a car and a house in the suburbs. A study in Pittsburgh in 1934 showed that fewer than half of the working people owned autos, and the same was probably true in other industrial cities. The majority of adult Americans apparently walked or took the trolley to and from work. As the nation approached World War II, most of its children still lived in car-less families. Some of the most impressive suburbs were built for people with comfortable incomes or for the very rich. The most famous example was Beverly Hills, California. When developers failed to find oil on land just west of Los Angeles, they turned it into an even bigger bonanza, selling spacious lots along broad, curving streets to wealthy Californians, including its most famous movie stars. Highland Park, north of Dallas, was a less expensive version for the upper middle class. Kansas City had its Country Club District, built on a former city dump and race track, a lushly landscaped area offering "spacious grounds for permanently protected homes, surrounded with ample space for air and sunshine."

Nevertheless, thousands of families with only modest incomes did take part in this vast exodus, and armies of middle- and working-class children made their homes and found their adventures along newly paved streets in neighborhoods that a year or so before had been cow pastures and corn fields.

The Great Depression brought the boom in home building to a crashing, grinding halt. Savings evaporated and incomes plunged or stopped altogether for millions of families. Among those who had any money to invest, very few had the confidence to take on a new home mortgage. Between 1928 and 1933, residential construction declined by a staggering 95 percent. Interestingly, the other part of the earlier change—sales of automobiles—continued to rise. In 1940 there were more than four million more cars registered than in 1930. Parents might postpone having babies, give up meat five nights a week, and sell the family silver, but autos had become so important that they were the last to go. As one housewife put it: "We'd rather go without clothes than give up the car."[11]

But if the flight to the suburbs stalled in the 1930s, it would pick up again later at an even faster pace. Even with the depression, American cities had changed their shapes dramatically by 1940. City people, especially families, spread themselves over a much larger area, and downtown was thinning out. A part of Brooklyn that had nearly 80,000 persons per square mile in 1920 was down to a mere 58,000 ten years later. New York City's Lower East Side, the most crowded place on earth in 1910 with a population of nearly 400,000 persons, dropped to about 147,000 inhabitants in 1940, a decline of nearly two-thirds.

With the help of the car, America's families were being flung outward, away from its inner cities, as if they were on a speeding merry-go-round. But that was only part of the change: the movement brought sifting and separation. The families moving to the suburbs were those who could afford it; they were also overwhelmingly white. From then on, the children of such suburban families would have little contact with the poor or with anyone of an ethnic or cultural background much different from their own. These revolutions in national life—the automobile, suburbs, and home ownership—were sorting American society into segments that were more and more isolated from one another.

All the changes described in this section were encouraged by the economic prosperity enjoyed by many families (but by no means all) during the 1920s. At the end of that decade, however, the good times ended abruptly as the nation entered the worst economic crisis of its history. The tougher times meant many changes for American children—to be discussed later with reference to their work, health, and legal status—but some of the most immediate and memorable adjustments were at home.

For some, the most traumatic change was losing their homes altogether. Thousands of families, unable to keep up with rent or mortgage payments, were forced to abandon their dwellings and search for alternatives. Parents and children took to the roads to look for work. Itinerant families slept outdoors in abandoned buildings or in camps with others in their situation. Many more gave up their homes to move in with others. "Doubling up," familiar to families in earlier eras, became much more common in the 1930s as younger families moved in with parents and grandparents and poorer relatives crowded in with others slightly better off. Frequently, this also meant separation, as mothers and children accepted invitations from kinfolks while fathers took off in search of a job and a new start.

Those who managed to hold on to their homes still faced profound adjustments, often surrendering much of what had been taken for granted— small and larger extras and luxuries, from vacations to special desserts, entertainments to new clothes. Many families eventually were reduced to the basics, and some below that. Jane Yoder was the daughter of a blacksmith for an Illinois mine that closed in 1930. After months of unemployment, her father left to look elsewhere, leaving Jane, her mother, and six brothers and sisters to get along as well as they could. They found the brutal winters especially trying:

> We were struggling, just desperate to be warm . . . I had one coat. It must have been a terrible lightweight coat or what, but I can remember being cold, just shivering. And came home, and nothing to do but go to bed, because if you went to bed, then you put the coat on the bed and you got warm.
> The cold that I've known. I never had boots . . . In rainy weather you just ran for it, you ran between the raindrops or whatever. . . . You simply wore your old shoes if it was raining. Save the others.[12]

In the most desperate circumstances, parents were forced to give up children they could not feed and clothe. One father appeared at the Children's Aid Society of New York with a daughter of three months and a two-year-old son. "I don't want to give up my children," he explained, "but they must have food." Their mother had suffered a mental breakdown, and he had been out of work for months. During the past three days the children had eaten nothing but bread with tea. He had to leave them at the agency while he went off in search of a job, although he promised to "work my hands off" to repay the costs of rearing them.[13] This father was one of thousands of parents in similar dilemmas. By one estimate more than half a million homeless children needed help and shelter from welfare agencies during the winter of 1931, which was still a year away from the worst of the depression.

Some of these children were placed in orphanages. These institutions, as discussed in chapter 1, had been the preferred means of dealing with homeless or abandoned children during the 19th century, and they continued to operate in the 20th. Dorothe Bernstein entered an orphanage in 1933 when she was ten. Her memories were not unpleasant: "I had clean clothes all the time and we had plenty to eat." On their way to school every morning she and her friends would pass unemployed vagrant men standing along the railroad tracks. If the girls did not like the lunches prepared for them, especially on Friday when they were given sandwiches of mashed sardines and mayonnaise, they would hand the small brown bags to the grateful men.[14]

By the 1930s, however, many officials no longer thought orphanages were the best means of providing for homeless children. For years there had been complaints that conditions in these places were a lot harsher than those experienced by Dorothe Bernstein. But something more fundamental had changed as well. The family increasingly was seen as the cradle of society and the ideal place for children to learn moral values and the virtues of citizenship. When a family suffered a great blow, it was now thought better to take children away temporarily, while parents healed the damage, so they could once more care for their sons and daughters. If parents were killed or the family was hopelessly broken, then the young should be placed with something as close to a natural family as possible.

The result was a movement away from institutions to foster care. The idea that "any reasonably good mother is the best and most economical caretaker of her children" was a major step beyond the orphanage system, declared the Children's Bureau in 1936. The trend to foster homes was well underway by the end of the 1920s, when the onset of the depression brought a swelling flood of children into state and private agencies. Besides those orphaned or removed from parents who were abusive, mentally ill or otherwise incompetent, now there were those given up by mothers and fathers unable to care for them. By a kind of compensation of suffering, however, the depression brought with it more parents willing to take in foster children. Foster parents, after all, were paid a stipend. The Children's Aid Society of Pennsylvania paid families up to four or five dollars a week, and although that money was supposed to cover the foster child's room and board, it also eased the strain on everyone in the household. Not surprisingly, the society had three to four times the usual number of families applying by 1932. Most such agencies supposedly refused to place their boys and girls with parents interested mainly in the money that came with them, but such regulations were largely ignored during these difficult years.

Coming hard upon what had seemed to be the most prosperous decade in U.S. history, the calamities of the 1930s were grim reminders of the limits of the American dream and the complex parts that children played in achieving them. As thousands of families faced the ultimate failure of admitting they could not support their sons and daughters, others took those youngsters in, partly out of devotion to the new ideal of giving children loving care, partly as an old impulse to use girls and boys to bring in precious cash.

## AT PLAY

During the 20th century, manufactured toys became a steadily greater part of a child's world of play. The growth of toy manufacturing, in part, reflected the general expansion of industry and, in part, a growing middle class with extra money to spend on such things. Like those who produced and showed motion pictures and who ran the urban penny arcades, toy manufacturers showed that American business was coming to recognize young people as an important and growing market of consumers. As with other aspects of children's lives, this industry also gave adults more opportunities to regulate and influence the experiences of children in their care.

Some manufactured toys were continuations or revivals of traditional and even ancient playthings. "Pull toys," usually miniature iron vehicles pulled by a string, were popular throughout the 19th century and variations of them seem to have been around for centuries. Variations after 1900 reflected the grand changes of those years. Automobiles, buses, and airplanes were made of lighter materials like steel, tin, rubber, and, finally, plastics. While some were still pulled or pushed by hand, others were powered by wind-up mechanisms and, after around 1915, by the friction wheel. When a toy with this device was pushed back and forth along the floor, a large balance wheel was made to spin inside, so when a child let the toy loose, the wheel sent it moving on its own. For nearly half a century, friction-wheeled playthings would be a common part of the American toybox.

One of the most popular "new" toys of the 1920s in fact was very old. The origins of the yo-yo are unclear. By one theory it appeared first in China, by another, in ancient Greece. Some authorities claim it was borrowed from a weapon used in the jungles of the Philippines. A four-pound round of wood was dropped out of a tree onto an animal's or enemy's head, then it rebounded back up a twenty-foot thong. By this theory, "yo-yo" meant "come-come" in a Filipino dialect. Yo-yos apparently were play-things of European royalty in the 16th and 17th centuries, and they show up in toy books of the late 19th century, but the modern mass use of them began in the late 1920s when Donald Duncan began their manufacture. Duncan, who also invented the parking meter, began marketing wooden yo-yos, demonstrating them to curious customers in department stores. The toys sold in huge numbers during the depression years, perhaps because they were cheap, but also because both children and adults discovered a nearly infinite number of tricks to be performed with them. Over time the public's affection dimmed; later, in 1959, Duncan began producing much more flamboyant plastic varieties—brightly colored, sparkly, even ones that glowed in the dark—and suddenly yo-yos were once again hot. At their new peak, in the mid-1960s, more than sixteen million were sold annually. Yo-yos remain a standard item in young America's toybox.

Other toys, mass-produced and mass-marketed, were entirely modern creations, miniature technical wonders, including diminutive versions of the very things that brought the toys to market—electric trains. Wind-up and pull models of locomotives were sold in the 19th century, and a few com-panies experimented with toy steam-powered trains. Then, just after 1900, the first trains with electric motors were marketed by the company that became the leader in the field, Lionel. Joshua Lionel Cowen began with an open freight car, and then a trolley, powered by dry cell batteries. The public clamored for them, but only in 1908 did Cowen's company, whose name was taken from his own middle name, introduce its first electrical locomotive. Competitors soon crowded into the action, and sales soared in the 1920s. Trains by Lionel were built of sturdy metals and plated in shiny nickel. They had headlights that actually shone, power stations, automatic switches, and whistles; and alongside the tracks were water tanks, train stations, and warning signals, as well as models of well-kept farms and suburban bungalows. Some of these models were astonishingly accurate in details. Virtually every part visible in a 1937 Lionel product, including the seats and benches seen through the windows, was an exact replication. When a customer discovered that Lionel's engine tender had 1,399 rivets on its side, while the original full-sized version had 1,402, the company corrected the error, then created the position of rivet-counter to check such things.

As toys, electric trains tell us a lot about the Americans who were buying them. This was an era when, even more than usual, people both celebrated their new technologies and looked nostalgically backward toward the "good old days," when life supposedly was simpler. A model railroad spoke of that longing for previous generations; in the 1930s a modernized version appeared, the shiny "Streamliner," but it was never as popular as the classics based on the black, smoke-belching railroads of the previous century. And yet the train itself was a mechanical marvel. At a time when electricity was being applied to so much else in daily life, from labor-saving appliances to radios, its use in this child's toy was natural enough. As parents set up an electric railroad late on Christmas eve, they were celebrating both the national past and the wizardry of its present and future.

Unlike the yo-yo, however, electric trains obviously were limited to a relatively small part of the buying public. Most children could only dream of such an expensive plaything, especially after the Great Depression destroyed other, much grander dreams. Even if they had the purchase price, furthermore, many families did not have the room for the elaborate layout of tracks and equipment that were part of even a modest set. That would change after World War II, and electric trains would become even more a part of children's playlife.

In any case, by the end of the first two decades of the century, toys had become a major American industry. Stores began devoting shelves, then entire sections to an expanding inventory of toy manufactures. By World War I, businesses were offering quite a Christmas array. One child recalled:

> There were tables of toys; one table alone of cowboy suits and cap pistols, and another with soldier suits and of machine guns that fired wooden bullets, a dozen bullets to a belt. There were new boots . . . and fireman's hats, alongside of baseball suits with heavy red sweaters. Mechanical sets with real screw drivers and metal braces. . . . But best of all was a brown truck-line machine, a miniature army tank on real rubber wheels.[15]

Quite a lineup. But toys like these were never simply playthings. Toys designed, produced, and marketed by adults and usually bought by parents for their children told as much about grownups as about the young. These items encouraged children to play in certain ways and to mimic certain adult activities. Girls and boys always have "played at" being grownups, but the particular roles emphasized in those playthings also suggest that manufacturers were stressing some activities and occupations—soldiering, sports, and mechanical arts—that were a compromise between respectable and useful jobs and what the young shoppers considered exciting. Toys, in fact, contained all sorts of complicated messages.

"Construction" and "mechanical" toys were good examples. Building blocks had been around for a long time and are still popular today. They varied a bit—some featured pictures of animals or odd faces—but, basically, they were simply wooden cubes that children could stack and line up into whatever formations occurred to them. Early in the 20th century a new kind of construction toy began to appear, which allowed a greater range of possibilities and more elaborate and realistic creations. Tinker Toys, which first hit the market around 1914, consisted of smooth, thin wooden sticks of different lengths sized to be pegged into round connector wheels. These sets were simple enough for young children, and the possible shapes and combinations (and so the possible imaginings of young builders) were endless. Tinker Toys became one of the most successful and enduring children's amusements of the century.

Another hugely popular construction toy had more of a message. Lincoln Logs appeared for sale in 1918, and over the next several decades the sets sold by the millions. Their inventor was John Lloyd Wright, son of one of the most famous and influential architects in American history, Frank Lloyd Wright. Each set consisted of a series of reddish-brown wood cylinders notched on the ends so they fit together, like the notched tree trunks of a classic log cabin. A child patiently built up walls and added a roof from other wooden pieces. Besides giving the young builder a sense of achievement, Lincoln Logs called up nostalgic images of an earlier America. At a time when so many were worried about the rise of cities and the threats of modern American life, this toy spoke of the myth of sturdy pioneers and old-fashioned virtues of self-reliance and courage. Supposedly, Lincoln Logs encouraged youngsters to imagine a simple life of an earlier day—a dream that plenty of parents were eager to feed their children. (There was an irony here. Wright's inspiration came not from pioneer cabins but from watching construction of the foundations of the Imperial Hotel in Tokyo, Japan, designed by his famous father to resist earthquakes.) Whatever the messages in them, girls and boys loved them, and would continue to. In 1975 more than a million sets a year were being sold.

Another construction toy, however, looked in the other direction. "Meccano sets" were imported from England first in 1909, and by 1915 an improved American version appeared: Erector Sets. These had multiple perforated metal pieces connected with bolts and nuts to form scaffolding or the bare structures of buildings. Also included were winches, pulleys and other mechanical devices, and, eventually, small electric motors. With these, boys and girls could construct buildings, bridges, even skyscrapers like those transforming urban skylines. If Lincoln Logs recalled a vanished

First marketed in 1918, Lincoln Logs® have remained a favorite of generations of boys and girls who have used them to construct their own fantasies. *Lincoln Logs® is a trademark of Hasbro, Inc. © 1996 Hasbro, Inc. All Rights Reserved. Used with permission.*

America, Erector Sets celebrated the new nation and encouraged fantasies of plunging into its construction. One child recalled:

> With the sheets of metal and the girders we could build almost anything, but we wanted to make something which needed some of our pulleys. . . . No matter what shape our construction took, it turned out to be a lifting crane. It would lift objects large in comparison to its size. . . . Finally we left it as a dock crane to supply the fleet with food and ammunition.[16]

Toys carried other kinds of messages too. Most obviously, guns, hobby horses, and tool sets were pitched to boys, telling them not so subtly that fighting, riding, and building were men's work. Girls, on the other hand, were expected to buy dolls and doll houses, tea sets, miniature irons, and other domestic playthings. And so, at a time when many adult men and especially women were challenging traditional roles of the sexes, toys were reinforcing the idea that women were supposed to work and behave in particular ways, men in others. The editors of *Playthings* suggested that toys might be used in another campaign to regulate and encourage some children's behavior—"Americanization," the efforts, described elsewhere in this chapter, to instill particular values and ways of living among youthful immigrants. A writer proposed that youngsters newly arrived from Sicily, Russia, or Romania be set to work making toys in settlement houses. Not only would they learn useful skills; the right kind of toys would also cultivate proper values and conduct.

As in so many other areas of American life, adults were trying to shape and direct how children acted as they grew up, in this case through encouraging certain kinds of private play. But, as always, children did not necessarily respond as toymakers hoped. The memory of the "Meccano" or Erector Set, quoted above, with its tiny girders and cranes and ammunition loaded into ships, is from a woman's girlhood, although those toys obviously were meant more for boys. "My prized possession," wrote another woman of her early years, "was a white leather two-gun holster, studded with fake stones."[17] Boys and girls took what was offered, then put it to their own uses. They played with dolls, but acted out scenes that would have shocked their parents. With electric trains and cap pistols, they fantasized acts of crime and rebellion. They put aside an expensive gift, then fantasized its box into a palace or a pirate ship.

Toys, ultimately, were not what factories made but what children imagined them to be. Play remained a richly independent and creative part of child life. In buying toys and receiving them as gifts, young people were, in a sense, negotiating with grownups, accepting some of their elders' intentions but adapting them to their own needs and purposes.

Among the most popular children's entertainments of these years was the board game Monopoly. Although there is some controversy about its origins, Monopoly's official inventor was Charles Darrow, an out-of-work heating engineer who sold the idea to the nation's leading board game manufacturer, Parker Brothers, in 1934. (Darrow later used his fortune to travel the world in search of rare orchids.) At first it was assumed young people would be uninterested or confused by the rather complicated rules, but it quickly became clear that youthful players were its most enthusiastic market.

Monopoly was a creation of the Great Depression. Appearing when the nation was on its knees, it allowed its players to fantasize about making their fortunes by wheeling and dealing—and also to act out in a harmless setting the sickening economic calamities that struck millions of families. Children and adults moved their pieces around the board, each step named for a street in Atlantic City, New Jersey, where inventor Charles Darrow had spent his vacations. In what became an American ritual, they bought and sold streets, collected and paid rent, built houses and hotels, profited from windfalls and suffered setbacks, went to jail, and collected two hundred dollars each time they passed "Go." The stacks of play money beside each player—divided from a total of $15,000—gave each contestant the heady feeling of the highroller. The rapid swings of fortune and the exhilaration of winning proved addictive to millions of players, and Monopoly only increased in sales after the depression gave way to good times.

Movies continued to attract the passionate attention of children during these years. As was discussed in the previous chapter, the earliest moving pictures were forbidden pleasures for most young people. Adults usually considered them morally dangerous, and reformers pressed for laws to keep boys and girls out of the theaters. City children were just as determined to see those short films about train robbers, wild Indians, and fearless detectives.

In the 1920s, however, moviegoing became much more a family entertainment. Motion pictures became part of the nation's entertainment mainstream, and as Hollywood studios turned out hundreds of features every year, a visit to a nearby theater became something close to a weekly ritual for millions of Americans. This popularity grew still more when silent films gave way to "talkies," movies with sound, around 1926. During the next four years attendance doubled, from about 50 million visits per week to 100 million. Then ticket sales sagged, as the depression began to take its toll, but by 1935 attendance was on the rise again. Americans, it seemed, decided that a couple of hours spent in a darkened theater watching a romantic, exciting, funny fantasy on the screen was worth the price of admission—usually around twenty-five cents for an adult and as little as a dime for a child. Theater owners also held drawings for prizes or sold dinnerware and other products at wholesale prices. They often showed more than one film for the price of a single admission; in 1935, half of all theaters in the country were showing double features.

Children attended movies with their parents. They likely were denied entry to what were considered the more daring films of the day, such as *It Happened One Night,* with its famous scene of Clark Gable in his undershirt, and Mae West's *She Done Him Wrong;* but in later years they recalled watching the great stars of the day playing in popular gangster films, such as Edward G. Robinson and James Cagney in *Little Caesar* and *Angels with Dirty Faces,* and "screwball" comedy classics like the Marx Brothers' *A Day at the Races, Duck Soup,* and *Animal Crackers* and W. C. Fields's *The Fatal Glass of Beer.* Certainly they saw films of prominent child stars. The most famous of them, Shirley Temple, appeared in a series of relentlessly cute roles that highlighted her considerable talents in singing and dancing. In fact, juvenile stars like Temple, Jackie Cooper, Judy Garland, and Mickey Rooney were among the most popular actors of the depression years; Rooney was the movie industry's leading male ticket-seller in 1939.

Though movies generally were family entertainment, children chose some kinds of films as their favorites and gave them their own enthusiastic loyalty. It was as if they were determined to hold on to part of the film industry for their own, apart from their parents. The children's special favorites were westerns. Western action films had been among the industry's first and most popular, and the earliest western stars, like Broncho Billy Anderson and William S. Hart, emerged well before 1920. Westerns flourished especially in the 1920s, with Buck Jones, Fred Thomson, Hoot Gibson, Ken Maynard, Tim McCoy, and Tom Mix appearing in dozens of films with titles like *Rider of Death Valley, The Ivory Handled Guns, End of the Trail, Wheels of Destiny,* and *Durand of the Badlands.* Occasionally, these dealt with historical themes, but typically they stressed simple plots in which the hero fought against the odds to overcome some villainous threat, and almost invariably there was a beautiful girl to be won in the process.

Any romance, however, was secondary to action. Some stars, like Mix, were genuinely talented riders and athletes who performed impressive stunts on horseback. In any case, the pace rarely slowed for very long. There were a few westerns with women as heroines, such as *The Fighting Shepherdess* with Anita Stewart, and some were played for laughs with comedy giants of the day, like Buster Keaton's *Go West* and *Way Out West* with Laurel and Hardy. But most stuck to a successful formula that young audiences apparently could not get enough of: a handsome hero, lots of riding and fighting and gunplay, with courage rewarded in the end.

The voracious appeal gave rise to the "B" western, so called to distinguish it from the classier "A" versions. These "B" westerns were the particular favorites of the young. They were made quickly and cheaply, and it showed. If an actor missed his lines, the scene often was used anyway.

Studios used the same sets over and over, so a boy or girl might see the same ranch house and saloon in several movies a year. Filming an entire movie might take barely a week, sometimes just a few days, and often the running length was less than an hour. Some of these cheap westerns were produced by major studios, but many came from independent companies with little money to invest. Actors in the "B" movies included many of the stars of the day, as well as somewhat less popular figures, like Rex Bell, Jack Randall, and George O'Brien.

Cheap and predictable as they were, young viewers loved them. Their cheapness, in fact, was part of their appeal, as their low budget meant that tickets were inexpensive too, often only a few cents. The "B" westerns were shown most often in theaters on Saturday afternoons. This was another device to increase attendance; besides the traffic of adults and families during the week and on weekend evenings, young audiences could be crowded into the theaters during the few hours of the week not consumed by school, church, chores, or homework. Saturday at the movies became one of the most common—and one of the fondest—memories of growing up in the period from the 1930s through the 1950s, when another medium, television, began to dominate children's attention. In addition to western feature films, theaters screened "serials," longer stories shown in short installments, each ending with some desperate, seemingly fatal crisis, with the hero apparently tumbling over a cliff, gunned down by outlaws, or trampled by stampeding cattle. The purpose, of course, was to draw the audience back the next week to see how in the world their favorite would manage to save himself. Some serials, like *The Painted Stallion* and *Overland with Kit Carson,* were substantial, expensive productions, while others were cheaper versions. All inspired plenty of speculation and guesswork during the week between the delicious few hours inside the dark theater every Saturday.

Another form of popular movie fantasy flourished during the 1920s and 1930s, becoming a basic part of American children's visual literature: animated short subjects, or "cartoons." Primitive animation had been part of the motion picture business from its earliest years, but during the 1920s cartoons began to come into their own. Some enduring characters emerged, like Felix the Cat. A common technique blended real and fantasy worlds, with animated characters interacting with photography. A popular series of cartoons, "Out of the Inkwell," showed animators themselves, with invented figures jumping out of the bottles of ink and taking off into their own adventures. At the end of the decade, the golden age of cartoonery was ushered in with the rise to fame of Walt Disney and his most famous creation, Mickey Mouse.

After working as an animator for several years, in 1928 Disney tried out a new character, a humanoid mouse living in a world of magic and invention. The cartoon that established Mickey Mouse's fame was *Steamboat Willie*, one of the first cartoons with sound, an animated "talkie." In it, Mickey, already with his characteristic four-fingered, white-gloved hands, was captain of a steamboat. As he would be for generations, he was courting the beautiful Minnie. Disney combined the characters' antics with a soundtrack of both dialogue and music and, most of all, strange and even bizarre manipulations of reality. When a goat ate Minnie's sheet music, she cranked its tail, and "Turkey in the Straw" came out of its mouth. This combination of familiar characters and inspired fantasy became the formula for Disney's success.

During the 1930s, Disney emerged not only as the dominant force in animated films, but as a towering figure in American popular culture. His influence in virtually all aspects of media would be difficult to exaggerate. The year after the success of *Steamboat Willie*, Disney animators made sixteen cartoons; then they really began to crank them out. Between 1930 and 1939, they averaged one about every three weeks, nearly two hundred in all, roughly half of them starring Mickey and the others in a series called the Silly Symphony. Critically acclaimed as well as popular triumphs, Disney's work won every Academy Award for cartoon shorts between 1932 and 1939.

The most famous of these, and perhaps the best known short cartoon feature ever made, was *The Three Little Pigs*. It had the usual Disney trademarks—humanized animals, plenty of action and bending of reality. It also had good music; its theme song, "Who's Afraid of the Big Bad Wolf?," quickly became a popular hit. The cartoon was based, of course, on a well-known folk and fairy tale, but it was also a reflection of its times. *The Three Little Pigs* appeared in 1933, at the depression's lowpoint. On the one hand, its story assured its audience that hard work and planning for the future would pay off in the long run. More generally, it was an expression of confidence that at the darkest moment of this national crisis—literally with the wolf at the door—the American people would survive and go on to enjoy even better times. Buck up, young America was told, and have faith in the old virtues.

As this famous short suggested, as Disney's films became more successful, they increasingly took on a loftier moral content. His earliest cartoons were wild and sometimes even a little rough. Mickey might make music by pulling a cow's teats, for instance. The emphasis was on action and, more than that, fantasies in which all things were possible. This imaginative humor was close to a child's heart. There were no lessons here, just a mind having fun by turning ordinary things into fantasies. Soon, however, the stories began to take on a point of view. In *Lullaby Land* (1933), a child dreamed of entering a garden of forbidden household objects: scissors, razors, matches, and more; after a series of mishaps, he is rescued. The point of this cartoon, and of more and more of those that Disney produced, was to encourage good behavior and traditional values, even as they were becoming more technically inventive and sophisticated.

The culmination of these trends came near the end of the 1930s with the release of *Snow White and the Seven Dwarfs* (1938). This film was a landmark, the first full-length feature cartoon. Many predicted financial disaster, but *Snow White* turned out to be spectacularly successful. Its dense animation, with each movement composed of multiple drawings, gave the action what was, for that era, an unprecedented lifelike appearance. Animation freed Disney to create magnificent special effects—storms that tore at mountains, forests more threatening than anything real, fantastic spirits. Through facial expressions and body language, the director and animators also managed to create characters of surprising depth and individuality. Young audiences (and some older ones) were terrified of the evil queen and charmed by the various dwarfs.

With these unmatched technical accomplishments came clear moral lessons. The main story line was a romance, with Snow White finally united with her handsome prince, but the film was woven through with encouragements: have faith in yourself, care for one another, virtue will be rewarded, selfishness is deadly. Cartoons had changed. From their free-wheeling beginnings, expressing a childlike all-things-are-possible view of reality, they had become both big business and another way that adults nudged children toward approved kinds of behavior.

The 1920s also saw the birth of one of the most familiar types of young people's literature, comic books. Like "B" westerns, comics were a popular entertainment that children could afford with their own pennies, and so these creations spoke for the boys' and girls' own needs and feelings.

The roots went back earlier, to just before the turn of the century. Starting in 1893, the *New York World* began publishing a one-panel cartoon, called "Down Hogan's Alley," drawn by Richard F. Outcault. Showing the farcical side of life in the city's slums, it featured as central character a strange figure who always wore a nightshirt, usually with comments written on it in street slang of the day. A few years later, as an attention-grabbing device, the *World* started printing the nightshirt in bright yellow ink. The "Yellow Kid" soon was a smashing success (and, according to some authorities, the source of the term "yellow journalism" for the gaudy, sensationalist, and often irresponsible practices of the newly popular daily newspapers).

The Yellow Kid inspired other newspaper cartoons. Readers of all ages were drawn to them, but, from the start, they seemed the special domain of urban youngsters. The newspapers that provided children with one of their most common and distinctive jobs also gave them one of their most beloved amusements. After World War I many papers began publishing a separate "comics page," with strips in garish reds, greens, and yellows, which youthful readers justifiably considered their own domain, an island of juvenile humor and adventure within the colorless pages of stories about events shaping the adult world. As with all popular culture, the kids' comics reflected their larger world. Many early strips—"Alphonse and Gaston," "The Katzenjammer Kids," and "Happy Hooligan" for instance—suggested the surge of immigration that had made America into a continental ethnic stew. Often immigrant characters were pictured as fools and clods, and blacks were portrayed as clownish, naughty infants, reflecting both the intolerance of the day and the pressures of conformity and "Americanization."

A new type of cartoon strip emerged in the 1920s, featuring running plots that emphasized not so much humor as drama and adventure. Their central figures were not dolts or tricksters but brave, heroic, clever, and sometimes mysterious characters. Probably the most popular was "Little Orphan Annie," first published in 1924. Millions of readers followed the trials and dangers of Annie and her faithful dog; by the 1930s the strip had spun off two feature films and a regular radio show (and in the 1970s a smash stage musical, *Annie*). Other enduring adventure comics included "Dick Tracy," "Gasoline Alley," "Mandrake the Magician," and "Prince Valiant." These, too, suggested something about what was happening in the lives of their readers. Several appeared, and enjoyed phenomenal popularity, during the 1930s. At a time when Americans, young and old, felt they were at the mercy of calamitous developments, swept along by forces that most neither recognized nor understood, they could identify and fantasize about heroes who were supremely in command of their worlds, or who at least managed to think and maneuver their way out of seemingly hopeless jams. These strips were also a kind of pure escape. For a few minutes each day, the reader could leave a distressing (and for some, an apparently hopeless) daily routine and spend time among courageous crime fighters and, in the case of Prince Valiant, the chivalrous knights, powerful sorcerers, and beautiful maidens of King Arthur's round table.

Out of this tradition was born the comic book, the first of which appeared in the late 1920s. In a sense comic books were simply expanded versions of newspaper strips—and smaller variations of another important phenomenon of the times, popular magazines and periodicals. Yet they were able to develop more intricate stories, introduce a greater range of characters, and provide more elaborate illustrations than anything found in comic strips. Initially, at least, they tended toward drama and adventure more than humor, so "comic" was not a very accurate term (and given the usual length of twenty or so pages, neither was "book"). Some were based on popular characters in radio and movies, such as the western heroes Gene Autry and the Lone Ranger. Even more than the strips, comic books tended toward powerful, mysterious protagonists, such as The Shadow, also the subject of a fabulously successful radio program.

The next logical development was the superhero, a comic book figure possessing astonishing strength and abilities. Some superheroes, like Superman (in 1938, the first creation of Action Comics, which came to dominate the industry), were aliens from other planets; others were earthly mortals who somehow had acquired an almost otherworldly prowess as well as dazzling skills, astounding inventions and devices, and apparently limitless wealth. (Batman, who made his debut in 1939, was an example of the latter.) Regardless of origin, all had double identities. Only a very few companions and helpers (and, of course, the reader) knew the superhero for who and what he was. The rest of the world saw him mostly in disguise—an ordinary citizen and usually, in fact, something of a dullard, inept and bumbling. Then, at a moment of crisis, the hero changed in a flash to his true self and sped to save helpless good folk from the foul plots of fiendish villains.

Superheroes, like other powerful and savvy fictional figures who appeared in the 1930s, doubtless reflected feelings of frustration among Americans who felt they had lost control over their own fates. On the other hand, many of these characters would remain popular for more than fifty years, not only through bad times but also years of unmatched prosperity and national power. That kind of appeal was not based on the times but on the needs of children everywhere and in every era. Through superheroes, children could indulge in two of the most delicious fantasies of the young. Following the adventures of Superman or Batman, any boy (and, in the case of Wonder Woman, any girl) could imagine having irresistible strength and command in a world full of larger, dominating adults who always seemed to be telling them where to go and what to do. And with that came the secret conviction that, in spite of all the ridicule, bad grades, and rejections that might come from others, "I am the only one who *really* knows who I am."

## AT WORK

Between 1910 and 1930, American children appeared to be working less and less—at least as measured by the standards of the government census. Nearly two million young persons between ten and fifteen were listed as "gainfully employed" in the federal census of 1910, accounting for just over 18 percent of all children their age. By 1920 the number had dropped substantially to just over a million (1,060,858), or 8.5 percent; and during the next ten years the figures slid again by roughly a third, so that in 1930 the census reported that 667,118 young people, or about 5 percent, were "gainful workers." The next decade, from 1930 to 1940, was the most economically disastrous in U.S. history, yet, even in those years, the number of child workers continued its decline, down to 1 percent at the eve of World War II.

According to these figures, nearly one child out of five was put to work in 1910; by 1930 the same could be said of only one child out of twenty; in 1940, one out of a hundred. On the face of it, this seemed to be one of the most sweeping and dramatic changes that American children would ever know.

That change was real, but the census, as usual, did not reveal some important facts about working children. The most striking decline in child labor came in heavy industries, notably coal mining, and in certain kinds of manufacturing. These industries provided some of the clearest examples of abusive and dangerous conditions. It was difficult, after all, to dispute that working as "breaker boys" for ten or twelve hours a day, stooped over coal conveyors in frigid, dust-filled rooms, was hazardous to the young people involved. Furthermore, because this labor was concentrated in mines and factories, it was more easily identified, observed, and regulated. Once child labor laws were passed, it was difficult for owners of these businesses to disobey them, and as children were taken off these jobs, the reduction in numbers was shown more clearly in official reports, like the census.

Young people continued to work in other kinds of jobs, probably in much greater numbers than showed up in the official figures. Especially as hard times settled over the country, parents looked for help from their sons and daughters, especially their older ones. Young women and men of fifteen or so often picked up what part-time work they could, trying to make up for some of their fathers' losses. One study took a close look at families in

Oakland, California, during the dark days between 1929 and the depth of the depression in 1933. Incomes in these households dropped by at least 15 percent and as much as 64 percent. Among the poorest families with unemployed fathers, more than 70 percent of the sons and 40 percent of the daughters helped out with extra jobs. One boy delivered newspapers, sold ashtrays he had made, and helped with household chores. A girl baby-sat for neighbors and clerked in local stores and restaurants.[18] These children, and probably tens of thousands of others, were important contributors to their families' economic survival during those grim years.

The work done by those Oakland young people was not reflected in the census. In fact, many kinds of child labor were difficult to document and control. The 1930 census reported nearly 100,000 young people working in trade and domestic-personal service (about 50,000 and 46,000 respectively), as well as about 17,000 in clerical jobs and 9,000 in transportation and communication. Most of this work was far more difficult to detect and regulate. "Trade," for instance, included boys and girls selling goods on the streets and door-to-door. "Domestic" jobs were not those done around a child's own house, but rather working, usually full time, as a servant for another family. Children at work as "clericals" were mostly messengers and errand and office boys. In all these kinds of jobs, it was extremely difficult to determine how many young people were at work, not to mention how they worked and for how long and what kinds of problems and dangers their work involved.

Much of the real world of working children was invisible, at least in the columns and tables of the census. In the street trades discussed in the previous chapter, for instance, tens of thousands of young peddlers, vendors, and "newsies" obviously went uncounted. The census of 1930, for instance, included 21,783 newsboys between ten and fifteen, but in 1934 the newspaper industry reported that more than 250,000 boys and girls under sixteen were selling and delivering papers. The same was true of the "home trades" or "tenement work," also described previously, in which children worked, usually with their families, to piece together ready-made clothing and to make cigars, artificial flowers, lace, jewelry, and other such items. This kind of labor, which took place in private rooms, was virtually impossible to measure or control. When regulatory laws were passed, they were easily evaded. Home work on infant clothing was illegal in New York and some other northeastern states in the 1930s, for example; the response of New York manufacturers was simply to send out the work to be done in other states, usually to dozens of small, impoverished towns desperate for any sort of employment. One firm alone shipped material to more than six hundred such communities. Families in a town in Maine with a population of only 3,500 did piecework for twenty-seven out-of-state companies.

The statistics that showed a steady decline of child labor, in other words, measured only part—the most visible, easily regulated portion—of the American workplace. Those statistics were misleading in another sense. Even for that labor most easily measured, changes came far more in some parts of the country than in others. The region with the highest rates of working children, by far, was the South. One out of four Mississippi boys and girls between ten and fifteen were "gainful workers" in 1930, well above what had been the national average in 1910, the census high point of child labor. The seven states with the highest percentages of laboring children in 1930 were Mississippi (24.9 percent), South Carolina (18.3), Alabama (17.5), Georgia (14.7), Arkansas (12.2), North Carolina (11.2), and Louisiana (10.1). Those with the lowest were Ohio (1.0 percent), California (1.1), Michigan (1.2), Maine (1.2), New Hampshire (1.3), and Indiana (1.3).

Clearly the pattern differed considerably, depending on where a child lived. Part of the reason lay in the South's continuing efforts to promote industry, in particular textiles, which, as already noted, employed huge numbers of young people. As more and more mills shifted their operations southward, poor rural families were tempted to find work in them. Companies were making this move partly because of the attraction of cheap labor—and children, of course, were cheapest of all—so those who were dedicated to boosting southern economic growth naturally discouraged any attempts by reformers to keep young people out of the mills. The South, as a consequence, was heading in exactly the opposite direction from the rest of the nation in this regard. The number of children working in textile mills in America at large shrank by 59 percent between 1920 and 1930, while in South Carolina their numbers grew by 24 percent and, in Georgia, by 12 percent.

Another reason for this backward movement toward child labor in the South was that, despite the growth of some industries, this region remained the most rural part of America and its families in the countryside were among the poorest in the nation. Impoverished farmers were the ones most tempted to keep their children in the fields for the longest hours, either as laborers on their own farms or as stoop workers for others. Child labor was so much a part of southern life both because of growing industry and the persistence of agriculture.

On the other hand, young people worked on farms not only in the South but in every part of the United States, in Nebraska wheatlands and Indiana cornfields, cutting hay in Montana and picking fruit in New Jersey, milking and hoeing in Washington and Pennsylvania as well as picking cotton in Mississippi. Nevertheless, the percentages of child workers were low and getting lower in many of those states, a result of some of the most important and controversial issues of child labor and its reform.

Children had worked—and worked hard—on farms since the first European colonial settlements. (For that matter, they had also helped in farming, hunting, fishing, and gathering among Native American peoples for thousands of years before Europeans showed up.) Millions of families depended on the help of sons and daughters; it is fair to say, in fact, that the nation's economy probably would have collapsed if young people had suddenly stopped lending their hands in the many tasks of making and running farms. Virtually everyone agreed, furthermore, that working on farms was potentially healthful and constructive. This opinion hearkened back to beliefs rooted deep in American history, voiced by influential figures from Thomas Jefferson to many contemporary politicians, that farmers represented the moral backbone of the nation, and working the land, doing honest toil close to nature, brought out the best of human qualities. The belief that most farm work was inherently good for children was embraced even by reformers who were critical of many other kinds of child labor. Senator Albert Beveridge led a congressional investigation of abuses of child labor in 1906, but he was careful to emphasize that he was not concerned with conditions in the countryside: "I do not for a moment pretend that working children on the farm is bad for them . . . there can be no better training."[19] More than thirty years later, Homer Folks, chairman of the National Child Labor Committee, basically agreed. Working around the family farm—milking cows, feeding chickens, pitching hay, and helping in the fields—was "part and parcel of a child's education," he wrote in 1938: "It helps him learn how to live and take his place in this world of ours. . . . No person in his right senses would consider such things as 'child labor.' "[20]

But by the time Folks ventured that opinion, disturbing, complicated questions were being asked. Several investigations in the 1920s revealed that many farm children, instead of doing a modest amount of chores, were working long hours under grueling conditions. A survey of more than eight hundred North Dakota boys and girls found that the majority often worked at herding, digging postholes, building fences, and butchering, as well as at field work and their usual chores. Sometimes this work was fit in around their school days. A nine-year-old "built fires in the morning, swept the floors of a two-room house, and brought in fuel and water; in addition, before he made a two-mile trip to school, he helped feed stock (5 horses and 12 cows) and chopped wood; in the evening he did the chores and washed dishes." Many children, however, were kept home from school from time to time. Another investigation in the same state showed that six out of ten youngsters between ten and fourteen had been held out of classes to work at some time during the year.[21]

Similar situations could be found in southern cotton country. Besides weeding (or "chopping cotton") in the summer, children were pressed to work long hours when the plants matured. Many school systems simply declared "cotton vacations" or "crop vacations," canceling classes for up to eleven weeks during autumn harvest. Otherwise, children simply stayed home to work. A study of Missouri cotton farms in 1940–1941 found that in districts without "crop vacations" students missed nearly one out of every five schools days because of the need to work in the family fields.

Here, then, were boys and girls working in ways usually considered good for them and for the nation, doing chores and helping to keep their own family farms productive. And yet there seemed to be little difference between this labor and other kinds that were roundly condemned. After all, what was the difference between a girl working ten hours a day in a tenement making cigars or cheap suits and one kept home from school to pick cotton for twelve hours? Was a boy herding cattle seven days a week in the hammering summer sun better off than one running errands or peddling candy on the streets of Philadelphia or Louisville? Were not all these situations ultimately harmful? The Missouri study, for instance, found that 15 percent of seventeen-year-olds who were not kept home to help pick cotton were classified as backward and poorly developed in their schooling; among those who were kept home, the figure was 60 percent.

Investigations revealed another type of rural child labor that many people found even more disturbing. In many parts of the nation, young people labored in large-scale commercial agriculture. The workplace here was not the family farm but extensive land holdings, usually owned by large corporations, which produced such crops as tobacco, onions, sugar beets, berries, fruits, and hops. Some of these children were "hired out" to work on their own; in many cases entire families were hired to work together. Unlike boys and girls on family farms, they did not work year-round but during the planting, growing, and harvesting seasons, between April and October. For some, most work was done during three or four weeks, but others stayed in the fields for four months or longer.

Children as young as seven or eight, investigators found, were set to work at backbreaking, exhausting tasks. An example follows of an ordinary day at harvest time in the sugar beet fields of Colorado around 1920. After a plow-like machine loosened the soil around these underground tubers, a child would walk down the long rows, grasping with each hand the leafy tops of the plants and pulling the beets from the earth. After knocking the two plants together to loosen the clinging dirt, the child threw the beets into a nearby pile, then moved on to the next pair. Once a few rows had been pulled and piled, the child would take up a large knife, about sixteen inches long, and with a vigorous swipe cut the tops off each beet plant, which was held for chopping on his or her knee. The child then would move on to the next rows. A mature beet weighs as much as five pounds, and with its tops and the sticky soil around it, the full weight pulled and thrown could be as much as twelve pounds. In a typical instance, a ten-year-old girl harvested five tons of beets daily, which meant she in fact was lifting between twelve and fifteen tons, or up to thirty thousand pounds, every day.[22]

During the sugar beet harvest, children spent an average of nine to ten hours in the fields, often longer, sometimes starting at dawn and working into the dark by lantern light. Harvest work, furthermore, was just the culmination of months of other labor. Usually a family, including the parents and five or six children, was contracted to maintain fifty or sixty acres. In spring, after planting, children thinned the sprouting clusters, leaving one beet plant every eight inches or so. During the following weeks, hundreds of hours were required for hoeing and weeding as the plants grew and matured. All told, a youngster would work hundreds of hours each season. A study of conditions in Colorado's South Platte River valley found that six-year-old children spent almost nine hours a day for three weeks at thinning, then more than two weeks of hoeing at nearly eleven hours a day. Finally came harvesting for three and a half weeks, nine hours daily. For this a family was paid between twenty and forty dollars per acre in 1915 and allowed to live in a one-room house. Earnings for the year usually came to between two and four hundred dollars.[23]

Similar situations could have been found in the tobacco fields of Kentucky, North Carolina, and the Connecticut River valley; on onion farms of Illinois, Ohio, and Massachusetts; on berry farms in Maryland, New Jersey, Virginia, and Washington; and in hop fields and fruit orchards in Washington and Oregon. The extent of this kind of children's labor has been difficult to measure, because much of it was done by migrant families, who moved around the agricultural regions, sometimes following tested seasonal patterns and sometimes drifting to wherever work was to be found. Census takers, who usually made their rounds in April, either missed or overlooked many of them. The official figures for Colorado in 1930, for instance, showed just over two thousand working children, while a single large sugar beet company reported that it employed at least six thousand boys and girls under sixteen.

Where had these migrant working families come from? Many, especially those in the western fields, were part of groups that had recently immigrated to the United States. The large majority of Colorado beet workers around the time of World War I, for instance, were "Germans from Russia," ethnic Germans whose ancestors had immigrated to the Black Sea region of Russia. During the same period, thousands of Japanese entered California before a new U.S. immigration law in 1924 effectively stopped this movement. Japanese families provided much field labor on the Pacific coast, especially in California. Then in the 1920s came a huge wave of immigration from Mexico into California, Colorado, and other parts of the West, tens of thousands of men, women and children who worked for appallingly low wages—from thirty-five cents an hour in 1928 to fifteen cents an hour at the low point of the Great Depression in 1933. More than thirty thousand Filipinos also arrived, mostly in California, during the 1920s.[24]

Those immigrant families provided nearly all the labor needed. But then many sharecroppers, tenants, and small farmers in the South and on the Great Plains were driven off their land by the Great Depression and the Dust Bowl, an environmental disaster on the plains brought on by a brutal drought and massive soil erosion. A new flood of displaced persons washed westward to the Pacific coast. An estimated six hundred thousand migrants arrived in California, Oregon, and Washington, all looking for some sort of work and most hoping for jobs in the fields. The result, of course, was disastrous: far too many people and far too little work. "Here we git short jobs and long waits; I reckon there's one picker for every tree," as a migrant from Texas to California put it: "Looks like we jes' jumped from the fryin' pan into the fire."[25] In this vicious competition, families had an advantage. A single man could offer only his own efforts. Desperate families, however, could provide the work of several persons, often including five, six, or seven girls and boys, for a combined wage that was not much more than what was paid one man. Such migrant families, working as a group for a single rate, were called "rubber tramps."

Living conditions among "rubber tramps" were, predictably, poor to abysmal. Many lived in tents and shacks in makeshift camps, in town dumps, and along the roads. They drank water from ditches and ate whatever food they could buy at inflated prices with their low wages. Rates of epidemic disease were high and school attendance was low. Educational surveys in several California counties revealed that migrant children scored consistently below local residents in all areas tested. Roughly half of the migrant students had been kept back at least one grade because their sporadic schooling had been inadequate. In Kern County, eighth-grade children from "rubber tramp" families were, on the average, sixteen months older than classmates who had grown up in the area.

Local studies like these raised extremely troubling questions about both the nature and extent of child labor. The term "child labor" had come to mean not family chores and moderate, character-building effort. Rather, it referred to work in which young people performed roles usually assigned to adults. Specifically, "child labor" meant work for which boys and girls were paid a wage. It included also labor for the mass production of goods in an industrial system. Finally, it usually referred to work that interfered in some fundamental way with a child's appropriate physical, intellectual, and emotional development.

Those standards usually had been applied to children working in towns and cities, the boys and girls in glass factories and textile mills, those in the tenement occupations, and others in the various street trades; but it became increasingly clear that similar conditions could be found in the countryside. Contrary to the old prevailing impression, a child laboring in agriculture was not necessarily a smiling, freckle-faced lad whose body, mind, and character were growing strong as he worked the family farm. The problems, dangers and limitations of scores of thousands of young rural workers were as severe as those of the girls and boys who worked in centers of industry and on city streets. The settings were different, but all were part of the same economic system. Eight-year-old girls pulled and trimmed beets that were shipped to factories to make sugar for family dinner tables; young boys in Oregon cultivated hops fermented into beer sold in Chicago saloons; cotton picked by sharecropper children went next to mills, where other youngsters helped turn it into thread and material for clothes and bed linens (including cheap pants and dresses sewn by children in tenement sweatshops) that were sold throughout the United States and Europe. And all these young people—factory workers and stoop laborers in the fields—faced severe physical strain, fell behind in their education, and were denied part of the recreation and freedom usually associated with a normal childhood.

Investigations have shown that the census reports of children "gainfully employed" were much underestimated. The Census Bureau's definition of a gainful occupation—one "by which the person who pursues it earns money or a money equivalent, or in which he assists in the production of marketable goods"—obviously applied to many thousands of young people who did not show up in the census tally. Migrant workers were especially easy to overlook, as were children who worked mainly in the late spring, summer, and fall, not in early spring when the census was taken. In short, the percentage of American youngsters engaged in "child labor" surely was substantially larger, perhaps even double or triple the five percent reported in the 1930 census.

That, in turn, raised other questions. What should be done to measure more accurately the number of working children? And more fundamentally, what were the rights of these young people, and what were the responsibilities of governments to protect those rights and interests? What sort of regulation of agricultural labor, if any, best served the national good? To what degree would such regulation, like that aimed at boys and girls working in mines and mills, interfere improperly with the prerogatives of parents and the privacy of family decisions? Questions like these would not be answered easily or soon. In many ways, lawmakers and officials would continue to argue and puzzle over them for the rest of the century.

## AT SCHOOL

Many educational trends apparent during the first two decades of the 20th century continued during the next two. An ever-growing number of American young people were attending school. Between 1920 and 1940 the portion of persons between the ages of five and seventeen enrolled in public and private schools rose from about 80 percent to nearly 95 percent. These young men and women were attending school longer, partly because new laws in state after state made this compulsory. Of every thousand students enrolled in the fifth grade in 1940, nearly five hundred would be graduated from high school; this was a dramatic increase from twenty years before, when about three hundred of every thousand remained for the full twelve years of schooling.

This expansion of education was having some effects, at least as measured by crude standards. The illiteracy rate, which had fallen from 20 percent in 1870 to 6 percent in 1920, dropped still farther, to barely 2 percent in 1940. Schooling also cost more. After a spectacular rise of spending on public education between 1900 and 1920 (from $215 million to $1.036 billion), this cost more than doubled again by 1930, to $2.317 billion. To put it differently, in 1900, Americans spent about $2.80 on education for every man, woman, and child in the country; in 1920, that figure had risen to almost $10.00 and, by 1930, it was nearly $19.00.

Just as before, however, not all American children were taking part equally in these changes. Nearly 13 percent of all white men and about 17 percent of all white women in 1940 had completed high school; the figures for black men and women were roughly 4 and 5 percent. And while the illiteracy rate among native-born white men and women had shrunk to barely 1 percent in 1940, that for foreign-born persons was 9 percent. Of all black Americans, nearly 12 percent could not read or write.

The debate and ferment over new ideas continued. The "progressive" school, most associated with John Dewey and his followers, had a spreading influence on public education. Dewey's doctrines—that education was inseparable from a changing society and that American education ought to promote pragmatically the ideals of democracy—increasingly were basic to the training of teachers. These approaches, however, did not go unchallenged. Opponents were loosely grouped under the heading of "essentialists," and their best known spokesman was William C. Bagley, who, like Dewey, was associated with Columbia University.

Essentialists were a varied bunch who often disagreed among themselves, and they had different complaints about Dewey's progressivism; but they generally agreed that the primary responsibility of education was the transmission to the young of the essentials of a common culture, the values, principles, and heritage that were at the core of civilization. These were best taught through the study of language, philosophy, literary classics, a common history, and the fine arts. Equipping young people for adulthood in more practical ways, through manual training and promotion of social skills, was fine, the essentialists argued, but such matters should always be secondary to the real business of education: passing on the fundamental truths of civilization.

One result of these broad-ranging disagreements was a remarkable experiment, the Eight Year Study. Administered by the Progressive Education Association, its purpose was to test the effectiveness of the different styles and philosophies. Beginning in 1930, two groups of students were followed and periodically examined from the time they entered high school until their graduation from college. One group was taught by more traditional, essentialist techniques, the other by the goals and methods of the progressives. The report in general gave the nod to the progressive approach. Predictably, essentialists argued that the experiment was tilted in favor of the other side, and they continued to call for a renewed emphasis on a core of study based on the cultural values and heritage they believed were paramount. The fundamentals of the debate in many ways continue until the present day.

As this debate showed, deciding what kind of education was more effective depended on the questions asked. More basically, the pushing and shoving among essentialists and progressives was part of an attempt to evaluate both education and students. After all, if educators wanted to create a national system of schooling that offered sound education for all children, they needed a way to measure both the abilities of students and the quality of the training they were getting in the classroom.

Out of this need has come a familiar part of school life, educational testing. Once or twice a year most students today undergo a series of tests designed to discover how they measure up against the standards for their grade level. Educational testing, like so much else in children's history, involves more than it seems. On the one hand, the story of testing reveals something about what was troubling many adults, some of their fears and prejudices as well as their ideals. These tests also provide an excellent example of some of the complexities and pitfalls of democratic education. By trying to offer the best schooling possible for all American children, sometimes the rights and interests of those children can be harmed.

Of all the many tests devised for school-age children, probably the most influential has been the intelligence quotient, or IQ, test. It originated with experiments by the French psychologist Alfred Binet shortly after the turn of the century. The French government had asked Binet to devise a way to identify schoolchildren whose poor classroom success indicated that they needed special attention and instruction. As he knew very well, others had tried many techniques at finding some physical basis for measuring intelligence. Most common was measurement of skulls (and thus, brains) and close attention to the shape of heads. Binet himself had worked in "craniometry" but had turned away, disillusioned.

Taking a different approach, Binet devised a series of questions and short tasks for young children of various ages. None supposedly required any training or education; rather, they called on a child's fundamental processes of reasoning. That way, Binet said, the results would show something of a boy's or girl's basic mental abilities at that particular time. Those tasks, furthermore, were arranged from simple to more difficult, with each level of difficulty reflecting the abilities of a particular age. A child taking the test would move through the tasks, from easier to harder, until he or she could do no more.

The age level of the most difficult problem completed became the "mental age" of the student, as compared to his or her actual, chronological, age. Eventually the mental age was divided by the actual age. The result (with the dividend taken to two places and the decimal point removed) was the intelligence quotient, or IQ. So a twelve-year-old who completed tasks to the twelve-year level received a score of 100 (12 divided by 12 = 1.00), which reflected "normal" mental abilities. An eight-year-old who made it only to the six-year level, on the other hand, had an IQ of 75 (6 divided by 8 = .75), while another eight-year-old who reached the ten-year level scored 125 (10 divided by 8 = 1.25).

Binet's purpose was simply to decide which students were in need of special attention. He was seeking a crude, but helpful, means of identifying children with mild mental difficulties so teachers could help them. He never meant these tests to measure "intelligence," which he believed was far too complex and elusive to be summed up so simply. He also feared that others might use his test to label and stigmatize students rather than to help them.

Binet had good reasons to be uneasy. Especially in the United States, the IQ test took on very different purposes and meanings from those originally intended. An early popularizer was Henry H. Goddard, a researcher first with a New Jersey school for "feeble-minded" children and later with the Ohio Bureau of Juvenile Research. In Goddard's hands, Binet's approach was now said to measure the intelligence of those who took it. That intelligence, furthermore, was said to be an innate, basically unchangeable part of each person's mental makeup. And finally, that fundamental mental capacity, according to Goddard and others, was now described as inherited, like eye color or baldness.

Goddard was especially interested in using such tests to identify and classify the "feeble-minded," not only the most severely retarded, whom he called "idiots" and "imbeciles," but also "high-grade" defectives. For them he coined the term "morons" (from the Greek "foolish"). Morons, Goddard said, were in most ways indistinguishable from other persons. They were a bit slower in thought, however, and also more likely to engage in immoral and criminal behavior. More alarmingly, he classed as morons many who just did not fit prevailing standards of what was normal, "all persons," Goddard wrote, "who are incapable of adapting themselves to their environment and living up to the conventions of society or acting sensibly."[26]

Lewis M. Terman of Stanford University took this approach a couple of steps farther, advocating testing children on a mass scale and then channeling them into future roles according to the results. The most clearly feeble-minded, he argued, were potential criminals—in his words, "morality cannot flower . . . if intelligence remains infantile"—so low-scorers on the tests ought to be confined to institutions and, above all, forbidden to bear children. Professions like law, teaching, and medicine should be closed to anyone who did not score very well, while lower marks identified boys and girls who should be limited to the simplest (and the poorest paying) labor.

More people became aware of—and alarmed by—the IQ test when it was given to thousands of recruits during World War I. The results were shocking on two counts: The average "mental age" of all whites who took the test was thirteen, which was particularly embarrassing because the standard definition of an adult "moron" was one with the mental age of twelve. Furthermore, even lower scores were made by African Americans (10.4 years) and by immigrants from eastern and southern Europe, such as Italians (11.0 years), Russians (11.3 years), and Poles (10.7 years).

A closer look at the test, however, shows that it was terribly flawed. It was given under exceptionally stressful and rushed circumstances, and, although it claimed to evaluate inborn intelligence, many of its questions required specific knowledge. A question to test reasoning, for instance, depended on knowing the names of the first and second U.S. presidents. Other items referred to particulars of American life (as in the multiple choice below):

Crisco is a: *patent medicine, disinfectant, toothpaste, food product.*

Christy Mathewson is famous as a: *writer, artist, baseball player, comedian.* [Mathewson was a professional baseball player.]

It was no surprise that someone who had just arrived from Lithuania or a black sharecropper's son would be stumped by such questions—and it was just as clear that their wrong answers said absolutely nothing about their innate mental skills.

Nonetheless, the test results had widespread consequences. They fed the ideas of racial superiority that received growing support during the 1920s, as well as the fears that America was being overrun by dangerous and inferior peoples from elsewhere in the world. Advocates of the Immigrant Act of 1924, which cut back drastically on the number of eastern and southern Europeans admitted to the country, pointed to the IQ findings to support their case.

Some of the most profound and longest-lasting effects, however, came in the area of education. Terman, in particular, argued that the IQ test offered the opportunity for a nationwide system of student evaluation, with an eye toward plotting the future course of individual children. His revised and expanded version of the Binet procedure became the Stanford-Binet test. Behind such testing was a perfectly reasonable concern. If public education was to be extended to all young Americans, surely there would have to be some means of sorting through these millions of students, discovering which needed what kind of help, locating the most promising ones so their talents might be encouraged and sharpened. That kind of mechanism theoretically would allow diligent teachers to provide instruction tailored to every child's unique gifts and problems.

But there were always darker possibilities. Terman, for instance, recommended a "multiple-track plan" in which students would be grouped into five classes (gifted, bright, average, slow, and special). This grouping would be based on the children's basic intelligence, as revealed in tests he devised. By the eighth grade, those in each category would be channeled into different courses of study, with the brightest headed for college preparation and the "slow" group for vocational training. The problem lay in confusing "intelligent" students with those who simply were better acquainted with information much more likely to be part of some children's backgrounds than others. One series of questions, for instance, asked about the busiest American port cities and characters from *David Copperfield*. Depending on whether a boy or girl had been exposed to that sort of information, he or she could be denied an education that would lead to the better pay, greater power, and higher status of doctors, lawyers, and other professionals. There were far more ominous possibilities. Students scoring especially poorly might be classified as "high-grade defectives," who, Terman advised, should at least be brought under the "surveillance" of society and maybe even confined. Eventually, he suggested, his tests should result "in curtailing the reproduction of feeble-mindedness and in the elimination of an enormous amount of crime, pauperism, and industrial inefficiency."[27]

Following World War I, intelligence testing of students suddenly was all the rage. Devising and distributing tests became a multimillion dollar industry. In 1902, only two mental tests were on the market. By 1924 there were seventy-six, thirty-eight introduced in the last year alone, and by 1930 more than 130 tests were available. For less than a dollar and a half, one prominent company advertised, administrators would receive twenty-five examinations, twelve pages each, and a couple of grading keys. Intelligence tests were being used to some degree in 85 percent of all towns and cities of more than ten thousand persons by the middle of the decade. Millions of children took them. Their most common purpose was to separate "subnormal" students into special classes and, to a lesser extent, to sort all pupils into different groups according to their scores.[28]

By then serious doubts were being raised. Opponents charged that the research and conception behind the tests were sloppy, and so the findings were misleading and certainly not the objective, scientific measurements they were claimed to be. And because students' lives were to some degree dictated by these misleading results, critics said, the whole system was often unfair, potentially dangerous, and fundamentally undemocratic. The idea of intelligence as a fixed and measurable quality, mostly passed on through heredity, tempted too many teachers to write off low-scoring students as beyond help, some said. Indeed, by the 1930s, even Goddard and Terman had turned away from most of their earlier claims. Both spoke out strongly on the severe limits and pitfalls of measuring human intelligence through anything as simple as an examination.

But testing was here to stay. Some system was needed for evaluating students, getting a sense of their strengths and weaknesses, comparing them with others in their own schools and across the country, and trying to assess how well the goals of education are being met. The trend turned away from measuring intelligence and toward evaluating how well each student was learning particular skills and bodies of knowledge. "Achievement tests," in fact, quickly outnumbered the "intelligence tests"; by the early 1930s, nearly 1,300 such exams were available.

In the end, educational testing, its origins and purposes and the controversies around it, tell us most of all about the dilemmas and contradictions of democratic education. If a basic education is a right of all American children, how can teachers best provide that right among students who come to them with varied talents, vastly different preparations, and a bewildering mix of origins? Is it possible, in the same classroom, to respect and fulfill the rights and needs of both the girl of dazzling brilliance and the boy who has trouble with long division? And most important, how do we go about achieving the goals of educational democracy in a world of deep and lingering prejudice and unrecognized intolerance among even our best educated adults?

As throughout American history, education reflected larger currents of change in national life. An important debate during the years after World War I, for instance, concerned the enormous influx of immigrants that had swelled the country's population during the previous few generations. Many of those who had arrived since 1870 were of the "new immigration." Unlike the "old" immigrants from the British Isles and northern and western Europe, the "new" immigrants hailed from such southern and eastern European origins as Italy, Sicily, Poland, Russia, the Baltic countries, Turkey, and the Balkans. Few spoke English. Their religions (most were Catholics and Jews) differed from the nation's Protestant majority. To "old stock" Americans, the customs and lifeways of the "new" immigrants seemed especially alien—and often somehow threatening.

The result was a deepening anxiety over these newcomers, which found extreme expression in anti-foreign organizations. The Ku Klux Klan, a re-invigorated version of the group that had terrorized newly freed slaves after the Civil War, railed against the threat of "un-American" peoples flooding our society and supposedly undermining the nation's basic values. Uneasiness over this question also resulted in a law that would profoundly affect the course of immigration during the next forty years. The "quota law" of 1924 limited the immigration from any particular country in any year to 2 percent of the number of that country's natives living in the United States in 1890. The practical effect was to reduce to a trickle the inflow of "new" immigrants.

At the same time, those worried about immigration were raising another question: What ought to be done with immigrants already here? Since a "nation" implied a collection of people with some identity in common, would there be any national life at all if those waves of new arrivals continued? From one angle, those who asked such questions were concerned with helping new arrivals adjust and acquainting them with the nation's basic institutions; from another, they were expressing a fear that their own beliefs and lifeways were being overwhelmed by the fresh influx of peoples with very different cultural traditions. The flood of immigrants from eastern and southern Europe seemed to threaten the heritage—the very meaning, in fact—of the "true" United States. These concerns gave birth to an effort to refashion immigrants according to the "old stock" standards that, until recently, had dominated national life.

This movement to reshape immigrant lifestyles was called "Americanization." The most obvious strategy was to concentrate on those whose values and customs were just being formed—that is, the children—and one especially obvious place to conduct that crusade was the school. Rather than attempting to create a cultural blend absorbing the new influences, the goal was to assimilate immigrants by encouraging and compelling their children to adopt the major features of Anglo-American culture.

Americanization through education was a formidable task. The U.S. Immigration Commission in 1909 surveyed classrooms in thirty-seven of the largest cities in the country and found that nearly six out of ten schoolchildren (57.8 percent) had one or both parents born outside the United States. In Boston schools the proportion was 63.5 percent; in New York City, 71.5 percent; and in Duluth, Minnesota, 74.1 percent. These young people came from a wide variety of backgrounds—Italian cities and Polish villages; Jewish, Roman Catholic, and Russian Orthodox families; households of Dutch shopkeepers and Czech farmers. Somehow, educational Americanization was supposed to produce a common ground out of this rich diversity.

An obvious starting place was language. Many immigrant youngsters knew little or no English—Edward Bok, who would become the editor of the most popular magazine of its day, the *Saturday Evening Post*, could not speak a single word of it when he started school—yet English was required in the classroom and virtually no effort was made to accommodate those unable to speak it. Improper usage and accents, in fact, were generally ridiculed, and other languages were sometimes forbidden. In public schools of New York City's Lower East Side, the center of the city's Jewish community, the district superintendent ordered that no Yiddish be allowed anywhere on school property. Those who broke this rule had their mouths washed out—with kosher soap. Many adults later recalled the terror of being left at school as young children unable to understand or be understood. Older students unable to speak English often were automatically assigned to the first grade. There a boy or girl of twelve or even fifteen suffered the humiliation of sitting at an undersized desk among much younger classmates. Others were given intense English classes of several weeks, then sent into classrooms and given a full load of work in their new language. A large number, understandably, failed badly.

Instruction in English often was woven together with other lessons about personal habits, respect for authority and institutions, behavior, and even standards of appearance. A text entitled *English for Foreigners* (1909) included such lines for practice as:

This is the family in the sitting-room.

That is the father who is reading . . .

The mother and the father are the parents.

The sister is playing the piano . . .

The family makes the home.

A gentleman is neat in his dress. He does not dress in loud colors. He likes better the kind of clothes that do not attract attention. . . . [O]ften a man is judged by his clothes.

The law tells you what is best for you and for everybody else. You must obey the law, and you should help others to keep the law.

The American flag means liberty and justice for everybody. It is honored by all citizens on the land and on the sea.[29]


A Wisconsin law of 1921 forbade the adoption of any school text that "defames our nation's founders . . . or which contains propaganda favorable to any foreign government."

Schoolchildren, of course, did not always assimilate these lessons as efficiently as teachers planned. Leonard Covello attended a private "soup school"—so called because students were given a bowl of soup and some white bread daily—organized in New York City by the Female Guardian Society of America. Chanting in unison with his classmates, he learned English by reciting poetry and geographical facts that had little or no meaning to him. Before eating his bowl of soup he recited the Lord's Prayer, although "I had no inkling of what the words meant." And in assembly, as an adult waved an American flag, he and his friends sang lustily a song with more phrases that had no meaning to him whatsoever: "Tree Cheers for de Red Whatzam Blu!"[30]

Children often had their names anglicized as well. Josef became Joe and Jerzy became Jerry. The dress and hair styles favored by their parents' generation were discouraged, as were the foods and eating habits of immigrant cultures. Jewish children were chastized for the crumbling leavings of the matzo sandwiches they ate during Passover, and Italian students were mocked for the grease-stained paper wrapped around their lunches. School prayers and religious songs almost invariably were to the God of Protestant Christians. As for the classes themselves, great emphasis was placed on the superior virtues of English literature and the political and historical traditions of Great Britain and its American outgrowth. Examples used in learning to read and even in mathematics extolled the excellence of American government and stressed the values of dedicated citizenship.

In home economics classes, young girls were taught that certain foods and dishes were preferable (including pork and combinations of meat and dairy products forbidden to Orthodox Jews) and were drilled on certain styles of food preparation, table manners, costume, and personal appearance, all patterned on the ways of life of middle-class Anglo-American homes. Americanization was extended even onto the school playgrounds. After the turn of the century, a movement for organized play stressed the need to control as much as possible the way children found their fun, and part of the reason was to discourage the survival of immigrant customs, games, folktales, and jokes. Instead, supervisors were to teach traditional

"American" games and gather children around to hear stories that stressed moral lessons and patriotic themes.

Predictably, all this led to tensions in the lives of immigrant children. The lessons they learned and the pressures they felt in school often conflicted with their lives at home. Many parents, to be sure, believed that it was necessary and valuable for their sons and daughters to learn about their new country, its customs, government, history, and certainly its language. In fact, many expected their children to teach them, in turn, about American life and lifeways. But, predictably, there were misunderstandings. Covello once brought home a bag of oatmeal his teachers had given him as the makings of a hearty breakfast. To his father, however, it resembled what he had fed to his pigs as a boy in Italy. "What kind of a school is this?" he raged. "They give us the food of animals to eat and send it home to us with our children!"[31]

Parents sometimes resented how their youngsters were changing. When a son named Powlowska came home to report that Poland had been a backward country that no longer existed, or when a Jewish daughter told about learning to fry bacon, or when a girl criticized her mother for not setting the dinner table correctly, with salad forks and water glasses placed just so, things could get tense. Just as children were caught in the contradictory demands of adjusting to a new and rapidly changing life, their mothers and fathers were divided between their loyalty to their own pasts and their desire to see their children adapt and succeed as well as they could.

One result was the growth of "ethnic schools" and religious classes meant to preserve and cultivate the languages and traditions of parents' origins. In Chicago in 1930 there were twenty Irish Catholic and thirty-three German Lutheran and Catholic schools operating, as well as others organized for Czech and Polish children.[32] Outside regular school hours, children in these classes were instructed in some of the very customs and values that their public education teachers were working to discourage. Formal schools of this type were attended by only a small minority of immigrant youngsters, but many more families did much the same thing informally at home. Immigrant sons and daughters grew up pulled and divided between these various influences. If this bred conflicts between the generations and within individual children, it also showed that American society remained one of diverse cultures and traditions. Efforts to Americanize this society according to one set of values and one history could never be fully effective.

Newly arrived immigrant families were not the only ones feeling the pressure to adopt certain standards of culture and behavior. A similar program was aimed at Native Americans. It might seem ludicrous to attempt to Americanize descendants of the first peoples to inhabit what would become the United States, but during the first third of the 20th century, the federal government stepped up its efforts to eradicate tribal customs and assimilate American Indians into the dominant white society. As with recent immigrants, these efforts concentrated on the young. So it was, ironically, that Americanization campaigns were directed at the newest arrivals and the oldest inhabitants of the country.

Until late in the 19th century, the formal, institutionalized education of Native Americans had been left up to religious missionaries, although from 1819 the federal government had subsidized their efforts. These mission schools still were operating at the start of the 20th century, but by then three other types had appeared, all sponsored by the federal or state governments. In off-reservation industrial boarding schools, Native American children lived far from their parents and relatives under conditions designed to surround them with European-American culture and ways of life. The first and most famous of these, Carlisle Indian School in Carlisle, Pennsylvania, was founded in 1879 by Richard Henry Pratt, who patterned it after Hampton Institute, which had been established after the Civil War for children of freed slaves. By 1900 there were twenty-five of these institutions. Indian students also attended schools on reservations. Some of these were boarding schools and others held day classes; more than a hundred of the former and more than two hundred of the latter were operating at the turn of the century. Finally, some children went to public schools, funded and run similarly to those for non-Indian students. In fact, Native American and white children typically attended school together, as most public schools for Indian children were on or near reservations whose land had been opened up to occupation by others.

All these schools were intended to educate Indian children in the basics of reading and writing, mathematics, science, and other subjects, much as anywhere else in the country. But, in another sense, the purpose of Indian schools was fundamentally different. Government-sponsored Native American education was based on four assumptions. First, Indians were considered culturally inferior to white Americans; they were thought to be simpler, less sophisticated people. "The Indian is an adult child," President Theodore Roosevelt told the National Education Association. "He has the physical attributes of an adult with the mentality of about our fourteen-

Chiricahua Apache youths on arrival at Carlisle Indian School and a few months later. The goal of Indian education was to transform the values and behavior as well as the appearance of young Native Americans. *Courtesy of National Anthropological Archives, Smithsonian Institution.*

year-old boy."[33] Second, it was also believed that this condition could be changed. Native Americans could be helped along the path toward advanced "civilization"—as defined, of course, by European-American culture. Third, the key was to concentrate on changing the children, whose attitudes and behaviors were still being formed. However, as adults would be expected to resist efforts to lead their young people along such a different path, the fourth assumption was that Indian children should be removed as much as possible from their elders' influence during schooling.

Boarding schools were seen as most effective in implementing this approach. In those off the reservations, Indian children might be taken hundreds of miles from their parents and remain for several years; even in reservation schools, boys and girls were often kept in isolation for months. Many went voluntarily or after pressure from authorities, but for some the process was harsher. Talayesva, a Hopi who grew up in Arizona, remembered his village being surrounded by agency police, who captured the children "and herded us all together at the east edge of the mesa. . . . The children and the mothers were crying and the men wanted to fight." A Hopi woman described how her husband was taken to the same school:

> He was sleeping with his little brothers on the second floor terrace of his home in Old Oraibi. One September morning, early, without his mother's knowledge, the school police took little Emory, still asleep, wrapped in a brand new blanket that his grandfather had made for him. . . . The "catch" that day was Emory, another six-year-old boy, and six girls who had not gone back to school after the summer vacation. . . . They were soon loaded into a wagon for the thirty-mile trip to Keems Canyon.[34]

Transplanted children had their clothes burned and hair cut. They were given new names—Talayesva became "Max"—and were allowed to speak only English. They were to worship only as Christians.

The hope was that a total and rapid immersion in the lifeways of white society would speed up their acculturation and boost them quickly up the ladder of civilization. Emphasis also was placed on training in the manual arts rather than advanced academic subjects. "To train the average Indian as a lawyer or doctor," Theodore Roosevelt said, "is simply to spoil him." Learning to be farmers and skilled workers, on the other hand, would turn them into proud and useful citizens. An editorial in 1909 in the *Journal of Education* summed up the opinion: "When the red man becomes skilled at bench, lathe, or anvil he is not anchored to a life of toil but he is ballasted for a successful voyage on civilization's sea."[35]

In fact, the results were rarely what the planners anticipated. Uprooted and thrust into unfamiliar surroundings, students suffered wrenching emotional traumas. Crowded together and living in new and often unhealthy conditions, Indian children also had terribly high rates of disease. Those taken from the arid West to the more humid East were especially susceptible to illnesses of the lungs. Late in the 19th century, 112 Chiricahua Apache boys and girls were taken to the boarding school at Carlisle. Within only a few years at least thirty-seven had died, thirty-four from tuberculosis and the other three from unknown causes. Several others had been sent home when they were near death.

Although many of the surviving children learned the ways of white people, those that later returned home found it difficult to fit back into their families and societies. They were, in effect, young people between two cultures and truly part of neither. On the other hand, life at the boarding school provided an opportunity for these young people to come into contact with Native Americans from other tribes and regions. As a result, some developed a sense of kinship and broader Native American identity they would never have felt otherwise.

So it was, ironically, that schools designed to remove the "Indian" from these young girls and boys actually encouraged a feeling of American Indian community among the many diverse native peoples of our diverse nation. Native American children, like European-American youngsters, were using adult institutions to pursue their own needs and purposes.

## HEALTH

If life wasn't necessarily getting a lot better for most American children during the 1920s and 1930s, at least it seemed to be getting longer. In 1920, out of every thousand babies born, eighty-six died before the age of five; in 1940, about forty-seven suffered that fate. There were several reasons for this improvement. Medical science continued to make significant contributions. Diseases that had taken murderous tolls a generation or two before were, if not entirely eliminated, at least largely subdued. There was a better understanding as well about the connections between living conditions—including the health of parents, the family's economic security, and its diet—and children's well being. That expanded knowledge opened the way for even greater advances in child health, but it also raised difficult questions that would continue to confront Americans for the rest of the century.


Advances in our understanding, for instance, led to questions about the responsibility of governments toward the health of our young people. Children's health was threatened on many fronts, but as discussed in the previous chapter, babies faced some of their gravest dangers even before they were born. Study after study showed that when mothers-to-be lived on poor diets, worked long hours, and when they had little or no prenatal medical care, their babies were far more likely to be stillborn or to die soon after birth. An important solution to the problem of infant mortality clearly was giving support to infants while they were still within their mothers' wombs.

Such care, however, was beyond the reach of many poorer mothers and those in areas isolated from medical facilities. Some state governments were attempting to provide some help for expectant mothers, but many others showed little interest or lacked the necessary funds for such an ambitious program.

In 1921, Congress acted to help remedy this situation by approving the Sheppard-Towner Bill, which then was signed into law by President Warren G. Harding. This pathbreaking legislation established the first federally funded health care program in the nation's history. The Sheppard-Towner law provided federal "matching funds" for states—money, that is, that would be made available if states also pitched in their own funds—that would be used "in promoting the welfare and hygiene of maternity and infancy." This funding and its resulting programs would be overseen by a new Board of Maternity and Infant Hygiene, and the chief of the Children's Bureau would be the executive officer.

The specific goals of the law were kept vague, doubtless because conditions and problems differed greatly from state to state. In general, however, administrators of the act encouraged certain actions and programs. They pushed hard for official registration of all births, something still not done then in some states. Gathering such information in the long run was of great benefit, if for no other reason than for studying more completely the dangers of infant mortality and the early death of babies. Administrators also strongly urged the establishment of "maternity centers" and "infant welfare centers," places where pregnant women and mothers could find helpful information on prenatal care and the proper care of their newborns. These centers might also have on their staff public nurses who were available for house calls. Finally, classes were organized for mothers, midwives, and "little mothers," older children who frequently were left in charge of caring for infants.

Beyond these general purposes, programs differed with circumstances. In states with more funds available, and where state programs already were underway, nurses were sent to visit nearly every mother who requested help. Nurses gave instructions on exercise, diet, and personal and domestic hygiene; they advised pregnant women on how to prepare for labor and delivery; they took the women's blood pressure and provided urinalyses; finally, they urged expectant mothers to consult with a doctor. In a southern state with fewer resources and programs, the concentration was on training the thousands of midwives who were most likely to be on hand at the time of an infant's delivery. Such classes stressed how midwives might offer good prenatal care and, when the time for the birth arrived, how they might use sterile procedures to discourage infections.

From its beginnings there was strong opposition to the Sheppard-Towner Act. Some warned that such federal help for mothers-to-be would open the way to much more ambitious actions on behalf of others. Might not Congress next turn to creating bureaus for "the foodless . . . the clothesless . . . the houseless," asked one congressman?[36] Behind this was the fear, commonly expressed in the 1920s, of a global trend toward socialism, which, in turn, was associated in the minds of many with the communist revolution in Russia and the rise of the Soviet Union. Fear of socialism was often linked with a concern that this new law would permit nurses and doctors to intrude into people's homes, meddling with the most private family matters, although the legislation made clear that no interference with parental activities or rights would be allowed. One senator objected to birth registration as an invasion of privacy—or, as he put it, a "poor, blushing little woman is compelled to register upon the public records the fact of her pregnancy"—while an article in *The Woman Patriot* in 1928 denounced the law as a "cold-blooded, calculated socialist feminist scheme." Some of the strongest reactions came from the medical community. Many doctors feared any federal sponsorship of health care and, in particular, objected to nurses working with patients outside the supervision of physicians. In 1922, the American Medical Association (AMA) passed a resolution lashing out against the law as "an imported socialistic scheme unsuited to our form of government," and for the next several years the AMA worked vigorously in opposition to the measure.[37]

Ultimately, the enemies of the act were successful. Originally scheduled to expire in 1927, the Sheppard-Towner Act was extended for two more years. In the meantime, the U.S. Supreme Court, in the case of *Common-*

*wealth of Massachusetts* v. *Mellon* (1923), declared the law legal and constitutional. Nonetheless, the persistent opponents were able to block proposals to extend the bill's life beyond 1929. The effects of the law, however, had been considerable. The number of states registering births increased from thirty (with about 70 percent of the national population) to forty-six (about 95 percent). In 1919, sixteen states had child-hygiene agencies; six years later forty-seven states and the territory of Hawaii had them. Nearly 1,600 local prenatal and child-health consultation centers were established. County programs already established were expanded; the number of rural nurses available for consultation doubled, for example.

Once the law expired, some states picked up programs and expenses on their own, but elsewhere the help for pregnant mothers and new babies was cut back or stopped altogether. Efforts to enact a new bill were unsuccessful. In 1935, however, the Social Security Act was passed, and, included in its provisions, were programs that basically recreated the system of support for state programs first offered by the Sheppard-Towner Act.

Some of the most significant medical developments concerned not direct assaults on diseases but rather changes in the daily habits of Americans. Nowhere was this shown more clearly than in one of the most fundamental functions of life, eating.

During the quarter century after 1910, for instance, discoveries were made that would affect profoundly the health and eating habits of the American people. These investigations concerned what was destined to become a familiar term to most Americans—vitamins. The previous generation, as discussed in the first chapter, had witnessed remarkable and far-reaching breakthroughs in the science of diseases, their detection, cure, and prevention. Those discoveries had centered on the "germ theory" and the part that bacteria and viruses play in ill health. The emphasis was on alien organisms that invaded the body and caused it harm. The lessons, naturally, stressed what people ought to avoid.

The new investigations, on the other hand, concerned the opposite, the harm caused by what people were *not* eating. Between 1911 and 1922, scientists, led by Elmer McCollum of Yale University, isolated and identified elements in foods that were essential for proper health. In 1912, a European researcher labeled these elements "vitamines" (the spelling was later changed to "vitamins"). The earliest were identified by a simple alphabetical system: Vitamins A, B, C, and D. Later, when it was found that these really were groups of related elements, some were classified accordingly, such as Vitamin B-1. With these discoveries came an understanding that some health problems stemmed from the lack of these elements, or vitamin deficiencies. A child who got too little Vitamin A, for instance, might grow up with impaired vision. Vitamins C and D were linked to healthy development of bones, teeth, and hair. In time, researchers isolated more vitamins as well as minerals and trace elements helpful or necessary for the proper development and maintenance of the human body. In most cases it was emphasized that getting vitamins early, during infancy, childhood and adolescence, was critically important for a long, healthy life.

Only later did scientists figure out how to synthesize vitamins, so, for the time being, these vital elements could be taken in only with the foods that contained them. Vitamin A was found in carrots and some other vegetables, Vitamin C in citrus fruits, Vitamin D in milk. Until well into the 1930s, however, there was no way to measure accurately the vitamin content in these foods. Careful consumers would eat considerable amounts, just to be safe.

Looking back, the dangers of vitamin deficiencies clearly could be exaggerated. For the most part, diseases directly linked to extreme vitamin deficits—scurvy (Vitamin C) and beri-beri (Vitamin B-1), for instance— were very rare or nonexistent in the United States. Help did come, nonetheless, for two important concerns. A chronic problem among poor southern farmers, for instance, was pellagra. This condition arises among people who are severely deficient in niacin, and it is most common among families who rely heavily on corn meal, which has no niacin, instead of wheat bread, which provides plenty. Once the connection was established between pellagra and corn diet, the problem could be alleviated by greater consumption of Vitamin B-3. Programs for more and better milk (and thus Vitamin D) reduced the incidence of bone-deforming rickets among children of the urban poor.

Awareness of vitamins and concern for balanced diets also offered a grand opportunity for some food manufacturers and retailers to play on parents' fears about their children's health. Middle-class mothers and fathers whose incomes allowed them to choose among the many items available at the local grocery were bombarded by a variety of astounding claims made by self-styled nutrition experts. Both Fleischmann's Yeast and Quaker Oats were said to be rich in Vitamin B, which supposedly increased children's appetites and "brain power" and, more substantially, battled against all sorts of blights and ailments, from pimples, acne, and boils to constipation, "fallen stomach," and "underfed blood." (This campaign proved a wondrous revival for the yeast industry, which had been hit hard by national prohibition and the end of the legal brewing of beer, and by the trend toward buying bread in stores rather than baking it at home.) Vitamin G (later classified as Vitamin B-2) was said to lengthen life and postpone senility. Fruit-growers claimed that Vitamin C protected youngsters from tooth decay and gum disease, and that down the road it would lessen chances of alcoholism. Vitamin D reportedly could help in similar wonders, including avoidance of lead poisoning.

Fascination with vitamins contributed to another important dietary trend for children—the vigorous promotion of cow's milk. Milk consumption had declined considerably early in the century, probably because of the better understanding of the dangers of contamination discussed in the previous chapter. The low point was reached about 1915. Then milk producers, especially corporations like Borden's and Sealtest, began aggressively advertising their products as not only pure and safe but also "the most important single food for a child," a source brimming with vitamins and other elements crucial for youthful growth. In the mid-1920s it was said that youngsters should drink at least a pint a day; and, by 1937, "experts" had upped the recommendation to a daily quart. This naturally was more feasible for the middle class, especially during the depression years; a family on welfare would have spent half its relief check to pay for the twenty-eight quarts of milk it supposedly needed every week. Regardless of a family's income, there was another problem: many children did not like the taste of this "miracle food." Their aversion gave birth to another growth industry, additives and flavorings to convince "Little Milk Rebels" to drain their glasses gladfully. Among the most successful was Baker's Cocoa, which also was claimed to contain "indispensable food elements."

Regardless of inflated claims for the miraculous properties of vitamins and the foods that contained them, the campaigns of the 1920s and 1930s reflected a greater awareness of the importance of diet in promoting good health among the young. Parents learned of the need to consume enough of a diversity of foods. A child's good health (and an adult's) depended not only on avoiding germ-infested items but also on the balanced consumption of nourishing foods. As always, America's poorer families were not in a position to act on that knowledge; but among those with moderate incomes, parents were paying much closer attention to what their children ate, even during the lean years of the 1930s when putting food of any kind on the table was difficult. This concern would continue to shape the daily life of boys and girls, particularly when they drew their chairs up to the table for a meal. The food campaigns of those decades produced one of the century's most enduring family refrains: "Eat your spinach (or broccoli, carrots, brussel sprouts, peas, or turnips). You need the vitamins."

These mealtime revolutions—the passion for vitamins, expansion of possibilities through improved transportation, modern processing, and the selling of food in boxes and cans—were felt far more by some Americans than by others. All depended on parents and children having access to new products and, more than that, having the money to pay for them. It was among the middle classes, consequently, that these changes had their greatest effect. For those Americans with fewer resources, breakfast and dinnertime remained much the same—and just as potentially unhealthy—as in previous generations.

Among families with the lowest incomes, regardless of what part of the country they lived in, meals shared certain characteristics. They were cheap, they varied little, and, for the most part, they were insufficient for a full and healthy life. Southern sharecroppers, black and white, continued to live by the "three M's": meat (usually salt pork), meal (processed corn meal and white flour), and molasses. In summer this might be supplemented by turnip and collard greens and a little fruit. During the winters, between harvest and planting, itinerant tobacco workers survived on a relentless regimen of fat meat, cornbread and dumplings, and a few greens. Much the same was true of Appalachian mountain families. Studies in the early 1920s revealed that the situation there was little different from the turn of the century, when each person's daily intake was about a pound of flour or corn meal, plus three or four ounces of lard. The situation was strikingly similar among the poorest westerners. Hispanic children, especially migrant workers and day laborers on farms, ate mainly corn tortillas, beans, chiles, and perhaps some tomatoes.

Even worse were meals of Native Americans living on reservations. Most food came from government subsidies, which consisted mainly of surplus items. Except for potatoes, beans, and some squash and canned tomatoes, vegetables were almost wholly absent. Most common was deep-fried white flour dough, or "fried bread." A government ration of beef usually was gone well before month's end. Indians typically tried to provide part of their own food, but that was not easy, as they were living on some of the poorest land in the country. When drought struck the Fort Yates Sioux reservation in 1912–1913, the corn and potato crops failed and most cattle died. As starvation neared, an agent paid fifty cents apiece from his own pocket for pictures children drew of their lives. One poignant example shows boys and girls around a meal inside a tipi, while outside a man holds out his hands and pleads, "w.oh jni w opyn B oh nowpin coyopi [I want food]."[38]

Scattered across the continent, varied in culture and lifeways, the children in all these families sat down to eat foods that had a lot in common. Most obviously, breakfast, lunch, and dinner offered few fresh vegetables, milk or other dairy products, and little, if any, fresh meat. The most familiar part of the diets, meal made from corn or wheat, usually was processed, which robbed it of much of its nutritional worth. The outward results of these diets, paradoxically, was a tendency toward both being underweight, because of small portions and lack of essentials for growth, and being over-weight, because of the preponderance of starches and animal fats. Investi-gators on a Sioux reservation in South Dakota estimated that 27 percent of the boys and girls were "extremely thin," while 11 percent were "dis-tinctly fat." Just as revealing was the prevalence of poor eyesight and blind-ness, tooth decay, and low levels of energy. Much the same could be seen among southwestern Mexican-American communities, black farmers in the South, and Appalachian whites—flabbiness and obesity mixed with a bony, sallow appearance.

This was the case before the onset of the Great Depression. Common sense would seem to indicate that the greatest economic crisis in American history must have hit hard at the diets of all Americans and hardest of all at the poorest families. Millions of jobs vanished, family incomes plum-meted, parents and children cast around for the basic means of survival. Surely the toll on the health of the nation's children was heavy. However, actually determining the depression's impact on the nation's eating habits and health is difficult and complex.

Government spokesmen, at least, were convinced that the depression was robbing families of nutritional essentials and thus undermining the physical basis of the American people. In President Franklin Roosevelt's ringing phrase from his second inaugural address in 1937, "one-third of the na-tion," a society that was arguably the wealthiest and most powerful in history, was "ill-nourished." The national government, he argued, must take up responsibility to insure a basic level of protection of its people, and that included the fundamentals of decent meals on the table.

There was little agreement, however, on what "ill-" and "well-nourished" really meant and how "nourishment" should be measured. The science of nutrition was still in its infancy. What were the "basic needs" of a child? What was an "adequate" diet, a "superior" or "poor" one? The standards were vague and open to debate.

Compounding the problem of vague nutritional standards was a lack of solid information on the diets of Americans across the nation. Most inves-tigations during the New Deal were limited to certain groups, most of them living in cities. Rural Americans, especially those in remote areas, were largely left out. And many of those studies, wherever they were made, ignored the very poorest families—migrant workers, city-dwellers without well-established homes, sharecroppers and the rural poor who lived in the more isolated parts of the South and West.

The coming of hard times certainly must have worsened the diets of millions of Americans. When fathers lost their jobs, parents squeezed every dollar to meet daily needs, and that meant reducing meals to the cheapest basics. Mothers cut back on (and often cut out entirely) fresh fruit and other items that had begun to lend variety to youngsters' diets. Milk consumption, after soaring during the 1920s, plunged after 1929. Meat, even the cheapest cuts, became a rare luxury, replaced by eggs, pancakes, corn meal and corn bread, pasta, and beans. Butter was left at the store and skillet drippings used instead.

To the extent that some standards could be agreed upon, several studies concluded that children of unemployed workers were living by diets woefully lacking in crucial nutrients. But if that were so (and if the standards were accurate to begin with), it still would be hard to say whether the depression was responsible for the problem. Instead of suffering because of cuts in the family budget, children might have been poorly fed because their parents did not know how to feed them properly. Millions of mothers and fathers still had little exposure to the findings of nutritional science, which was, after all, still unsure of its own conclusions. These studies, furthermore, were conducted mostly among the middle and urban working classes who benefited the most from government relief and re-employment programs. Whatever good and bad that could be found in these investigations, in other words, missed almost entirely the most deprived citizens of the nation.

Many of those poorest Americans surely must have been a lot hungrier because of the depression. Pushed off the land with their families and set to wandering in search of work, some children were reduced to eating boiled wild plants and whatever their parents could find in garbage dumps. And yet, ironically, the depression probably hurt the eating habits of the poor less than those of the middle classes. Impoverished farmers and day laborers had never eaten well, even under better conditions in earlier years, and had less of a distance to fall. Most continued to dine on fried and baked variations of corn and flour, a few beans, a little meat, and occasional vegetables, just like their parents and grandparents before them.[39]

In other words, there is no conclusive evidence that the Great Depression caused substantial numbers of children to become "ill-nourished." But a more important point is that the diets of the poorest Americans—tenant farmers and sharecroppers, day laborers and migrant workers, squatters, itinerants, and Native Americans on reservations—had always been unhealthy and inadequate. As living standards of other Americans had risen in the past, theirs had stayed much the same; and now, as times got a good bit worse for others, the grim, debilitating diets of the very poor remained as bad as ever. There were plenty of undernourished Americans, but their plight could not be blamed on the times. They were, instead, continuing reminders of those who had always been left out of the American dream.

## CHILDREN AND THE LAW

As described in chapter 1, some reformers had begun to use the power of law and government to help children they believed were threatened by the sweeping changes in American life. The best examples of that effort were in child labor reform, and those campaigns continued between 1920 and 1940. After the Supreme Court struck down the Keating-Owen Act of 1918, the first federal child labor law, reformers began to work for a suitable amendment to the U.S. Constitution. Opposed by influential leaders of industry and business and spokesmen for the nation's farmers, their campaign for a child labor amendment appeared to be dead by 1925.

With the coming of the depression, the number of working children suddenly began to rise, as families felt the pressure to bring in as much income as they could and businessmen looked for ways to hire cheaper labor. President Franklin Roosevelt and leaders of the Democratic party, in turn, made regulation of child labor part of their political program. One of the most important early laws (1933) under Roosevelt's New Deal administration created the National Recovery Administration (NRA), which set standards for many aspects of American industry; and as part of that regulation the NRA forbade employment of persons under sixteen years in virtually all industries.

Here was the first effective federal child labor law since the Keating-Owen Act, but, once again, this one was erased by the Supreme Court when the justices declared the NRA unconstitutional in 1935. Investigations showed that the child labor situation was drifting backward toward that of the turn of the century, with more and more children employed in unhealthy, dangerous jobs for pathetically low wages. Some reformers again pursued a constitutional amendment on child labor, and several states approved one; but the Roosevelt administration instead passed yet another law. The Fair Labor Standards Act of 1938 regulated several aspects of labor conditions for all ages, and one of these provisions forbade hiring anyone under sixteen in any industry engaged in interstate commerce. In industries classified as especially dangerous, no one under eighteen could be employed. Unlike the first two federal efforts, this one was accepted by the Supreme Court.

That still left hundreds of thousands of working children beyond any federal regulation, and many of those were outside state laws, too. Boys and girls in rural America and those working close to their homes, on the streets, and in smaller businesses—they were mostly ignored by the growing body of child labor law. Their jobs could be just as dangerous and abusive as the ones now forbidden to children. Plenty of problems surrounding child labor remained, as did the deeper causes of those problems. Young Americans usually labored in ways that were bad for them because their families were too poor for them to do anything else.

Some New Deal programs were created and designed specifically for young (or relatively young) persons. The National Youth Administration (NYA), whose first head was the future president Lyndon B. Johnson, offered four different sorts of programs for persons between sixteen and twenty-five. Besides vocational training and work-study arrangements for young men and women still pursuing their educations, there were also employment programs in public works and recreational activities. During its lifetime (1935–43), the NYA put more than 2.5 million young people to work and provided work-study assistance to more than 600,000 persons in high schools and 1.5 million in colleges. Hundreds of thousands received vocational training, including skills in defense industries after 1939. The Civilian Conservation Corps, one of the earliest federal work relief programs, eventually put more than 2.5 million young men to work on conservation projects—planting trees to prevent erosion on the plains, laboring in national forests, and building cabins, shelters, and other facilities in thousands of public recreation areas.

Other programs were concerned with younger Americans, ones vulnerable to difficulties other than unemployment. One of the most significant laws during the 1930s—in fact one of the most important in the 20th century—was the Social Security Act (1935). Its best known provisions set up a mandatory program of contributions that would be given back to individuals as benefits when they retired and as temporary income if they lost their jobs. In a sense, these broad-based commitments, by trying to relieve some of the worst economic pressures on the family, were intended to help children, who were some of the depression's most vulnerable victims. With outside help for the elderly and during bouts of unemployment, parents could devote more resources to taking care of their sons and daughters.

The Social Security Act also established a program of Aid to Dependent Children (later called Aid to Families with Dependent Children), the first direct federal aid to the young. Such support was nothing new at the state level. The special White House Conference on Children in 1909, recognizing how poverty was undermining families headed by single mothers with low incomes, often leading to children being sent away to orphanages, recommended some sort of public support to keep these young people at home. Illinois led the way in 1911 with the Funds for Parents Act, which created state pensions "to enable the parent or parents to properly care for such a child."[40] Twenty states followed suit within a couple of years, and by 1935 only two states, Georgia and South Carolina, had failed to pass "mother's aid" or "mother's pension" laws. State support was spotty and in virtually all cases far too limited, however. Nearly twenty thousand families were helped in New York, but fewer than five hundred received aid in Texas and less than a hundred in Louisiana. As usual, there was a clear racial twist to the help given: although African-American mothers were among those most desperately in need, only 3 percent of families receiving state aid were black; and more than half of those were in Ohio and Pennsylvania, far outside the deep South where poverty was the deepest.

Aid to Dependent Children (ADC), which held out matching funds to the states, was meant to support and enhance those state programs and to provide more consistent help. Black families were much more likely to receive help under these early federal programs. Funds were given only to states that set up an administrative structure and operated by guidelines laid down under the law. Later, especially after World War II, ADC would balloon into one of the most extensive and costly programs of the national government. In its early years, however, it was quite limited. Fewer than half a million families participated initially, receiving only an average of less than ten dollars a month. As with most such laws, this one was also something of an invasion of the family's private sphere, as, almost from the start, some states insisted that aid be given only to families that met certain standards of behavior, including what officials considered proper discipline of boys and girls.

Children were aided, directly and indirectly, by other New Deal programs. Certainly one of the most famous agencies of the 1930s was the Works Progress Administration (WPA), through which millions were hired to do everything from building highways and airports to painting murals and composing symphonies. Included were women hired to run nursery schools for the young children of other women working to support their families. These nurseries, some of the most popular programs of the New Deal, established a precedent for later federal funding of daycare centers.

There was a puzzling contradiction at the heart of the story of children's rights during the 1920s and 1930s. That contradiction was especially plain during those years, but it had been there since the earliest stages of the movement to protect children's interests. In many ways, it remains today. On the one hand, many men and women in positions of influence were dedicated to guaranteeing certain rights for American children; on the other hand, this inevitably led to some encroachments on their freedom.

In the past those essential rights of children had included the right to an education, to protection from gross abuse, and to reasonably good health. By the 1920s that list was expanding to include the right to the broader, but vaguer, notion of healthy growth and development—not merely protection from disease and physical harm, but promotion of psychological and emotional well-being too.

Protecting such rights naturally involved studying children and their difficulties, then classifying children and making decisions about their characters, their intelligence, their emotional stability, their habits, and their lifestyles. With that necessarily came opinions about how young people ought to be treated in order to correct any problems that "experts" believed they had found.

In order to defend children's rights to healthy growth of character, sympathetic authorities had to determine what "healthy" was, then measure children according to that standard; they also sought to correct deficiencies of behavior and improper environments of those who were not measuring up. Potentially, that meant prying into some of young people's innermost privacies and trying to regulate and change some of the most personal aspects of their lives. Expanding and protecting children's rights, in other words, seemed to lead to restricting their rights.

One example, discussed in the "At School" section of this chapter, was intelligence testing. Educational authorities, believing that IQ tests accurately and objectively measured the raw brain power of children, used the results to help determine the educational "tracks" different students should take—whether toward the professions, for instance, or toward the manual arts. In fact, the questions and problems in those tests proved to favor white boys and girls of stable, nuclear middle-class families. Based on faulty assumptions, the tests resulted in a violation of the very right—that of a proper education that opened life's opportunities—that they were supposed to protect.

This problem also was in evidence in the juvenile justice system. Juvenile courts supposedly were dedicated to treating youthful offenders in a manner that would help them grow up into useful, well-adjusted citizens. Rather than punishing young people, they were supposed to encourage proper and healthy behavior. To do that, judges were given remarkable powers. Without following the usual courtroom procedures or the laws governing adults, a juvenile judge could place a child under "probation," the close supervision of authorities, for months or years. He could also sentence a young person to a long term in a reformatory for the vaguest reasons or for behavior that was perfectly legal for adults. With usually good intentions, juvenile courts were supposedly protecting young Americans by taking away some of their rights.

Looking back, it also seems that courts judged some young people by tougher standards than others. Juvenile offenders brought before the judges were overwhelmingly from the poorer working classes, and a disproportionate number of those boys and girls were from particular ethnic and racial groups, especially the "new" immigrants, the Italians, Russians, Poles, and others from eastern and southern Europe who had poured into the country during the early years of the century. About nine out of ten young people brought before the juvenile court in Milwaukee during these years, for instance, were children of immigrants, and three out of four were either German or Polish. In this sense, the juvenile courts apparently were singling out those groups to enforce certain standards of behavior, just as educators were working to "Americanize" immigrant youngsters and Native American youths, as previously discussed.

Similarly, juvenile courts were treating one half of their young people, girls, differently from the other half. Concern about youthful misconduct in the 19th century had focused mainly on boys. Then, during the first three decades of the 20th century, there was a mounting worry about "female delinquency." This new attention to girls reflected general changes in society as well as new roles that young females were playing. In the growing cities, children of both sexes led more independent lives, spending considerable time away from their parents. In the urban economy, young girls also were finding jobs in a variety of occupations outside the household, such as waitresses, clerks in stores, and unskilled factory laborers. Many parents, moral spokesmen, and juvenile officials were alarmed, believing that children were more likely to fall into immoral and criminal ways if they passed much of their formative years apart from the watchful eyes and discipline of their mothers and fathers. Girls were of special concern as, by the belief of that day, they were more easily corrupted, and, in particular, more likely to yield to sexual temptations.

As worries grew about female delinquents, more and more girls showed up in juvenile courts. A close study of courts in three cities revealed a clear pattern. Boys typically were brought in on grounds of common criminal activity, accused of theft, vandalism, robbery, assault, and similar offenses. Girls, however, were almost never charged with such crimes; generally they were accused under the vague term of "immoral conduct." Often this meant frequent disobedience of parents; in fact, girls usually were brought to court by fathers and mothers who complained that they could not control their daughters. New York's Wayward Minor Act, passed in 1923, provided that females between the ages of sixteen and twenty-one could be convicted of disobedience or immorality entirely on the testimony of their parents. Those young women then were either placed on probation or sent to reformatories.

"Immorality" almost always involved sexual matters. A young single girl might be accused of having sexual intercourse, but she could get into serious trouble much more easily than that. To be brought to court she only needed to show "signs" that she might become sexually active in the near future. Likely signs might be obscene language, masturbation, disrespect for elders, or "provocative" dress; sometimes it was enough just to show evidence of thinking too much about sex.

Furthermore, although girls rarely were accused of criminal actions, they received harsher punishment than boys. In Chicago courts about 60 percent of the boys were put on probation but only 37 percent of the girls. "Immoral" females were likely to hear a judge say something like this (from a case of a fifteen-year-old girl accused of having sex):

Well, Deborah, this is a very serious matter. If you would live a good life you would be a good woman, and be useful to society, but you have started out very bad. There is only one way to reform you and this is to send you to an institution. I cannot let you go home to your parents.[41]

In Milwaukee about 20 percent of males and 50 percent of females brought before juvenile courts were sent to reformatories. A girl usually was sentenced to two or three years. This kind of power was not exercised only on younger adolescents. When Evelyn Blackwell, twenty, became pregnant in 1926, a New York juvenile court sent her to an institution, even though she had borne two other children and had been briefly married.

In reformatories girls were kept far away from boys. In California a new female facility was built when it was decided that the old one was too close to the boys' reformatory (one mile away) to prevent "the influences that mysteriously emanate from the proximity of the sexes."[42] During their terms, female inmates were kept to rigid standards of behavior and trained in such domestic tasks as cooking, making beds, and sewing—the same training emphasized in educational Americanization programs. Girls who rebelled against authorities could be kept longer, some indefinitely. As was discussed elsewhere in this chapter, immorality was linked with low intelligence. Suspicious persons who scored very low on IQ tests could be confined to homes for the "feeble-minded," even though those tests were slanted against persons of certain cultural backgrounds. Young girls in reformatories sometimes were given IQ tests, and if they performed poorly enough, they might be sent for an indefinite stay in other institutions.

Children's legal status reflected how their place in American life was changing. Nowhere was this shown more dramatically than in the ways that courts wrestled with a basic legal question: How much was a dead child worth?

Since early in the 19th century, American courts, drawing on precedents in English law, had compensated parents when a son or daughter was killed through someone's negligence. The principle was simple: At an early age children became important, valuable contributors to their families' economies. Although there were expenses in child rearing, as boys and girls worked in the fields, around the house, and at various jobs in towns and cities, they brought in more than was being spent on them. Until they left home to pursue their own fortunes, they were crucial economic assets. A dead child, then, meant lost income, and a person or business responsible for a child's "wrongful death" would naturally be expected to pay.

As seen in this chapter and the one before, a son's or daughter's monetary value could be substantial, especially among those families farther down the economic scale—farmers who worked by the older ways, city folks relying on day labor, immigrants without marketable skills, and others. Courts recognized this fact of life. Wrongful death awards could amount to several thousands dollars, substantial sums at the turn of the century. The figure to be given was based on a basic reckoning: a child's potential earning capacity from the time of death until the age of twenty-one, minus the parents' estimated costs of support. As one historian puts it, "the price of each life was literally bargained in court."[43] Here, for instance, is an exchange in court between an attorney and a father asking for ten thousand dollars for the death of his son, aged five:

Q. I ask you now, what do you think [this child] is worth in money? . . . You have a step-son about twelve years old: what would you consider him worth—$10,000 from five to twenty-one?

A. Yes, I would; boys between twelve and sixteen and twenty are worth $75 or $80 a month.

Q. Is this not rather an unusual thing, and an extraordinary boy who will get it?

A. I suppose it is not ordinary.

Q. Taking $720 per annum as the best rates a boy can earn on an average for the last six years of his minority . . . it would amount to $4,370. Deduct six years' expenses at $360 per annum, making $2,160, and it leaves the net earnings $2,210.

The jury, apparently siding more with the questioner, allowed the father $2,265.[44]

States usually placed ceilings on the amount that could be awarded, ranging from five to twenty thousand dollars in 1900, but courts often ordered considerable payments, grim recognition of how much children meant to their parents, at least in terms of dollars and cents. Wrongful death cases became increasingly common during the last decades of the 19th century and first years of the 20th, mainly because of the threats children faced from new technologies and from dangers in the cities. Railroads and trolley companies were especially likely to find themselves in court to pay for young persons crushed and mangled beneath the wheels of their cars.

Then, around the turn of the century, some court decisions suddenly went in what seemed to be the opposite direction. In some cases, judges drastically reduced generous awards that juries had given to bereaved parents; in others, the juries themselves ordered payments that were, compared to similar cases in the past, tiny. After a race car swerved into a crowd at the 1911 New York state fair and killed several persons, including a nine-year-old boy, the child's parents were paid only $500 (while families of adult victims received several thousand dollars). In another widely publicized case, the father of a boy killed by a New York City streetcar was awarded six cents for his dead child—although, on appeal, the man eventually received $7,500. Parents in Missouri who lost their twelve-year-old were given a single penny.

From the courts' point of view, the reasoning had not changed. The rule had always been that fathers and mothers were to be compensated simply for the economic value of their children. But as discussed in the "At Work" sections of chapters 1 and 2, many children, especially those of the middle classes, were contributing less and less to the income of their families, even as their parents were spending more and more on them. These children were being taken out of the workplace, kept in school, and reared in other expensive ways. Economically speaking, middle- and upper-class children were worth little or nothing, and, in fact, were an ever larger drain on their parents' pocketbooks. In explaining the six-cent award for the New York streetcar victim, the jury pointed out that the father was relatively well-to-do, and the man himself testified that his boy "never earned a dollar in his lifetime. . . . All the time, up to the date of his death, he had been a source of expense to me." Why, then, should mothers and fathers in such a case be paid for their children's deaths?

By the same logic, the courts occasionally made economic distinctions between the sexes. A father who sued a condensed milk company for the death of his twins, aged three months, was given $2,000 for the boy and $1,000 for the girl. An appeals court in New Jersey upheld an award of $6,000 for a young man killed in a trolley and train wreck, but it reduced an award for a female victim to $3,000. A girl, said the judge, might eventually mature into a breadwinner, but a boy certainly would, so even if the young girl had grown up to be a schoolteacher, her market value was at best only half that of the dead male.

These decisions, in other words, reflected the economic realities of modern America, the changing lives of millions of American children, and the new meanings they had for their parents. The trend of shrinking income from children and rising expenses for them continued as the century progressed. By an estimate in 1930, a family that made $2,500 a year would spend nearly $7,500 to rear a child to the age of eighteen. Strictly by a dollars-and-cents measurement, a child's death often meant a massive savings to parents.

But such an approach, of course, represented only part of a child's worth. While the economic value of American children was shrinking, boys and girls were also playing an increasingly prominent role in their parents' emotional lives, as they were kept closer to home. Many families became more and more "child-centered." Middle-class parents tended to bear and rear fewer children, and they invested more of their attention and affection in their small families. As a child's immediate monetary worth shrank, his or her emotional value expanded.

The courts adjusted. After trending generally downward, awards began to move back up, and by the 1940s amounts paid for wrongful deaths of children, even when those young people were demonstrably without financial value to their parents, were typically quite large. In an important decision by a federal appeals court in 1961, the court rejected the "cold-blooded deduction" used to calculate the difference between a child's income and his cost and argued that parents should be compensated for losing the incomparable emotional opportunity of watching their offspring grow up: "What makes life worth living more than the privilege of raising a son?"

# BIBLIOGRAPHICAL ESSAY

## General Works

A reader interested in further research on the topics in this chapter might start with N. Ray Hiner and Joseph M. Hawes's *American Childhood: A Research Guide and Historical Handbook* (Westport, Conn.: Greenwood Press, 1985). It offers two chapters covering childhood generally from before World War I through World War II, as well as two others touching on children outside the national mainstream—Native Americans and immigrants from Europe and Asia—who were the objects of the Americanization programs discussed in this chapter. All these essays contain interpretive accounts of their subjects and excellent bibliographies that will steer researchers to pertinent books and articles. There is also a chapter on children's literature in the 20th century, a subject I have not pursued here at length. The chronological chapters pay special attention to public agencies and the "child saving" movements that were such an important part of political and social reform during these years.

For background on the history of these years, there are some excellent works readily available in many libraries. A couple of older accounts of the 1920s, both available in revised editions, have become modern classics. Frederick Lewis Allen's *Only Yesterday: An Informal History of the Nineteen-Twenties* (New York: Harper and Row, 1964) is entertaining, vigorously written, and filled with vivid details of that colorful period. William E. Leuchtenburg's *The Perils of Prosperity, 1914–1932,* a somewhat more formal history, is highly readable and offers insights and interpretations that have held up well over the years. For an excellent overview of the Great Depression, students should consult Robert S. McElvaine's *The Great Depression: America, 1929–1941* (New York: Times Books, 1993), as well as Gerald D. Nash's *The Crucial Era: The Great Depression and World War II* (New York: St. Martin's Press, 1992); and, on the political movements and changes that dominated that era, Paul K. Conkin's *The New Deal* (Arlington Heights, Ill.: Harlan Davidson, 1992). The man whose personality and power dominated this period, Franklin Roosevelt, has had many excellent biographers. The best of recent years is Kenneth S. Davis; see his four-volume biography, *FDR* (New York: Putnam, 1972, and Random House, 1985–93). For overviews of the history of Mexican-Americans, with especially good material on the 1920s and 1930s, a student should look up Rodolfo Acuna's *Occupied America: A History of Chicanos* (New York: Harper and Row, 1988) and a classic in its field, Carey McWilliams's *North from Mexico: The Spanish-Speaking People of the United States* (New York: Praeger, 1990).

The pertinent volume in The Everyday Life in America Series, noted in the bibliographical essay for chapter 1, is Harvey Green's *The Uncertainty of Everyday Life, 1915–1945* (New York: HarperCollins, 1992). Like the others in the series, it is a trove of information and enlightening details on topics ranging from childhood and family life, to eating habits and dress styles, to work, sports, and recreation. For information on how ordinary people responded to the greatest economic disaster in American history, see Carolyn Bird's *The Invisible Scar* (New York: Longman, 1978). Finally, anyone of any age who hopes to get a "feel" for life during the dismal 1930s should turn to a moving and fascinating book, Studs Terkel's *Hard Times: An Oral History of the Great Depression* (New York: Avon Books, 1971). A superb interviewer, Terkel collected and transcribed his conversations with a wide array of Americans from that era—farmers and miners, millionaires and transients, politicians and artists. His book has a special focus on young people. Not only does it include interviews with adults who were children during the hard times, but, interspersed among the depression veterans are conversations with young people of the late 1960s, who speak of their impressions of a time they knew only from history lessons and family stories.

## At Home

The student interested in daily life in American homes can choose from several good sources. On eating and foodways, two excellent social histories are available, both by Harvey Levenstein: *Revolution at the Table: The Transformation of the American Diet* (New York: Oxford University Press, 1988) and *Paradox of Plenty: A Social History of Eating in Modern America* (New York: Oxford University Press, 1993). Both are well written, often entertaining, yet also full of fascinating morsels and well-grounded conclusions about changes in our collective eating habits. The first volume covers the period from the late 19th century through the 1920s; the second takes its topic from the coming of the Great Depression into the 1980s. In both, Levenstein shows how the things we eat and how we eat them reveal much about broader currents of American life: technological transformations, changes in the job force, even our perceptions of ourselves. He also emphasizes how diet differed according to the economic assets of breadwinners. An amusing and instructive history of the breakfast cereal industry is Gerald Carson's *Cornflake Crusade* (New York: Arno Press, 1976).

Unfortunately there is no one, full modern history of the radio and its role in American life. J. Fred MacDonald's *Don't Touch That Dial!: Radio Programming in American Life, 1920–1960* (Chicago: Nelson-Hall, 1979) provides a useful sense of radio's changing offerings to its audience and its daily impact on their lives, while Alice G. Marquis's *Hopes and Ashes: The Birth of Modern Times* (New York: Free Press, 1986) devotes several pages to radio's role in transforming American mores. Edward A. Herron's *Miracle of the Air Waves: A History of Radio* (New York: Messner, 1969) emphasizes the technical side of the subject; and an older work, available in some libraries, contains some interesting detail on the social aspects of the radio, as well as the automobile and motion pictures: Lloyd R. Morris's *Not So Long Ago* (New York: Random House, 1949).

The automobile, on the other hand, has had an excellent historian in James J. Flink, whose *The Car Culture* (Cambridge: MIT Press, 1986) is a splendid work on the transformation brought by this, the most significant technological development of the 20th century. Jean Pierre Bardou's *The Automobile Revolution* (Chapel Hill: University of North Carolina Press, 1982) stresses some of the car's broader, global implications. One of the consequences of the automobile revolution, the modern suburb, is the subject of a superb history that illuminates much more in American life than housing patterns: Kenneth T. Jackson's *Crabgrass Frontier: The Suburbanization of the United States* (New York: Oxford University Press, 1985). Jackson takes his history from the mid-19th century to the 1970s, but some of his most revealing chapters concern the period of this chapter.

General historical surveys have very limited coverage about the difficulties of children in impoverished families during the Great Depression. The excellent published set of documents mentioned in the bibliographical essay for chapter 1, *Children and Youth in America: A Documentary History,* edited by Robert H. Bremner (Cambridge: Harvard University Press, 1971) has some compelling material early in its third volume covering the years 1933 to 1973. Geraldine Youcha's *Minding the Children: Child Care in America From Colonial Times to the Present* (New York: Scribner, 1995) provides excellent detail on family life (among the rich as well as the poor), child care, and institutions dedicated to improving the lives of the young. Especially useful on these years is a chapter on foster care during the depression.

## At Play

For an excellent discussion of the nature of toys and their place in children's lives, see an essay by Bernard Mergen, "Made, Bought, and Stolen: Toys and the Culture of Childhood," in *Small Worlds: Children and Adolescents in America,*

*1850–1950*, edited by Elliott West and Paula Petrik (Lawrence: University Press of Kansas, 1992). And as for the toys themselves, the best sources are those mentioned in the first bibliographical essay. Richard O'Brien's *The Story of American Toys: From Puritans to the Present* (New York: Abbeville Press, 1990) has some especially good sections on some of the toys emphasized in this chapter, such as electric trains, as does Gil Asakawa and Leland Rucker's *The Toy Book* (New York: Alfred A. Knopf, 1992), which is rich in delicious detail and some obscure facts. An older work, now out of print and more difficult to find, is especially good on toys and games of the 1920s and 1930s: Ruth and Larry Freeman's *Cavalcade of Toys* (New York: Century House, 1942).

Anyone interested in the history of films and the relationship between movies and American culture should consult Robert Sklar's *Movie-Made America: A Cultural History of American Movies* (New York: Random House, 1975). While his book covers the years from the birth of the film industry until after mid-century, much of his focus is on the years of this chapter, between the world wars. His chapter on movies and youth and the debates over films' effects on the young, "Movie-Made Children," will be especially interesting to young readers. Sklar also has a brief, but insightful, discussion of Walt Disney and the evolution of Disney's cartoons, subjects that have also drawn the attention of several other scholars. Disney, himself, is the subject of two biographies with somewhat different views of their subject: Bob Thomas's *Walt Disney: An American Original* (New York: Simon and Schuster, 1976) and Marc Eliot's *Walt Disney: Hollywood's Dark Prince: A Biography* (Secaucus, N.J.: Carol Publishing Group, 1993). On the large body of Disney's work, there are several useful works: Russell Merritt, *Walt in Wonderland: The Silent Films of Walt Disney* (Baltimore: Johns Hopkins University Press, 1993), Christopher Finch, *The Art of Walt Disney: From Mickey Mouse to the Magic Kingdoms* (New York: H. N. Abrams, 1975), Richard Schickel, *The Disney Version: The Life, Times, Art, and Commerce of Walt Disney* (New York: Simon and Schuster, 1968), and Leonard Maltin, *The Disney Films* (New York: Crown, 1984). For an intriguing argument about expression of social and political values in film and newspaper cartoons, including those of Disney, take a look at Eric Smoodin's *Animating Culture: Hollywood Cartoons from the Sound Era* (New Brunswick, N.J.: Rutgers University Press, 1993). And to learn something about the youthful movie stars who were enormously popular during these years, see Norman J. Zierold's *The Child Stars* (New York: Coward-McCann, 1965). For the ways young people have been portrayed on the silver screen, see Ruth M. Goldstein and Edith Zornos's *The Screen Image of Youth: Movies about Children and Adolescents* (Metuchen, N.J.: Scarecrow Press, 1980).

Westerns, particular favorites of young people over the years, have also been a popular topic of students of American movies. Three large, well written and amply illustrated books offer plenty of information: John Tuska, *The Filming of the West* (Garden City, N.Y.: Doubleday, 1976), George N. Fenin and William K. Everson, *The Western: From Silents to the Seventies* (New York: Grossman, 1973), and

James Robert Parish and Michael R. Pitts, *The Great Western Pictures* (Metuchen, N.J.: Scarecrow Press, 1976). For even more illustrations, see William K. Everson's *A Pictorial History of the Western Film* (New York: Citadel Press, 1969). Two books discuss how Native Americans have been portrayed (and usually misportrayed) on the screen and how their filmic distortions can teach us something about broader public values: Gretchen M. Bataille and Charles L. P. Silet, eds., *The Pretend Indians: Images of Native Americans in the Movies* (Ames: Iowa State University Press, 1980), and Ralph E. Friar, *The Only Good Indian: The Hollywood Gospel* (New York: Drama Book Specialists, 1972).

Comics, even more than westerns, reveal a great deal about children and their world and values. Less has been written on comic strips and books than on movies, but there are some useful works. For a scholarly approach, see David Kunzle's *History of the Comic Strip* (Berkeley: University of California Press, 1973); and on the technical side of comic illustration, there is Scott McCloud's *Understanding Comics: The Invisible Art* (Northampton, Mass.: Tundra Publishers, 1993). A famous cartoonist himself, Jules Feiffer has given us an insightful look at *The Great Comic Book Heroes* (New York: Dial Press, 1965). For a useful general work, read *The Funnies: An American Idiom*, edited by David Manning White and Robert H. Abel (New York: Free Press of Glencoe, 1963).

## At Work

Basic numbers about children at work, at least in American industry, are most easily found in government documents, and the most accessible of these in libraries typically is *Historical Statistics of the United States,* published by the Census Bureau (see bibliography for chapter 1). There is extensive excellent material as well in Robert H. Bremner's *Children and Youth: A Documentary History,* cited above. Those interested in the history of work around the house (by children as well as parents) can turn to an invaluable source: Susan Strasser's *Never Done: A History of American Housework* (New York: Pantheon Books, 1982), which covers the subject from the mid-19th century nearly to the present, with fascinating discussions and rich detail on household tools and appliances, cooking and clothes-making, child care and household servants. An older work, now out of print, takes a more formal look at family economics; although not as entertaining, it contains important insights into the history of how families have supported themselves and the roles that children have played: Hazel Kyrk's *The Family in the American Economy* (Chicago: University of Chicago Press, 1953). On the changing working life of children, and, more than that, on evolving attitudes toward their economic value, see a fine work cited in the first bibliographical essay, Viviana A. Zelizer's *Pricing the Priceless Child: The Changing Social Value of Children* (New York: Basic Books, 1985).

Glen H. Elder, Jr.'s *Children of the Great Depression: Social Change in Life Experience* (Chicago: University of Chicago Press, 1974) is a sociological study of young people in one American city, Oakland, California, during the calamitous 1930s. As its title suggests, it considers many aspects of children's lives and their responses to the crisis, but its main focus is on the changing economic roles and responsibilities of girls and boys, especially in helping support their families. On the working life and family economy in a very different part of America, a fine source is Jack Temple Kirby's *Rural Worlds Lost: The American South, 1920–1960* (Baton Rouge: Louisiana State University Press, 1987). This excellent study contains much more on the nature of rural southern communities and the drastic changes they experienced during the pivotal years from 1920 to 1940.

Although most available works on child labor emphasize the earlier years of the 20th century, some sources on this period are accessible in larger libraries. Probably the most useful documents were produced by the federal government, through the Children's Bureau and other executive and congressional bodies, as part of its effort to publicize conditions among working children. See, for instance, Helen Wood's *Young Workers and Their Jobs in 1936*, Children's Bureau Publication No. 249 (Washington: Government Printing Office, 1940). Especially rewarding is *Child Labor: Report of the Subcommittee on Child Labor*, based on the White House Conference on Child Health and Protection, which was published privately (New York: Century Company, 1932). A more accessible source, concentrating on child labor on family farms and among migrant laborers, brings together earlier publications from the National Child Labor Committee and other groups: *Children in the Fields*, edited by Dan C. McCurry (New York: Arno Press, 1975).

## At School

On the general history of education during these years, the works of Lawrence A. Cremin, mentioned in the bibliographical essay for chapter 1, are essential for these years: *American Education: The Metropolitan Experience, 1876–1980* (New York: Harper and Row, 1988) and *The Transformation of the School: Progressivism in American Education, 1876–1951* (New York: Alfred A. Knopf, 1961). For a more specific look at the 1930s, see C. A. Bowers, *The Progressive Educator and the Depression: The Radical Years* (New York: Random House, 1969).

Among the most controversial aspects of educational planning and policy was the use of intelligence testing and other such measurements to evaluate students and to channel them along certain paths of training. An especially good book on the history of such tests (and one of the most critical assaults on their uses) is Stephen Jay Gould's *The Mismeasure of Man* (New York: Norton, 1981). Another very useful study is Raymond E. Fancher, *The Intelligence Men: Makers of the IQ Controversy* (New York: Norton, 1985). To learn more specifically about a key figure in the testing phenomenon in the United States and about the application of tests to education and to the "tracking" of students, see Paul Davis Chapman's *Schools as Sorters: Lewis M. Terman, Applied Psychology, and the Intelligence*

*Testing Movement, 1890–1930.* This book also covers the move away from intel-ligence testing toward an annual evaluation of skills and aptitudes.

Although no single history of the Americanization movement is available, stu-dents can learn about the experiences of immigrant children in education and how they were pressured to conform to new habits and values in Selma Berrol's *Immi-grants at School: New York City, 1898–1914* (New York: Arno Press, 1978) as well as *American Education and the European Immigrant,* edited by Bernard Weiss (Urbana: University of Illinois Press, 1982). Far and away the best book on Native American education during these years and up through the 1960s is Margaret Con-nell Szasz's *Education and the American Indian: The Road to Self-Determination since 1928* (Albuquerque: University of New Mexico Press, 1974). For a fine case study of a program of attempted Americanization, see Robert A. Trennert, Jr.'s *The Phoenix Indian School: Forced Assimilation in Arizona, 1891–1935* (Norman: Uni-versity of Oklahoma Press, 1988). The memoir of the man most responsible for shaping the policy to assimilate Native American youth through education, Richard Henry Pratt, has been edited and republished: *Battlefield and Classroom: Four Dec-ades with the American Indians, 1867–1904,* edited by Robert M. Utley (New Haven: Yale University Press, 1964). And for the account of a woman who experienced such schools firsthand as a child, see Louise Udall, *Me and Mine: The Life Story of Helen Sekaquaptewa* (Tucson: University of Arizona Press, 1969).

## Health

Once again, the literature on the history of children's health and public health generally is sadly lacking. Students will find excellent documentary sources in the first, second, and third volumes of Robert H. Bremner's *Children and Youth in America: A Documentary History,* cited above. No book has yet appeared on the important experiment in government support of maternal and infant health, the Sheppard-Towner Act, but Bremner's collection offers valuable material on this law, its application, and the debates surrounding it. Two books noted in the previous bibliographical essay also will be helpful here: Richard A. Meckel's *Save the Babies: American Public Health Reform and the Prevention of Infant Mortality, 1850–1929* (Baltimore: Johns Hopkins University Press, 1990) and a more technical work by Sam Shapiro, et al., *Infant, Perinatal, Maternal, and Childhood Mortality in the United States* (Cambridge: Harvard University Press, 1968). For basic statistics on declining rates of so many diseases common among children in the past, *Historical Statistics of the United States* is again the most accessible source, along with other publications of the U.S. Census Bureau.

On the relationship between diet and health and the changes that occurred during these years, you should turn to two books mentioned earlier in this essay, Harvey Levenstein's *Revolution at the Table* and his *Paradox of Plenty.* In these, Levenstein considers the craze over vitamins and how that concern was used by manufacturers and other businessmen to promote consumption of milk, fruit, and other items in the name of better health. In the second book, especially, he also discusses the ways that diet changed (and more often did not change) among the poor, and he considers the complicated task of evaluating the effects of the Great Depression on children of poverty.

## Children and the Law

If far too little has been written on children and public health, there is a bounty of good books on youth and public programs and the law during 1920–1940, some of the most important years in the evolution of our government and its relationship to our people. For information on child labor reform legislation, two basic works, mentioned in the earlier essay, apply here as well: Walter I. Trattner's *Crusade for the Children: A History of the National Child Labor Committee and Child Labor Reform in America* (Chicago: Quadrangle Books, 1970) and Jeremy Felt's *Hostages of Fortune: Child Labor Reform in New York* (Syracuse: Syracuse University Press, 1965).

The broader topic of how children fared in these sweeping reforms of social policy has inspired two helpful books, although neither are easily available in school and public libraries: Emma Octavia Lundberg's *Unto the Least of These: Social Services for Children* (New York: Appleton-Century-Crofts, Inc., 1947) and Gilbert Steiner's *The Children's Cause* (Washington, D.C.: The Brookings Institution, 1976). Two of the best surveys of the general topic of social welfare and reform, including those problems and solutions especially significant for children, are Walter I. Trattner's *From Poor Law to Welfare State: A History of Social Welfare in America* (New York: Free Press, 1979) and Roy Lubove's *The Struggle for Social Security, 1900–1935* (Cambridge: Harvard University Press, 1968). Another excellent study, written much earlier and difficult to acquire, concerns one New Deal agency created especially for young people and adolescents: Betty Lindley and Ernest K. Lindley's *A New Deal For Youth: The Story of the National Youth Administration* (New York: Viking Press, 1938).

Of the specific programs for children that grew out of the New Deal years, probably the most significant was that regarding public child care and, specifically, Aid for Dependent Children. A recent book cited above, Geraldine Youcha's *Minding the Children*, will give you a fine summary of these developments. Other books can fill in the details, including Margaret O. Steinfels's *Who's Minding the Children? The History and Politics of Day Care in America* (New York: Simon and Schuster, 1973) and Winifred Bell's *Aid to Dependent Children* (New York: Columbia University Press, 1965).

On juvenile delinquency and the juvenile court system during these years, students should start with two sources mentioned in the previous bibliographical essay, Joseph M. Hawes, *The Children's Rights Movement: A History of Advocacy and Protection* (Boston: Twayne Publishers, 1991) and Ellen Ryerson, *The Best-Laid Plans: America's Juvenile Court Experiment* (New York: Hill and Wang, 1978). In this chapter, I have stressed some of the paradoxes and problems that came with the juvenile justice system. The scholar who has worked most extensively with this topic is Stephen Schlossman. Readers should consult his book *Love and the American Delinquent: The Theory and Practice of "Progressive" Juvenile Justice, 1825–1920* (Chicago: University of Chicago Press, 1977). Less accessible is his excellent article (with Stephanie Wallach) "The Crime of Precocious Sexuality: Female Juvenile Delinquency in the Progressive Era," *Harvard Educational Review* 48:1 (February 1978), pp. 65–94, which reveals how this system worked against young women. Another very useful look at the treatment of older girls in this system can be found in Ruth Alexander's chapter " 'The Only Thing I Ever Wanted Was Freedom': Wayward Girls in New York, 1900–1930," in a book cited above, *Small Worlds,* edited by Elliott West and Paula Petrik.

Finally, most of the material in this chapter on the fascinating, disturbing, but highly revealing subject of the changing monetary value of boys and girls in "wrongful death" lawsuits in American courts is covered in Viviana Zelizer's *Pricing the Priceless Child,* also mentioned earlier in this essay.

## Personal Recollections

A good starting place for personal recollections is the collection of interviews cited above, Studs Terkel's *Hard Times: An Oral History of the Great Depression.* Terkel has a section devoted specifically to children's memories as well as many interviews with parents about family life and child rearing. One of the best and most widely praised memoirs of recent years (and winner of the prestigious Pulitzer Prize) is Russell Baker's *Growing Up* (New York: Congdon and Weed, Inc., 1982). Baker, who went on to become one of America's most respected journalists (and winner of another Pulitzer Prize for his newspaper commentaries), was born into a poor Appalachian family. In this family reminiscence, he tells of his early childhood, his move with his mother to Baltimore during the Great Depression, and of his teenage years. His beautifully written book is brimming with telling detail about youth in these years and about American life generally during this turbulent time.

Another prizewinning author, Maya Angelou, has written a powerful memoir about growing up as an African American in this period: *I Know Why the Caged Bird Sings* (New York: Random House, 1969 and later editions). Angelou's book is especially interesting because in her youth she moved between two ways of life among black Americans, spending her earliest years in a small town in southern Arkansas and later moving to a major urban gathering place for blacks, East St. Louis. Her reminiscence is among the finest in our autobiographical literature. Another African American memoir by a prominent figure in the arts is Gordon Parks's *A Choice of Weapons* (New York: Harper and Row, 1966). As was the case with Angelou, family difficulties required him to move from one part of the country to another. Parks, who became one of the nation's most respected photographers as well as a successful writer and composer, grew up in a small town in Kansas; then on the death of his mother he went to live with his sister in St. Paul, Minnesota.

A fine memoir by a Japanese-American writer who grew up as part of a middle-class family in the Pacific Northwest is Monica Sone, *Nisei Daughter* (Boston: Little, Brown and Co., 1953). For a superb remembrance by the son of other immigrants, Jews from Russia, living on the other side of the continent in Brooklyn, New York, there is Alfred Kazin's *A Walker in the City* (New York: Harcourt, Brace and Co., 1951 and later editions). In time, Kazin would become a leading literary and social critic. His account of urban life is vital and sensual, full of memories of smells and sights as well as commentary on the significance of religion, family, and neighborhood in his early life. A classic memoir by the product of yet another immigrant experience is Ernesto Galarza's *Barrio Boy* (Notre Dame: University of Notre Dame Press, 1971). Galarza was born in a small mountain town in Mexico and immigrated to the southwestern United States with his family. His account provides a fascinating look at life from both sides of our southern border.

## NOTES

1. Steven Mintz and Susan Kellogg, *Domestic Revolutions: A Social History of American Family Life* (New York: The Free Press, 1988), 141.

2. Robert L. Griswold, *Fatherhood in America: A History* (New York: Basic Books, 1993), 101.

3. Ibid., 133.

4. Monica Sone, *Nisei Daughter* (Boston: Little, Brown and Company, 1953), 69–70.

5. Vicki Ruiz, " 'Star Struck': Acculturation, Adolescence, and Mexican American Women, 1920–1950," in Elliott West and Paula Petrik, eds., *Small Worlds: Children and Adolescents in America, 1850–1950* (Lawrence: University Press of Kansas, 1992), 69.

6. Ibid., 71.

7. Kenneth T. Jackson, *Crabgrass Frontier: The Suburbanization of the United States* (New York: Oxford University Press, 1985), 157.

8. Ibid., 162.

9. Ibid., 173.

10. Ibid.

11. Ibid., 187.

12. Studs Terkel, *Hard Times: An Oral History of the Great Depression* (New York: Avon Books, 1971), 107–08.

13. Geraldine Youcha, *Minding the Children: Child Care in America from Colonial Times to the Present* (New York: Scribner, 1995), 286.

14. Terkel, *Hard Times*, 123.

15. Flannery Lewis, *Brooks Too Broad for Leaping: A Chronicle from Childhood* (New York: Macmillan, 1938), 257.

16. Bernard Mergen, "Made, Bought, and Stolen," in West and Petrik, eds., *Small Worlds,* 102.

17. Ibid., 86.

18. Glen H. Elder, Jr., *Children of the Great Depression: Social Change in Life Experience* (Chicago: University of Chicago Press, 1974), 66–67.

19. Viviana A. Zelizer, *Pricing the Priceless Child: The Changing Social Value of Children* (New York: Basic Books, 1985), 77.

20. Homer Folks, *Changes and Trends in Child Labor and Its Control* (New York: National Child Labor Committee), 9.

21. Zelizer, *Pricing the Priceless Child,* 77–78.

22. Dan C. McCurry, ed., *Children in the Fields* (New York: Arno Press, 1975), 182–86.

23. *Child Labor: Report of the Subcommittee on Child Labor* (New York: The Century Company, 1932), 219–61.

24. McCurry, *Children in the Fields,* 8–9.

25. Ibid., 10.

26. Stephen Jay Gould, *The Mismeasure of Man* (New York: Norton, 1981), 161.

27. Ibid., 179.

28. Paul Davis Chapman, *Schools as Sorters: Lewis M. Terman, Applied Psychology, and the Intelligence Testing Movement, 1890–1930* (New York: New York University Press, 1988).

29. Robert H. Bremner, ed., *Children and Youth in America: A Documentary History,* Vol. II (Cambridge: Harvard University Press, 1971), 1325–26.

30. Ibid., 1321–22.

31. Ibid., 1321.

32. Harvey Green, *The Uncertainty of Everyday Life, 1915–1945* (New York: HarperCollins, 1992), 125.

33. Frederick E. Hoxie, *A Final Promise: The Campaign to Assimilate the Indians, 1880–1920* (Cambridge: Cambridge University Press, 1984), 198.

34. Louise Udall, *Me and Mine: The Life Story of Helen Sekaquaptewa as Told to Louise Udall* (Tucson: University of Arizona Press, 1969), 31–32.

35. Hoxie, *A Final Promise,* 106, 201; Arrell Morgan Gibson, *The American Indian: Prehistory to the Present* (Lexington, Mass.: D. C. Heath and Co., 1980), 432.

36. Bremner, ed., *Children and Youth in America,* Vol. II, 1011.

37. Ibid., 1016, 1120–21, 1024–25.

38. Fort Yates Children's Drawings, Ayer Collection, Newberry Library, Chicago, Illinois.

39. Harvey Levenstein, *Revolution at the Table: The Transformation of the American Diet* (New York: Oxford University Press, 1988), 27–9, 178–81; Harvey Levenstein, *Paradox of Plenty: A Social History of Eating in Modern America* (New York: Oxford University Press, 1993), 60–61.

40. Winifred Bell, *Aid to Dependent Children* (New York: Columbia University Press, 1965), 5–6.

41. Stephen Schlossman and Stephanie Wallach, "The Crime of Precocious Sexuality: Female Juvenile Delinquency in the Progressive Era," *Harvard Educational Review* 48:1 (February 1978): 75.

42. Ibid., 75–76.

43. Zelizer, *Pricing the Priceless Child,* 156.

44. Ibid.

# Chapter 3

# 1941–1960

## INTRODUCTION

The Great Depression ended in the late 1930s with the onset of war in Europe. On one side were the Axis nations, led by Germany, Italy, and Japan, and, on the other, the Allied powers, England and France. By the end of 1941 the Allies were joined by the Soviet Union and the United States after those countries had been attacked, respectively, by Germany and Japan. After Axis countries first occupied most of Europe and north Africa and much of eastern and southeast Asia, the Allies gradually regained the initiative. During 1944, the reconquest of Europe began with invasions from both west and east, and, in the Pacific, the United States began to press toward Japan. In May 1945, Germany surrendered. Early in August, the United States dropped atomic bombs on two Japanese cities, and within days of the second, Japan's government asked for peace. The bloodiest and most costly war in human history was over.

In the United States, World War II brought massive government spending and a surge of demand for many kinds of goods. The number of unemployed, which had never fallen below eight million since the early depression year of 1932, dropped to virtually nothing by 1942. Wages surged and banks began to fill once more with Americans' savings. Our country was entering an era of unprecedented affluence. The price for the return of good times was a terrible one, however. Nearly 300,000 American soldiers died, far more than in any other conflict except the Civil War, and hundreds of thousands more were seriously wounded. (Our toll was not nearly as great as that of others; the Soviet Union alone lost an estimated twenty million persons.)

The war ended with the United States as the most powerful nation in the world. By 1947, however, our government, Great Britain, and other western European nations found themselves increasingly at odds with the Soviet Union, its allies, and the countries it controlled. This confrontation, the "Cold War," became far more ominous in the early 1950s when the Soviet Union developed its own atomic weapons. The Cold War dominated world diplomacy throughout these two decades and beyond. Its most violent episode was the Korean War (1950–1953), in which the United States fought with South Korea and other allies against invading forces of North Korea and the People's Republic of China. More than 33,000 American troops died in the conflict. The 1950s proved to be years of both power and insecurity, anxiety and affluence.

During the years between 1941 and 1960, one thing can be said with certainty about children: There were a lot more of them. As mentioned at the start of the last chapter, during the Great Depression, many men and women put off marrying and having children. The reason was obvious: they were worried about paying the bills that marriage and children always bring. But starting in the early 1940s, millions of couples changed their minds and began marrying and making babies at a pace the nation had not witnessed for decades. The war brought a boom in jobs, so the main reason for postponing the decision—economic uncertainty—disappeared. Couples also chose to marry, and often to begin a family, before the man headed off for war, hoping to have some intimate life together in the face of the terrible possibility of the husband's death on the battlefield. The result was a large number of "good-bye" babies born between 1942 and 1946.

The real surge, however, would come during the heady and confident years after the Allied victory. Japan surrendered in August of 1945; nine months later, during May 1946, 233,452 babies were born in the United States—a jump of about 13 percent from a few months earlier. A month later, in June, births increased by another ten thousand; in October, nearly 340,000 American mothers bore babies. The nation had embarked on a birthing frenzy, one of the greatest population booms in modern history.

A poll taken at the end of the war showed that women wanted to have an average of 4.2 children. The postwar years brought better times (economically, at least) than many had dreamed possible, and that affluence fueled a desire to pursue another part of the American dream: a fulfilling family life, including plenty of daughters and sons. In fact, there was a huge demand during these years for "black market babies," infants, usually illegitimate, bought for as much as $2,000 by parents unable to produce their own. Such transactions were illegal in only a minority of states. The fertile American family quickly made useless all predictions about the national population. Experts in the 1930s, looking at sagging birth rates of their day, had thought that the U.S. population would never reach 200 million, a level it was to attain by 1968. A study by highly respected researchers in 1943 estimated that the 1980 population would be 153 million; in fact, it would be more than 226 million.

The great fertility turnaround happened during, and partly because of, the world war. In 1932, at the depth of the Great Depression, about 56 marriages occurred for every thousand unmarried women. That number was rising as times got better—it was up to 73 by 1939—but then it really jumped, up to 93 in 1942 and 118 right after war's end, in 1946. That figure was far higher than at any time in the 20th century. With all those marriages, one result was sure to follow—many more babies. One way to show this is to look at the number of births in a year for every thousand women of prime child-bearing age, between fifteen and forty-four years old:

### Annual Births per Women, 15–44 Years

| | |
|---|---|
| 1932 | 81.7 |
| 1940 | 79.9 |
| 1943 | 94.3 |
| 1945 | 85.9 |
| 1946 | 101.9 |
| 1947 | 113.3 |
| 1950 | 106.2 |
| 1955 | 118.5 |
| 1957 | 122.9 |
| 1960 | 118.0 |
| 1965 | 96.6[1] |

The figures for the 1950s were the highest since before World War I. Not only were more couples deciding to have children, they were also producing larger families than in the past. Between 1940 and 1960, the birth rate for third children doubled, and that for fourth children tripled.

This was the famous "baby boom," one of the most important features of American life after World War II. It reflected the popular mood during what was surely one of the most optimistic, self-confident eras of our past. An expert in family life wrote that parents "believe in themselves, believe in America, and believe in babies."[2] In a sense the jump in birth rates was a burst of national energy and emotion, a release of pent-up restraint and a dispelling of doubt.

Yet the "baby boom" had its troubling aspects. Americans were also producing children at a much younger age—too much so, according to some opinion. More recently, during the 1980s and 1990s, there was mounting concern over teenage pregnancies, but the birth rate among teen-age girls was higher—much higher, in fact—during the 1950s. Out of every 1,000 females in 1957 between the ages of fifteen and nineteen, 97 delivered a baby. (The figure for 1983 was only 52.) Many of those young women were married (and often pregnant at the time they exchanged vows); many others, however, bore children outside of wedlock. The number of infants born to unmarried women, then put up for adoption, increased by 80 percent between 1944 and 1955.[3]

The grand rise in marriages and births, furthermore, eventually led to an equally impressive increase in another institution—divorce. There was a startling burst of divorces in 1946, nearly 18 per 1,000 married women, twice the rate of 1940. The divorce rate then settled down for more than twenty years before starting to rise again sharply in the late 1960s—just as all those babies born in the boom began maturing and leaving home.

Fueling this surge in births was another kind of boom—economic. The postwar years were the most affluent by far in American history up to that time. The most fundamental measurement of our economy is the gross national product, or GNP, which represents the total monetary value of all goods produced and services rendered by American workers. During the fifteen years after the end of World War II, the GNP shot upward, increasing more than two and a half times. Americans' average "disposable income," or money available to spend, nearly doubled.

The most startling result was the growth in that part of the public classified as "middle class." (In the 1950s, that meant people with incomes between $3,000 and $10,000 in "constant dollars," or income adjusted for the rise and fall in prices.) In the 1920s, a decade also known for its prosperity, 31 percent of our population was middle class; in the 1950s, the figure was 60 percent. Another traditional definition of a middle-class person is one who is paid on the basis of an annual salary instead of an hourly or daily rate, the usual wages for the working class. Between 1947 and 1957, the number of salaried employees grew by more than 60 percent.

Year by year, more and more families found themselves able to buy material comforts and pleasures unthinkable in an earlier time. To many, the American dream seemed to be at hand.

Yet many Americans remained in desperate poverty. Statistics, as always, could be misleading. Although the middle class grew dramatically, the number of poor people in this country increased as well, and their share of the nation's wealth remained appallingly low. In 1947 the most impoverished 20 percent of the population (about 28 million people) received only 3.5 percent of all personal income. In 1960, the figures were actually worse: the poorest 20 percent (now about 36 million persons) got only 3.2 percent. (The richest 20 percent, on the other hand, got 45.6 percent in 1947 and 44.0 percent in 1960.) America as a whole, in other words, was making a lot more money, and more families were crowding into the middle class; but the distribution of wealth, the way money was spread over the nation's families, stayed pretty much the same.

World War II and its aftermath did much to set the course of family life for the rest of the century—its restless movement, its prolific birth rate, and some of its stresses and the seeds of its later difficulties. Persistent problems and old contradictions remained, with grinding poverty amid prosperity, great promise and enduring limitations.

## AT HOME

World War II, the baby boom, and postwar prosperity combined to effect great changes in the daily lives of American young people. For one thing, families were set in motion. To millions of boys and girls, "home" was a moving target.

Americans have always been fond of moving from place to place, but rarely, if ever, had families moved around the country at as vigorous a clip as they did during World War II. In the spring of 1945, as the war in Europe wound to a close, about 15,000,000 people, or roughly one out of every ten Americans, lived in a different county from the one they had lived in when the Japanese attacked Pearl Harbor. (These figures do not include an even greater number of men and women who were moving about because they were in the armed forces.) That frenzy of movement continued, stimulated by wartime activity. All told, about 25,000,000 people left home during and right after the war and did not go back. Nearly half of them moved to a different state.

The most common reason, of course, was to take new jobs. During the harsh years of the Great Depression, families took to the road and fathers left home to wander in an often fruitless search for work. Now, people were on the move because all of a sudden there was plenty of work. Fathers left for one kind of guaranteed government employment—service in war. Many families pulled up stakes and migrated to booming areas where jobs were waiting to be filled. Ironically, the war also took jobs away, as some civilian products were considered unnecessary in the face of mobilizing for the military effort. Hundreds of thousands were laid off—about 175,000 were set loose from automobile plants in the first month of 1942, and those workers set off in search of new positions that quickly appeared in other industries.

The result was a series of great tidal shifts in the national population, just as there had been during and after World War I, when huge numbers of African Americans, for instance, had left the South for northern cities. The trend in the 1940s was to the West, where many new wartime industries were located. A few remarkable statistics suggest just how great this movement was. In only two months of 1942, January and February, a million persons moved to the three states along the Pacific coast. The older states, the ones where the great concentrations of people had always been, grew too, but not nearly so fast. Pennsylvania increased by barely half a million in the 1940s, New York by a little more than a million. California, on the other hand, had an increase of over 3.5 million between 1940 and 1950. In those booming states, families were crowding into places that turned, almost overnight, from fairly sleepy towns into congested cities. Between 1940 and 1943, the population of Richmond, California, near San Francisco, soared from under 24,000 to more than 135,000 as the government and private industries built several wartime facilities. Four shipyards alone employed 90,000 persons. (The California boom has been one of the most significant national events of this century. Its increase in population between 1900 and 1970, about 19 million, was roughly equal to all immigrants who came to America during the entire 19th century).

Children were an important part of the massive wartime migration. People who cut their roots and headed for better opportunities were likely to be young couples with sons and daughters to take along. The U.S. Census Bureau classified more than one out of every five children born between 1941 and 1947 as a "migrant." In a nation frantically on the move, children were the most mobile Americans of all.

More remarkably yet, the American people kept moving during the years that followed. As the country continued to change dramatically after the war—as new opportunities opened and new difficulties arose, as more automobiles were driven along more and better highways, and as air travel expanded—families had both the reasons and the ability to change their place of residence. By the 1960s, the typical American family would move five times during one generation, sometimes across town, but often to another part of the nation. The percentage of Americans who moved during a year from one state to another was 3.2 in 1960, actually higher than the 3 percent in 1947, during the frenzy right after the war. In 1969 the number was higher still (3.5 percent). We have always been, to some degree, a people on the move. But World War II set Americans more actively in motion, and they have not slowed down since.

This mobility naturally was encouraged by—and in turn encouraged—the automobile. Car sales had increased almost every year before World War II, even during the depression. They slowed during the war because the government limited production, but afterwards, with money to spend and a renewed emphasis on moving around, Americans once again turned to cars with a great passion. At war's end there were 25 million cars registered in the country; five years later there were 40 million, and in 1960, 60 million. For the first time, in fact, families began buying second cars, so both parents could go about their auto-business independently. The number of two-car families doubled between 1951 and 1958. If the car had become a familiar part of most children's lives before 1941, by 1960 it was virtually inescapable.

The spread of the car culture, plus the baby boom and the return of good times, inspired millions of families not just to move but to seek out new styles of home life. During the war, couples had postponed the pursuit of many dreams. One of the dearest was the desire to own a roomy house where they and their children could find comfort and privacy. After 1945, many of the barriers that had stood in the way of that dream vanished. These couples had money and a job. Moreover, the arrival of babies quickly pressed them to find more room.

The result was one of the greatest housing shortages in American history. Builders had to start almost from a dead stop, as the nation's productive efforts during the war had been diverted from producing houses. Demand for houses ran far, far faster than the supply, just as the need for schoolrooms, teachers, and pediatricians increased much faster than their availability. There were some strange consequences. In Chicago, 250 families bought abandoned trolley cars for houses, while others in North Dakota were living in old grain bins. An advertisement in an Omaha newspaper offered a "Big Ice Box" for sale, seven by seventeen feet, which "could be fixed up and lived in." A desperate, but imaginative, newlywed couple in New York City lived for two days in a department store window; their plan was to find someplace to live through the publicity.

But help was on the way. The intense housing shortage quickly produced a phenomenal construction boom. In 1944 only about 144,000 new single-family houses were begun; in 1950, there were nearly 1,700,000 such housing starts. Some of these new homes were built in older areas of cities, but the most frenzied activity by far was taking place on the metropolitan outskirts—in the suburbs, where millions of acres of farmland and other open country were converted into neighborhoods of family houses. Suburbs, as mentioned previously, had first appeared in the late 19th century, when public transportation lines allowed families with enough money to live outside the congested centers of cities. They had boomed earlier, during the 1920s, another prosperous period when the automobile first liberated families to look for houses away from the city center and the rail lines.

Now, after World War II, the suburban migration of middle-class Americans leapt forward again. Population growth in the new housing developments, or "subdivisions," was fifteen times greater than in any other segment of society. By 1955, three out of four new houses in metropolitan areas were being built in suburbs in these outlying areas. For more and more American children, "at home" meant the suburbs.

These houses and neighborhoods would be home to millions of young Americans who grew up during these postwar years. They would be at the center of their memories of childhood. The model, in many ways, was one of the first suburban communities, and certainly one of the most famous: Levittown, built on four thousand acres of potato farmland on Long Island, New York. The builders, Levitt and Sons, applied the techniques of mass production to house building. Each house was built in twenty-seven precise steps. Land was bulldozed, cement slabs laid down, then the houses assembled from parts largely pre-assembled elsewhere. The Levitts also cut their own lumber, made much of their own materials, even grew their own trees. At their peak of production, the company was building about thirty houses every day. The typical dwelling was of "Cape Cod" design; each had a living room with fireplace, a kitchen, bath, and a couple of bedrooms. Houses also came with many appliances, including clothes washer, outdoor barbeque, and television with a twelve-and-a-half-inch screen built into the wall. The first Levitt houses sold for $7,900, with no down payment and installments of $60 per month for veterans. The price was attractive, as rent for a modest apartment in nearby New York City often was $90 to $100 a month. Eventually, more than 17,000 houses were built and sold

Rushing by the millions to the fringes of the cities, middle-class parents and their children chased the American dream in blossoming suburbs like this one outside Dallas, Texas. *From the collections of the Texas/Dallas History and Archives Division, Dallas Public Library.*

in Levittown. They were home to a population of more then 82,000, a very large percentage of them children.

Levittown was unusual in its size and scope. It was, after all, an entire town built from scratch, with meeting halls, several swimming pools, parks, and recreational facilities. On the fringes of most cities were smaller new developments and subdivisions. All, however, shared certain traits. First, they were on the periphery of urban centers, where the techniques of mass construction worked best. From 1945 to 1954, an estimated 9 million people shifted to these outer areas. Second, people and houses were spread out in these suburbs, with homes built on relatively large lots with spaces between them. Third, in these neighborhoods, the architectural styles were strikingly similar. A few basic patterns and plans were repeated over and over, block upon block. Fourth, these houses were relatively inexpensive, as compared to housing in many parts of the city. Suburban living was financially accessible to a huge portion of the American middle class.

Fifth and finally, these developments were also economically, racially, and culturally homogenous. The poorest Americans could not afford these houses and the rich could afford better. Government policy aggravated this tendency. The Federal Housing Authority (FHA), begun under the New Deal of the 1930s, and the Veterans Administration provided support for mortgages to help families trying to find their own new housing. The policies of these agencies, however, clearly favored the middle class. After 1948, the FHA spent most of its funds to help build single-family, privately owned homes—the housing, that is, of the expanding middle class—and cut back drastically on support for the kinds of rental units that poorer Americans could afford. The FHA also "red-lined" large areas of American cities, drawing boundaries around older urban sections and refusing to guarantee loans within them. The reason, they said, was that a possible black migration into such places, a "Negro invasion," would threaten property values. The effect was further to encourage development outside the city centers and to deny African American families the chance to finance new housing.

Meantime, out in the suburbs, the new subdivisions almost always officially excluded black families. Not a single African American could be found among Levittown's 82,000 inhabitants. Other new subdivisions also barred Jews and Catholics from purchasing houses. Segregation by race and cultural background, of course, had been a fact of life throughout the century. But suburbanization brought a new level of separation, with the distance between different peoples measured more in miles than in city blocks. To the growing middle class on the fringes of the American city, poverty and people of other racial and ethnic origins were virtually invisible.

So a boy or girl growing up in the mid-1950s, especially if he or she was of the middle class, was far more likely to be a suburbanite, compared to even ten years earlier. In those subdivisions, nicknamed "babyvilles," children were surrounded by other children. America had become increasingly "child-centered," and this was most obvious on the city fringes. Much of suburban social and community life was focused on schools, young people's sports, and other children's activities. Polled on why they had chosen to live where and how they had, suburban parents answered over and over: "It's a better way of life for raising kids."

The houses themselves, compared to those of earlier generations, were roomier. Before, as discussed in the previous chapters, families often doubled up, with relatives, boarders, and unrelated families crowding into one dwelling. That pattern was even more prevalent during the hard times of the Great Depression and the housing crunch in boom areas during World War II. Now, in the postwar era, new opportunities set families on the move, often taking them from their children's grandparents and other relatives; but the same opportunities also gave families adequate money to live on their own and to buy the space to spread out. In 1950, America's 38 million families were living in 46 million dwellings, or 1.2 families per unit. Even more remarkable, in nearly 85 percent of all households, there was at least one room for each person living there. A child might have to share a bedroom with a brother or sister—although sons and daughters having rooms entirely to themselves were increasingly common—but the space available to play and find privacy within the house still was far greater than in previous generations.

Houses, in fact, had enough room to feature different "zones" of activities. One of the most popular housing models of the 1950s was the "ranch house." Usually one-story, these homes featured low pitched roofs, large rooms, open space indoors, and lots of windows. They were associated with the more informal lifestyles of the West Coast, California in particular, where so many newly mobile Americans continued to establish their homes. The emphasis was on "livability." Through ranch-style houses, built by the tens of thousands in suburbs from North Carolina and New Jersey to Illinois, the California boom was influencing the rest of the country.

Coming home from school to such a house, a girl or boy might enter through a kitchen door. (The kitchen often faced conveniently onto the front yard and the street, so busy mothers could look out and check on their playing children.) This was the family's working zone, where many household labors took place—the kitchen and utility area, with washer and dryer. From here, the child would pass quickly into a second area, the zone of play and family leisure. There was at least a living room and, near it, often a "family" or "recreation" room. Where there were younger children, the floor might be cluttered with toys; with older ones, games, sports equipment, maybe a ping-pong table. In these years, with their emphasis on companionship among family members and the freedom of boys and girls to express themselves and have fun, there was room for romping and, increasingly, to enjoy the new technologies of television and phonograph recordings. Some called this part of the house the "don't say no" space, where children could let loose. (And with loud television and then rock and roll music, parents sought their own space for quieter relaxation and reading.)

Beyond this leisure zone lay the zone of privacy, the bedrooms and baths. The son or daughter could head for his or her own room to listen to records or radio, read comic books, or, depending on the mood, to daydream or sulk. This daily fact of life—a child's separate bedroom of private space— was in some ways the era's most revolutionary development for middle-class youth. More often than not, a boy or girl would share that room with a brother or sister. But still, the privacy and sense of independence and territorial possession, the unquestioned assumption that there was some place to go to be away from adults, would have been strange, indeed, for most American children in the past. In some ways that room became the center of the growing child's life and identity.

The middle-class parents, too, had their own "master bedroom," an is-land of privacy, usually further enhanced with a "master bathroom," con-taining toilet, bath, and sometimes a dressing area exclusively for their own use. Often the master bedroom suite was slightly isolated from their chil-dren's rooms by a hall. With their respective doors shut, and perhaps locked, parents and children could withdraw into their own spheres.

Houses, as always, reflected prevailing attitudes and values. The subur-ban home celebrated the importance of children, the companionship among older and younger family members, and the comforts that America's new wealth could buy. But these houses also showed how American parents and children were becoming increasingly isolated. The lives of new suburbanites were turned more and more inward, away from the world outside their freshly painted walls. Even neighbors were often something like strangers, and as suburbs spread farther and farther from other parts of the cities, white middle-class youngsters were growing to maturity with little or no contact with others their age from different racial, ethnic, or economic ways of life. Inside their suburban homes lived only the nuclear family. Not only did relatives live in different houses; they very likely lived in another town or state, perhaps on the other side of the country. Visiting grandma and grandpa became a special occasion, indeed. And even at home, there was now space for the family to break apart for several waking hours in the day, with parents going one way, children another, all under the same roof. Children and parents, urged to be companions and fellow playmates, had never lived so separated from each other.

In the new American home, a particular piece of technological furniture was quickly becoming the center of family life: the television set. Americans had carried on a passionate love affair with radio and movies. Television, however, spread through our national culture more quickly than any other innovation. It soon altered children's patterns of living, their language, their education, even their ways of looking at and thinking about the world.

The technological basics of television date from early in the 20th century, and the first experiments in broadcasting took place in the 1920s, about the time of the spread of radio. The earliest regular television broadcasts came in the 1930s, and, by the end of that decade, sets were available for sale. Initially, television sets were expensive and programming was limited and primitive. In 1940, there were fewer than four thousand sets in the entire country.

That soon changed. After World War II, television rapidly became an essential and unavoidable part of American life. In 1946, about 6,000 sets were manufactured. Seven years later annual production had grown to 7 million sets. In 1948, 100,000 households had televisions. Two years later, 3.9 million did, and in 1960, 50 million. That figure represented about 86 percent of all American families, and the numbers continued to climb. Ten years later nearly 99 percent of the nation's households had at least one set, and many had two or more. In America of the 1980s, there were more televisions than bathtubs.

Some reasons for television's rocketing popularity were obvious. It was a medium that went beyond radio to bring both sound and visual images into the home. As the number of sets increased, more programming became commercially viable, and the range of possibilities expanded. Not only was a wide variety of entertainment televised, but other traditional national pastimes, diversions and interests, from sports to politics to holiday parades, appeared on the home screen. Television widened enormously the possible exposure of ordinary people to the world.

Television also was perfectly suited to other trends and traits of this period of American history. For one thing, this fairly expensive piece of entertaining furniture became available just as more people had more money to spend. Many of the more affluent families were determined to own their own homes and to spend more time there, finding amusement among themselves. In the suburbs, there was less public life easily available, no shops or saloons or markets within a short walk. Families turned inward and found their "public" life, their connection to the world, increasingly through electronic media inside their houses. A television set became the evening gathering place for parents and children.

One consequence was a growing danger to other kinds of amusements and activities that earlier children and families had enjoyed. Radio had delivered a blow to the phonograph recording industry. Television, in turn, threatened both radio and another entertainment staple, motion pictures.

By the late 1950s, the time spent listening to radio had dropped by more than half since the previous decade. In 1946, the baby boom's first year, 90 million people went to at least one movie every week, and, to meet that demand, more than four hundred films were produced in that year. Then, with millions of more babies to care for at home, all of those new mortgages to pay, and so many families heading for the suburbs and away from the downtown theaters, movie attendance crashed. By 1953 the crowds buying tickets for films had thinned by half. Business in America's restaurants also shrank alarmingly as families tended more to stay at home, often watching their favorite evening programs while eating appropriately named "TV dinners" served on "TV trays."

Children proved to be the most enthusiastic television viewers of all. By 1960, nine out of ten six-year-old girls and boys were watching "the tube" every day. By age twelve, the typical American child was spending almost as much time in front of the television as in the classroom—nearly four hours. And by no means did they confine their time to shows intended only for them. A survey in 1960 revealed that children typically spent the majority of their watching hours on "adult" programs—crime, variety, westerns, and "situation comedies," or "sitcoms."

That last category became television's most enduring type of program. Reflecting the postwar focus on the home and rearing children, sitcoms almost always concerned families and family life. These programs also conformed to the images and values of middle-class families in the suburbs. Just as those neighborhoods were dominated almost entirely by white Americans, so virtually all sitcom families had one thing in common: they were white and showed little if any influence of minority ethnic experiences. On radio, Jews and African Americans had often been portrayed in undignified and unflattering stereotypes, but at least their presence was recognized. Now, on this new medium, an audience could watch weekly comedy and dramatic programs without ever suspecting that Asians, Hispanics, eastern and southern Europeans, or African Americans existed within the national boundaries. (The great exception was one of the most popular shows of the time, "I Love Lucy." Its stars were Lucille Ball and Dezi Arnaz, husband and wife in real life, who played Lucy and Ricky Ricardo, she a scatterbrained housewife and he a Cuban bandleader. Producers at first had been extremely reluctant to include Arnaz, but Ball, an extremely popular performer, pressured them into writing him into the storyline.)

Within that sameness, however, there were interesting differences in the family images shown in those programs. In some, especially those set among the working class, fathers and husbands were clownish figures.

Chester Riley in "The Life of Riley" was easily manipulated by his wife, children, and friends; and Ralph Kramden and Ed Norton in "The Honeymooners" were forever hatching hairbrained schemes to increase their skimpy paychecks and to chase impractical daydreams. Ozzie Nelson in "The Adventures of Ozzie and Harriet" and Dagwood Bumstead in "Blondie" (based on a popular comic strip) were suburban equivalents of these likeable, but bumbling, characters. Dagwood was frequently fooled even by his dogs. Wives and mothers in these shows often were stronger, shrewder, and more self-confident characters. But other programs, invariably set among the middle class of the suburbs, showed both parents, but especially fathers, in a much more idealized and positive light. In "Father Knows Best" and "The Donna Reed Show," for instance, parents were financially untroubled, stable, good natured, and always a source of wisdom and understanding.

These programs, then, reflected both uncertainties and aspirations about parents' roles in an age of rapid change. Just what were fathers supposed to do? Working in traditional blue-collar labor or on the farm earned them little respect. Fathers who tried and failed to exert authority in the home were scorned and ridiculed, and so were those who did not have what it took to move up the social and economic ladder. The ideal families, on the other hand, were always headed by middle-class parents living, naturally, in the suburbs. Fathers seemed to make money effortlessly in distant occupations that were never really identified. At home, they helped maintain the household, doing odd jobs and mowing the lawn. Mothers kept house immaculately, doing a great deal of dusting and vacuuming and producing hearty meals and after-school snacks. Both parents' main tasks seemed to be to provide for and watch over their children—making their youngsters' lives secure and comfortable, exerting modest discipline, and dispensing sound, helpful advice.

Those sons and daughters were invariably clean-cut and good spirited. Their difficulties were those of anyone growing up wholesome—acceptance among school friends, early romantic involvements (free of all but the most innocent sexuality), homework, and making a little spending money. There was no hint of darker worries of the day, such as juvenile delinquency. Symbols of youthful rebellion, such as dress and rock and roll, were treated in a sanitized, nonthreatening way. One popular member of a television family, Ricky Nelson, joined a well-dressed rock and roll group on "The Adventures of Ozzie and Harriet," then went on, outside the series, to establish his own career as rock singer and guitarist Rick Nelson. Perhaps the best known and most characteristic of these idealized programs was

"Leave It to Beaver," which ran originally between 1957 and 1963 and has continued successfully in re-runs ever since. The Cleaver family lived at 211 Pine Street in Mayfield, the essence of stable suburbia. Theodore, nicknamed "Beaver" or "Beav" by his older brother, Wally, and his parents, Ward and June, experienced the usual range of safe adventures and resolvable crises basic to television's view of family life. The closest thing to a threat to established order was Wally's friend Eddie Haskell, an obsequious and sly teenager always up to some mild mischief.

Family sitcoms expressed the confident goals of middle-class America in the prosperous postwar years. They offered a comfortable escape from the anxieties of an often turbulent and uncertain world. (By an appropriate coincidence, the first episode of "Leave It to Beaver" appeared the same day the Soviet Union launched Sputnik, the first man-made satellite ever put into orbit, an event that triggered something close to a panic about national security and America's world leadership.) These shows soothed the worries of their viewers. Their firm implication was that the young Americans on the screen—and, presumably, those watching from their own living rooms—would grow up to live well-adjusted, prosperous lives with families of their own in some future middle-class neighborhood. An exchange between Ward and June Cleaver, the parents on "Leave It to Beaver," summed up this ideal:

*Ward:* What type of girl would you have Wally [their elder son] marry?

*June:* Oh, some very sensible girl from a nice family . . . one with both feet on the ground, who's a good cook, and can keep a nice house, and see that he's happy.[4]

Here, in these confident sitcoms, was the essential expression of the baby boom ideal.

Children's mealtimes, like their entertainments, revealed much about their life at home. For one thing, on average, boys and girls were eating considerably more, a reflection of what has been called our "age of affluence." During World War II and the fifteen years that followed it, politicians and public spokesmen boasted that the United States had become the best-fed society in history. Rising incomes gave more families more to spend on food, and they took advantage of it, even more so than the experts predicted. Usually, economists have found, when people make more money, they tend to spend it on things other than what they eat; that is, as people bring home larger paychecks, their food budgets might go up, but they also buy a lot of other goods and the portion of their income spent for the dinner table actually goes down. However, in 1953, with incomes way up, a typical family was spending 26 percent of its paycheck on food, as compared with 22 percent of a leaner paycheck in 1941. The result was a stunning increase in the actual dollars that Americans put down on the counter for groceries.

Although there remained too many Americans who did not have enough to eat, millions of American children sat down to meals that were larger than ever in the past, if not necessarily as healthy as they might have been. Besides sheer bulk, there was another clear trend in family eating habits during the postwar years, which was parallel to similar trends in housing, clothing, entertainment, and other aspects of daily life: American children and their parents, no matter where they lived, tended more and more to eat the same things.

Surveys showed that in the vast majority of American homes, the evening meal, the heftiest of the day, consisted of some form of meat (most often beef), some starches (usually potatoes or corn with bread), a vegetable, and a dessert. For a special occasion, dinner might feature roast beef or beef steak, with whipped potatoes, beans, and pie; at a more ordinary dinner, hamburgers, french fries, peas, and jello might be served. The basic components varied little. Lunch and breakfast also were remarkably predictable. Food preferences had not changed much over the previous twenty years, and they would be much the same in the early 1960s. Americans' ideal meal remained startlingly consistent—and uninventive—during the middle decades of the century. As a people, we were a no-nonsense, meat-and-potatoes culture.

This tendency toward sameness of eating habits became even more pronounced after World War II. Families now had the funds to buy those preferred meals, but there were other reasons as well. American customs were being knit ever more tightly together as improved transportation and new systems of mass communication eroded regional differences. Mass marketing spread the same kinds of products throughout the nation and beyond. As families became increasingly mobile, shuffling from one part of the country to another several times a generation, customs and lifestyles naturally became more homogenous from coast to coast. As noted in the previous chapter, this trend could also be seen in eating habits.

Another new development was accounting for this creeping sameness of

By the 1940s the great American meal was well established at most dinner tables, even for pets—white bread, canned fruits or vegetables, perhaps some sliced cheese, and some kind of meat, often in a casserole. *Courtesy of Library of Congress.*

diet—one of the most important developments, in fact, in the American family during the second half of the 20th century: the changing roles of mothers.

Middle-class wives and mothers of the 1950s were far more likely to have jobs outside the home than ever in the past. Working-class women, especially in the poorest urban families, had always had to find employment to help put food on the table. Among the middle classes, however, mothers typically stayed home, seeing to the many household chores. Rarely did they contribute directly to the family income. That situation began to change in the early 1940s, and, by 1960, working mothers had become common in American life.

Once again, the world war was partly responsible. With so much work to be done, and with men sailing off to fight, women in the millions went to work in factories, offices, and stores. At war's end, it was assumed that these women would once again be "housewives." Public spokesmen of the 1950s celebrated the "traditional" family arrangement with the father as the sole breadwinner while the mother cared for children and saw to domestic chores. Many women did return to the home, but others stayed in the workplace.

Parents of the baby boom discovered that pursuing the dream of their own house and car and the best of life for their children was expensive. A father's income often was not enough. Moreover, women were more likely to search for personal fulfillment through an occupation in the commercial or professional world. In 1953, 30 percent of housewives worked outside the home, up from 24 percent at the start of the war. The numbers of working women continued to rise. By 1957, a third of the entire work force were women, and more than half of these were married. The number of working wives doubled between 1950 and 1960, and the number of working mothers increased four times over. For the first time, this phenomenon—both mother and father working to support their families—became a familiar part of life among the vast American middle class.

In another sense, however, the family arrangement remained much the same: wives and mothers still were expected to handle most household duties. A tired and harried housewife would arrive at home after a full work day. Within an hour or so, she would have to have dinner on the table. Obviously, the old methods, with varied shopping and lengthy preparation of raw foods, became exceptionally difficult and impractical. Instead, working wives turned to processed, or "ready-made," foods. In a way, dinner was waiting when mother came home from work—in cans and boxes in the cupboard or packaged in the freezer.

The result was what has been called "the golden age of food processing." As noted in the previous chapter, frozen foods had first become available in the 1920s, but their quality was often poor, and few families had freezer space to store them. Refrigerators of the 1950s, however, featured ever larger freezer compartments to stack goods that had become a more common sight in grocery stores and supermarkets. Frozen vegetables and fruit juices led the way. The predictable extension was the appearance of entire meals frozen, appropriately called "TV dinners," as most were consumed while watching a favorite television program. Just as predictable were the contents of this prepackaged frozen meal: a meat, a starch, a vegetable, and a dessert. By 1960, sales of frozen foods approached $3 billion annually, a staggering increase of 2700 percent over the previous decade.

Other meals were easily made with the help of the contents of a box or can. A fresh meat might be quickly cooked and combined with powdered or canned soup and frozen vegetables, and perhaps dried pasta that had been soaked and boiled, with all of it baked into a casserole. Ending the meal would be an "instant" dessert of gelatin or pudding. The rushed worker-mother could turn to a wide range of cookbooks especially designed for hurried meal making. These featured "quick 'n easy" recipes for "heat 'n serve" lunches and dinners. Popular magazines such as *Good Housekeeping* also did their part, offering plenty of advice and hints in every issue. *The Joy of Cooking,* which had first appeared early in the 1930s, became one of the bestselling books of American history, partly by responding to the needs of the day and adapting its offerings to mothers pressed by "the continuous shrinkage of housekeeping time."

As a consequence, American postwar children, whether living in Detroit, Lubbock, Tampa, or Phoenix, were likely to sit down before virtually the same foods at mealtime. For the most part, those dishes were notoriously bland. The "ideal" meal of beef and potatoes, even when carefully prepared from scratch, was hardly known for its spiciness, and the processed, quickly prepared variations tended to be even more neutral-tasting. Corporations like General Foods already were developing all sorts of preservatives to prolong their products' "shelf life"—the time that goods could remain in the store without spoiling. They also developed artificial flavoring and other chemicals that gave packaged foods a more colorful, appealing look. Between 1949 and 1959, more than four hundred new additives were devised and pumped into mass-produced groceries.

Even so, meals had a numbing sameness of taste and appearance. Magazine and cookbook recipes tried heroically to bring some zest and variety to family mealtime. After school and play and before homework, a boy or girl might sit down to a dinner of "Frankaroni Loaf," a baked concoction of boiled hot-dogs, bread crumbs, macaroni, processed cheese, and milk. Serving up something different was especially difficult because very few dishes of other cultures had made their way into the American mainstream. As the "frankaroni" example suggests, a few Italian pastas, such as elbow macaroni (one of the earliest processed foods was the Kraft Macaroni Dinner, first marketed in 1937) and spaghetti (served to the army by the millions of pounds during the war) had made it to the American table. But even these were usually served with the blandest cheese and tomato sauces. A slightly more "exotic" dish was patterned on the Chinese—chow mein, or chop suey, consisting of fried meat, canned fried noodles, and canned bean sprouts, flavored sometimes with ketchup but often with a new addition to family spices, soy sauce. Children were probably thankful that other efforts never caught on. One flop, for instance, was a "quick 'n easy" form of homemade pizza: a baked English muffin covered with tomato sauce, cheese, and salad oil.

Nor did restaurants offer much greater variety. As in the 1930s, Italian-American dining was about the only departure. Most others served variations of what was usually offered at home. Dining out on a special occasion typically meant eating steak or roast beef, with fancier versions of the inescapable side dishes of potatoes and standard vegetables, salads, and desserts. A visit to a restaurant, in any case, was fairly unusual for most middle-class children, and the rarest of events for poorer families. With so much income going into housing and home recreation, and with parents and children giving much of their evenings to television, Americans of the 1950s were dining out less and less. That meant, among other things, that restaurants had to cut costs to survive. And they shaved expenses in part by serving customers the same easy-to-prepare products used by working mothers in a hurry—frozen, powdered, canned, and processed dishes.

Variety did not entirely disappear. Distinctive regional and ethnic variations survived, ironically, in part because of continuing American poverty. Some children and their parents did not dive into the meat-and-potatoes mainstream because they could not afford to. The diet of African American and poor white children in the rural South was different, although unvarying in its own way, with some pork and lots of beans, greens, cornbread, and molasses. Some children hunted wild game and gathered native vegetation, such as poke, a large plant that was poisonous when mature but safe and succulent early in the spring.

There were also islands of distinctive foods among larger ethnic communities. Midwestern children of German ancestry grew up eating sausages and pastries that would have seemed strange, indeed, at the typical suburban dinner table. Mexican-American youngsters in small towns and cities of the Southwest knew dishes spiced with chiles and other flavorings that were alien to restaurants in even the largest cities. The most elaborate of such cuisine could be found among some of those ethnic groups that were most shunned and confined to communities of their own. The Chinese-American novelist Maxine Hong Kingston recalled her foodways while growing up in San Francisco's Chinatown:

My mother has cooked for us: raccoons, skunks, hawks, city pigeons, wild ducks, wild geese, black-skinned bantams, snakes, garden snails, turtles that crawled about the pantry floor and sometimes escaped under refrigerator or stove, catfish that swam in the bathtub. "The emperors used to eat the peaked hump of purple dromedaries," she would say. "They used chopsticks made from rhinoceros horn, and they ate ducks' tongues and monkeys' lips." She boiled the weeds we pulled up in the yard. . . . Once the third aunt who worked at the laundry ran out and bought us bags of candy to hold over our noses; my mother was dismembering a skunk on the chopping block. I could smell the rubbery odor through the candy.[5]

## AT PLAY

As American society became more caught up in technological change, so did its children's amusements. Among the several changes in children's playtime after World War II, one was especially significant: boys and girls spent less time outdoors in games with others and more indoors in front of the television screen.

As mentioned in the previous section, television in some ways brought the generations together, with children and parents gathering around the family set, laughing at the same jokes on "I Love Lucy" and cheering the same heroes in early adventure shows. Almost from the start, however, television broadcast programs pitched to younger audiences. Producers were reaching out to a large and growing group of viewers, the toddlers and preteens of the baby boom who were learning to flip through the channels by the early 1950s. Here was a vast potential market representing many millions of dollars waiting to be spent on the toys and other products advertised on these shows. Just as in the early days of penny arcades and one-reel silent movies, young America was helping to change the national marketplace and to shape our popular culture.

Children's shows were clustered at certain points in the week when the young were most likely to have free time, especially Saturday mornings and on weekdays during hours between school's end and dinnertime. Saturday mornings were dominated by action-filled shows much along the same lines as the movies that many of these same boys and girls would pay to see a little later in the day. Westerns were especially popular. Some western film stars, such as Roy Rogers and Dale Evans and William Boyd as Hopalong Cassidy, had their own shows. Among the most successful was "The Lone Ranger," which had originated on radio and had some limited exposure in the movies but found its greatest popularity on television, with Clayton Moore as the Lone Ranger and Jay Silverheels as Tonto. An unusual variation was "The Cisco Kid." Played by Duncan Reynaldo, the Kid was dashing and handsome and resplendent in a black-and-silver outfit and broad sombrero. With his comic saddle buddy, Pancho, he was the only leading character on television of Latino heritage other than Ricky Ricardo of "I Love Lucy." Like "B" westerns, Saturday morning westerns emphasized fast-paced plots with dark-hearted villains foiled, and usually under arrest, by the end of the half-hour format.

Other children's shows introduced young viewers to original characters, who appeared week after week in a familiar format, with ongoing gags, long-running comic plots, and predictable personality clashes. Among the earliest and most popular children's shows was "Howdy Doody," which first appeared in late 1947. Hosted by "Buffalo Bob" Smith, the show aired for half an hour Monday through Friday, in late afternoon, just in time for young viewers to tune in after school. Howdy Doody, himself, was a marionette dressed in a flannel shirt and bandana. Some other characters were also puppets—Phineas T. Bluster, a thickheaded carpenter named Dilly Dally, and several more. Human characters included a mute clown, Clarabell, an Indian chief, Thunderthud, and a wrestler, Ugly Sam. All lived in Doodyville, a town inhabited mainly by circus performers. A live audience of children, the "Peanut Gallery," sat in bleachers and cheered lustily. Beginning in 1956, "Howdy Doody" was broadcast only on Saturday mornings; its final show (the 2,343d) was aired in September 1960.

Young children's shows have remained a staple of television. The longest-running of them, "Captain Kangaroo," premiered in 1955 and remained on the air for three decades, until the end of 1984. The Captain, Bob Keeshan, had played Clarabell the Clown on "Howdy Doody," but the tone and pace of "Captain Kangaroo" was much calmer and gentler than the frenzied, often satirical "Howdy Doody." The show featured other adult characters, most notably the farmer, Mr. Green Jeans, as well as puppets. Its mild humor, educational approach, and warm moralism made it a favorite of parents.

The content and interests of children's shows naturally changed as the baby boomers matured. In the late 1950s, programs like "Howdy Doody" gave way to others appealing more to young people moving into adolescence. The most popular of these was "The Mickey Mouse Club," which ran from 1955 to 1959. Produced by Disney Studios, it was unusual on two counts. It produced its own serial stories, usually teenage adventures such as "Corky and the White Shadow" and, most popular, "The Adventures of Spin and Marty," about two young boys at a summer camp. What set this show most apart, however, was its use of young people as both stars and hosts—the Mouseketeers. There were two dozen Mouseketeers during the first season. Two adults, Jimmie and Roy, were around, but they were on the edge of the action, like camp counselors. The Mouseketeers, dressed in tee-shirts showing their names and wearing caps with mouse ears, were in charge. They sang and danced in their own production numbers, acted in some of the series, and introduced guest performers. In its way the show was an assertion of youthful independence and power.

By the end of the 1950s, as the earliest offspring of the baby boom edged into adolescence, the maturing interests of young viewers influenced programming in other ways. The simply plotted, half-hour westerns of Saturday morning began to lose some of their appeal. In their place, a new breed was appearing during prime evening viewing hours. This new wave began on Tuesday evening, September 6, 1955, at 8:30 (EST), with the first episode of "The Life and Legend of Wyatt Earp," starring Hugh O'Brien (who earlier had been the youngest drill instructor in the history of the U.S. Marine Corps). Four nights later, James Arness appeared as Marshall Matt Dillon in the initial program of "Gunsmoke," introduced that first evening by the western demigod, John Wayne.

While still offering plenty of fights and gunplay, these programs dealt with more serious themes and presented somewhat more complicated characters. This earned them the label of "adult" westerns, although they are better understood as family shows, with young people, especially baby boomers moving into their teen years, a larger part of the audience. Polls showed that children composed about 30 percent of the millions of viewers. The success of those first programs inspired others, which also drew impressive audiences. By 1957, a third of all prime viewing hours were taken up by thirty-three westerns. Two years later, eleven of the twenty most popular television shows were "horse operas." The passion for westerns began fading by 1962, although "Gunsmoke" would last for twenty years, longer than any prime-time program in television history.

These years also demonstrated dramatically how children, through television, were becoming an increasingly powerful force in the American marketplace. As this new medium became a pervasive presence in children's lives, businesses used it more and more to reach their youthful market. A dedicated young viewer was bombarded with scores (and later hundreds) of commercials for the whole range of toys and juvenile products. Those appeals then were passed on to parents. A study in 1980 reported that television-viewing youngsters asked their mothers and fathers for an average of thirteen products every week, all based on televised advertisements.[6]

But televisions were more than just a means of advertising various items sold in stores. This new medium created demand for its own images. Chil-

Through a haze of gunsmoke, television audiences of the 1950s could spend most of their evenings watching "adult westerns" that were especially popular among baby boomers entering their teenage years. *Photo © 1996 Capital Cities/ABC, Inc.*

dren were drawn into taking part in what they saw. In a sense, they were lured into stepping through the screen and into the video land beyond. They played board games named after and mimicking such popular television quiz shows as "Twenty One," "Jeopardy," and "Concentration," not to mention others drawing on programs having nothing to do with games, such as "Dr. Kildare," "The Beverly Hillbillies," and even "Alfred Hitchcock Presents."

Imagination and reality were blurring together, and businessmen found that the result was a money-making proposition. Children could participate in television by making their heroes' clothes and tools their own. In 1950, Americans spent $40 million on outfits, guns, and other paraphernalia patterned on just one television western hero, Hopalong Cassidy. By the end of the decade, cowboy duds and guns based on various Saturday morning stars were bringing in $75 million a year; their total sales for the last half of the 1950s, $283 million, were more than $100 million above the annual value of all toys, games, and sporting goods produced twenty years earlier. At the height of the popularity of "The Life and Legend of Wyatt Earp," a special toy edition of Wyatt's pistol was selling at a clip of eighteen thousand a day.

The most dramatic demonstration of this wedding of television with children's marketing came in 1955. "Disneyland," a popular program that will be discussed further in the next chapter, had introduced "The Adventures of Davy Crockett," a series of weekly episodes based loosely on the life of a Tennessee frontiersman, folk hero, and failed politician, who had died at the Alamo during the Texas revolution against Mexico in 1836. The shows were a smash hit. Millions of children sat glued to the unfolding story, which included fights with bears, plenty of Indians, exploits among rowdy boatmen on the Mississippi River, and, finally, the dramatic last days in Texas. Merchandisers discovered that just about any item associated with Crockett suddenly had a market. Most popular were children's versions of Davy's trademark, a coonskin cap. The wholesale price of raccoon skins shot up from twenty-six cents a pound to eight dollars. Reportedly, more than three thousand different items associated with Crockett could be found on the shelves, not only clothes and plastic firearms, but lunch boxes, hairbrushes, fishing rods, "whistling peace pipes," hunting spears, and wall-paper. Total sales topped $100 million. It all seemed to happen in an instant. The future film director Steven Spielberg, a third-grader at the time, recalled:

> Suddenly the next day everybody in my class but me was Davy Crockett. And because I didn't have my coonskin cap or my powder horn, or Old Betsy, my rifle, and the chaps, I was deemed the Mexican leader, Santa Anna, and they chased me home from school until I got my parents to buy me a coonskin cap.[7]

And yet, as Spielberg was suggesting, children were taking this craze and making it into their own collective experience. As they always had, girls and boys were negotiating as they played, taking the toys given them, using them in the intended ways, yet also giving it all their own twist. A record of "The Ballad of Davy Crockett," based on the show's theme song, had become an overnight hit. Quickly boys and girls took the song as their own, rewriting the lyrics in mild rebellion:

> Born on a tabletop in Joe's Cafe,
> Dirtiest place in the U.S. of A . . .

Folklorists reported that the children's altered version cropped up virtually simultaneously throughout the nation, in England, and even in Australia.

The Davy Crockett craze was only part of a much larger phenomenon, the increasing orientation of American business toward children and young people. This was partly a continuing trend mentioned all along in this book, starting with city children lining up for tickets to the earliest movies, but after World War II, merchants and manufacturers really turned their attention to younger customers. The reasons were obvious: more children, more money to spend on them, and parents more dedicated to meeting their children's needs and desires. A four-year-old was more than a toddler, as a writer for *Life* magazine put it. He or she was "a backlog of business orders that will take two decades to fulfill."[8]

That growing market would include all sorts of products, starting with the physical needs of young America: first baby food and diapers ($50 million annually in 1957, up from $32 million ten years before), then clothing, books, and pediatric medicines. Specialists calculated the "juvenile market" at $33 billion a year at the peak of the baby boom about 1960. For a businessman looking for a chance to cash in, the most obvious part of the national store was the toy department. Throughout the 1950s, each year's toy sales surpassed those of the year before. By the late 1950s, Americans were spending $1.25 billion annually on children's playthings, fifteen times the amount they had paid out in 1940.

Some of the popular toys of the baby boom were inspired indirectly by World War II. While aboard a ship in 1943, a naval engineer named Richard James watched a torsion spring fall off a table and bounce on the floor. It gave him a multimillion-dollar idea. After experimenting with different types of metal, he and his wife, Betty, produced a coil of lightweight steel that seemed to have an uncanny ability to move on its own, down stairs and across sloping boards. They called it the Slinky. At their first demonstration at Gimbel's department store in Philadelphia in 1945, the James's sold four hundred in an hour and a half. Since then the Slinky has become one of the most familiar American toys. It still sells millions every year.

Another product, equally famous, began as part of a wartime experiment to invent a synthetic substitute for rubber. An engineer for General Electric came up with a substance with a combination of odd traits. It could stretch, but it broke cleanly when pulled too far. When rolled into a ball, it bounced. It could erase pencil marks and, strangely, when pressed against printed matter, like newspapers, it took the images onto itself. After the war, the engineer named it Gooey Gupp and sold it in small amounts through a local toy store in New Haven, Connecticut. There another businessman found it in 1949. He bought the rights to the product, began producing it in much larger quantities, packaged it in small red plastic eggs, and changed the name to Silly Putty. In five years he sold 32 million eggs. Like the Slinky, Silly Putty's popularity has endured.

Among the most popular children's entertainments of these years were board games. In one sense they were nothing new. Early examples could be found in American homes even in the middle of the 19th century. During the postwar years, however, their number and popularity soared, partly because children and parents now had more money to buy them, but also because board games were one more example of a meeting ground between what young people enjoyed and adults approved. Boys and girls liked to compete, to "play grownup," and to imagine their way into other identities through these games. Parents appreciated board games as unthreatening and, in many cases, subtly encouraging values they favored.

The golden age of board games came after World War II. The field was dominated by two companies, Milton Bradley and Parker Brothers, which had been in the business since the 19th century, prospering by sensing the mood of the times. Parker Brothers' Monopoly, which was discussed in chapter 2, was an obvious, fabulously successful example. The companies had devised games to match events of the day, like The Siege of Havana during the Spanish-American War. So in the get-ahead years of the baby boom, they produced popular board games like Careers, Risk, and The Game of Life. In Careers, players moved around the board, pursuing their dreams of fortune, fame, or happiness by trying to buy yachts, discover uranium or run for office. In Risk, competitors worked on a grander scale, moving armies against opponents and trying to dominate the world. The Game of Life was an updated version of Bradley's first game, the Checkered Game of Life, first marketed in 1860, but its changes were revealing. In the original, a player won by avoiding Ruin and reaching Happy Old Age through moral living and frugality. The postwar version, by contrast, sent its players on a headlong pursuit of wealth, material comforts, and maximum possessions. Winning was simply defined: having the most money and things at the end.

Other board games played on more enduring themes. Introduced from England in the 1950s, Clue put its players in a plush mansion in the wake of a murder, then tested their deductive reasoning as they gradually eliminated potential killers, weapons, and the rooms in which the dastardly crime might have taken place. Over the years children grew up familiar with Colonel Mustard, Mrs. White, Professor Plum, and other sometime murderers. More than thirty years after Clue's first appearance, a film comedy was made based on its setting and figures. Its mental demands limited Clue mostly to older children and to adults, as was the case of another hugely popular game, Scrabble, which continues to sell about two million sets a year. Developed in the early 1930s, Scrabble did not take off until 1948, after it was revised, renamed, and marketed by the same company that had created an old favorite, Parcheesi, in the 1860s. Within its bag of small wooden squares, each with a letter of the alphabet, are 3.2 billion possible combinations of the seven letters a player is given each turn.

These amusements were not entirely limited to youngsters of eight and older. One of the most significant developments of the postwar years was the appearance of board games easily enjoyed by preschoolers. Candy Land was invented by a California woman while she was recovering from polio. Introduced in 1949, it has sold more than twenty million sets. Because players determine their movement along a path according to matching colors rather than by reading instructions or even counting, Candy Land has been a favorite of toddlers as young as three. Children only slightly older could play Chutes and Ladders, first marketed early in the 1940s (although supposedly based on a prototype from the colonial period).

Board games were an old way of playing that fit beautifully the mood and values of postwar American families, which celebrated a home-oriented, child-centered, increasingly private generation. Whether simple, like Chutes and Ladders, or challenging, like Scrabble, which today inspires international competitions, the games could bring together parents and all but the very youngest children. The whole family could spend hours huddled around a table, casting dice, flicking spinners, winning and losing, and, all the while, visiting, laughing, and arguing. As families turned increasingly inward, away from the public world and into apartments and the dens and playrooms of suburban houses, the appeal of this kind of entertainment naturally increased. Clue and Candy Land, Risk and The Game of Life all embodied a fond belief of the baby boom years: the family that plays together stays together.

Even the board games and television programs targeted mainly at children in large part expressed the views and values of adults. The Game of Life spoke for parents' dreams of material comforts and success. The programs watched most by boys and girls invariably stressed mainstream values and an optimistic outlook respectful of national institutions. In the America on the glowing screen, as in the suburban life portrayed in "Ozzie and Harriet" and "Leave It to Beaver," there was little sense of serious tension between the generations. Society seemed homogenous, placid and happy, and the future looked rosy.

Children absorbed those values held by their parents, but they also had their own view of life, one that rarely showed up on television. Obviously, television was a medium that children did not control. In a day of relatively few networks, there were not many program options each afternoon and evening; and, for the most part, parents influenced or controlled completely what was watched. So when television producers and programmers pictured the audience they had to please, they thought of parents first, children second.

Other amusements, however, were much more the children's. All were relatively cheap, so girls and boys could buy them on their own, with some pocket change scraped together from odd jobs, selling soft drink bottles, or leftover allowance. Looking at this market, businessmen responded with products that revealed more clearly America as it was perceived by the young—scenes, attitudes, and aspects of national life invisible elsewhere in popular culture.

A flourishing survivor from earlier years was the comic book. Comics first became popular in the 1920s, and from the start they reflected the concerns and fantasies peculiar to the young. This was young people's own literature, one they could afford. After World War II, sales of comics rose to more than sixty million a month; and, throughout the 1950s, comics remained cheap enough to be bought by children who could spare a dime or so. "Superheroes" like Superman and Captain Marvel, which had first appeared in the late 1930s, still flew and fought their way to rescue whole cities from the forces of evil. Some of the most popular new comics were extensions of other entertainments, like film cartoons. The Disney empire turned out comics by the millions featuring their most popular characters: Donald Duck and his mischievous nephews, and, of course, Mickey Mouse. Like all of Disney's productions, these might contain occasional sarcasm toward authority, but their values were staunchly traditional. (Disney's most spectacular achievement of the 1950s, the opening of Disneyland in California in 1955, will be taken up in chapter 4.)

In the late 1940s, however, a new type of comic appeared that could hardly have been more different from the Disney format and style. These "crime" and "horror" comics featured stories of murder and mayhem. Characters were depraved and psychotic. Drawings were elaborate and remarkably graphic, showing victims screaming in agony as blood gushed and as gore splattered the scene. Many of these were inspirations of publisher William M. Gaines, who had inherited his father's comic publishing house and quickly began experimenting with new formats. He tried romance and westerns, with some success, but the "horror" comics, with such titles as *Weird Fantasies, Crime SuspenStories,* and *Tales From the Crypt,* quickly began to sell in astounding numbers. Young readers probably were responding mainly because the topics were normally forbidden, though certainly some were fascinated by the lurid crimes and gory illustrations. A typical issue, for instance, had stories about a homicidal maniac and his sister boiled to death, a man murdering his best friend to steal his girl, and an animal-torturing sadist, who in the end is burned to death in an auto accident.

Within a few years crime and horror titles represented more than half of all comic sales. Predictably, there was a howl of protest from some authorities. Newspapers published editorials condemning them as dangerous and immoral. As this chapter's section on children and the law will show, it was argued that these comics were contributing to a rise in juvenile crime and rebellion. Influential books warned of the comics' threat, and the U.S. Senate held hearings on the matter. Responding to this pressure, publishers formed the Comics Magazine Association of America and issued a code that forbade words like "Horror" or "Terror" in titles and extreme bloodshed in the stories and pictures. Within a few years horror comics had largely disappeared from the mass market.

Another new comic production of these years, however, survived and flourished. *Mad Magazine,* in fact, is one of the most enduring successes in the history of American publishing. Another product of the Gaines publishing enterprise, its first issue appeared in the summer of 1952. Adolescent readers quickly began snatching up copies, and *Mad* quickly developed a loyal, even fanatical following. Soon it was changed from a comic book to a "slick" format—longer and more elaborate—and, beginning in 1954, books of reprinted material from the magazine were published.

In its way, *Mad* was much more a threat to established authority than any crime comics. It poked fun at virtually every familiar part of American life, from parents and politicians to television, movie stars, popular music, and education. Among its earliest targets were other comics. Some of the first issues featured "Mickey Rodent" and a bumbling "Superduperman." The teenage cartoon character "Archie" became a gun-toting juvenile delinquent, "Starchie." *Mad*'s symbol, invariably depicted on each cover, was Alfred E. Neuman, a boy with a freckled face, ears sticking straight out from his head, and a gap-toothed, slightly idiotic grin. The face would become instantly recognizable in most parts of the world, as would Neuman's slogan, "What, Me Worry?"

*Mad Magazine*'s Alfred E. Neuman, with his jug ears and dopey grin, became a symbol of young Americans' enjoyment of poking fun at much they saw around them, including the "counterculture" of the 1960s and their own rebellion. *Courtesy of E. C. Publications, Inc.*

*Mad*'s humor was (and is) always iconoclastic and occasionally outrageous. That style, as well as the innovative, exaggerated, often manic drawings, have appealed to young customers for more than forty years. Adults sometimes buy and read the magazine, but its real significance has been as an expression of youth culture that is consciously and defiantly different from that of grownups.

Besides comics, another form of popular culture, music, gave young America a chance to express its own tastes and views. The 1950s, in fact, witnessed the birth of what arguably has been the most persistent and powerful expression of youthful identity and rebellion in the second half of the century: rock and roll.

Popular music in the late 1940s and early 1950s was dominated by the smooth singing style of "crooners" and by lyrics celebrating romantic love and cute, sentimental themes. Among the hits of the day were "Hernando's Hideaway," "How Much Is That Doggie in the Window," "Ghost Riders in the Sky," and "Oh, My Papa." The sentiments behind these songs reflected mainstream adult values of the generation, such as optimism and idealized relationships between the sexes and between generations.

But popular music was about to change. For many years there had been a vigorous market among African Americans for what many whites called "race music," recordings performed and produced by black musicians and promoters. Very rarely one of these records sold well to a wider audience; "One Mint Julep" by the Clovers was an example in 1952. In 1951, a white disk jockey in Cleveland, Ohio, Alan Freed, was told by the owner of a local record store that many young white customers were listening to and buying the music broadcast on African American radio stations. Freed was host of a late-night classical music program, but that summer he changed course dramatically and began broadcasting "The Moondog Show." Blasted out over much of the Midwest, Freed's program for the first time featured "race records" on a major white station. His teenage audience loved it, and Freed eventually devoted his programs exclusively to black recording artists. The more of this music he played, the more his listeners liked it.

Freed called the music "rock and roll." The term, like that of another earlier form of black music outside the mainstream, jazz, was taken from sexual slang. Freed next gave his fans the real thing, a live performance by some of the musicians featured on his radio show. To the promoters' astonishment, more than 25,000 customers, most of them white teenagers, bought tickets. This marked the birth of the rock and roll concert, the first of many thousands to come over the next decades. When Freed moved his show to New York City, he attracted a far greater following and promoted more concerts that drew huge crowds from surrounding areas.

Other stations in other cities quickly followed Freed's lead. Soon the old lines between "black" and "white" music began to blur and fade. In 1954, Bill Haley, a white musician, recorded a version of the black classic "Shake, Rattle and Roll." It sold a million copies, rose to the top of *Billboard* magazine's main record chart, called the "white" chart, and to number four on the black "rhythm and blues" chart. The next year, something even more amazing happened: a black guitarist and singer, Chuck Berry, released "Maybellene," which shot up to number one on the "rhythm and blues" and to number five on the "white" charts. The same year the manic, piano-pounding, outrageously dressed black singer, Little Richard, had a hit with "Tutti Frutti." Rock and roll had arrived.

Its success was partly the result of two themes stressed throughout this book: technological change and more control of money by young people. Rock and roll records sold well and radio programs flourished because young consumers, with their part-time jobs and allowances, had money to buy them. Technology, in the meantime, was helping transform and revive two industries. The phonograph recording business had been hurt badly by radio, and radio, in turn, had lost part of its appeal to television. That began to change within a decade of the end of the war. Most radios and, especially, record players had been fairly expensive, affordable only by adult wage earners—and therefore essentially controlled by parents. In the early 1950s, the first transistor radios appeared, followed by smaller versions of record players. Radios cost as little as twenty-five dollars; record players, about twice that; and companies were offering them on credit for as little as a dollar a week. As the 1950s closed, merchants were selling ten million portable record players a year.

In other words, while adults controlled the purchase of and programming of television, radios and phonographs suddenly slipped beyond their grasp and into the reach of their sons and daughters. Young America was seizing control of part of the broadcasting and recording market, and those industries quickly began to give them what they wanted.

Technology was also changing record production. Recording was becoming a far less expensive process; a businessman with a small studio could compete, at least on a local scale, with the giants that had dominated the field for years. This change opened the way for one of the most important figures in American popular culture in these years, Sam Phillips. In his small studio in Memphis, Tennessee, and with portable equipment, Phillips made a modest living recording weddings, bar mitzvahs, and funerals (at eighteen dollars each). He also recorded dozens of hopeful singers and musicians. His passion was the music of black rhythm and blues performers of the Mississippi delta, music he called "ugly and honest," sung and played by people he later described as "politically, economically and musically disenfranchised."[9] Phillips recorded some of the earliest work of black musicians who would go on to vast popularity, including B. B. King and Ike Turner.

Phillips's greatest influence, however, was in finding, recording, and promoting white musicians who became some of the greatest early rock and roll stars. Southerners from rural backgrounds, their musical roots were in gospel, rhythm and blues, and Appalachian, or "hillbilly," traditions. They fused those strands together into something new, a style of rock and roll that dominated these early years. Among those Phillips recorded for his Sun Records label were Carl Perkins, Johnny Cash, Jerry Lee Lewis, and Roy Orbison, all of whom would go on to international fame and fortune. None, however, approached the sensational popularity and influence of Phillips's greatest find, Elvis Aron Presley.

Born in 1935, Presley grew up poor in Tupelo, Mississippi, and learned to play guitar in high school. In 1953 he came to the Phillips studio to make a record as a birthday present for his mother, Gladys. The secretary asked him about his singing style: "Who do you sound like?" Presley answered: "I don't sound like nobody." Phillips signed him to a contract and put out his first record. On one side was a song originally recorded by the black bluesman Arthur Crudup, "That's All Right," and, on the other, a bluegrass classic, "Blue Moon of Kentucky." Presley was an instant hit in Memphis, then soon across the South. Phillips sold Presley's contract to RCA for $35,000 (a poor business decision, perhaps, but the promoter later became rich with an early investment in a friend's motel chain, Holiday Inn); and, within months, Presley was on his way to the most meteoric success in the history of popular music. "Hound Dog" (originally recorded by Big Mama Thornton) and "Don't Be Cruel" sold millions of copies; even more important, they both rose to the top of all three of *Billboard*'s charts: the white "pop" list, country and western, and rhythm and blues. Propelled by demand from America's young consumers, these songs were shattering old categories and transforming a major national industry.

What was rock and roll? In its roots as well as its words, it was the music of outsiders. It drew together the musical traditions of African American blues, gospel, and "boogie woogie" and the "hill" music of poor whites. It fused those parts into something new, however. Rock and roll had a simple, powerful, driving beat that was easy to dance to; in fact, it

The King of Rock and Roll meets his adoring young fans. By blending musical styles of blues and southern country music and by giving the world a unique and ambiguous personal image, Elvis Presley became the most successful figure in the history of popular music. *Courtesy of The Dallas Morning News/Joe Laird.*

was difficult *not* to move while listening. Lyrics were simple, and adults ridiculed them as silly or gibberish. There was plenty of sugary, first-love sentimentality, but critics charged that rock was also full of raw sexuality. They were right, and sometimes this was quite open, as in Presley's early recording of "Baby, Let's Play House" and Gene Vincent's "Woman Love," the flip side of "Beebop a Lula." Sexuality was also evident in the sensual, slurred delivery of otherwise tame lyrics and in the hip-grinding movements on stage by Presley and others. Besides this rebellion against sexual standards of the day, rock and roll told of other irritations, like the teenager's menial jobs, as in Chuck Berry's "Too Much Monkey Business," and complaints about lack of power, as in Eddie Cochran's "Summertime Blues." More than anything else, from its birth and throughout its history, rock and roll has had the explosive energy of the young, their sense of ownership—"we found and made this music, and it's *ours*"—and their determined independence and separation from institutions and rules that otherwise controlled their lives.

## AT WORK

One of the clearest facts about American work during these postwar years was how little of it was done by children. At the opening of the century, young boys and girls had been laboring in virtually every major area of the American economy. They played crucial roles in industrial production, agriculture, communication, and merchandising. By the middle of the century, the importance of children in the workplace, at least the youngest of them, had diminished dramatically. The scope of the change is shown in the reports of the U.S. census:

### Percentage of Children, Ages 10–15, Gainfully Employed

| | |
|---|---|
| 1900 | 18.0 |
| 1910 | 18.0 |
| 1920 | 8.5 |
| 1930 | 5.0 |
| 1940 | 1.0 |
| 1950 | 2.0 |

Ten years deep into our century, children of ten and even younger were commonly seen working long hours in coal mines, cotton mills, shoe factories, slaughter houses, and glass factories. Forty years later, they had all but disappeared from those places.

The reasons for this remarkable change have been touched on in the first two chapters. Some new laws kept children out of much industrial work. Other laws indirectly kept them off the job market by requiring them to be in school. Labor unions were active in keeping potential young workers away from workplaces so more jobs would be available for adult union members. Many middle-class parents did not require the income of their children; moreover, these parents had dedicated themselves to providing a better future for their children by prolonging their education rather than sending them off to help the family income. Finally, technological changes in many cases made child labor impractical and even economically dangerous for businessmen. As industrial factories became increasingly sophisticated—and more and more expensive to build and maintain—they demanded more highly skilled workers and technicians. No child had the years of training needed to work with much of this machinery. Putting a

boy or girl of twelve or fifteen in charge of a complicated piece of equipment costing $50,000 was not a happy prospect for a businessman, re-
gardless of how cheaply that young person would work. Technology, laws,
and changing attitudes combined to pull the great majority of younger
children out of the American workplace.

As also mentioned earlier, children had been much more likely to continue working and playing important economic roles on American farms.
Agriculture had always provided the means of laboring for a very large
portion of the nation's youth—a majority, in fact, until well into the 20th
century. Reformers against child labor had focused almost completely on
urban and industrial work. Sweating on the farm, they thought, especially
when children were working side-by-side with parents and siblings, was
good for both the physical and moral health of the young laborers. The
pressure to reduce the amount of child labor consequently was directed
elsewhere. Nonetheless, American farms and farmers were being changed
by some of the same forces transforming cities and industries. For one
thing, children were doing less agricultural work because every year
thousands of families were leaving farms. Fewer children were in agricultural labor, that is, because many fewer people were in it. The census of
1940 showed that about 17 percent of American workers were farmers or
agricultural laborers; by 1960, that figure had slipped to only 6 percent.
The effect was shown even more dramatically in labor statistics among
sixteen- and seventeen-year-olds. In 1940, nearly half of all employed
Americans of that age worked on farms. But then, the bottom dropped out:

### Percentage of Employed Persons, 16–17, Working on Farms

| | |
|---|---|
| 1940 | 48 |
| 1950 | 29 |
| 1960 | 15 |
| 1970 | 5 |

By the last third of the century, the great majority of the nation's children
had lost all personal contact with the work and experiences that had defined daily life for most young people only a few generations before.

For those who stayed on the farm, many chores remained much the same
as in the past. They fed and cared for stock raised for market and the home
table—feeding hogs, cattle, and chickens—and helped in chores around the
house and farmyard. In other ways, however, farm life and labor were
changing rapidly. The effect of many of these changes was to reduce the
economic contributions of young people, just as was happening elsewhere

in the nation. Most of the food on the family dinner table now came from local groceries, not from hunting that had been done partly by children in the past. Clothes were mostly bought in local stores rather than being made by mothers and daughters working together. Children didn't draw water or gather fuel; those things came from indoor faucets, gas pipes, and electrical lines. In many ways, most farmers were living a lot like suburban middle-class families: on both an Indiana farm and in a Houston suburb, a new way of life was phasing children out of most jobs they had performed for decades.

Another important force had the same effect. Even as tens of thousands of families were fleeing the countryside for the cities every year, American farms were producing much, much more food. With more sophisticated equipment and techniques being applied to the nation's farmlands, fewer workers were needed. Farm children were less likely to work with new machinery that, after all, was expensive and complicated to operate. In an earlier generation, sons and daughters had taken on important tasks not long after they could walk, and by puberty they could handle about anything their parents could. On the new American farm, young children could help with chores, but the real productive work was beyond their reach until they were in their middle or late teens. Farms, in other words, were being increasingly mechanized, just as industries were, and farm and factory owners were equally hesitant to put such an investment into the hands of youngsters.

As costs of farming went up and boys and girls were phased out of much of the work, the expenses of rearing children were rising too, just as in the cities and suburbs. The prices of clothes, taxes for education, doctor bills and medicine, and so much more—they all were taking larger bites out of the parents' bank accounts. The bottom line was that the economics of farm families was following the same trend already described for city families: children cost more and they contributed less. A study in 1954 estimated that parents were spending $2,829 a year for all of a farm family's needs; a good portion of that was spent on their children, nearly $12,000 for a boy by the time he was sixteen, and about $13,000 for a girl. Sons and daughters, however, did not start contributing to the family income until the age of ten or so, and the money they produced was slim for the next few years. A young man began to bring in more than he cost only at about the age of eighteen—and that, of course, was about when he was likely to leave home; his sister, even if she remained to work on the farm throughout her thirties, never did produce enough to offset her parents' expenses for her.

By mid-century, family economics on the farm had become the opposite of what it had been for most of the nation's history. Instead of being valuable economic assets to American farmers, boys and girls were expensive investments that often packed up and left just when they were starting to pay off. Farm children had become a losing proposition according to these crude economic measurements.

The family farm economics just described were true among farmers who were fairly well off, who owned their own land and produced a reasonably good income much of the time. As was true in earlier decades, however, many who worked the land were not nearly so fortunate. In certain parts of the country, especially the South, rural Americans lived and labored under very different circumstances. There the children remained crucial to the family's working life, but there, too, things were changing.

At mid-century, much of the South still was farmed under the sharecropper and tenant systems, arrangements mentioned in the first two chapters of this book. These systems had appeared in the South in the aftermath of the Civil War, and they had dominated much of the region ever since. Both African American and white families worked the land under these arrangements, but blacks predominated, especially among sharecroppers.

In both sharecropping and tenant farming, those who worked the land did not own it. A sharecropping family worked a piece of land (generally five to ten acres) for the owner, who provided housing, fuel, tools, sometimes livestock, and, usually, a cash advance, or "furnish," for living expenses. The family, in turn, provided all the labor. Owner and sharecropper split the costs of seed, fertilizer, and, if cotton was grown, the ginning and bailing of the crop. At the end of the working year, the income of the harvest was divided evenly, half to the owner and half to the family. After the owner deducted the "furnish" and the workers' share of costs from their half, the sharecroppers had the rest as their year's income. A "share tenant" came into the arrangement with more to invest. He provided all equipment, seed, fertilizer and costs, as well as the labor. He got the house but no "furnish." On the day of reckoning he would usually get three-fourths of the income, with the other fourth going to the owner. In another arrangement, a cash tenant simply rented the land and house for a set price, and he got all the profit (if there was any).

Sharecroppers had the least going into these arrangements, and they got the least when it was time to tally up the profits. They were also the most vulnerable. What if drought, or flood, or insects, or collapsing prices ate away at the income from the harvest? A sharecropper, getting half of very little, and with other costs and loans, would be left with a pathetically few dollars at the end of the work season. Often, in fact, expenses and loans were greater than his share of the profit; so, after months of brutal work, he actually ended up in debt. Here is an entry for a Mississippi sharecropper, Mimy Stells, from a landowner's ledger during the cotton season of 1940:[10]

| | | |
|---|---|---|
| account brought forward [in debt] | 8.31 | |
| December, Cash, (furnish) | 5.00 | |
| March 1, Cash, (furnish) | 5.00 | |
| April 1, Cash, (furnish) | 5.00 | |
| May 1, Cash, (furnish) | 5.00 | |
| June 1, Cash, (furnish) | 5.00 | |
| July 1, Cash, (furnish) | 5.00 | |
| | 38.31 | |
| interest | 3.08 | |
| | 41.39 | |
| September, 1 yd. cotton sack | .13 | |
| | 41.52 | |
| credit account for cotton sold | | 16.21 |
| carried forward [in debt] | 25.31 | |

Share tenants were a little better off than sharecroppers, but not much.

Sharecropping and tenant farming tended to keep families tied to a piece of land. Rarely could they accumulate sufficient resources to move and start over elsewhere. Many black farm children grew up on land their relatives had worked for generations. The labor of working that land, furthermore, was of the old style. Only the most primitive equipment was used, often only a mule and plow for getting the seed in the ground, with hoes for chopping weeds and back muscles and a bag for picking. Cotton cultivation was one of the last agricultural endeavors to feel the force of mechanization. Work was basic and hard, much as it had been in all farming in an earlier America, accomplished not through investing money in equipment but by applying thousands of hours of human energy to a tough job.

On these nonmechanized cotton farms, children remained important. Before his teenage years, a boy could handle a plow. Girls and boys both spent hours "chopping cotton," hoeing out weeds during the long growing season. At harvest, all children except the youngest moved up one row and down the next, stooped over, pulling cotton from the bolls and filling they large sacks they dragged behind them. Speed was important; the young cotton pickers were in the fields before dawn and left only, by tradition, when it was "too dark to tell a black mule from a brown one." Their

Like these boys living along the Mississippi River in Arkansas, many African-American children continued to work with their parents in the fields until well after World War II. *Courtesy of "Arkansas Giant" Collection, #3993. Special Collections Division, University of Arkansas Libraries, Fayetteville.*

memories are full of what surely was some of the most merciless drudge labor of any children in the country—the summer sun hammering them fifteen hours a day, muscles screaming from bending over and pulling the sack, hands bleeding and raw from pulling cotton from the sharp bolls. Only infants were spared this labor. Set at the end of cotton rows, under trees when possible or in a tub and shaded by sack cloth propped over them, they spent their first years watching what awaited them dead ahead.

Sharecroppers lived on the slimmest margin, scraping by on a few dollars a month, growing or hunting most of their own food. On these farms, unlike the modestly comfortable mechanized midwestern farms described above, the economic value of young Americans wasn't shrinking. On the contrary, a family without child workers was in serious trouble. The children's value as farm laborers operated to their detriment. Their usefulness was one reason the quality of education for the southern poor, especially African Americans, was so low. As in the past on most farms, here parents had to keep their sons and daughters out of classes much of the year to help with work that had to be done. As long as much of the South continued to be farmed in this marginal, labor-intensive way, child workers would continue to fill the fields—and suffer for it.

There were probably more children working on farms than the official figures showed. The table of children "gainfully employed" printed at the opening of this section shows a striking decline between 1910 and 1920. A closer examination of the census figures indicates that two-thirds of that dramatic decrease was in southern agriculture, but it's a good bet those figures were exaggerated. For one thing, the census was taken in January; children might be reported as nonworking then, even though a few months later they would be toiling in the fields. Youngsters working as "unpaid family labor," furthermore, have been frequently undercounted in the census. Child labor after 1910 may not have decreased nearly so much as it seemed, and many of the "hidden" workers were probably among poorer southern farm families. In 1930 even the official figures showed that more than half of all working children between ten and fifteen were on southern farms, most of them African Americans. The table shows that among all American youngsters in 1930, only 5 percent were "gainfully employed," but among Mississippi blacks, the rate was about 35 percent.

This part of our national farmland, however, was also about to feel the impact of new technology. It started with tractors, used to plow and cultivate more of the land every year, especially land used for corn, soybeans, and other food crops. The number of tractors in the South increased nearly four times in the 1920s (from about 30,000 to 112,000), then doubled again in the 1930s, and then again in the next five years, to more than 400,000 by the end of World War II. Mechanization came more slowly to the part of southern agriculture where family labor was most common, the cotton fields. In the 1930s, rotary hoes and "sweep blades" were first used for mechanical weeding and cultivating. Early in the decade, two Memphis brothers, John D. and Mack Rust, introduced a "spindle picker." At first it harvested only a bale a day, but, with improvement, it soon could pick five bales, then even more. It was only in the 1940s, however, when giant national firms like International Harvester and Allis-Chalmers developed more efficient and marketable pickers, that the impact of mechanization really began to be felt. The number of mechanical pickers in operation soared during the 1950s.

Machines replaced families in the fields with mixed consequences. Many thousands, including huge numbers of young children, were freed from the crushing work of chopping and picking; but it was not at all clear what they were to do instead. The Rust brothers had worried that "in the share-cropped country . . . 75 percent of the labor population would be thrown out of employment" by their inventions.[11] Many poorer families, especially blacks, were leaving the land and, often, the South in search of work and better lives elsewhere, particularly in northern cities. Thousands in the Mississippi delta headed upriver to St. Louis and, beyond that, to Chicago and Detroit. This exodus helped persuade landowners to turn to machines to take over work in the fields. In one of the most dramatic changes in the history of American agriculture, sharecropping virtually disappeared in the South in little more than a generation. In 1940, the census reported more than 540,000 southern sharecroppers; by 1960, the number had shrunk to 121,000; and after that the category disappeared from the census.

By the end of the 1950s, then, many thousands of children from the South's poorest farming families were putting behind them a way of life and labor known for generations, just as better-to-do youngsters in other agricultural areas were breaking with their past. Modernization of the American farm was changing all their lives. And yet the old patterns had not disappeared entirely. Today the largest number of employed children under fifteen are those who work on other people's farms, many of them in the South. Many others are part of another large group considered in the previous chapter and in the one to follow—migrant workers, especially those in western agriculture.

As children and young people were excluded from some kinds of work, they continued to do other jobs. Some of that work was done around the house, but the nature of domestic labor, like so much else in family life, changed considerably during the 20th century. The most obvious developments had to do with the technology of housework. Just as on the farms, new "labor-saving" machines, these powered by an expanding electrical industry, took over some of the heaviest work and made other tasks much easier. Automatic washing machines ended the drudgery of washing clothes and linens by hand. Housewives previously had devoted a full day a week, traditionally Monday, to the wash. Now they could do the job in a few

hours spread over the week. Refrigerators eased the tasks of food preparation, canning, and preserving, and frozen and processed foods shrank the
time needed to put meals on the table. Vacuum cleaners reduced the time
and effort previously given over to sweeping and beating rugs.

All this cut down greatly on the hours needed by a typical middle-class
housewife to perform some of the basic tasks of homemaking. Ironically,
another change in domestic life was having the opposite effect: the rise of
what historians call "consumerism." In one sense, the term means simply
that Americans were buying more of what they needed rather than producing those things for themselves. But in its broader definition, "consumerism" refers to the growing pressure to purchase more and more goods
and, just as important, to replace older items, not because those things were
worn out or useless, but because newer ones were available. Like nearly all
important changes in habits, this one had been building for a long time, at
least since the middle of the 19th century. Consumerism really gathered
strength in the 20th century, and although the Great Depression naturally
slowed it down, the years after World War II proved to be its golden age.

Essential to this change has been the modern advertising industry. By the
end of the 1950s, advertisers were spending $2.2 billion a year to pitch
their goods to the public, and a recent study showed that the average American is exposed to about 1,500 advertising appeals every day, on television
and radio, in magazines, on billboards and in many other forms. Advertising fuels consumerism by stimulating demand for goods and by helping to
persuade customers to buy products that are not essential for their families'
daily life.

Children and young people became very important in the new postwar
consumerism as the nature of work in the middle-class home changed. If
mothers were doing less of the old physical labor, like washing and sweeping, they now began spending more and more time at the tasks of consumption—shopping, looking for bargains, managing households in more
efficient ways. With more children and more attention given to their needs
and activities, mothers were also spending far more time taking boys and
girls to lessons, sporting events, and school activities. It added up, and
repeated studies have shown that, despite all the new labor saving devices,
women were spending more time, not less, at the jobs of wife and mother.

As already noted, many of those same mothers were also working at jobs
outside the house. They were doing double duty, and one result was that
there was less time spent, as the years passed, on keeping the middle-class
house spotlessly clean and orderly. By the 1960s and 1970s, the typical

home was more cluttered, its clothes less likely to be cleaned and ironed, its dishes more often unwashed and in the sink, its general appearance somewhat messier than in the 1930s and 1940s.

This also meant that sons and daughters were often expected to help out more at home. Chores around the house became a greater part of a child's working time. That work might be washing dishes, general housecleaning, and special attention to cleaning one's room, helping with the laundry, and mowing the lawn. This trend would continue until the present day. A sampling of families at the end of the 1970s revealed that about nine out of ten children made their beds and cleaned their rooms at least once a week, seven of ten cleared the tables and washed dishes, and about half worked in the yard and cared for pets. At least as important was babysitting for younger sisters and brothers; two-thirds of the young people polled cared for siblings at times, about half of them at least once a week. Significantly, babysitting was considerably more common among those children whose parents worked, especially in single-parent households.

Unlike much of children's work in previous generations, this did not add directly to a family's income. Rather, it was an indirect contribution: young household workers were filling in for mothers who now were making (and spending) money as they never had before. Caring for younger brothers and sisters, cutting the grass, washing and folding laundry, making sandwiches for lunch or helping cook dinner, these young workers in their way remained vital members of the family work force, as others had at the opening of the century. Nevertheless, their contribution should not be exaggerated. Whatever help they gave was often offset by the demands on their parents of looking after the needs of youngsters in a "child-centered" age. A close investigation of 1,300 two-parent families in one city found that when the children's help was balanced against extra hours their parents (mainly their mothers) spent taking care of them, working parents gained time only in households with a lot of older children.[12]

During the 1950s, another trend in the working life of young America, particularly among the middle class, became clearer. A growing number of children, especially older ones, were finding some work outside the home. At first this seems to contradict what has been said in most of this section. True, the youngest children, those under fourteen or so, rarely took part in much work outside their houses, and children of all ages were pulled almost entirely from the types of work done by millions of youngsters early in the century—industrial labor, many street trades, and field work on farms—but young men and women, fifteen and older, were taking jobs and making money. There were two big differences in this employment, however: These young people were working in occupations in which adolescents had never worked before in great numbers, most of them in retail sales and in the "service" industries. Sixteen-year-olds stood behind counters in stores, pumped gas in automobile service stations, and cooked food and waited on customers in franchise restaurants. A second difference had to do with how they used the money they earned. In the past, children had spent some of their income on themselves, but a lot of their pay went to help meet their family's needs. Now, however, teenage workers were keeping their earnings almost completely for themselves. Like their parents, they were enthusiastic consumers, and the money they made flipping hamburgers and sacking groceries paid for their entertainment and other desires.

So the years from 1941 to 1960 marked an important transition in the history of working children. As young people continued to move out of some kinds of labor, they began to enter others, the "new workplace" of teenagers that will be described more in the last chapter. Young America's part in the nation's economy was changing, and, as always, teaching us something about the wider and deeper currents of national life.

## AT SCHOOL

If the big story in America during the 1940s and 1950s was the "baby boom," the implications for education were obvious. In a few years the millions of babies born soon after the war would be leaving home every morning, September to May, and heading for the classroom. The challenge, in fact, was even greater than it might seem on the surface. Not only were there many more children, but, as the table below shows, a larger portion of those children would be attending school.

**Percentage of Persons, 5–19 Years Old, in School**

| | |
|---|---|
| 1940 | 74.8 |
| 1950 | 78.7 |
| 1955 | 86.5 |
| 1960 | 88.6 |

The greatest increase was coming at the lowest levels. Children of five and six years old were much more likely to begin school in kindergarten and start the first grade on time in 1960 than twenty years earlier:

### School Enrollment Rate, Ages 5–6

| | |
|---|---|
| 1940 | 43.0 |
| 1945 | 60.4 |
| 1950 | 58.2 |
| 1955 | 78.1 |
| 1960 | 80.7[13] |

The huge wave of boys and girls washing toward American schools would have to be accommodated. Educators were at best only partly successful. The first table above shows that a very large proportion of school-age Americans were in school—and, indeed, in 1950 and 1960, 99.2 and 99.5 percent, respectively, of boys and girls between the ages of seven and thirteen were enrolled, but what sort of schools were they in, and how well were they being educated? Unfortunately, the years after World War II showed that American parents could make babies a lot faster than educators could get ready for them.

Because the baby boom really got underway from 1946 to 1947, American schools began to feel its greatest impact in the early 1950s. First kindergartens, then elementary schools, and, finally, in the early 1960s, high schools were engulfed. For a dozen years each September saw at least 1.5 million more students, and in some cases 2.5 million more, than the year before. In 1964, the year the first squalling newborns of 1946 were in their senior year of high school, one out of every four people in the entire nation was a public school student.

Where were all those students to go? The problem was serious everywhere, but in those parts of the country to which Americans were migrating, the situation was close to overwhelming. California opened one school a week during the 1950s, and, by 1965, Los Angeles alone was spending a million dollars a week on new construction. Even so, classrooms were overcrowded; a national survey estimated that 60 percent had too many students. At the height of the swelling attendance, harried school officials were borrowing 78,000 empty stores, church halls, and other facilities to hold the overflow of students.

Besides classrooms, a large problem was finding teachers to put in charge of them. A teacher shortage began building during World War II, as thousands of teachers joined the armed forces and thousands more left their posts for the better pay of wartime industries and other newly available jobs. As was true throughout the century, those parts of the country most in need of teachers were often the ones least able to attract them. Birth

As thousands of schools were built every year for the flood of students from the baby boom, classrooms in the poorer parts of rural America remained outmoded, as for these schoolchildren in Arkansas. *Courtesy of Arkansas History Commission.*

rates usually were highest—and, thus, the number of students was greatest—where people were poorest. Impoverished districts could only offer salaries well below the national average. "States with the most children have the least wealth," explained the *Journal of the National Educational Association,* while "states with the most wealth have the fewest children."[14] Some of the deepest poverty, furthermore, was in rural America, where the isolation, as well as the poor pay, made teaching posts even less attractive to many qualified men and women.

The troublesome trends during the war accelerated once it was over. As the United States entered into its exhilarating economic growth, public education had to compete with many high-paying occupations. Even if the number of students had remained fairly stable, there likely would have been a teacher shortage; but enrollments were skyrocketing. The result was a yawning gap between the number of teaching jobs and the number of people to fill them. In the early 1950s, as the baby boom was just beginning to hit the schools, American schools already were short an estimated 72,000 teachers.

One solution was to loosen standards and put less qualified persons to work. During the war emergency permits—permissions to hire teachers who did not meet the usual standards—rose from fewer than 5,000 in 1941–1942 to nearly 70,000 in 1944–1945.[15] The situation worsened during the postwar crunch. In 1959 an estimated 100,000 teachers, or about one in every dozen, were on the job without the proper credentials.

The strain on educational facilities, as the baby boom turned into a student boom, naturally would have influenced the ongoing debate about how students were being taught. But another development made the discussion over the quality and approach of education more heated. World War II ended with the Soviet Union as the only nation in the world with power in any way comparable to that of the United States. Within a year of Japan's surrender, it was also clear that these two superpowers were increasingly at odds. As the Soviet government consolidated its control of eastern Europe, many in the United States came to believe that its goal was to control all of Europe and, beyond that, to encourage Soviet-style governments in other parts of the world.

In that climate of opinion, public education became even more crucial. The great contest between the United States and the Soviet Union would be decided, in part, by how well each nation prepared its young people for dealing with the rapidly changing world at mid-century. Poor education, it was argued, would cripple America's capacity to meet the Soviet threat. These worries were especially alarming because of the new technology of destruction that had ended the great war. By the early 1950s, the Soviet Union had developed its own atomic and hydrogen bombs. Suddenly, it seemed that, for the first time in U.S. history, it was possible for its enemies to inflict terrible destruction on most parts of the country. That placed a new emphasis on education in the sciences, which seemed to provide the key to national security.

Debates over education were expressed through a theme that was now several decades old. Some critics charged that policies originating during the progressive era, especially those associated with John Dewey, were neglecting too much of the basics of the intellectual tradition, and, by so doing, were not meeting the challenges of the day. The emphasis on practical skills and social adjustment, these critics said, was robbing children of basic training in mathematics, foreign languages, science, history, and other areas. There was also criticism of Dewey and other progressive educators for their sympathy for socialism—and thus, it was implied, an ideological connection to the Soviet Socialist-Communist government.

In 1957, the concern that American students were ill-prepared turned to something close to panic. That fall the Soviet Union became the first country to launch objects into orbit around the earth—two satellites, Sputnik I and II. These satellites, themselves, circling the planet and sending back electronic signals, posed no threat to the United States, but they had disturbing implications. They demonstrated that the Soviet Union had rockets of tremendous power; and the amount of thrust required to send the Sputniks into orbit could also, perhaps, allow the Soviets to propel atomic weapons deep into the United States. The rockets, in fact, were called "intercontinental ballistic missiles," or ICBMs—devices, that is, that were capable of sending destructive payloads from one continent to another. Beyond that, the satellites suggested that the Soviets were well ahead of this country in their scientific and technological achievements. The spectacular demonstration of the orbiting Sputniks was a grand propaganda victory for the Soviet Union; for the United States, it was a psychological Pearl Harbor, as the atomic scientist Edward Teller called it. It brought the criticism of American education sharply into focus. We seemed to be lagging badly behind, and something, the critics said, had to be done. A book published two years earlier, *Why Johnny Can't Read—And What You Can Do about It,* by Rudolf Flesch, a blistering attack on the educational system, suddenly became a best-seller. *Life* magazine featured a cover story with photos of a Russian high school student working hard for long hours at his books while an American youth enjoyed himself at sports and other nonacademic activities.

One result was a massive flow of money from the federal government into public schools and higher education. Another was a series of reforms recommended in reports by two prestigious figures, Admiral Hyman Rickover, a prominent military leader, and a former president of Harvard University, James Conant. They urged higher standards for graduation from high school and greater attention to basic training in the social and physical sciences. Through this more rigorous schooling, the United States would embark on what Rickover called the "Great Talent Search" to identify the most able students. Such a program, reformers said, would be an essential weapon in our Cold War with the Soviet Union. That, in turn, called for a better way to evaluate students throughout the country by some common standard, which brought a renewed emphasis on something discussed in the second chapter—educational testing. The purpose here was not to measure raw intelligence, or a person's IQ, but to test a student's skills and level of performance. The Educational Testing Service (ETS), founded in 1947, devised the Scholastic Aptitude Test (SAT), which was designed to evaluate high school students as they headed for college, and, by the late 1950s, many colleges and universities were requiring applicants for admission to submit SAT scores. Taking these tests was rapidly becoming a common experience for all young Americans hoping to move into higher education. These tests, however, raised the same difficult, troubling questions asked about earliest testing programs: Did the tests favor certain groups of young Americans, the white middle class in particular? Did the answers and scores reflect only ability and training? Or cultural experience?

The broader issue, of course, was determining how the full potential of American young people could be realized as long as some were offered a far poorer education than others. If the United States was involved in a global struggle, called the Cold War, wasn't this effort thwarted if some children were not given the chance to do their best? The most obvious differences in educational opportunity, as shown in previous chapters, had to do with race. School systems in most of the country were segregated, with African American students attending classes that were generally funded far below those of white children. This division of schooling by race had been upheld in 1896, when the U.S. Supreme Court, in the case of Plessy v. Ferguson, ruled that public facilities (like schools) that were "separate but equal" did not violate the Constitution.

On May 17, 1954, the Supreme Court, in the case of *Brown v. Board of Education of Topeka,* unanimously reversed that earlier decision. The new ruling not only drew on evidence about the difference in quality of black and white school systems, it also emphasized the psychological and emotional damage done to children required to attend separate schools merely because of their skin color. Chief Justice Earl Warren concluded that

> To separate [black children] from others of similar age and qualifications solely because of their race generates a feeling of inferiority as to their status in the community that may affect their hearts and minds in a way never to be undone. . . . We conclude that in the field of public education the doctrine of "separate but equal" has no place. Separate educational facilities are inherently unequal.

The *Brown* decision set in motion profound changes in the educational experience, eventually affecting millions of American youth. At the time, seventeen states required segregated schools, as did the nation's capital. Four other states allowed racially separate systems, and, in other states, many or most schools were segregated in practice. Some of these systems began to dismantle their separate systems quickly and quietly. President

Dwight D. Eisenhower immediately ordered schools in Washington, D.C., desegregated.

Other regions and school systems, however, vowed to resist, and there was talk of making that resistance violent. The FBI reported a drastic rise in firearm sales in the South, in some places by as much as four times over. Some southern political figures threatened to shut down schools entirely rather than allow white and black children to attend together.

The Supreme Court ordered administrators to desegregate schools not by any precise timetable but as soon as was "practicable" and "with all deliberate speed." As implementation of the order spread, there was trouble. In the small Tennessee town of Clinton, when twelve black students tried to enroll in schools, seven tanks and several hundred troops from the National Guard were needed to control a mob of a thousand persons that attacked the local police force (which had eight men). The most famous incident came in Little Rock, Arkansas, when nine African American students enrolled in the city's Central High School in the fall of 1957. Crowds shouting racial insults, beating black reporters, and surging up to the steps of the school quickly grew beyond the control of local and state police, and President Eisenhower ordered a unit of paratroopers from 101st Airborne Division into the city. The nine students were protected and escorted to classes, and, by November, the situation had simmered down enough that most troops were withdrawn.

Elsewhere the order to desegregate schools was resisted in less dramatic, but highly effective, ways. Many school districts passed "pupil placement laws," which gave officials the power to assign students to different schools according to their perceived scholastic ability; and, to no one's surprise, the difference in abilities coincided with the pupil's race. White parents withdrew their children from public schools and placed them in newly formed private all-white "academies." District funds sometimes were then taken from the old schools, now mostly black, and given to the new ones.

At the opening of the 1957 academic year, barely a fifth of the South's school districts—637 out of more than 3,000—had even started to desegregate their schools. Change had certainly begun, but it was change affecting public education in many different, often contradictory ways. The legacy of racially separate schools and the High Court's demand that segregation be ended would remain with the nation for decades to come.

Of the long list of authors who have shaped the thoughts and language of American children in the 20th century, probably none has had a greater influence than Theodore Geisel. Hardly a girl or boy in the country would recognize his name, but millions would instantly know him by the name he chose to put on the title pages of his roughly sixty books: Dr. Seuss.

Geisel was born in 1904 in Springfield, Massachusetts. His father worked his way up through the ranks at a brewery and finally was named president—on the day national prohibition went into effect, outlawing the making and sale of beer and other liquor. Possibly from that, Geisel learned that it was important to be flexible in making occupational plans. After graduation from Dartmouth College, where he had edited the humor magazine, he studied literature at Oxford University in England and toured Europe before returning to the United States to draw advertising cartoons for a widely used insect repellent, Flit. He also wrote humorous essays for several prominent publications.

In 1936, Geisel and his wife crossed the Atlantic on an ocean liner. As he later related, the peculiar, insistent rhythm of the ship's engines stuck in his head, and he composed a simple story in verse to match the rhythm, then drew a series of cartoons as illustrations. The result, *And To Think That I Saw It on Mulberry Street,* was turned down by twenty-seven publishers before the twenty-eighth (whose editor was a college friend) took it. It did well. Geisel published it as "Dr. Seuss," a pseudonym he had used on some of his essays. Seuss was his own middle name and his mother's maiden name; the "Dr." perhaps alluded to the doctoral degree he never got at Oxford.

During World War II, Geisel served in the Army Signal Corps, working with the popular film director Frank Capra to produce informational films, including the famous series *Why We Fight.* After the war he worked as a journalist, including time as a foreign correspondent, and continued to make films. In fact, he won three Academy Awards for his work in documentaries and animated cartoons.

His longest-running and greatest contributions came in his children's books, however. All were popular; some were read so widely they became virtually part of the national language, including *Horton Hears a Who, McElligot's Pool, Green Eggs and Ham, If I Ran the Circus,* and *How the Grinch Stole Christmas.* One of these, *The Cat in the Hat,* had a significant impact on education. Geisel wrote it in the mid-1950s, in the middle of the national uproar about public schools and what many considered the poor state of teaching. He set out to give children a book with the basics for beginning readers, but one that also would draw those fresh students into the excitement of reading. As that, this story of a troublemaking cat was a brilliant accomplishment, providing the fundamentals of reading in a storyline children loved, told in simple, amusing rhyme. At the end, he even managed to ask his readers to consider a moral question. When the errand-running mother returns, just as the outlaw cat has cleaned up the wrecked house, the narrator wonders whether to tell her what has gone on. Then he turns to the young reader and poses the question: What would you do? With the book's enormous success, Geisel became head of Beginner Books, a special division of Random House publishers dedicated to putting out simple, entertaining books for early readers. He, himself, wrote more than twenty books for the series.

What was the secret of their appeal? Geisel understood language—words, their rhythms, their wonderful sounds—and used it skillfully. He later gave a lot of credit to high school classes in Latin, which, he said, "allows you to adore words—take them apart and find out where they come from." He had an uncanny gift for inventing words that sounded as if they ought to be in somebody's language. The rhythm of the verses were beautifully suited for reading aloud. Parents liked them as much as their children. Plenty of them continued turning the pages, reading the perfectly phrased rhymes, long after the young audience had nodded off to sleep.

As for the stories and their lessons, Geisel had a knack of seeing the world from a child's-eye view. There were jibes at adults, especially ones who thought they were smarter than they were. Marco, the young boy who narrates *McElligot's Pool*, sits fishing in a pond barely larger than a puddle. A passing farmer ridicules him and calls him a fool. You might be right, Marco answers, but then again, he reminds the man, we can never really know what wonders the world holds, just out of our sight. Marco proceeds to picture an aquatic world that could be down there, just below his dangling bait. Even if the boy catches nothing, his inspired fantasy lifts him above the man who looks down on him, physically and in his attitudes. As in this story, Geisel's books were monuments to unrestrained youthful imagination. Anything—the most fantastic creatures or outlandish machines—was possible, and the more ridiculous and improbable, the better. The stories honor and celebrate wild fantasies and cultivate in children a sense of their own capabilities and worth.

The messages also have emphasized toleration and awareness of the points of views of others. This may have reflected in some way Geisel's childhood: as a boy, during World War I, he was insulted and had rocks thrown at him because of his German name. In *Horton Hears a Who,* a compassionate elephant with sharp hearing saves a tiny world of inhabitants no one else knew existed. The themes of listening to others, trying to see things as others do, and the idiocies of pride and pomposity come through in other books. *The Butter Battle Book* was an obvious play on the nuclear arms race and the lunacies it had produced. In an escalating confrontation between the Yooks and the Zooks, the two sides finally face each other with the final weapon, the Bitsy Big-Boy Boomeroo. Will they wipe each other out? We'll have to wait and be patient, the old warrior in the story tells his grandson. We'll just have to wait and see.

Some of Geisel's books were performed on television, notably *How the Grinch Stole Christmas,* but they remain, most of all, a tribute to the pleasure of reading, especially aloud, and to language itself. In 1956, Geisel became officially a "Dr." when he received an honorary doctorate from his alma mater, Dartmouth. In 1984, he was awarded a special Pulitzer Prize, the nation's highest literary award, "for his contribution for over half a century to the education and enjoyment of America's children and their parents."

## HEALTH

The baby boom brought many changes—not all for the better—to children's health care, just as it did for most aspects of their lives. During the twenty years after 1940, the tremendous upsurge in the number of children ideally should have been matched by a roughly equal growth in the number of doctors to treat them. Unfortunately, the number of students in medical schools and the number of doctors licensed by the American Medical Association did not begin to keep pace with the increase in children. In 1960, in fact, there were fewer doctors per 100,000 persons than there had been in 1950—this in spite of the fact, as any parent can testify, that children tend to get sick more often than their elders. The flood of babies during the ten years after World War II brought with it 38 million possible sore throats and 76 million ear aches. At the end of the 1950s, hospitals had more than five thousand positions waiting to be filled by doctors. As always, inadequacies in medical care was felt most painfully by those who could least afford to pay for it, but virtually all young families felt the squeeze. The baby boom, in short, produced a doctor crunch.

In other ways, however, the years between 1941 and 1960 continued the happier trends in medicine described in earlier chapters. Further medical advances promised longer and healthier lives for American youngsters. Still, medical breakthroughs were of little use to children who lived in isolation and deep poverty. The disparities between richer and poorer, and often between the young of different races and ethnic groups, continued to plague the nation's health care.

In the early 1940s, medical researchers achieved what is probably medicine's greatest single accomplishment of the 20th century—the development of antibiotics. The term "antibiosis" means that one organism is used to resist the growth of another one. In the late 19th century, it had been discovered that certain kinds of bacteria in the soil fought against and often destroyed other bacteria, like that causing the deadly animal disease anthrax. Over the years, scientists found that this "antagonistic action" came when bacteria produced chemical compounds. By 1939, soil bacteria was being isolated, purified, and applied to a few human diseases. Perhaps the greatest step came in 1942, when a team at Oxford University reevaluated the possibilities of penicillin, an antibiotic discovered in 1928 by Alexander Fleming. Penicillin, they found, could be unleashed against numerous infections and infectious diseases. An American research group developed another powerful antibiotic, streptomycin, in 1944.

At the time, antibiotics were called "miracle drugs," and for good reason. Until then even mild infections—a cut on the foot, a sore throat, or a hand burned while cooking breakfast—might escalate into a massive assault on the body. A healthy girl or full-grown man might die—and did—from a blister on the heel or a lung infection that began with a slight cough. Graver wounds and illnesses, such as a bad burn, a puncture of the stomach, or meningitis, proved fatal in a large percentage of cases. With antibiotics, the war against such infections turned into a rout. Penicillin proved effective against a remarkable range of infections, especially those from staphylococci (including pneumonia, bronchitis, laryngitis, meningitis, and infections usually following wounds and burns), as well as diphtheria, anthrax, syphilis, and many others. It takes little to imagine the tremendous impact penicillin and other antibiotics had on medical practice during the carnage of World War II.

On the homefront, antibiotics had an equally dramatic effect, bringing some of their greatest benefits to mothers and children. Deaths of women in childbirth resulted mainly from massive infections following the trauma of labor and delivery. With antibiotics, doctors found it far easier to cope with that threat. The decline in deaths from childbirth was nothing short of astonishing: In 1940 the maternal mortality rate stood at 37.6 per ten thousand births; in 1960, it was 3.7. That is, for every ten women who died from bearing a child in 1940, only one suffered the same fate in 1960.

The benefits to children, if not quite so dramatic, were still impressive. Many "childhood diseases" proved vulnerable to antibiotics. General infections, furthermore, had always been more dangerous to children than adults. High fever and nausea often led to loss of fluids, or dehydration, which is particularly devastating to smaller bodies. Antibiotics, by stemming the effects of infection quickly, would spare millions of children that fate.

The development of new vaccines was another crucial, seemingly miraculous breakthrough. Vaccines and the strategy behind them had been used for generations. A well person was inoculated with a mild form of a disease. The body responded with its usual protective mechanism, producing a natural immunity to any further assault by the disease in its more dangerous forms. During the years after World War II, a series of new vaccines were developed for what had been some of the most common childhood illnesses, such as diphtheria and measles.

Along with these medical discoveries, programs continued to achieve better sanitation and healthier diets and behaviors. The first kind of knowledge focused on how to confront and defeat diseases directly; the second emphasized how to avoid getting diseases in the first place. Together, these efforts continued to improve the chances that children would survive into their adult years.

On the eve of World War II, our infant mortality rate stood at 47 deaths for every thousand live births. Twenty years later that figure was far lower, 26 deaths per thousand, a drop of more than forty percent. Illnesses that had been commonplace killers just a generation or two earlier, especially those susceptible to antibiotics, now were virtually unknown. Names of diseases that used to strike fear in the hearts of parents and children sounded strange to younger Americans. To a boy or girl in 1960, "diphtheria" was as exotic as "beri-beri."

Consider a few categories:

**Deaths of Persons Ages 1–14 (Per 100,000 population)**

|  | 1939–1941 | 1959–1961 |
|---|---|---|
| Infective diseases | 29.8 | 3.7 |
| Respiratory diseases | 27.8 | 8.4 |
| Influenza & pneumonia | 24.3 | 6.3 |
| Circulatory diseases | 9.0 | 1.4 |
| Tuberculosis | 7.7 | .3 |
| Rheumatic fever | 5.6 | .5[16] |

These remarkable accomplishments meant that for many millions of American children—though not all—serious disease and early death were only a remote possibility. That, as shown in earlier chapters, was very different from the facts of life, and death, in the early 20th century.

One of the most devastating child-killers, diphtheria, was practically wiped out. As described in chapter 1, in 1900, diphtheria was a familiar and dreaded part of growing up. Thousands of parents every year watched their sons and daughters suffer its horrors and sometimes slowly suffocate. But in the next forty years, improved hygiene and treatment had the disease on the run. The rate of death had shrunk from 40 per 100,000 in 1900 to 1.2 per 100,000 in 1945, although about 20,000 persons still contracted diphtheria every year during World War II. Then, in 1945, a diphtheria vaccine, quickly termed the "DPT" shot, came into use. Mortality from the illness dwindled from 1.2 to .1 in six years, then to less than .05 (figures per 100,000). Diphtheria, in effect, disappeared. A similar story could be told about whooping cough. Nearly 200,000 cases were reported in 1940, and although its death toll had been cut dramatically (from 12.0 per 100,000 in 1900 to 2.2 per 100,000 in 1940), about one child victim out of a hundred still died. With the widespread use of a vaccine, whooping cough dwindled to fewer than 15,000 cases in 1960 and only about 2,000 cases in 1977.

Surely the most dramatic single breakthrough of these years—and one of the most significant in the long war against childhood disease—was the defeat of poliomyelitis. Polio is probably an ancient disease—a drawing from Egypt of 1400 B.C. shows, a priest with a foot seemingly deformed by it—but the disease was not clearly described by physicians until late in the 19th century. Polio viruses are communicated usually through the mouth, often by tiny droplets of water. Its most common victims are children and adolescents—its earlier name was "infantile paralysis"—although adults certainly are not immune. The most famous victim in the nation was President Franklin D. Roosevelt, who contracted it at the age of thirty-nine and whose legs remained paralyzed the rest of his life.

Polio begins with headaches, fever, weakness, and aching of muscles and limbs. In most cases, children survive with no lasting consequences; but in some, the disease affects the central nervous system and results in paralysis of muscles, sometimes permanent. When the muscles affected are those of the lungs, the victim either dies or must live with artificial help in breathing. In the 1940s and 1950s, that help was in the form of an "iron lung," a large metal cylinder enclosing all of the body except the head. More often polio left persons unable to move their legs. Therapy took the form of rigorous exercise to regain the use of muscles and the application of cloths soaked in extremely hot water. Because the paralysis does not bring with it the loss of feeling, such treatment was quite painful.

Polio was a terrifying disease, not only because of its symptoms, but also because its causes were unknown and because it could spread so rapidly through whole communities and families. For years it would recede, only to flare up again and rage through the country. Only in the 1950s did researchers learn for certain how it was contracted. Until then, its spread was variously attributed to insects, water supplies and sewage, personal contact, or contaminated food and milk. Here, then, was a killer and crippler of the young, striking apparently at random, always lurking, waiting to devastate families and cause immeasurable physical and emotional pain.

Epidemics had struck earlier in the century—more than 9,000 cases in New York City alone were reported during one in 1916—but the worst came during World War II and in the early 1950s. The rate of infection in 1942, 3.1 per 100,000 persons, more than tripled by 1944 as over 27,000 cases were recorded that year. "Parents were as frightened of polio as they were of the Germans and Japanese," a man recalled of his boyhood in those years.[17] The epidemic receded, then arose again between 1949 and 1954. The toll in 1952—nearly 58,000 cases, or 37.2 per 100,000 persons—was far and away the worst of the century. More than 1,400 persons died. Understandably, parents were deeply frightened, even panicked. Many kept their children inside houses, sealing windows and doors. Public swimming pools and theaters were closed. There was the feeling of a state of siege.

But the end was near. The wartime epidemics had inspired a massive research program, led by the National Foundation for Infantile Paralysis, which financed the efforts partly through a continuing fund-raising campaign, the March of Dimes. The medical assault was one of the most extensive (and expensive) in history, but it produced results. Major breakthroughs occurred in the late 1940s; and in 1953, as part of a program involving nearly two million boys and girls, Dr. Jonas Salk of the University of Pittsburgh tested a vaccine on more than 400,000 children. It worked.

At a news conference on April 12, 1955, Salk announced the victory. In towns throughout the country church bells rang, traffic stopped as car horns blared in celebration, even court trials were interrupted as judges gave out the good news. Newspapers printed the announcement under headlines as large and bold as those telling of the world war's end a decade earlier. And indeed, to many parents the relief from the news was equally great. Massive programs of vaccination began right away, and the next year the rate of infection plummeted. In 1962, a new oral vaccine developed by Alfred Sabin was approved. Even more effective and more easily administered, it soon was being taken by children throughout much of the world.

With that polio was virtually eliminated, at least in the United States. Its legacy remained in the mid-1990s in the tens of thousands of polio survivors, most of them adults who had suffered the disease as children in the early 1950s. As many as half of them had begun to experience "post-polio syndrome," with muscle pains, weakness, and other symptoms similar to the disease itself, although not as intense. Nonetheless, the ravages of this terrible killer were virtually ended. Between 1915 and 1955, about 357,000 cases were recorded in this country; between 1969 and 1979, only 179 new cases were reported, virtually all of them rare reactions to the oral vaccine. In the 1990s, the number of cases of polio, the disease that once terrified the nation, averaged about ten per year.

Nevertheless, nagging problems remained. The poorest children, which, as before, often meant many of those of certain racial and ethnic groups, continued to suffer and sicken far more often than those of more financially comfortable families. There were also hints that the war for improved children's health, having vanquished some of its most prominent enemies, now was confronting challenges that would prove more frustrating.

From one perspective, medical breakthroughs and improved sanitation benefited all Americans. No matter what segment of society is considered— rich or poor, black or white, new immigrant or longtime resident—the likelihood of getting seriously sick or dying was dropping during these years. But from another perspective, not all Americans shared equally in these advances. As indicated in the chart below, a gap continued to yawn between the situation for black Americans and the total population:

**Infant Mortality Rates (Deaths per 1,000 live births)**

|  | Total Population | Black |
|---|---|---|
| 1940 | 47.0 | 73.8 |
| 1945 | 38.3 | 57.0 |
| 1950 | 29.2 | 44.5 |
| 1955 | 26.4 | 42.8 |
| 1960 | 26.0 | 43.2 |

Maternal Mortality Rates (Deaths per 10,000 live births)

|      | Total Population | Black |
|------|------------------|-------|
| 1940 | 37.6             | 77.4  |
| 1945 | 20.7             | 45.5  |
| 1950 | 8.3              | 22.2  |
| 1955 | 4.7              | 13.0  |
| 1960 | 3.7              | 9.8[18] |

Being born and giving birth was far more treacherous for African Americans than for their white counterparts. Conditions were improving for everybody, but for black children and mothers, those improvements still lagged ten or twenty years behind.

Statistically, American Indians fared more poorly than blacks in terms of infant mortality. In the mid-1950s, the infant morality rate among Native Americans was 80 per thousand live births, more than three times that of whites and twice that of blacks. Among Indians in Arizona and New Mexico, the rates were much higher still: 127 and 121 per thousand, respectively. The death rate among Native American mothers in those states from childbirth was also triple that of the nation.

Native American children who survived their first months of life suffered much higher rates of disease than most American youngsters. About a third of all patients in Indian hospitals were under the age of fifteen. Most commonly they fell ill with respiratory maladies, especially pneumonia and influenza, and digestive illnesses, like typhoid, dysentery, and gastritis. Hospital care was woefully underfunded and understaffed. At a clinic on the Navajo reservation, for instance, a doctor often saw up to seventy-five patients in a session. Many hospitals had no laboratories and no provisions for blood transfusions. Far too few nurses had to cover far too much area and too many patients. Government investigators found health staffs grossly inadequate.

Medical care for another group, migrant workers, lagged far behind that for most other families. In a southern California county, a survey found that, even in 1960, six out of ten children under three had not yet received any of the standard immunizations for diphtheria, whooping cough, tetanus, or smallpox. In Texas, the Public Health Service found that only four out of eighty-three persons examined had ever been vaccinated for polio. Results of such poor care were predictable. In Minnesota, another investigation showed, two-thirds of migrants over age fifteen had positive tuberculin tests, compared to 13 percent for the nation.

These groups, though widely scattered, had certain conditions in common. They were nonwhites who exercised little political power, and they were poor and had few resources either to pay for good health care or to provide a heathier living environment. Another common denominator was that many of them—African Americans, Native Americans, and migrant workers—also lived in rural regions of the country. In many cases, they were far from medical care, even if such care was adequate and if they could pay for it. In the northeastern portions of the Navajo reservation, an area of more than 4,500 square miles was home to only 13,000 people. In much of the South, African Americans lived isolated on small farms far from modest-sized towns. Health conditions for children in these areas were among the nation's worst; yet, even so, considerable improvements were felt, especially when imaginative approaches were used.

Arkansas provides a case in point. That southern state lagged far behind the nation both in income and in the movement of its people toward the cities. The great majority of Arkansans continued to live in the countryside, far from dependable medical facilities. The poverty and isolation of African Americans in Arkansas were considerably worse—as was the quality of their health care. World War II only deepened these problems, as the government and the American Medical Association called for physicians to join the armed forces and care for the nation's fighting men and women. At the time of Pearl Harbor, there were about 1,800 doctors in Arkansas, or about one for every 1,113 persons. (The national ratio at the time was one per 750 persons.) Six months later, the number of doctors in the state had shrunk to barely a thousand; and, at the end of the war, only 990 physicians were practicing in Arkansas, or about one for every two thousand people. These doctors, furthermore, mostly worked in cities and larger towns. At the moment of the nation's greatest triumph, on the eve of a period of unmatched prosperity, rural Arkansans lived most of their lives without knowing anything resembling adequate medical care.

The situations surrounding childbirth in Arkansas were especially appalling. In 1941, fewer than a fourth of the births in Arkansas took place in a hospital, and about another fourth were delivered by midwives. That meant that a majority of babies were born with no medical attention whatsoever. The result, predictably, was a high rate of infant mortality. At least one death out of ten in the state was that of a baby under the age of one year, and because so many stillbirths and infant deaths went unreported, the situation was actually much worse than these figures indicate.

The response of the state government and its medical association was to concentrate on improving the quality of the most common form of help in childbirth among rural black Arkansans, that of midwives. In 1945, Mamie Hale, a graduate of the Tuskegee School of Nurse-Midwifery, was placed in charge of a training program, consisting of a seven-week course and ending with an examination. Her challenge was especially great because three out of four black midwives could not read or write and only one in twenty was literate enough to fill out a birth certificate. Hale used demonstrations, films, photographs, and songs to teach practical methods of dealing with situations her students would be facing. Newspapers, for instance, were put in a wood stove and cooked until they began to brown; these were placed under a mother in labor to provide more sterile surroundings for the birth. Tape for tying off a newborn's umbilical cord should be cooked, students were told, the same as a medium potato. Programs like these were extended to most counties, and after five years of classes, the great majority of midwife-assisted births were with trained and certified women. The infant mortality rate fell significantly, and the number of African American women dying from complications of pregnancy and childbirth in 1950 was only 43, down from 128 in 1930.[19]

In June 1946, a thirty-five-cent paperback book appeared on the market: *The Common Sense Book of Baby and Child Care*, by Dr. Benjamin Spock. It became one of the most influential—and eventually one of the most controversial—books of the century. It was also one of the most financially successful. Spock's book was the best-selling new publication in American history. Within six years, four million copies had been sold; the public bought at least a million copies a year for the next eighteen years in a row. Thirty million copies were in print in 1960, with editions in twenty-nine languages, including Urdu. Benjamin Spock became one of the most familiar names in the country.

Spock's remarkable book on caring for children had several things going for it. The author's credentials were impressive. A graduate of Yale (and, along the way, winner of a gold medal in rowing in the 1924 Olympic Games), he went on to earn a medical degree in pediatrics, then complete several years of psychiatric training. He had been in pediatric practice for ten years when he wrote his book. And Spock wrote very well. He was able to communicate his knowledge and experience in an easy, conversational style with touches of good humor. He had a gift for speaking compassionately (and, as the title announced, with common sense) about the fears and concerns of parents, mothers especially. His deepest interest, he explained later, was not in unusual cases, but in helping parents deal with the day-to-day challenges of child rearing. He obviously loved children and working with them. His warm personality and dedication came across to the reader, and readers responded.

But the book was also a phenomenal success because of what Spock said, not just how he said it. Glancing through the original edition, a reader would find a few clear themes running through its five hundred pages. Spock first urged parents to have more self-confidence in rearing their children. The opening words of *The Common Sense Book of Baby and Child Care* became some of the most famous in the history of popular literature: "You know more than you think you do." Trust your instincts, Spock was saying, as well as your observations, your practical sense, and your experience. In a way, his book was as much about women as children; mothers responded to it partly because it respected their insights and abilities. Self-trust, in turn, encouraged a flexibility toward children, their training, and treatment. Parents should have a toleration for a child's own pace of development and his or her own personality. Finally, Spock wrote to mothers and fathers, don't be afraid to show generous affection and to enjoy young children's company. Openly demonstrated love is natural and healthy.

Such advice might seem obvious, and it hardly sounds controversial. But, in fact, Spock's words struck a chord because they were an articulate and persuasive contrast to opinions that had prevailed until quite recently. The most influential manual of child care of the previous generation was John B. Watson's *Psychological Care of Infant and Child,* published in 1928. Where Spock told mothers to trust themselves more, Watson had urged them to question their instincts and to follow rigid regimens and rules. Those rules were based on experiments in behavioral psychology that left little room for individual differences among infants and young people. Daily care should be governed strictly according to iron standards and an exact schedule. An infant should be awakened, fed, and put to bed at precise times, for instance; water in its bath should be no less than four inches deep, no more than eight; weaning and toilet training should occur by a specific age and no later.

Of the various rules to be followed, the most important was: Don't give your baby too much affection. "Mother love is a dangerous instrument," Watson wrote. Cuddling, kissing, or simply touching a child threatened to make it overly dependent on parents and incapable of forging a successful adult life. Many modern ills, including divorce and men's unsuccessful careers, were blamed on the sympathy and excessive affection of mothers. So restrain yourself, Watson told mothers and fathers, and keep your babies at a healthy distance:

Treat them as though they were young adults. . . . Never hug and kiss them, never let them sit in your lap. If you must, kiss them once on the forehead when they say good night. Shake hands with them in the morning. Give them a pat on the head if they have made an extraordinary good job of a difficult task. Try it out. In a week's time you will find how easy it is. . . . You will be utterly ashamed of the mawkish, sentimental way you have been handling it.[20]

Well before Spock wrote his book, other authorities had been moving away from Watson's rigid behavioralism and his aloof treatment of youngsters. C. Andrews Aldrich and his wife, Mary, encouraged parents to respond warmly to their children's emotional needs. Their book, *Babies are Human Beings,* appeared in 1938, about halfway between Watson's and Spock's. *The Common Sense Book of Baby and Child Care* crystallized, in an appealing way, newer attitudes about parenthood and looking after children. It also provided a wealth of practical information about childhood diseases, preparation of baby formula, vaccinations, diet, teething, and diapers.

Spock—and before him, Watson—also reflected broader changes in attitudes toward children and their place in the family and society. Both had at least something in common: the assumption that rearing a well-adjusted child was a central responsibility of an adult. Watson dedicated his book to "the first mother who brings up a happy child." But Watson's stress was on fostering a fierce self-reliance, a goal more in keeping with turn-of-the-century values. The emphasis was more on strength of inner character and less on working within groups and communities. Parents should prepare a child for an independent life, and they should do so literally from the start. Soon after an infant's arrival, Watson suggested, leave it outdoors in a fenced yard much of the day, and when it learns to crawl, be sure to dig holes for it to fall into and crawl out of. "Let it learn to overcome difficulties almost from the moment of birth," he told mothers, "and if you are worried and *must* check on your backyard baby, don't let it see you. Watch through a peephole or periscope."[21]

Spock's advice was based, first, on the spreading ideal of a companionate and loving family, with plenty of affection openly expressed. He pointed out that both sons and daughters needed the close attention, friendship, and approval of fathers as well as mothers. A father's role was to "enjoy [his son] when he's around, give him the feeling he's a chip off the old block, share a secret with him, take him alone on excursions sometimes." Much of the material on behavior concerned getting along with others—table manners, social responses, meeting strangers, playing with friends, adjusting to school, and dealing with the awkwardness of puberty. The focus was on preparation for participation in society, as was the case with so much professional attention to childhood of the 1940s and earlier.

Spock's thoughts on education, for instance, were echoes of Dewey and other educational "progressives." A good school, he wrote, adjusts to a pupil's needs and abilities, teaches its students firsthand about the outside world, and encourages democracy through classroom practices. The family, too, should be more democratic, or at least less authoritarian. Children should be given room to establish their own identities, to "play at their own level," for instance, and explore through their own curiosity, all the while supported by friendly mothers and fathers. Parents ought to be moderately tolerant of what was traditionally considered improper behavior, such as using "dirty" words, moodiness, aggressive play, and occasional bad manners.

Spock originally thought he was bringing commonsensical advice based on extensive experience: "I was trying to take the psychoanalytic concepts I was studying and somehow fit them together with what mothers were telling me about their babies. . . . I really suffered and sweated trying to figure out the best advice to give."[22] His emphasis was on a pragmatic flexibility. He was especially concerned, for example, that rigid schedules of toilet training and weaning might do unnecessary harm to youngsters, in light of prevailing Freudian ideas about such things. (Ironically, breast-feeding was falling out of fashion altogether during these years, from 65 percent of newborns in 1946 to 27 percent in 1966; for most mothers, in other words, the timing of weaning was irrelevant.)

In time, however, critics accused Spock and his book of encouraging a rampant "permissiveness" toward babies and children. This overly lenient attitude on all aspects of behavior, it was said, produced spoiled, self-indulgent, irresponsible adolescents and young adults. This criticism grew especially intense during the 1960s, years of youthful "countercultural" rebellion against many institutions. Spock was accused of creating a selfish, ill-disciplined, unpatriotic generation—a charge many saw confirmed when he spoke out openly and often against the war in Vietnam.

Early on, Spock, himself, saw the need to emphasize, in revised editions of his famous book, that parents should guard against overindulgence and should provide firm, consistent, loving discipline. In 1994, when he published his seventeenth book at age ninety-one, he called for greater attention to family and less to material consumption and competition. Even then, however, nearly fifty years after his first and best-known book appeared, he reported being frequently accused of "permissiveness."[23]

Spock's significance, and that of *The Common Sense Book of Baby and Child Care,* was twofold. First, his role in the ordinary aspects of child health can hardly be overemphasized. Millions of mothers turned to the man and his book for answers about everything from mumps and tantrums to diaper rashes and stuttering. As families became more and more mobile and nuclear, Spock took the place of absent trusted relatives as a source of advice and comfort. In this sense, *Baby and Child Care* also was part of a democratization of medicine. In an era when doctors were seen less often as distant, unchallengeable experts, Spock was more of a collaborator who listened to what mothers had to say.

Spock's popularity and influence—and the criticisms leveled at him— should also be understood as part of questions and patterns, emphasized throughout these chapters, that reach far beyond issues of health and child care. What is the right balance between granting children freedom and directing their lives in their best interests? If the family is, among many things, a relationship of power, where should a parent's authority stop and a child's begin? When does loving control become unhealthy (and ineffective) repression? As a child grows up, how best can he or she be encouraged to find a reasonable balance between his or her own needs and a responsibility toward society and family?

## CHILDREN AND THE LAW

During the 1940s and 1950s, there was a growing concern over youthful crime and general misconduct. A phrase that had been around for a while, "juvenile delinquency," became part of the common public vocabulary. Troubled youth, tending to lawlessness, showed up in popular movies and television programs. Authors of articles in popular magazines, prominent politicians, social critics, and educational authorities warned that American young people were behaving in disturbing—and in some cases dangerous and criminal—ways. With these warnings came all sorts of opinions about what was going wrong and what to do about it.

Part of the cause for concern over delinquency is obvious. The baby boom meant, in the first place, that there were many more young people to be concerned about. In this "child-centered" era, it was also natural to pay more attention to how children were acting, alone or in groups, and with that was bound to come some alarm. The profound social and economic changes of these twenty years were sure to raise some questions about how young people were being affected. War and the 1950s brought more prosperity and opportunity; it also put the family under new stresses. More and more mothers spent less time at home and more in the workplace. The result were millions of "latchkey" children, boys and girls left on their own for hours every day. This problem seemed especially threatening during the war, with so many fathers gone and, with them, it was feared, much of the family's discipline. Good times also pulled many young people themselves into jobs that some critics thought were not the best environments. Affluence and technology, finally, gave young Americans new freedom and exposed them to new influences. Some adults, inevitably, found some of the consequences worrisome.

Nonetheless, there is no firm agreement on how much juvenile crime and delinquency increased in this period. Both the Federal Bureau of Investigation and the Children's Bureau agreed that juvenile crime rose during the war, but the rise does not seem to have been nearly as great as many persons feared, and according to the Census Bureau, once the war was over, the number of arrests of persons under eighteen settled back to what it had been before:

|      | All ages | Under 18 |
|------|----------|----------|
| 1940 | 609,000  | 35,000   |
| 1942 | 586,000  | 38,000   |
| 1945 | 544,000  | 50,000   |
| 1947 | 659,000  | 34,000   |
| 1950 | 794,000  | 35,000[24] |

Local agencies reported dramatic increases during the 1950s, but this may have been because law enforcement bodies were paying more attention to perennial "delinquent" behavior, such as loitering, truancy, and general rowdiness. The statistics might also reflect not so much a change in the character of young people, but America's new affluence and changing lifestyles. "Joyriding," for instance, the taking of an automobile to cruise around for an hour or so, was usually included under the more serious category of auto theft. What seemed clearly to be a boom in juvenile crime, in other words, may have been largely changes in perceptions toward young people and larger developments in American life. When actual arrests in New York City of children under sixteen were analyzed, the "crime rate" of young people was found to be five times greater in 1907 than in 1950.

Alarm over juvenile delinquency, then, probably says as much about adults—parents, politicians, and social critics—and their anxieties as it does about young people and their behavior. There was a vigorous debate in the nation's newspapers and periodicals over the ways the media and popular culture supposedly encouraged delinquency. In the mid-1950s, the *New York Times* published more than fifty articles in a year on the subject, an average of one a week. This criticism focused on those entertainments that, as shown in the earlier chapters, young people had embraced enthusiastically. Hollywood, as usual, reflected the nation's worries by putting out films about rebellious, troubled youth, including the extremely popular *Rebel without a Cause, The Wild One,* and *Blackboard Jungle.* Although these movies all ended with fairly uplifting moral messages, some authorities charged that they glamorized and encouraged youthful disrespect and misbehavior. City fathers in Memphis, Tennessee, went so far as to forbid theaters from showing *Blackboard Jungle.*

Another target was comic books. Frederic Wertham's *Seduction of the Innocent* (1954) was a widely read assault on comics generally, but especially "crime" and "horror" comics and others that featured violence and aggression. Comics, Wertham claimed, were popular culture's greatest influence on children, and that influence was not a good one. In particular Wertham and others claimed that the graphic portrayals of violence stimulated similar behavior in youthful readers. Many parents who read his book and articles wrote the psychiatrist letters of agreement, like this one from a California mother:

> We have two boys, 7 and 13, with unusually high intelligence and excellent ability in school and in sports . . . yet in the presence of comic books they behave as if drugged, and will not lift their eyes or speak when spoken to. . . . My boys fight with each other in a manner that is unbelievable in a home where both parents are university graduates and perfectly mated. We attribute the so-called "hatred" they profess for each other to the harmful influence of these books, plus movies and radio.[25]

The highpoint of the debate came in a series of hearings of the U.S. Senate's Subcommittee to Investigate Juvenile Delinquency. The hearings attracted a huge popular audience, especially after Senator Estes Kefauver of Tennessee became chair of the subcommittee. One reason for this wide attention was television; at one time an estimated 86 percent of daytime audience tuned in to hear the testimony. This was ironic, because another reason for all the attention was the subcommittee's questions about the role of the media and its power over American society. Testimony concerned many causes of youthful crime, including troubled home life and poor schools; but, from 1954 to 1956, it concentrated on the role of the media.

In these hearings, Wertham and others laid out their arguments that the mass media was a major cause of the alarming spread of delinquency. Special attention was given to comic books, particularly the "crime" and "horror" variety that Wertham and so many parents worried about. The graphic and gory illustrations and the stories featuring brutal murders appalled some of the senators. In one exchange, William Gaines, the most successful publisher of such comic books, was questioned by Senator Kefauver and two committee investigators, Herbert Beaser and Herbert Hannock:

> *Beaser:* There would be no limit to what you'd actually put in the magazines?
>
> *Gaines:* Only within the bounds of good taste.
>
> *Kefauver:* Here is [the cover of] your May issue. This seems to be a man with a bloody ax holding a woman's head up which has been severed from her body. Do you think that's in good taste?
>
> *Gaines:* Yes, sir, I do—for the cover of a horror comic. A cover in bad taste, for example, might be defined as holding the head a little higher so that the blood could be seen dripping from it, and moving the body over a little further so that the neck of the body could be seen to be bloody.
>
> *Kefauver:* You've got blood coming out of her mouth.
>
> *Gaines:* A little.
>
> *Kefauver:* And here's blood on the ax. I think most *adults* are shocked by that. Now here's a man with a woman in a boat and he's choking her to death with a crowbar. Is that in good taste?
>
> *Gaines:* I think so.
>
> *Hannock:* How could it be worse?[26]

Other experts replied that delinquency was not nearly so widespread and that its causes were far too complicated to be blamed mainly on popular media, even comics with decapitations on their covers. The committee's report in 1957 did not advocate any drastic legal intervention—it called, instead, for further study of the problem—but there were plenty of local efforts to regulate or ban altogether controversial comics and movies. Pressure on publishers seems to have been especially successful. Of the twenty-nine companies producing crime comics at the time that *Seduction of the Innocent* appeared, twenty-four were out of business within a few years.

The alarm and arguments over delinquency and the media reflected new developments, such as the rise of new technologies and troubling changes in the family, but also expressed continuing questions about children and society. Were boys and girls manipulated and controlled by outside forces, such as films and comics, or did those things reveal the demands of children who were making up their own minds about what they wanted to see and read? Were critics worried about a surge in crime and a youthful threat to society, or was there also a deeper hostility toward children who were, as always, exerting their independence?

Looking back, World War II probably brought more changes to American society than any other four years in our history. Among those changes was the federal government's new and expanded responsibility toward children and their mothers. Some of these new responsibilities were cut back for a time after the war, but most have been continued in some form until the present.

During the war years, for instance, Washington embarked on an unprecedented experiment in government support of child health. The Emergency Medical and Infant Care Program (EMIC) provided maternity care for wives of servicemen in the lowest ranks. This program was a response to the great dislocations brought about by drafting men into the armed forces on a scale never dreamed of before. Soldiers' wives not only were often short of funds, they also might find themselves strangers in cities distant from their homes and with no friends or family to direct them to medical help. Although the main motive of this program was to boost the morale of husbands far away at war—and by that to improve the military effort—the effects nonetheless were felt by families on the home front, who could more easily find and afford medical care. By the time the EMIC was phased out in 1949, more than a million and a half mothers and babies had received some kind of aid.

During the war, the national government made a similar commitment in the area of children's day care. Before 1942, day care had been mostly the concern of private organizations. Policies and goals also had shifted and changed over the years. Late in the 19th century, middle- and upper-class women began organizing the first centers. Their concern was as much for mothers as for children. Especially in the cities, they saw many lower-class women who had to work to help support their families. By watching over girls and boys as young as two, these women set out to help these mothers through a difficult time—and also to teach the children their own values and ideals.

By the time of World War I, however, day care was mostly being run by social workers, who had different goals. Public child care, they thought, should be mainly for "pathological" family situations, for children of parents who (in the opinion of the social workers) were not rearing their boys and girls correctly. No longer was the purpose simply to help out poor families in a fix. Putting a child in such a nursery, of course, became a humiliation, an admission that something was very wrong at home. Enrollments in day care facilities dropped drastically.

Then, after 1933, the situation changed again. Under the Works Progress Administration (WPA), the federal government funneled money into day care centers as part of the New Deal effort to create jobs for those thrown out of work by the depression. For the first time, public funds, both federal and state, were used to pay for this service. The official goals of day care also changed once again. Now the purpose was said to be mainly educational, and most centers were set up in schools. Enrollments surged; by 1937, forty thousand children were given day care in more than nineteen hundred centers.

The coming of war once again changed the purposes and policy of children's day care. Suddenly it was the patriotic duty of women, including mothers, to work outside the home for the war effort. This created a problem for mothers of preschoolers, and the obvious solution seemed to be that national and state governments should provide some means for watching over those children whose parents were away in the armed services and at the factories. In 1941, Congress passed the Community Facilities Act, often called the Lanham Act, which provided federal funding for all sorts of social services necessitated by the war. A court decision in 1942 held that such services could include day care for children of working mothers, and by year's end hundreds of centers were being opened. On the eve of the Japanese surrender, a million and a half American children were in day care facilities. The government had spent nearly fifty million dollars building and running those centers. Several state governments had spent millions more, and some wartime industries, for example many Pacific coast shipyards, were providing space and supervision for workers' children. Child day care had become a common and widely accepted aspect of family life.

The assumption behind such care, however, was always that it was a temporary expedient, a sacrifice, like rationing of sugar and automobile tires, that would be ended as soon as victory was at hand. Federal money for day care was administered through the Federal Works Agency, whose job was to bring women into the factories, not to oversee children's well being. Support, in other words, did not reflect any fundamental change in the underlying assumptions about working women and their youngsters.

So once the war was over, funds under the Lanham Act were withdrawn and more than 2,800 day care centers were quickly closed. Mothers were expected to resume their roles as homemakers and tend to their daughters and sons while husbands, home from the battle, would resume their peacetime jobs. In fact, however, large numbers of women remained in the workplace, and during the years that followed more and more left their homes to take jobs. Many of these were mothers who had to support children on their own. By 1956, a million American women were widowed, deserted, divorced, or living apart from their husbands; and half of these were holding down jobs while supporting preschool children. In many other cases, wives living with husbands worked outside the home, often to help meet the expenses of a middle-class lifestyle. In 1948, of all mothers who had young children and lived with their husbands, roughly one out of ten had a job outside the house. By 1966, one out of every four did. In short, in the postwar years a large and growing number of women needed some sort of daytime care for their preschool children.

Getting such care, however, was difficult. In the vast majority of cases, children were left at home, sometimes to look after themselves. Those kept outside the home usually were cared for by relatives. Only about two percent of such children were kept in day care centers or nursery schools in 1960. By then, furthermore, the official policy toward day care had returned to what it had been during the years after World War I. Facilities should be available for "socially deviant" families. "The child who needs day care," according to the Children's Bureau in 1963, "has a family problem which makes it impossible for his parents to fulfill their parental responsibilities." Nonetheless, if public facilities for young children of working parents were sparse, there was a basis for change. The policy of agencies like the Children's Bureau rested on doing what was best for the child. Day care, the bureau argued, was a way of strengthening family life and preventing neglect of some boys and girls. Here was a beginning for the change in attitudes toward working mothers that would later open the way to a broader acceptance of professional day care as a benefit for millions of children in ordinary families.

# BIBLIOGRAPHICAL ESSAY

## General Works

Fortunately for researchers, there are many excellent histories covering the period of the 1940s and 1950s, including: John Patrick Diggins, *The Proud Decades: America in War and Peace* (New York: Norton, 1988), William Manchester, *The*

*Glory and the Dream: A Narrative History of America, 1932–1972* (Boston: Little, Brown, 1974, and later editions), and Richard Polenberg, *One Nation Divisible* (New York: Penguin Books, 1980). A good history of the greatest war of this century is Gordon Wright's *The Ordeal of Total War, 1939–1945* (New York: Harper and Row, 1968), and for the story of the home front, consult Richard Polenberg's *War and Society: The United States, 1941–1945* (Philadelphia: Lippincott, 1972) and John Morton Blum's *V Was for Victory: Politics and American Culture during World War II* (New York: Harcourt, Brace, Jovanovich, 1976).

Sherna Berger Gluck's *Rosie the Riveter Revisited: Women, the War and Social Change* (Boston: Twayne Publishers, 1987) deals with the changes and opportunities open to women during World War II. On the detention of thousands of loyal Japanese American citizens after Japan's attack on Pearl Harbor, see Roger Daniels's *Concentration Campus USA: Japanese Americans and World War II* (New York: Holt, Rinehard, Winston, 1981).

There are two fine narrative histories, both full of fascinating detail, on the decade of the 1950s, a period historians today consider one of modern America's most eventful and significant: David Halberstam's *The Fifties* (New York: Villard Books, 1993) and Douglas T. Miller and Marion Nowak's *The Fifties: The Way We Really Were* (Garden City, N.Y.: Doubleday and Co., 1977). For an insightful, if sometimes troubling, account of the nation's economic and social trends and its popular culture, see George Lipsitz's *Class and Culture in Cold War America: "A Rainbow at Midnight"* (New York: Praeger, 1981). Finally, an invaluable book on these years, one explicitly recognizing the role of children both as driving forces in their parents' lives and as actors in their own right, is Landon Y. Jones's *Great Expectations: America and the Baby Boom Generation* (New York: Ballantine Books, 1980). Highly readable and insightful, it has much material on many of the subjects that are the focus of this chapter, from child-rearing and television, to rock and roll, suburban housing, and fast foods.

Readers can also find solid information in some of the basic sources mentioned in the previous bibliographical essays. Two chapters in Joseph M. Hawes and N. Ray Hiner's *American Childhood: A Research Guide and Historical Handbook* (Westport, Conn.: Greenwood Press, 1985) cover the years of World War II, the baby boom, and the 1950s. Robert H. Bremner's essential volumes, *Children and Youth in America: A Documentary History* (Cambridge: Harvard University Press, 1971), bring together invaluable material on many of the topics considered in this chapter, including social history, education, health care, public policy, and juvenile delinquency.

## At Home

On the American family during these transforming years of our society, readers should consult an outstanding book mentioned earlier, Steven Mintz and Susan Kellogg's *Domestic Revolutions: A Social History of American Life* (New York:

Free Press, 1988), which has two fine chapters on families during World War II and the 1950s. A history of the American family that focuses more specifically on these years is Elaine Tyler May's *Homeward Bound: American Families in the Cold War Era* (New York: Basic Books, 1988). On the war years, an absolutely essential work on children and families is William M. Tuttle, Jr.'s *"Daddy's Gone to War": The Second World War in the Lives of America's Children* (New York: Oxford University Press, 1993). One of the most intelligent and perceptive looks at young people and American society in any period, this book provides both broad analysis and vivid detail on topics ranging from home life and games to work and relations among young people, mothers, and fathers. Another crucial source is Robert L. Griswold's *Fatherhood in America: A History* (New York: Basic Books, 1993). Griswold covers a vast span from the early 19th century until the 1990s, and his book should be read for a better understanding of the entire period, but some of his most insightful and important chapters concern the years of the Great Depression, World War II, and the baby boom generation. Like the best works cited in these essays, Griswold's integrates the history of children with that of the society in which they lived. Yet another book on families and societies during these years is Stephanie Coontz's *The Way We Never Were: American Families and the Nostalgia Trap* (New York: Basic Books, 1992). Coontz argues that the idealized image of families, rooted especially in the popular view of the relatively prosperous years from 1945 to 1960, was always distorted and remains an unrealistic standard for many Americans. Families, she writes, have always been more diverse, unstable, and troubled than our nostalgic view of the past would have it.

Excellent sources are also available on the housing revolution. A good general survey noted in an earlier essay, Clifford Edward Clark, Jr.'s *The American Home, 1800–1960* (Chapel Hill: University of North Carolina Press, 1986) has two chapters that are particularly pertinent to this period, one on "ranch style" houses and another on the "suburban complex." On the modern suburban era and the sprawling development that ushered it in, see Herbert Gans's *The Levittowners: Ways of Life and Politics in a New Suburban Community* (New York: Pantheon, 1967). And no research on this topic will be complete without consulting Kenneth T. Jackson's splendid *Crabgrass Frontier: The Suburbanization of the United States* (New York: Oxford University Press, 1985), which also was mentioned earlier. His discussions of postwar suburbs, the "drive in culture" of those years, and the withering of community life are the most valuable on these subjects. For an entertaining, occasionally fascinating, and frequently angry commentary on postwar trends in housing and community development, read James Howard Kunstler's *The Geography of Nowhere: The Rise and Decline of America's Man-Made Landscape* (New York: Touchstone Books, 1993).

On television, the great transforming force of these years, the best accessible history is Erik Barnouw's *Tube of Plenty: The Evolution of American Television* (New York: Oxford University Press, 1982). All social histories of this period contain much material on television, and discussions in the books by Manchester,

Halberstam, and Jones, mentioned above in this essay, are particularly good. See also Ella Taylor's *Prime Time Families: Television Culture in Postwar America* (Berkeley: University of California Press, 1989). Far and away the best work on American foodways during this generation is Harvey Levenstein's *Paradox of Plenty: A Social History of Eating in Modern America* (New York: Oxford University Press, 1993), with chapters on the "golden age of food processing" and on other aspects of life at the American dinner table.

## At Play

Histories of television, including the ones mentioned just above, deal with children's programming and situation comedies (or sitcoms), and David Halberstam's *The Fifties* has a particularly good discussion of sitcoms. Landon Jones's *Great Expectations* includes a description of the Davy Crockett phenomenon. The two sources on American toys recommended in the earlier chapter bibliographies, Richard O'Brien's *The Story of American Toys: From Puritans to the Present* (New York: Abbeville Press, 1990) and Gil Asakawa and Leland Rucker's *The Toy Book* (New York: Alfred A. Knopf, 1992), are just as useful for this period. Each deals in some detail with board games and with toys spawned by technological innovations so much a part of material life during those years.

Histories of newspaper comics and comic books, such as *The Funnies: An American Idiom*, edited by David Manning White and Robert H. Abel (New York: Free Press of Glencoe, 1963), do not discuss in much detail the rise and fall of "horror" comics. More on this subject can be found in works on the controversy those comics inspired, such as James Gilbert's *A Cycle of Outrage: America's Reaction to the Juvenile Delinquent in the 1950s* (New York: Oxford University Press, 1986), which has an excellent chapter on the issue. The influential book written at the time as a dire warning about the danger of comics, Frederic Wertham's *The Seduction of the Innocent* (New York: Rinehart, 1954), remains important for any study of this subject. Fortunately, there is also an informative, and often very funny, book on the central figure in this controversy, William M. Gaines: Frank Jacobs's *The Mad World of William M. Gaines* (New York: Bantam Books, 1973). This book also deals with the rise and spectacular success of Gaines's subsequent publication, *Mad Magazine*.

Rock and roll, its rise and evolution, and its major figures, has attracted a huge number of writers. Basic reference works include Norm N. Nite, *Rock On: The Illustrated Encyclopedia of Rock 'n Roll* (New York: T. Y. Crowell Co., 1974–1978), Nick Logan and Bob Woffinden, *The Illustrated Encyclopedia of Rock* (New York: Harmony Books, 1977), and Phil Hardy and Dave Laing, *Encyclopedia of Rock* (New York: Schirmer Books, 1988). An indispensable source on the history of the recording industry and the economic dynamics behind the rise of rock and roll is Russell Sanjek and David Sanjek's *American Popular Music Business in the 20th Century* (New York: Oxford University Press, 1991). The best single piece of writing on rock and roll and how it reflects American society is Greil Marcus's *Mystery Train: Images of America in Rock 'n' Roll Music* (New York: E. P. Dutton and Co., 1976 and later editions), a brilliant, if sometimes difficult, collection of essays. Among other topics, it focuses on the blues roots of rock, a few performers like Randy Newman and Sly and the Family Stone, and concludes with a lengthy essay on Elvis Presley. Presley is the subject of several biographers. Eric Goldman's *Elvis* (New York: McGraw-Hill, 1981) has good material on Presley's early years, but much better is a recent biography that takes Presley's life through his first successes to his induction into the U.S. Army: Peter Guralnick's *Last Train to Memphis: The Rise of Elvis Presley* (Boston: Little, Brown and Co., 1994). On the course of rock and roll during the years considered in this chapter, see Arnold Shaw's *The Rockin' 50s: The Decade That Transformed the Pop Music Scene* (New York: Da Capo Press, 1987) and Richard Aquila's *That Old Time Rock & Roll: A Chronicle of an Era, 1954–1963* (New York: Schirmer Books, 1989).

## At Work

For raw statistics on working children and young people, readers should again begin with reports of the U.S. Census Bureau and its summary, *Historical Statistics of the United States: Colonial Times to 1970* (1975). Another source on more recent periods that is readily available in most libraries is the *Statistical Abstract of the United States,* another Census Bureau publication issued annually. Although its main focus is on a later period, some good background on these years can be found in Ellen Greenberger and Laurence Steinberg's *When Teenagers Work: The Psychological and Social Costs of Adolescent Employment* (New York: Basic Books, 1986). Two journal articles available in larger libraries or through interlibrary loan provide useful information and statistics: David Stern, Sandra Smith and Fred Doolittle's "How Children Used to Work," *Law and Contemporary Problems* 39:3 (Summer 1975): 93–117, and James D. Tarver's "Costs of Rearing and Educating Farm Children," *Journal of Farm Economics* 38:1 (February 1956): 144–53. On southern agricultural life, including the importance of child labor and the technological changes that revolutionized the rural southern economy by the end of the 1950s, see Jack Temple Kirby's *Rural Worlds Lost: The American South, 1920–1960* (Baton Rouge: Louisiana State University Press, 1987).

Domestic labor in the home is the subject of Susan Strasser's *Never Done: A History of American Housework* (New York: Pantheon Books, 1982), and, although she concentrates on women's work, the significance for children is clear enough. Strasser also has an excellent discussion of consumerism and its significance not only for housework but also for relationships among parents and children. Further comments on changes in household labor can be found in Stephanie Coontz's *The Way We Never Were,* cited above. For some valuable insights into the ways World War II affected the responsibilities of young Americans including some in the domestic economy, see the book noted above, William Tuttle's *"Dad-*

*dy's Gone to War."* As for the role of boys and girls in this new domestic work-place during the postwar era, the most ambitious study takes a look at a later period, in the 1970s, but what these researchers find clearly began during the years considered here: Elliot A. Medrich, et al., *The Serious Business of Growing Up: A Study of Children's Lives Outside School* (Berkeley: University of California Press, 1982).

## At School

Probably the best brief discussion of the overcrowding of American schools caused by the baby boom can be found in Landon Jones, *Great Expectations,* cited above, and for the raw numbers of youngsters flooding the classrooms, see *Historical Statistics of the United States* or *Statistical Abstracts* for those years. A well-written, provocative commentary on education since World War II is Diane Ravitch's *The Troubled Crusade: American Education, 1945–1980* (New York: Basic Books, 1983). Readers should be alerted that Ravitch expresses strongly held opinions, but her remarks on educational progressivism, race and the *Brown* decision, and the loyalty controversies of the 1950s are very worthwhile. Useful comments on education during these years also can be found in a general work on the family by two distinguished historians, Oscar Handlin and Mary F. Handlin's *Facing Life: Youth and the Family in American History* (Boston: Little, Brown and Co., 1971), as well as in Willis Rudy's *Schools in an Age of Mass Culture* (Englewood Cliffs, N.J.: Prentice-Hall, 1965). There is also the excellent work on reform and its controversies in schooling, mentioned in both of the earlier bibliographical essays: Lawrence A. Cremin's *The Transformation of the School: Progressivism in American Education, 1876–1957* (New York: Alfred A. Knopf, 1961), as well as Cremin's masterwork on schooling in this century, *American Education: The Metropolitan Experience, 1876–1980* (New York: Harper and Row, 1988).

On the debates that swirled around education after the onset of the Cold War, both Cremin's and Ravitch's books are very useful, as well as the general works on the period, mentioned above, by Manchester, Halberstam, and Jones. One of the most prestigious and influential critics of education, James Conant, authored books that are worth examining if they can be obtained: *The American High School Today* (New York: McGraw-Hill Book Co., 1959) and *Slums and Suburbs: A Commentary on Schools in Metropolitan Areas* (New York: McGraw-Hill Book Co., 1961). Those debates also involved charges that Communist influence was spreading throughout the United States, and especially within the educational system. With that came demands that teachers pledge their loyalty to American ideals and assure their superiors that they were free of dangerous political influences. This phenomenon, not discussed in the text, is the subject of David Caute's *The Great Fear: The Anti-Communist Purge under Truman and Eisenhower* (New York: Simon and Schuster, 1978).

Out of those controversies also came fundamental questions of inequalities in education, especially regarding race and economic class, and from that came the *Brown* decision ordering desegregation of public schools. An extremely influential book published near the end of World War II played a crucial role in raising issues of racial inequality in American life: Gunnar Myrdal's *An American Dilemma* (New York: Harper and Brothers, 1944, and later editions). See also Christopher Jencks, et al., *Inequality: A Reassessment of the Effect of Family and Schooling in America* (New York: Basic Books, 1972). The best work by far on the *Brown* decision is Richard Kluger's *Simple Justice: The History of* Brown v. Board of Education *and Black America's Struggle for Equality* (New York: Vintage Books, 1975), which traces the history of educational segregation, its consequences, the elaborate and shrewd legal strategies of its opponents, and their eventual victory in 1954. Kluger's work is an essential source not only on the history of education but also on the story of race in America and the civil rights movement.

As for Dr. Seuss (Theodore Geisel), readers can turn to a new book, Judith Morgan and Neil Morgan's *Dr. Seuss and Mr. Geisel: A Biography* (New York: Random House, 1995), as well as an earlier interesting analysis of his life and work, Ruth K. MacDonald's *Dr. Seuss* (Boston: Twayne Publishers, 1988). And, of course, Geisel-Seuss's own books are worth reading by young and old.

## Health

The basic sources on children's health and public health generally apply here, as they did in the first two chapters: *Historical Statistics,* for changes in rates of various diseases; and for both statistics and fairly technical discussion of trends in health, Sam Shapiro, et al., *Infant, Perinatal, Maternal, and Childhood Mortality in the United States* (Cambridge: Harvard University Press, 1968) and Carl L. Erhardt and Joyce E. Berlin, eds., *Mortality and Morbidity in the United States* (Cambridge: Harvard University Press, 1974). Unfortunately, another point mentioned in the earlier essays also holds true: there is not much easily accessible historical literature on developments in children's health during these years.

One welcome exception is writing on the disease that inspired widespread terror among American families, poliomyelitis. The development of a vaccine that conquered this killer and crippler of children was one of the most dramatic stories in the history of American medicine. For a fairly technical work on the history of the disease itself, see John R. Paul's *A History of Poliomyelitis* (New Haven: Yale University Press, 1971). More accessible and easily read books are available on the drama of the successful search for a cure, including Jane S. Smith's *Patenting the Sun: Polio and the Salk Vaccine* (New York: Morrow, 1990) and Richard Carter's *Breakthrough: The Saga of Jonas Salk* (New York: Trident Press, 1966). For a study of the responses to this scourge by those most closely affected by it, see Fred Davis's *Passage through Crisis: Polio Victims and Their Families* (Indianapolis: Bobbs-Merrill, 1963).

Research on the man who arguably had the greatest impact on day-to-day care of American children after World War II should begin with his own breakthrough book: Benjamin Spock's *The Common Sense Book of Baby and Child Care* (New York: Duell, Sloan and Pearce, 1946; republished in dozens of later editions under the title *Baby and Child Care*). Spock published other books, some of them seemingly in response to charges that he was encouraging an ill-disciplined, spoiled generation. See in particular *Decent and Indecent: Our Personal and Political Behavior* (New York: McCall Publishing Co., 1970) and *Raising Children in a Difficult Time: A Philosophy of Parental Leadership and High Ideals* (New York: Norton, 1974). An invaluable source is his own account of his early life, his evolving interests, and the writing of his influential guide to child care, Benjamin Spock and Mary Morgan's *Spock on Spock: A Memoir of Growing Up with the Century* (New York: Pantheon Books, 1989). There is also a biography of Spock, Lynn Z. Bloom's *Doctor Spock: Biography of a Conservative Radical* (Indianapolis: Bobbs-Merrill, 1972). It would also be useful to look at an earlier influential work, one with attitudes Spock was rejecting when he wrote his own: John B. Watson's *Psychological Care of Infant and Child* (New York: W. W. Norton, 1928).

## Children and the Law

The basic work on juvenile delinquency, the debates generated by it, and the government's responses is James Gilbert's *A Cycle of Outrage: America's Reaction to the Juvenile Delinquent in the 1950s* (New York: Oxford University Press, 1986). Gilbert tries to give a realistic assessment of the actual extent of juvenile crime and whether or not it was, in fact, increasing. Then he deals with a variety of other issues, including the responses of the public and the intellectual community to perceived delinquency, sociological discussions, debates regarding comic books and movies, and congressional investigations and their consequences. There is a good, concise discussion also in Joseph M. Hawes's *The Children's Rights Movement: A History of Advocacy and Protection* (Boston: Twayne Publishers, 1991). Robert H. Bremner's *Children and Youth in America: A Documentary History,* cited several times already, has an excellent section of material from the period on the delinquency issue. The flap over "horror" comics is also covered in Frank Jacobs's *The Mad World of William M. Gaines,* cited above. On the juvenile court during these years, see the work noted in earlier essays, Ellen Ryerson, *The Best Laid Plans: America's Juvenile Court Experiment* (New York: Hill and Wang, 1978), as well as John R. Sutton's *Stubborn Children: Controlling Delinquency in the United States* (Berkeley: University of California Press, 1988). Finally, if available, some works on juvenile delinquency from the period would be very helpful in understanding both the arguments of the day and their emotional tone; see, for instance: Bernard Lander, *Juvenile Delinquency* (New York: Columbia University Press, 1954), Albert K. Cohen, *Delinquent Boys* (Chicago: Free Press, 1955), and Sheldon Glueck and Eleanor Glueck, *Physique and Delinquency* (New York: Harper and Row, 1956).

A good chapter on World War II child care and the Lanham Act, its consequences and repeal can be found in Geraldine Youcha's *Minding the Children: Child Care in America from Colonial Times to the Present* (New York: Scribner, 1995). A more detailed account is included in what remains the best single source on the history of day care programs, Margaret O. Steinfels's *Who's Minding the Children? The History and Politics of Day Care in America* (New York: Touchstone Books, 1973). Documentary material on public policy toward children, including the extension of New Deal programs on aid to dependent children into wartime and the baby boom years, is available in Bremner's *Children and Youth in America*, while the best and most complete history of such aid is Winifred Bell's *Aid to Dependent Children* (New York: Columbia University Press, 1965). If possible, readers should also consult two older works on these and related issues: Dorothy Zietz's *Child Welfare: Services and Perspectives* (New York: John Wiley and Sons, 1969) and Gilbert Y. Steiner's *Social Insecurity: The Politics of Welfare* (Chicago: Rand McNally and Co., 1966).

## Personal Recollections

Interestingly, the segment of our society that has produced the fewest memoirs of childhood have probably been that near the top of the social and economic ladder. A couple of welcome exceptions come from the period of this chapter, however. James Merrill, a son of America's cultural and intellectual elite who grew up to be a brilliant and widely celebrated poet, included his early years in *A Different Person: A Memoir* (New York: Knopf, 1993). Annie Dillard, the daughter of a well-to-do Pittsburgh family who matured into one of her generation's finest writers, wrote her memoirs in *An American Childhood* (New York: Harper and Row, 1987). Among the most understudied movements in our population has been the migration of poorer southern whites out of their region to northern cities and to the Pacific coast. A wonderful reminiscence that takes that movement as its centerpiece is Harry Crews's *A Childhood: The Biography of a Place* (New York: Harper and Row, 1978). And for an intelligent, richly textured memoir from someone who stayed in the South and grew up there, see Shirley Abbot's *The Bookmaker's Daughter: A Memory Unbound* (New York: Ticknor and Fields, 1991). From farther West, readers can turn to an entertaining look at a childhood in the Great Basin, Phyllis Barber's *How I Got Cultured* (Athens: University of Georgia Press, 1992); and by Wright Morris, one of the finest novelists of this century from the Great Plains, there is *Will's Boy: A Memoir* (New York: Harper and Row, 1981). A highly successful writer and historian, Richard Rhodes, told of his growing up in *A Hole in the World: An American Boyhood* (New York: Simon and Schuster, 1990). And for an amusing account of what it was like as a child during World War II, written especially for a juvenile audience, see James Stevenson's *Don't You Know There's a War On?* (New York: Greenwillow Press, 1992).

Probably because the civil rights revolution of the 1960s led to a greater curiosity about the black experience in this country, there has been an unusual number of memoirs by African Americans born during the baby boom or the years just prior to it. Surely the most famous is Malcolm X's *The Autobiography of Malcolm X* (New York: Ballantine Books, 1965, and later editions), written with the help of Alex Haley. Also well known, and justifiably so, are Claude Brown's *Manchild in the Promised Land* (New York: Macmillan, 1965) and Anne Moody's *Coming of Age in Mississippi* (New York: Dell Publishers, 1968). Daisy Bates, a courageous woman who played a pivotal role in the desegregation crisis in Little Rock, Arkansas, wrote of her own childhood memories as well as her experiences in that famous confrontation in *The Long Shadow of Little Rock* (Fayetteville: University of Arkansas Press, 1987).

Michael Ondaatje wrote of his less familiar ethnic roots, from Sri Lanka, in *Running in the Family* (New York: Vintage International, 1993). Japanese-Americans, whose experiences during the war years were, to say the least, troubling and poignant, have produced several good memoirs, including John Okada's *No-No Boy* (Seattle: University of Washington Press, 1981) and Lydia Yuri Minatoya's *Talking to High Monks in the Snow: An Asian American Odyssey* (New York: HarperCollins, 1992). Finally, students might seek out a collection of childhood memories that includes some from this period: *Childhood Revisited*, edited by Joel I. Milgram and Dorothy June Sciarra (New York: Macmillan, 1974).

## NOTES

1. *Historical Statistics of the United States: Colonial Times to 1970* (Washington, D.C.: Bureau of the Census, 1975), I, 49.

2. William M. Tuttle, Jr., *"Daddy's Gone to War": The Second World War in the Lives of America's Children* (New York: Oxford University Press, 1993), 24.

3. Stephanie Coontz, *The Way We Never Were: American Families and the Nostalgia Trap* (New York: Basic Books, 1992), 39.

4. David Halberstam, *The Fifties* (New York: Villard Books, 1993), 509.

5. Maxine Hong Kingston, *The Woman Warrior: Memoirs of a Girlhood Among Ghosts* (New York: Knopf, 1977), 90.

6. Landon Y. Jones, *Great Expectations: America and the Baby Boom Generation* (New York: Ballantine Books, 1980), 403.

7. Ibid., 50.

8. Ibid., 41.

9. Halberstam, *The Fifties*, 470.

10. Charles Sawyer, *B. B. King: The Authorized Biography* (London: Quartet Books, 1982), 187.

11. George B. Tindall, *The Emergence of the New South, 1913–1945* (Baton Rouge: Louisiana State University Press, 1967), 430.

12. Elliott A. Medrich et al., *The Serious Business of Growing Up: A Study of*

*Children's Lives Outside School* (Berkeley: University of California Press, 1982), chapter six.

13. *Historical Statistics of the United States,* I, 371–72.

14. Quoted in Tuttle, *"Daddy's Gone to War,"* 120.

15. Ibid., 121.

16. Shapiro, Sam, Edward R. Schlesinger, and Robert E. L. Nesbitt, Jr., *Infant, Perinatal, Maternal, and Childhood Mortality in the United States* (Cambridge: Harvard University Press, 1968), 341.

17. Tuttle, *"Daddy's Gone to War,"* 191.

18. *Historical Statistics of the United States,* I, 59.

19. Pegge L. Bell, "Making Do with the Midwife: Arkansas's Mamie O. Hale in the 1940s," *Nursing History Review* (1993): 155–69.

20. John B. Watson, *Psychological Care of Infant and Child* (New York: W. W. Norton, 1928), 81–82.

21. Ibid., 84.

22. Benjamin Spock and Mary Morgan, *Spock on Spock: A Memoir of Growing Up with the Century* (New York: Pantheon Books, 1989), 130.

23. Interview in *USA Today,* September 15, 1994.

24. *Historical Statistics of the United States,* I, 415.

25. James Gilbert, *A Cycle of Outrage: America's Reaction to the Juvenile Delinquent in the 1950s* (New York: Oxford University Press, 1986), 105.

26. Frank Jacobs, *The Mad World of William M. Gaines* (New York: Bantam Books, 1973), 136.

# Chapter 4

# —— 1961–the Present ——

## INTRODUCTION

The years since 1960 have been among the most turbulent in American history—socially, culturally, diplomatically, and politically. This period saw yet another war (1964–1975), this one in Vietnam, in Southeast Asia, in which more than 50,000 American soldiers died. The Vietnam War was one of several developments that served to create deep fissures in American society. Defenders saw the war as an important stand against the spreading influence of the Soviet Union, China, and world communism; opponents countered that American troops were sacrificed to prop up a corrupt South Vietnamese government in a civil war posing no threat to the United States.

Behind this division were deeper differences that ran along generational lines. Many children of the baby boom were growing up to criticize much in their parents' values and allegiances. They found fault, for example, in what they considered an excessive materialism and conformity. They questioned many dominant national institutions, from religion to education to standards of sexual behavior. This "countercultural" phenomenon was expressed not only through protests against the war but also in the adoption of "alternative" lifestyles, a creative blossoming in popular music, and even attempts to create new communities of fellow believers. Another development besides the war, a movement for expanded civil rights among African Americans, also contributed to this social unrest. Building since the 1930s, this movement culminated in the 1960s with the passage of federal legislation extending and protecting rights of blacks in voting and other areas of public life.

Concern for civil rights led, in turn, to a deeper awareness of a major national problem—poverty. As part of his call for a "Great Society," President Lyndon Johnson's declaration of a "war on poverty" in 1964 resulted in the creation of several federal programs designed to expand economic opportunities among the poor and to improve their health care and living conditions. Predictably, opinions varied widely on the success of these programs, but, by some measures, the gap between the rich and poor narrowed considerably during the following decade.

All these changes generated extraordinarily intense emotions among the American people, stresses that found tragic expression in domestic and political violence. President John F. Kennedy was assassinated in November 1963, and, less than five years later, his brother Robert and the civil rights leader Martin Luther King, Jr., were murdered within two months of one another. Race riots occurred in more than two dozen cities between 1965 and 1968. Some of the hundreds of civil rights and antiwar marches and protests turned bloody.

The movements and programs for reform always had their peaceful critics, and by the mid-1970s a more conservative climate was emerging. "Great Society" programs came under growing criticism, and, in the minds of many, the earlier youthful protests were expressions of a permissiveness and decline of moral standards that some thought contributed to a growing rate of crime and other social ills. Old fears of a large and powerful national government fed a growing concern over federal programs and a national budget that was massive and getting bigger. By the mid-1990s, the political pull and tug over these issues was becoming especially vigorous.

Beneath these political events, the broader outlines of our national population continued to change. The frantic surge in births after 1945, pushed by millions of young couples determined to make babies, slowed down by the 1960s. The number of babies born annually dropped from 4.3 million in 1961 to about 3.1 million in the mid-1970s. Then the number began to jump again, up above 4 million by 1985. This new bump in births was called the "baby boomlet," brought about by the children produced by the great boom from 1945–1960 entering their own child-producing years. Now it was their turn to create families and chase their version of the

American dream. Fed partly by this new growth, the national population surpassed a quarter of a billion by 1990.

Another source of population increase were the millions of new immigrants. Laws passed in the 1920s had severely restricted the number of immigrants allowed into the country, particularly those from eastern and southern Europe. Our national doors were opened much wider again in 1965 by the Immigration and Nationality Act, which abolished the national quota system set up forty years earlier and significantly increased the number of aliens allowed to immigrate—120,000 a year from the eastern hemisphere and 170,000 from the western.

Partly as a result of this law, the immigrant presence in the United States has increased dramatically. The number of persons entering this country has inched upward, although the official count remains well below that at the start of the century:

**Number of Immigrants Annually per 1,000 Residents**

| | |
|---|---|
| 1901–10 | 10.4 |
| 1911–20 | 5.7 |
| 1921–30 | 3.5 |
| 1931–40 | .4 |
| 1941–50 | .7 |
| 1951–60 | 1.5 |
| 1961–70 | 1.7 |
| 1971–80 | 2.1 |
| 1981–90 | 3.1[1] |

In some ways, this most recent wave of newcomers differs dramatically from that at the start of the century. Those earlier "new" immigrants were largely from eastern and southern Europe. The "newer" immigrants are much more likely to come from Asia and Latin America. Asians have arrived not only from China and Japan, the nations that had sent most in earlier years, but also from the Philippines, Korea, Vietnam, Laos, and India. An even greater number of immigrants have come from Mexico and other nations to the south. During the 1980s, the number of immigrants from Mexico alone was more than double that from all of Europe. These figures, furthermore, reflect only those who have entered the country legally. By even conservative estimates, many thousands more have crossed our southern border illegally every year, pushed by dismal economic conditions to the south and drawn by the hope of American jobs.

The Census Bureau estimates that at least 800,000 immigrants, legal and illegal, will arrive every year for the next six decades. Unlike the great wave in the early 1900s, most of these will probably stay. By the middle of the next century, at least 20 percent of our population will comprise either immigrants or their children; some authorities set that estimate much higher, as much as a third of all Americans by 2050. So after a mid-century lull we have moved once more, as in the early 1900s, toward a more ethnically and culturally diverse society. Today's children often grow up isolated among others of their own backgrounds, but they can hardly avoid realizing that they are part of a nation of great human variety. And as at the century's start, this has brought a rise in social tensions. Many demand tighter control of borders to keep out "illegals," while some recommend reimposing rigid quotas on immigration. Once again, there are warnings that a flood of aliens will threaten American institutions and values, and with that have come calls to "Americanize" the newcomers with lessons in proper behavior and customs.

During the years since 1960, American families have continued their vigorous, sometimes frenzied, movement around the country. As usual, economic opportunities (and the lack of them) have been the most important reasons. Beginning in the 1960s, many heavy industries languished where they had prospered during the war years and the 1950s, sending millions in search of work elsewhere. Parts of the Northeast and Ohio Valley came to be called the "rust belt." Lighter, "cleaner" industries boomed for a while, especially on the Pacific coast and in parts of the Southwest. Poorer families in the South, seeing their chances to work the land continue to wither in their native region, took off in search of better jobs in the North and West.

Simultaneously, many large companies left the North for the friendlier business climate in southern cities. A great surge of white collar workers and their families headed for states like Georgia, Florida, and Alabama. By the 1990s, the economy of the nation's most populous state, California, was sagging badly, triggering an exodus into the Pacific Northwest, the interior West, and the South. As farms and ranches have offered fewer opportunities for young families, many have left the Great Plains. So, as our population has grown in size, it has moved unevenly around the nation—blowing like drifting snow, as Peter Morrison has put it, mounting up and covering older patterns of living in some places, while leaving other places nearly bare.[2]

## AT HOME

From the perspective of children, the most important changes have come not in the size and makeup of our population or in our people's mobility, but rather in the character and composition of the American family. What many people have considered the "normal," or nuclear, family—a husband and wife living together with at least one child—is far less common than in the previous generation. In 1970 such families made up 40 percent of our households; in 1991, only 26 percent. The rate of divorce has continued to rise. Even more startling has been the growing number of children born to unmarried mothers. One result of each of these trends has been the rapid increase in families with single parents (which usually means families headed by mothers without husbands). In 1990, one child out of four lived with a single parent (22 percent with mothers), double the rate in 1960. This phenomenon is much more common among African Americans. Of all white households in 1991, 24 percent were headed by single parents; the rate among black households was 58 percent.

Families that fit the "normal" pattern have changed too. Where husbands and wives live under the same roof with a child or children, it is much more likely today that both parents will be working outside the home. Throughout the century, of course, women in poorer families had worked to help feed their families. The big change in these years was the mass movement into the job market of wives of the middle class. Some of these women worked in search of personal fulfillment beyond the role of house-wife and mother. Many others found jobs to help meet the rising cost of living. It has become harder and harder for families to pay for the basic elements of the middle-class life—a home, car, appliances, vacation, and entertainment—on a husband's income alone.

The working mother has become a fundamental feature of American life. In 1975, less than 40 percent of women with children under six were work-ing; by 1990, more than 60 percent were in the work force. Mothers were also heading for the workplace much earlier in their children's lives. In the mid-1990s, of all women between eighteen and forty-four who had borne a child within the last year, more than half were working in a job away from their homes.

So if there is a "normal" family of the 1990s, defined by the way of life of the majority, it is one in which children live with one parent, or with a parent who is not their biological father or mother, and one in which both parents are gone from the home much of the day and often in the evening. These changes in the family's structure and in its members' roles naturally have brought with them patterns of living quite unlike those from earlier generations. If children and parents today could travel back and visit with their recent ancestors thirty, fifty, or seventy years ago, they would quickly find that they spend their time differently and expect different responsibilities from one another. They would see that much has changed in the details of how they pass their hours and days: in who is home and when, in how tired people are and what they are tired from, in what they laugh and complain about at the dinner table (if they can find half an hour to sit down together), and in how they show their affection for one another.

Counting only the time during the work week, for instance, a recent study showed that America's preschool children typically spend much more time in day care or with babysitters than with their parents (1,715 hours a year versus 1,102 hours). Even when weekends and vacations are figured in, these youngsters still are with their mothers and fathers only about 60 percent of their waking hours. (And even when parents are around, children are often watching television.) As families move around the country, furthermore, they are usually separated by long distances from other family members. Only about 5 percent of American children see a grandparent regularly, according to one estimate.

Critics worry about the long-term effects of this lifestyle. Are girls and boys getting enough love and guidance from parents? Will they enter adolescence and adulthood with the sense of security and the values necessary for a successful life? Have men surrendered their essential roles as fathers?

Deepening the concern over these changes has been a rapidly rising rate of drug and alcohol use among young people. Especially disturbing has been the spread of more addictive drugs, in particular "crack," a form of smokable cocaine that has become the most common illegal drug in impoverished urban areas. Drug trafficking, in turn, has fed the increase in crime and violence, disrupting—and often destroying—life at all economic levels, but especially among the poorest Americans. Drinking and taking drugs are seen as both a symptom of and a contributor to the unraveling of the family and the alienation of young people from their parents, schools, and other social institutions.

All this is part of what is perhaps the greatest paradox of American childhood at the end of the 20th century. As mentioned at the outset of this book, this has been called the "century of the child." Parents have dedicated themselves to cultivating for their sons and daughters the best possible lives. They have sacrificed time, money, and emotional energy to that end. The child, in many ways, has become the centerpiece of a typical parent's world, and young people's interests and customs have come to dominate much of national popular culture. Never, in other words, has childhood seemed so important in American life.

And yet, other changes have had very different results. Children spend less time than ever with their parents. Especially in poorer households unable to afford child care, daughters and sons as young as eight are expected to look after their infant sisters and brothers for hours every day. Millions of school-age boys and girls come home in the afternoon to houses empty of voices except those on television. These "latchkey children" are left largely alone, with adult responsibilities but with youthful emotions and judgment. Teenagers are entering the workplace early in large numbers to pay for an unprecedented range of amusements and material possessions available to the young, including automobiles that offer unmatched independence (and temptations) and motion pictures portraying scenes and situations that would make critics of the first movie houses faint with shock. Birth control devices have reduced some (but by no means all) unwelcome consequences of sexual intercourse, even as films, television programs, and popular music often portray sexual contact more openly and explicitly than at any time in our history. Encouraged by the media or not, young people since 1960 have generally become more sexually active, and have begun having sex at an earlier age, although this trend seems to have reversed somewhat since about 1980.

All these changes press young people into adult roles and responsibilities while they are still children or adolescents. Some critics have warned that this generation is witnessing what Neil Postman has called the "disappearance of childhood."[3] Ironically, part of the pressure on young people has come about because their parents must spend more and more effort working longer so they can afford all that they think is needed to provide the best for their sons and daughters. While working hard for their children, that is, they are helping to shorten childhood itself.

This complaint that childhood is "disappearing" would have been familiar at the opening of the century. Then, too, critics warned that childhood was a unique period of development, one that must proceed at its own pace, a time requiring protection and loving attention from parents and other adults. Mothers and fathers, it was said, needed to dedicate themselves more to seeing to their youngsters' special emotional needs. They must bring their own time and energy into focus on their sons and daughters. Much of the family's history since then has been a story of parents dedicating themselves increasingly to children. The result, however, has been a situation in which many young people are not encouraged, or even permitted, to be children and to let childhood run its course. It is a trend in home life typically paradoxical in this century of contradictions.

Measured in the most obvious ways, the American people and American families have grown much richer since 1960. The gross domestic product, the total value of all goods and services produced, rose from just under $2 trillion to nearly $5 trillion (adjusted for inflation and measured in "constant dollars") between 1960 and 1990. Disposable income—the money that people actually have to spend—has nearly doubled, from $7,264 per person in 1960 to $14,101 thirty years later (once again adjusted into "constant dollars"). Families typically spend nearly everything they make. In 1992, a family with husband, wife, and children under six spent more than $37,000 on average, including nearly $5,000 for food, $1,686 for household furnishings, nearly $2,000 on clothing, and almost as much on entertainment. Our standing among other nations has slipped, as several other countries enjoy higher per capita incomes than ours. And as was always the case, our money has been spread unevenly among our people: poverty still blights American society.

That said, the remarkable affluence that began with World War II has continued for many families. Those families have continued to chase many of the same dreams that have been described throughout this book. The most enduring of these dreams has been that of a family home. More than a million new privately owned houses have been built every year since the 1960s, and in some years (1971–73, 1978) the number topped two million. Unfortunately, the money needed to buy those homes increased so rapidly that many families could not keep up. Especially during the 1970s, the price of houses rose at a dizzying pace, more than 50 percent between 1973 and 1977. In 1978 alone, the estimated increase in housing prices, $140 billion, exceeded that of the entire decade of the 1960s. California led the way. In the most desirable parts of that state the value of a typical house sometimes tripled in one year, and a modest ranch-style house usually cost at least $100,000. The rise of prices nationwide has leveled off, but increases have taken their toll. During the 1950s and 1960s, a typical thirty-year-old man would have had to spend about 15 to 18 percent of his income to pay for the principal and interest on a medium-priced house. By 1983, he had to spend more than 40 percent of his paycheck to make those payments. No matter how you measure it, buying a house costs far more and takes a much bigger bite out of a family's income than was true thirty years ago.

As a result, the goal of a family home has slipped a little farther out of the reach of many. In 1960, standard one-family dwellings made up nearly 70 percent of all housing. By 1990, that figure had slipped to 59 percent. The difference was taken up by homes that demanded much less of an investment. By the tens of thousands, families, especially the younger ones like those who had swarmed into newly built houses after World War II, now were renting apartments or were looking for cheaper alternatives. In 1960, mobile homes or trailers made up only 1.3 percent of all housing; in 1990, they accounted for 7.2 percent. Furthermore, a large gap still yawns between the ability of white and black Americans to buy their own homes. Whites own the housing they occupy in about 68 percent of cases; for blacks, the figure is only about 43 percent. These trends are likely to continue for the foreseeable future. The money families make just isn't growing as fast as the cost of buying a home, so more young parents with young children will probably be denied this traditional dream.

Popular housing styles have changed little during the past three decades. The "ranch house," or one of its variations, remains the most common, especially among younger families just starting out. Inside are the features that helped define middle-class life earlier in the century—private bedrooms for parents and children, at least a couple of bathrooms, kitchens bristling with appliances and with easy access to outside, a modest dining area and larger den or "family room," which has come to mean the room where the primary television is located. A small back yard allows minimal outdoor recreation. A front yard with little function faces the street. Some of the older features of family homes sometimes appear as ornaments without any real purpose. Downsized columns sometimes stand on either side of the front door. A tiny covered area around the door recalls the traditional porch, but there is not enough room for even one chair.

Nothing in the house's design, in fact, suggests that its family spends any time looking and reaching outward into the neighborhood around it. The focus is indoors. When not spending time inside, parents and children are likely traveling elsewhere in the family car, or one of them. So it makes sense that the most prominent feature on the face of the house is no longer a large and open porch, a place for gathering and conversing with others, but the door of an enclosed garage, usually large enough for two cars. Reflecting the automobile's significance in family life, the width of the garage usually stretches across nearly half the house's front.

A visit inside these homes would show that American families are continuing to accumulate technological products, devices which previous generations would have considered miracles but which modern children grow up accepting as part of their everyday world. A personal computer has rapidly become a standard feature in many middle-class homes. A typical household has between five and six radios. Other appliances, virtually unknown a few decades earlier, have become standard in most homes:

**Percentage of Households with Selected Appliances, 1991**

| | |
|---|---|
| Microwave Oven | 79% |
| Clothes Washer | 76 |
| Clothes Dryer | 53 |
| Dishwasher | 45[4] |

A poll in 1983 asked a sampling of Americans what household items were important to them. Of these, 87 percent said a clothes washer was a necessity, 71 percent noted aluminum foil, and 60 percent selected frozen foods. An electric toaster was considered essential by 64 percent of those polled.

Topping all such items in popularity are television sets. In 1993, there were more than 200 million sets in the country, or nearly one for every man, woman, and child. Virtually every American household had one (99 percent), and most, in fact, had more than one: the average family owned 2.2 sets. The typical American house today is more likely to have a television than a telephone. The average American watches the tube a total of 1,530 hours during the year. Children remain among the most enthusiastic viewers. Boys and girls ages six to eleven watch an average of twenty-three hours and seventeen minutes every week—almost exactly one full day out of seven. Their younger brothers and sisters, ages two to five, watch even more (twenty-five hours and forty-three minutes a week). The only age group that spends even more time viewing television are near the other end of life's cycle, those over sixty-five.

The extraordinary extent of children's viewing has naturally raised many questions that have brought some troubling answers. A common concern is that the content of many television programs, especially their violence, might encourage dangerous and destructive behavior among the young, or at least make them more accepting of violence. Studies reveal that even programs made especially for children have an average of seventeen acts of violence per hour; general programs during prime time average thirty-two violent acts. An American youth on average will witness more than 23,000 simulated murders on television before his or her eighteenth birthday.

Just as disturbing to some is television's effect on traditional relationships. Rather than spending time with their younger daughters and sons, mothers and fathers sometimes tend to turn them over to the television, which has been dubbed "the third parent." (Peak viewing hours for those two-to-five year olds are from ten in the morning to late afternoon, the busiest part of the day for mothers.) Even the hours that parents and children do spend together are often in front of the television, with virtually no conversation or interaction. As viewing has consumed more and more of a family's leisure time, persons of all ages have cut off many of their connections outside the home. Many traditional types of neighborhood and community social life have withered away. Even moviegoing, which had brought people together since early in the century, has suffered, especially with VCR machines allowing films, or "videos," to be rented or purchased for viewing on the home TV screen. With this more recent technology—more than three-fourths of all households have a VCR—the movie has been pulled into the private, isolated world of the home. Americans in the mid-1990s spend one-fourth less time in movie theaters than in 1984.

The paradox of television, apparent from the start, has only deepened. A window onto a far larger world, it has kept Americans progressively confined within the walls of their houses. Many children cannot recognize or identify the people living on their streets, but they usually can name all characters on their favorite programs. These actors, in a sense, have become their true neighbors.

The only other machine to invade Americans' lives as successfully has been the automobile. The car-buying passion that began in the 1920s and continued even during the Great Depression was still burning hot in the latter years of the century. In 1990 there were more than 143 million cars registered in our nation of about 250 million persons. This ratio of about one auto for every 1.7 persons surpassed that in any other nation and was far, far ahead of most of the world's societies:

#### Persons per Registered Auto, 1989

| | |
|---|---|
| United States | 1.7 |
| Great Britain | 2.6 |
| Japan | 3.8 |
| Mexico | 14.0 |
| Egypt | 127.0 |
| China | 822.0[5] |

The ratio in the United States is particularly startling as it is based on the total population, including children unable to drive. When those youngsters are taken out of the calculations, the nation has more than one auto for every person old enough for a driver's license.

Clearly, the car has become a standard feature of our national life. Our cities are built on the assumption that nearly anyone has access to an auto. Businesses assume the same. Invitations to social occasions and public events typically include directions or a map usable only by people with a car. And certainly much of the daily life of most American families rests on the premise that an automobile somehow will be available, gassed up and ready to go. In the 1983 poll noted above, cars outranked all other items arranged by their necessity. More than nine out of ten persons (91 percent) said that an auto was absolutely essential, far more than even televisions (64 percent). In fact, more than one person out of four (26 percent) said that life was unworkable without two cars.

Americans of all classes, but the middle classes above all, have evolved into a "drive-in" culture. Virtually all enterprises and services have accommodated to autos; there have even been a few experiments in drive-in mortuaries, where the deceased are propped up in windows so friends and relatives can pull up, view the corpse, and drive away, all without leaving their Dodge or Chevrolet. A California church that began in 1955 at a drive-in movie theater, with its minister speaking from atop a concession stand, had grown by the 1980s into a gigantic organization. Its congregation still could come and worship in their cars at a vast complex (appropriately, next to Disneyland), called by its admirers a "shopping center for Jesus Christ."

Shopping for more earthly goods today is rarely done in small groceries and other stores within walking distance of home. Much of what is needed is bought instead in shopping centers and malls located at a nexus of roads able to funnel thousands of cars into vast parking lots. Other goods and services are found in "strip malls," long stretches of stores and outlets strung along major thoroughfares in virtually every community in the country. Neighborhood movie theaters have given way to multiscreen complexes built in the same car-accessible clusterings of "superstores" and other businesses. To get money for purchases, customers go to drive-up windows at their banks, perhaps after stopping at one of their town's most common sights—a "service" or "filling" station, where they refuel what many of them consider their life's most important possession.

Children and their parents structure many of the day's activities through a scheduling of car trips. Younger sons and daughters are taken to school by auto or bus, are picked up and driven to friends' houses or to classes in gymnastics and piano or to practice soccer or basketball, then perhaps to an orthodontist appointment and to shop for supplies needed for school projects. During school hours, nonworking mothers drive around on many other errands. Urban planners have coined a term, "trip-chaining," to describe this sequential series of mobile chores. The auto, which initially was seen as a machine of escape and liberating movement, has become for many parents, especially mothers, a kind of rolling cage, where they are confined by family responsibilities for hours every day.

Nowhere is the car's influence better illustrated than in how it has affected family eating habits. For a long time cities have had low-cost eating places where customers could be served quickly, and during the 1950s there was a rash of automated restaurants with food sent out on conveyor belts and other novelties. Drive-in eateries, where "carhops" served customers sitting in their cars, had been familiar since the 1930s. But the modern "fast food" restaurant is nonetheless a product of the post-1960 era. Its basic features are the speed of service, the predictability of its products, its assurance of hygienic standards, and finally its location. While the earlier rapid-serve businesses were usually close to downtown areas, fast-food franchises normally are in the suburbs and along routes heavily traveled by autos.

The earliest innovator was Ray Krok, founder of what remains the most famous fast-food chain, McDonald's. Buying out a California business, name and all, Krok immediately went hunting for baby boomers, opening outlets in the suburbs. It was "a conscious effort to go for the families," a company president later explained, and "that meant going after the kids."[6] Surveys showed, in fact, that when families ate outside the home, children decided where to go in three out of four cases. Krok allowed nothing even vaguely threatening to parents; he banned jukeboxes, and, recognizing that female carhops had been associated with loose morals, he at first hired only young men to work behind the counters. A McDonald's seemed as safe as a sitcom. As the company symbol, he created a clown, Ronald McDonald, and he later built mini-playgrounds adjacent to the facilities. Massive advertising helped, too. By the 1970s Ronald McDonald was second only to Santa Claus among figures most readily recognized by American children.

McDonald's was only one of the most successful of many chains that suddenly blossomed during the ensuing years across suburban America— Burger King, Wendy's, Arby's, Jack-in-the-Box, and Kentucky Fried Chicken, among others. All catered both to those who came inside and ate quickly and those electing to "drive through"—ordering from their car into a microphone, pulling forward, paying and picking up the goods, then driving away. This mobile meal was consumed in either of the family's two most familiar and intimate spaces: at home, typically in front of a televi-

sion, or in the car. In 1983, there were more than 122,000 fast-food restaurants, triple the number only twenty years before; their sales, more than
$34 billion, represented about 40 percent of all money spent in public
eating establishments.

All this posed an obvious threat to supermarkets and other grocery outlets. They fought back, installing delicatessens and salad bars and offering
sandwiches, roasted chicken, lasagne, and other foods fully prepared and
ready for the table. Another innovation, the microwave oven, aided supermarkets by expanding the empire of processed foods. Cartloads of individual items or full dinners now could be taken home and stored, ready to
eat even faster than meals at the drive-through. "There are never any lines
at home," as an industry spokesman put it. "With the microwave you just
reach into your freezer, pop it into the microwave, and zap! it's done."[7]
So, at day's end, a mother or father could choose from several options on
the way home from work, pulling through McDonald's or making a quick
run among the supermarket aisles. Dinner could be on the table (or on
various laps in favorite televiewing chairs) within half an hour of arrival
in the driveway.

Children today are growing up in a society almost perfectly meshed with
the automobile and what it has made possible. All is arranged to permit
the easiest flow of effort in providing the family's immediate needs beyond
walls of the home. Supermarkets, for example, have added other facilities
besides takeout food—pharmacies, large racks of periodicals and romance
novels, extensive hardware displays, and video movie rentals. Middle-class
daughters and sons, fathers and mothers can spend days or even weeks
passing only a few fleeting moments outside schools, offices, stores, fast-
food eateries, and that heavily used room on wheels, the family car.

Besides the proliferation of fast-foods, the eating experience was evolving
in other ways for American children. What they found on the dinner table,
as discussed in earlier chapters, had already changed substantially during
the years before 1960. However, starting in the 1960s and gathering momentum in the 1970s, ethnic foods, largely shunned in the past in favor of
meat-and-potato staples, suddenly became all the rage, especially among
the middle-class and upper-middle-class families. Not only Chinese and
Italian, but also Japanese, east Indian, Ethiopian, Mexican, Vietnamese,
Polynesian, Thai and other cuisines were more than acceptable. Families
sat down to eat these foods in retail outlets, including vaguely named "continental" restaurants. (The humorist and gourmand Calvin Trillin, puzzling
over the menu, suggested that the continent in question was Antarctica.)
Many parents, however, chose to cook at home, using woks, bamboo

steamers, pasta makers, and libraries of ethnic cookbooks. Supermarkets began offering aisles of exotic makings and displays of new kinds of vegetables, from bean sprouts and bok choi to snow peas and cumino.

Fast-food entrepreneurs quickly picked up on this trend. Chains with Mexican themes, such as Taco Bell, sprang up beside others offering new variations on one of the earliest mass produced ethnic dishes—pizza. Pizza "parlors" had first become popular in the 1950s. In the next decade, spurred by new technologies allowing quicker preparation, they spread to the suburbs, now in chains appealing to the family market. By 1970, more than 800 million pounds of mozzarella cheese was being melted annually on nearly two billion pizzas. Seeking to expand their appeal, food chain executives toned down the spicier flavors and more unusual traits of these dishes. The idea was to make pizzas and tacos seem slightly exotic while keeping them fully predictable, offering little challenge to the mainstream family tastebuds. With that, these products cut off virtually all connection with the supposedly ethnic origins of the food. The most successful pizza chain of the 1990s, Pizza Hut, was founded in a city hardly known for its Italian roots, Wichita, Kansas.

Hard upon this ethnic celebration came a mounting concern over the unhealthy results of eating too much fat, cholesterol, and chemical preservatives. In the 1980s and 1990s both manufacturers and restaurants began advertising more "natural" foods and those low in the offending substances, often dubbed "lite." Now mothers shopping for dinner could find frozen entrees combining these trends: low-fat Oriental dishes, lite pastas with thin sauces, low calorie Mexican and Cajun foods. Instead of sitting down to breakfast with sugar-loaded cereals like Count Chocula and the sweet, multicolored Trix, popular since the 1970s, children might fill their bowls with products like Heartland, poured from boxes featuring pictures of waving grain and 19th century field hands, images of a world that the first packaged cereals, ironically, were meant to leave behind. Fast-food outlets installed salad bars and offered croissants and low-cholesterol french fries, as well as fish and chicken sandwiches along with the traditional beef. Even the vast market for "junk foods" adapted. In 1992, Americans ate gargantuan quantities of chips, cookies, and sweet concoctions like Twinkies and Ding Dongs—about twenty pounds of these things per person annually—and older children were among the most passionate consumers; but a marketing report in 1993 showed a tendency even among teenagers to switch more to fruit juices, unsalted snacks, and "natural" chips.

Eating, as usual, was a reflection of national life. What young people chewed and swallowed revealed a lot about broader developments in the world around them. So did the houses they lived in, the cars in the garage, the appliances in the kitchen, and the glowing screen they watched. All were also part of patterns of family life traced through much of this book.

The spread of technology and vigorous mobility has had many beneficial effects on children growing up throughout the United States. They have offered many comforts and exhilarating experiences. They have made life in some ways easier and potentially more interesting. Meals in chain restaurants and packaged food in supermarkets for the most part are inexpensive and prepared by rigorous standards of hygiene. Automobiles offer exciting possibilities undreamed of by earlier generations; like televisions, they can expose Americans of all ages to larger worlds, a far wider slice of experience, than ever before.

And yet, paradoxically, one result has been to make us more and more alike. Families in all parts of the country eat the same foods bought in the same kinds of stores and prepared in the same appliances. Even newly popular ethnic cuisines are mass produced by the same techniques and, when sold in fast-food outlets, homogenized to taste as familiar as possible. New houses and apartments throughout the country are almost indistinguishable in style and often built to the same dimensions. Children play with the same toys. Our national soundscape has become uniform, from Oregon to Delaware to Mississippi; largely insulated from birdsong and even the wind, children all grow up hearing the same popular songs, microwave timers beeping at precisely the same tone, auto engines and horns making the same racket, and the same electric breezes blowing from central air systems and from hair dryers. Television is perhaps the greatest homogenizer of all. Families everywhere have a common intimacy with talk show hosts and sitcom characters. They laugh and sniffle simultaneously at the same jokes and tragedies.

The same forces that have made American families more alike, however, have tended also to isolate them from one another. With the help of cars, parents have tried to settle away from congested areas—and away from groups different from themselves. Children often grow up without much contact with youngsters of other racial or ethnic backgrounds. Most of all, the middle-class family has become increasingly self-contained. Its life is focused within home, work, school, and a few other places, and in automobiles in between, with little spontaneous and unpredicted contact with persons not part of those worlds. Possessing much more than others in the past, children and parents seem poorer in the range and diversity of their experiences in their society and with the world at large.

Despite the impressive affluence among some American families, many others have continued to live in poverty. In fact, one of the most disturbing recent developments has been the growing inequality of wealth and income in the United States. From the 1950s to the mid-1970s, the distribution of wealth remained about the same. Then, in the late 1970s and especially during the 1980s, an economic shifting began. Those at the very top started getting a heftier portion of the nation's income. This situation did not drastically affect the large middle class partly because more wives went to work to shore up the family income. But those at the bottom, the lowest-paid 15 or 20 percent of Americans, watched their share of the economic pie shrink. By 1995, as the rich got much richer and the poor much poorer, the economic distance between the top and bottom of our economic heap had become greater than in any other industrialized nation.[8]

Between 1977 and 1988, for instance, the income (after taxes) of the wealthiest 5 percent of U.S. households increased by 60 percent, while that of the richest 1 percent grew by a whopping 122 percent. The poorest families, on the other hand, saw their incomes shrink drastically during the same years. By the start of the 1990s, the poorest two-fifths of American families were receiving less of the national wealth than at any time since the Census Bureau began calculating such things, in 1947. If we were to add up income earned by all families in 1992, we would see that the number of dollars taken in by the richest 5 percent was more than everything earned by the poorest 40 percent; the incomes of the wealthiest 20 percent were nearly 50 percent greater than those of the lowest 60 percent:

### Income Distribution of Families: 1992

| Level of Income | Portion of National Income |
|---|---|
| Poorest 20% | 4.4% |
| Second 20% | 10.5% |
| Third 20% | 16.5% |
| Fourth 20% | 24.0% |
| Richest 20% | 44.6% |
| Richest 5% | 17.6%[9] |

Those figures refer only to income. Considering all kinds of property and assets, the differences are even more startling. The most affluent 1 percent of Americans, for instance, own more than 35 percent of all wealth, including 60 percent of corporate stock.

These figures might seem abstract, but the basic facts behind them are clear and alarming: As a greater part of our income and wealth has gone to a few at the top, the number of the American poor has increased substantially. The Census Bureau reported in 1992 that 36.9 million persons, or 14.5 percent of the population, lived below the poverty level.[10] Of these, about 14.3 million were children, or roughly one American child out of every five. This rate of poverty among our young is among the highest in the industrialized world, significantly above that in the United Kingdom, Germany, Canada, Norway, Sweden, and Switzerland. All this has been happening as the overall wealth generated by our economy has increased substantially. Between 1979 and 1989, as the nation's Gross National Product was growing by about 25 percent, child poverty increased by 21 percent.

Poor children and their families did not fit any single stereotype. According to popular perception, most were African Americans depending heavily on government aid while living in large cities. In fact, the majority of children below the poverty line were (and are) white. The parents of most of them have jobs. The majority live outside our largest urban centers. Large parts of rural America today, as was true at the opening of the century, have limited and shrinking opportunities for work, particularly any kind that pays well. The relatively scattered population in places like southern Utah, the Maine woodlands, and the sandy pine barrens of Alabama may be much less visible than the poor crowded into the inner cities, but rural poverty remains one of the most enduring problems in our national life. Even more surprising are the many impoverished families in that cradle of the middle-class dream, the suburbs. The Census Bureau classifies areas of high concentration of poor families as "poverty areas." Of all our nation's poor, about a third live in these areas. Most of those, about 60 percent, are in the inner cities, and another 26 percent are in small towns and the countryside; the rest, roughly 14 percent, live in suburban areas. Poor Americans, that is, are scattered and spread throughout the American social landscape. Few families in our country, not even the wealthiest, live more than a mile or two from children of poverty.

Especially disturbing today is the increase in poverty among younger families—which are also, of course, the ones most likely to have children. The economic standing of families headed by persons under thirty declined dramatically during the 1970s and 1980s. Earlier, during the optimistic postwar days of the baby boom and the 1960s, these Americans had done rather well. Between 1949 and 1973, a typical man moving from his twenty-fifth to thirty-fifth year would watch his "real" wages—that is, his income adjusted for inflation—grow by a healthy 110 percent. But the pattern then was reversed: over the next ten years, the real wages among men of that age group went up only 16 percent. Young families, in fact, have been slipping backward financially. The median income of families headed by someone under thirty declined by about 27 percent between 1973 and 1986. To put this in perspective, that was almost exactly the decline of per capita income for all Americans between 1929 and 1932, during the onset of the Great Depression, the grimmest economic calamity of our history.

At the same time, of course, the prices of what these families had to buy were going up. The result has been that young husbands and wives have found it increasingly difficult to achieve—or even to hope for—the basics of the American dream that had inspired the previous generation. Some critics worried that they were seeing a fundamental watershed in American life. During this century—and, for that matter, throughout most of our history—most parents always had good reasons to believe that their children would be better off than they themselves were. They would find better jobs and enjoy more comfortable and fulfilling lives. Now, as the century drew to a close, more and more Americans saw that dream slipping away. The future seemed to hold progressively tougher times and narrowing opportunities, especially for those on the lower half of the nation's economic ladder.

And for those at the lowest levels, the changes in fashion and habits elsewhere in America had little meaning. Native American boys and girls on many reservations ate foods high in fat because that was what was available through government surplus. Parents taking home a thousand dollars a month to support three children did not look for lite, microwaveable entrees; they bought in bulk whatever was on sale. Teachers in rural West Virginia reported that many students kept part of each day's subsidized lunch to eat for dinner. Friday's lunch was packed away whole. For many children, it was all they would have to eat until Monday.


## AT PLAY

A scientific study in 1992 revealed that adult Americans laugh on the average of fifteen times a day. A typical child, on the other hand, laughs four hundred times. It's hard to avoid the conclusion that most children have more fun than their parents. It is also worth remembering that their playtime is one of the most revealing parts of their lives. If we want to understand young people and what life has been like for them in the 20th century, we should pay special attention to how they have amused themselves.

Like everything else about American children, the story of their amusements is one of both continuity and change. At the end of the 20th century, most young boys and girls continued to find some of their fun in ways that children in 1900—or in 1800, for that matter—would have recognized instantly. They lined up in streets and schoolyards to do mock battle in games that had been played on the Nebraska frontier and on Alabama plantations. They called out rhymes and guessed at riddles that had made their great-grandparents laugh and scratch their heads a century earlier.

They also played with toys engineered with the help of the technologies that were sending astronauts to the moon and revolutionizing the country's productivity and communication. Video games, some played in arcades reminiscent of those early in the century and others played through televisions at home, emerged as an enormously popular entertainment for children (and some adults). By 1992 Americans were spending more on these games than they were on tickets to motion pictures. Children's dedication to video fun—one California five-year-old, trying to enter his locked house to play, got stuck climbing down the chimney—caused some parents to worry their youngsters were becoming addicted to this new technology.

Playtime followed the broader patterns of changing American life. As children moved toward the center of the family's concerns, the amusements of young and old seemed to merge, leaning toward the preferred fun of sons and daughters. Enterprises that provided for children's play became some of the largest and most profitable in the nation's history, and the places of entertainment for girls and boys became some of the most familiar sights on our daily landscape.

By the 1990s the money spent by and for children on toys had become a major part of the national economy. Total sales in 1993 surpassed $23 billion, up from $15 billion only two years earlier. The industry dipped and soared with the rest of the economy. During the recession of the early 1990s, stores told of a shift away from pricier items toward cheaper ones, like the small dolls called Trolls and even pipe cleaners and plastic material for crafts. But year by year, the portion of the family income spent on children's playthings remained remarkably high.

The great annual buying spree came between Thanksgiving and Christmas, but, throughout the year, billions of dollars changed hands in the purchase of merchandise that, like so much else in the American marketplace, showed an increasingly sophisticated technology. Besides being sold in department stores and other general outlets, toys increasingly were marketed through chains of toy stores, thousands of square feet each, with shelves crowded with a dazzling variety of goods. The largest chain, Toys

"R" Us, reported nearly $5 billion in sales in 1993. Stores and manufacturers spent vast sums on advertising, particularly through television and pitched especially at consumers between the ages of six and twelve. "My kids want anything they see, especially on TV," complained one mother.[11] And parents typically came through.

Children's toys were of the usual wide array. Many were traditional, but during the years since 1960, manufacturers have been especially successful in developing and selling by the hundreds of millions a category of toys that in the past had rarely been seen on store shelves. They were extremely simple in design and construction, yet they held enormous appeal to youngsters. Though reminiscent of playthings that had been around throughout history, in a sense they represented something new—a new hybrid, a combination of earlier kinds of playthings.

In 1850, 1900, or 1950, toys might have been divided into two general groups. The first were those created and made by adults, fairly elaborate in design and relatively expensive, such as mechanical banks, metal and electric trains, and construction sets. The second group included toys found or fashioned by children themselves out of the stuff of their daily lives—spears from sticks, tiny wagons out of matchboxes, helmets out of melon rinds. Not long after mid-century, some businessmen began to cross the line between the two categories. It was as if these manufacturers suddenly began paying attention to how children amused themselves when on their own; and when they did, these entrepreneurs made a great deal of money.

No company has been more successful at this type of toymaking than Wham-O. In 1958, Wham-O's two founders were visiting Australia when they noticed some young students playing and exercising with a lightweight hoop made of bamboo. Back home in the United States, they produced a simple hollow plastic ring like the one they had seen. They named it the Hula Hoop, since a customer could twirl it around the waist by swiveling his or her hips, Hawaiian-style. Twenty-five million hoops were sold in four months, more than a hundred million in two years. Hula Hoops became a global phenomenon, sold in astonishing numbers in Europe, given away to poor children in the slums of South Africa, even carried to the South Pole by Belgian explorers. As with so much relating to children's lives in these years, they became enmeshed in the popular culture at large. Their appearance on television on "The Dinah Shore Show" boosted their appeal, and the hoops' required hip gyrations were associated with rock and roll and the performance style of Elvis Presley and other stars. Hula Hoops, in fact, helped inspire a new dance and a hugely popular song by Chubby Checker, "The Twist." (Their connection to the controversial music and dances also led the Japanese government to ban the toys from the streets.) By the end of 1959, the craze was fading fast, as if the exertion had tired out the nation, although Hula Hoops would continue to sell well for more than thirty years.

Another Whamo-O product has proved far more enduring. In the 1920s students at Yale University had amused themselves on the campus green by tossing around pie tins used by a firm in nearby Bridgeport, Connecticut— the Frisbie Baking Company. After World War II, a California building inspector, fascinated by recent advances in both aerodynamic design and lightweight materials, made a plastic disc that could sail long distances when flung with a strong flick of the wrist. Whamo-O bought the idea, and, after first naming the product the Pluto Platter, they revived the name of the baking company that had unwittingly provided the earliest prototype. (To warn unwary bystanders, Yale students had called out "Frisbie!" when flinging the pans.) First marketed in 1957, the Frisbee has become one of the most successful toys in history. More than a hundred million have been sold. They have been tossed and sailed on beaches, in fields, down streets, across ponds, not to mention in houses and shopping malls. They have been adapted to sports—Frisbee Golf and Frisbee Football— with their own rules, fields of play, and tournaments. As with the games Monopoly and Scrabble, careful records are kept of outstanding (and strange) Frisbee achievements: greatest distance thrown (623.5 feet), maximum time aloft (16.72 seconds), and longest distance thrown by two persons during twenty-four hours (362.4 miles). Cheap compared to other playthings, they have become part of the youth culture of play from the richest to the poorest Americans.

Wham-O's Super Ball, introduced in 1965, was another example of a traditional child's favorite plaything given something extra through postwar technology. Made of a new synthetic rubber substitute, developed for other commercial purposes, this small sphere bounced far higher and longer than the balls of anyone's fondest memories. Yet another familiar part of children's play, once again a scientifically enhanced version of an age-old amusement, appeared and flourished during these years. Inspired by his sister-in-law's complaints that the traditional art and modeling clay was difficult for her elementary school students to use, an Ohio man worked with various compounds and finally came up with one material that had two great advantages: it was easy to mold, and it did not dry out quickly. He began selling it in 1957, calling it Play-Doh. It took a few years to make it into the larger market, but once it did, Play-Doh became a standard part of millions of youngsters' fun time. Parents liked it because it was safe and it encouraged artistic talents. Children loved it because it allowed the free exercise of creative imagination as they rolled and shaped and squeezed the pliable "dough" however fancy struck them. It was like playing with mud indoors, except with more color.

Other traditional kinds of toys, updated with new technological wrinkles, continued to find success on the youthful market. Young builders continued to play with Tinker Toys, Lincoln Logs, and Erector Sets, and now they could turn to another medium: Legos. The company had been around since the depression years, and an early version of the famous building blocks had first appeared in 1949, but the current familiar design did not appear until the late 1950s. Its basic unit is a colorful plastic brick with eight round protruding studs on top and eight hollow tubes beneath. The bricks snap together easily and hold together with impressive stability, allowing the budding structural engineer or architect to construct a remarkable array of buildings and other creations. Their manufacturers claim that half of the nation's households have Lego sets. The company's name sums up the appeal of these simple but versatile toys. "Lego" is both Latin for "I assemble" and a contraction of the Danish *"leg godt,"* or "play well."

Toy vehicles had always had a wide appeal, and as Americans took to the road even more, auto playthings naturally became more prominent. Tonka Toys, begun around 1950 as an outgrowth of a garden tool manufacturer, specialized in large, sturdy metal trucks. As the 1960s wore on Tonka expanded its line to include dump trucks and moving vans, wreckers and logging trucks. By that time another phenomenon, slotcars, allowed an even headier fantasy of motoring along streets and highways. Basically slotcars represented the mechanism of electric trains applied to automobiles. Plastic tracks were laid out in infinitely expandable and complex arrangements. The small electrical engine in each car was powered by current running through grooves in the track, and cars ran faster or slower as boy or girl (or parent) pushed down a plunger or eased up on it. The sets were rather expensive—another similarity to train sets—and they sometimes seemed to appeal to adults almost as much as children. Throughout the 1960s and afterwards the popularity of slotcars continued to build, spurred on partly by national racing competitions sponsored by some toy companies.

Less expensive variations designed for younger children soon appeared. The most successful were Hot Wheels, introduced by Mattel in 1969, miniature cars that moved by gravity down their own plastic tracks. Their wheels, designed to drastically reduce friction, allowed them to move fast and far, even around loops, with barely a nudge. For those drawn to miniature versions of traditional model cars, there were Matchbox cars, introduced from England in the mid-1950s. Nicely detailed replicas made on a scale of one seventy-fifth of actual size, they quickly caught the fancy of young car fans. They were relatively cheap and came in a remarkable variety of types, so many that, by the late 1960s, children could store their collection in carrying cases that housed five or six dozen of their favorites. For slightly older children, there were remote-controlled cars (and boats and airplanes) that zoomed around rooms, streets, and parking lots, independent of tracks and directed from a hand-held panel. And for still older boys and girls, go-carts, miniature cars propelled by small gasoline engines, were available. Early on, children were permitted to drive these mini-cars on the streets, but soon they were confined to tracks built especially so young would-be automobilers could zip around the circuit, initiated early into the all-American fascination with the car culture.

As noted in the previous chapters, toys and play have always expressed an affectionate tension between the generations. Adults design, produce, and buy toys in part to encourage among their children particular values and behavior; boys and girls make their own toys or they use the ones given to them in their own ways, expressing their own aspirations and points of view. As manufacturers profited from Frisbees and Play-Doh, they were, in a sense, recognizing and surrendering to youngsters' own feelings and instincts about play. But the shelves of America's stores also continued to fill with other toys meant to instill lessons and messages in the girls and boys who played with them.

Dolls have always filled this function. They are inspirations for young girls whose parents hoped they would grow into dedicated, loving mothers. In this sense these dolls were part of a far larger industry of domestic playthings—diminutive ironing boards, tiny tea sets, plastic curling irons and hairdressing sets, as well as doll-size baby bottles, baby carriages and other nursery furnishings. There were also, of course, entire miniature houses, "doll houses," that adjusted with the times. Stores in the 1950s and 1960s offered ranch-style and other suburban models, just like the ones children were likely to be living in. With this paraphernalia, children, girls especially, could act out the whole range of home-oriented fantasies.

One of the best-selling toys of the 1980s were Cabbage Patch dolls, supposedly motherless children found in the garden among the vegetables, ripe for mothering. Updated versions of rag dolls with perky yarn hair—and perhaps a welcome relief from realistic dolls that could cry, eat, crawl, walk, and/or talk—Cabbage Patch dolls came complete with adoption certificates. Ironically, however, the most popular doll in history was not modeled on a child and not meant to inspire mothering instincts. It was a well-developed teenager living in her own world of fun and glamorous fashion. As much as any development of post-World War II America, this doll mirrored the rise of young people's independence, buying power, and determination to accumulate material goods that drew their fancy.

The doll was Barbie, named for the daughter of its creators, Ruth and Eliot Handler. Patterned on a German doll, Lilli, which, in turn, was based on the heroine of a newspaper comic strip, Barbie was slim, but shapely, so buxom in fact that many parents at first balked at buying. But preteen and early teenaged girls responded with unprecedented enthusiasm. Barbie first appeared in 1959. Two years later Barbie's boyfriend, Ken (named for the Handlers' son), appeared, and then a somewhat less stunning pal, Midge, a younger sister, Skipper, and others. Thirty-five years after the first production, sales were still growing. Surveys revealed that of the millions of preteen girls who had bought Barbies, each owned an average of eight of the dolls. With dolls available in 140 countries, annual revenue surpassed one billion dollars in 1993. In the mid-1990s, two Barbie dolls were sold every second.

The dolls, however, were only the beginning. Mattel, the company that produced Barbie, has emerged as one of the leading clothing manufacturers in the world, turning out dozens of outfits for the long-legged, 11 ½-inch figure and her companions. Some have emphasized the glamorous—jeweled ball gowns and fur stolls—and others the day-to-day, such as stylish school outfits and beachwear. Some, like the Barbie-Q set with utensils for outdoor grilling, looked forward to a domestic life, while many more envisioned exciting careers as a stewardess, model, astronaut, ballet dancer, and doctor. For surroundings, there were beach cabanas, ice cream store counters, a theater, and a variety of home settings. It was, in short, a Barbie universe, with her at its center.

This doll's fabulous popularity was, in one sense, a culmination and updating of one of the most traditional youthful playthings; yet, in another sense, Barbie was a dramatic and fundamental reversal of the meaning of dolls and many other manufactured toys. A baby doll had always been a means that adults were using to draw a young girl toward a future life that they thought was best. Such a toy, like most others made and given by grown-ups, were expressions of parents' values and dreams for their children. Barbie, however, in her looks and clothes and surroundings, spoke for children's fantasies. Dressed for the theater or ready to lead an expedition into space, she was more of a projection of dreams that girls were

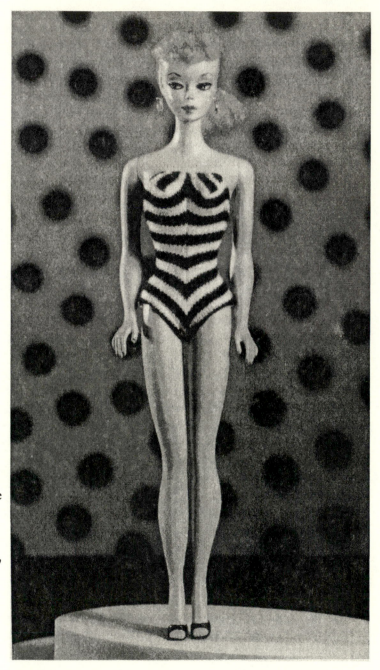

The most popular doll in history, the Barbie doll, allows American girls to fantasize lives of glamor, popularity, and achievement. Two Barbie dolls are sold every second. *Courtesy of Mattel, Inc. BARBIE is a trademark owned by Mattel, Inc. © 1995 Mattel, Inc. All Rights Reserved. Used with permission.*

fashioning for themselves. Here, as in so much of America's play, its entertainment, and daily life, the perspectives of the young seemed to be taking command.

Barbie, of course, is bought mainly (but not entirely) for girls. Boys, however, have had their own variations. The 1960s saw the booming of a huge market in plastic masculine figures. They were not called "dolls," presumably because that term was rejected as too feminine; nonetheless, the parallels to the Barbie phenomenon are obvious. If Barbie stood tall in the ideal female form, these heroes—and the villains—were superb, heavily muscled specimens. Barbie's outfits and extras placed her in exciting, exotic, and romantic settings, while the male characters similarly were portrayed as living sensationally dramatic lives.

The pioneer of these male "action figures," G.I. Joe, appeared five years after Barbie, in 1964. Exactly Barbie's height, he featured flexible arms and legs and a fairly deadpan expression that the manufacturer, Hasbro, claimed was a composite of the faces of twenty winners of the Congressional Medal of Honor. Also available—another parallel to successful girls' dolls—was a vast assortment of uniforms, firearms, and various military equipment, from jeeps to dog tags. Although his success never matched Barbie's, G.I. Joe helped turn Hasbro into one of the world's leading toy manufacturers, and he inspired whole platoons of imitators. Some were modeled on prime-time television programs, such as "The A-Team," and on films like the James Bond series. Many drew upon fantasy TV cartoon series, which now were standard fare on Saturday mornings. He-Man and Skeletor were especially popular. Then, in the late 1980s, Hasbro released action figures based on what seemed an outlandish premise—muscular turtles, grown large by some scientific aberration, trained in the martial arts, and named after cultural leaders of the Italian Renaissance. The Teenage Mutant Ninja Turtles quickly became the hottest items on the shelves, a tribute to the powers of advertising. Meantime G.I. Joe, phased out in 1978, had been called back into duty (although shrunk to only four inches) in 1982 as the leader of a new line of fighting men, the Real American Heroes.

Inevitably, these popular toys have aroused controversy. Some critics wondered whether action figures encouraged violent behavior. Others believed Barbie came to stand for an ideal of feminine beauty and body type impossible to achieve. The journalist Anna Quindlen and others suggested a connection between the self-image associated with the doll and potentially fatal eating disorders such as bulimia and anorexia. Behind these charges was the opinion that both categories of dolls reinforced male and female stereotypes. To dramatize their point, a group of performance artists in 1993 switched microchips in dozens of talking Barbies and in soldier action figures called Talking Dukes, then replaced them on the shelves. When children opened their new toys and pushed the "talk" buttons, the battle-ready Talking Dukes said "Let's plan our dream wedding!" and "Will we ever have enough clothes?" Barbie barked out, "Eat lead, Cobra!" Barbie's defenders have countered that, on the contrary, the many varieties of the doll have encouraged young girls to imagine a future full of diverse possible careers, including many that in the past have been largely closed to women.

These fabulously successful products, then, offer us one more lesson in the complexity of "reading" toys to find their meaning. Barbie and her friends are, on the one hand, reminders of how dolls and other toys have been given to children to teach them how they ought to behave and what they ought to be when they grow up. But on the other hand, they tell us how young Americans have steadily expanded their control over their own lives, in this case by demanding and getting dolls that express youthful independence and fantasies.

Whatever we choose to call them, these products have been some of the most revealing playthings of recent years. Skeletor, G.I. Joe, and the Ninja Turtles were dolls, in that they were idealized figures that children used to act out dramatic scenarios playing in their imaginations. (In a lawsuit involving tariffs on imported toys, a federal court in 1989 ruled that these figures were, indeed, "dolls.") And Barbie and Ken, as much as He-Man, were "action figures," used by boys and girls to dramatize their own fantasies, not ones of ultimate adulthood but of the imagined present and the immediate teenage future—achieving the victories of superheroes, living in perfect popularity as a glamorous seventeen-year-old, and enjoying all fruits of adolescent consumerism.

Another prominent part of children's play also was revealing about changes in American families and the children's roles within them. While Barbie and G.I. Joe were small, but telling, details in a girl's or boy's daily life, this other entertainment was on a far grander scale—amusements and excitements spread over hundreds of acres, with sights and sounds and imaginative creations sometimes towering toward the sky or plunging into dark caverns and tunnels. This form of entertainment created its own world, one that tells us much about childhood and the world in which children grow up.

The entertainment in question is the updated and greatly expanded version of the amusement park described in chapter 1, now known as the theme park. The old-style amusement park had begun to decline in the mid-1920s. As the birth rate fell and society aged, youthful amusements naturally suffered. The Great Depression bit deeply into the cash reserves people had to spend on what was, after all, something of a luxury. The automobile was another culprit. With a car, families, and eventually young people, did not have to choose their public amusements according to where they could go on a trolley line. During the summer, the months when the parks attracted most of their business, parents and children increasingly turned to another alternative, the family vacation. After setting aside money during the months of poor weather, they would pile into the family Chevrolet or Oldsmobile and take to the road for a couple of summertime weeks, to bask on the beach, camp in the mountains, or see the sights out west.

The lowpoint came in the late 1930s, when the number of amusement parks had shrunk from about two thousand to some 250. The return of better paychecks brought a modest revival by the late 1940s, but a new age of the industry lay just ahead. We can pinpoint its birth exactly: July 17, 1955. On that summer morning, the gates opened for the first day at Disneyland Park.

Over the past year, teams had worked frantically, often twenty-four hours a day, converting a 160-acre orange grove into a revolutionary entertainment "kingdom." Located in Anaheim, California, near Los Angeles, Disneyland was divided into five imaginative regions: Main Street USA, Frontierland, Adventureland, Fantasyland, and Tomorrowland. Each had its own rides, shops, and, just as important, its own distinctive landscaping, decor and "feel." Customers, officially called "guests," felt immersed in each as they moved through portals from one "land" to another. Reinforcing this illusion of total participation were earthworks, more than two stories tall, surrounding the park, isolating those inside from any sense of connection with the world beyond.

A few bugs had to be worked out in the beginning; on opening day, people's feet stuck in the newly-laid asphalt and gate receipts were carried to the bank in fire buckets. Quickly, however, Disneyland proved to be one of the great success stories in American entertainment and enterprise. A million customers attended within the first six months, and four million the next year. A decade after its opening, more than fifty million persons (a number roughly equal to a quarter of the national population) had paid to visit the Jungle Cruise, the Submarine Voyage, and other showpieces.

Entrepreneurs were surprisingly slow to follow up on Disneyland's success. Only in the 1970s did a series of highly successful "theme parks" open up other options for the public. All reflected to a large degree Disney's lessons. In an environment buffered from the world outside, customers are caught up in elaborately designed settings centering on themes of escape and adventure. A feeling of spontaneity, paradoxically, arises from designers' careful attention to detail and manipulation of emotions. Some parks, like Knotts Berry Farm in California, were independently operated. Many more were part of chains owned and operated by large corporations: the Anheuser Busch brewing empire (Busch Gardens), Bally, a firm best known for making pinball machines (Six Flags), Marriott Hotels (the Great America parks), the respected publishing house of Harcourt Brace Jovanovich (Cypress Gardens), and the movie and entertainment giant, MCA (Universal Studios). Revenues and attendance have marched steadily upward, especially in the 1980s:

**Amusement Parks & Attractions (Attendance and Revenues, in Millions)**

| Year | Attendance | Revenues |
|------|-----------|----------|
| 1970 | 151 | $  321 |
| 1976 | 173 | 832 |
| 1980 | 178 | 1,400 |
| 1986 | 215 | 2,000 |
| 1989 | 254 | 4,000[12] |

The ultimate expression of the theme park phenomenon, and far and away its greatest success, has been the Walt Disney World Resort, built in 1971 on part of forty-three square miles of land acquired by Disney near Orlando, Florida. The original park was an expanded version of its predecessor, Disneyland. In the early 1980s, a huge addition was opened on neighboring land, EPCOT Center, designed as a showcase for new and emerging technologies and as a tour among several world cultures. In 1989, the Disney-MGM Studios theme park opened nearby. Altogether, this vast complex, supplemented by hotels with thousands of rooms, amounts to an empire of amusements. It has become the most popular tourist attraction in the United States and one of the most popular in the world. More than 30 million persons paid to enter during 1989. (In second place was Disneyland, with 14.4 million; Universal Studios Hollywood was a distant third, with 5.1 million.) In 1981, before the opening of EPCOT Center, Walt Disney World ranked sixth among international tourist attractions— and the first five were entire countries (Spain, Italy, France, Canada, and the United States). During the previous decade, more persons had visited Disney's Florida kingdom than the Eiffel Tower, the Taj Mahal, or the pyramids of Egypt. The money generated was enormous. In 1990, the merchandise sold within Walt Disney World—not including what was paid for admission or food—brought in more than $580 million.

The appeal of these new amusement parks is clear and understandable, an enhancement of the reasons behind the old parks' popularity. Some of the rides, for instance, are genuine technological wonders. Disney once again has been the pioneer, creating such astounding illusions as three-dimensional holograms that move and speak to the "guests." Intricate landscaping creates exotic locales for boat trips, with mechanized creatures and human predators rising from the water and lurking in the underbrush.

Virtually all theme parks feature increasingly elaborate variations on one of the oldest amusement park thrillers, the roller coaster. Modern roller coasters are designed to mesh with the themes of their parks; they are no longer rides on tracks but runaway trains and tours through magic mountains. As with recent children's playthings, they utilize space-age materials and technologies, in this case durable, lightweight plastics and tubing of metal alloys as well as computer-assisted engineering design. The rides plunge customers in and out of dark caves and tunnels, send them flipping through double and triple loops, leave their feet dangling free below them, and generally carry them deliciously close to the edge of stark terror. These "megacoasters" themselves are case studies of what has happened in American pleasure parks. From their wild, chaotic, barebones beginnings, they have become more and more technologically sophisticated, while providing, like the parks around them, illusions with a message.

Besides excitement machines like the megacoasters there are other reasons for the enormous success of theme parks. The timing of their construction meshed perfectly with baby boom demographics. Disneyland opened its gates just as the first waves of postwar children were reaching the age when the park would seem most magical. Disneyland and its imitators fit America's blossoming car culture and the age of the family vacation—the very things that had helped undermine the older amusement parks. Families flocked from across the country, especially in the summer, planning their time at Six Flags or Great America months, even years, ahead. Vacations elsewhere killed the traditional parks; Walt Disney World *is* a vacation. Most parks are run with highly impressive efficiency. Once again the Disney kingdoms have set the pace. Sophisticated analysis allows the easy movement of customers. There are plenty of restrooms and water fountains. A relentlessly cheerful staff keeps the grounds immaculately clean.

The appeal of the new amusement empires have tapped deeper than that, however. Disneyland, first of all, was a brilliant extension of the new modes of entertainment that spoke especially to America's young. In a way, its

The Steel Phantom of Pittsburgh's Kennywood Park. Modern "scream machines" continue the popular tradition of roller coasters that have thrilled customers in amusement parks throughout the century. *Courtesy of Kennywood Park.*

"guests" were allowed to step into and take part in a world they previously could only sit and watch in movies and on television. The park's history had been entwined with television from its inception; it had been partly financed by the American Broadcasting Corporation (ABC), and, as part of that deal, Disney agreed to create a weekly TV show, "Disneyland," during the months prior to opening day. The show quickly shot to the top of the charts. With that, viewers could watch segments on "Tomorrowland" and "Fantasyland" during the school year, then travel to California in summer to walk and ride in those imagined realms. In "Frontierland," one could partake, through fantasy, in television's fabulously popular "Davy Crockett" series. There, too, were all the other characters familiar from years of Disney cartoons and comics, some of them walking around the park, ready to pose for a photograph with vacationers. Other parks have followed this lead. The new breed of amusement park is the culmination of a technology of entertainment that has drawn its customers always closer in its embrace, making them full partners in illusion.

The parks also pulled generations together. On the one hand, they have been landmarks in the expansion of children's influence over their families' lives. Parents, sons, and daughters joined together in a commercial world born from fantasies of twelve-year-olds. Adults spent precious days away from work, not to mention large amounts of hard-earned money, to pass time walking around in their children's cartoons. But on the other hand, these youthful living daydreams were ones cleansed and kept in control by adults. Earlier amusement parks, like turn-of-the-century arcades and cheap movie houses, had been runaway places for adolescents, offering enticing possibilities well outside the rules laid down by parents. But these corporate playworlds, like Disney's films and television's family sitcoms and the newly policed comic books, celebrate values applauded by parents. There are no side shows on Disneyland's Main Street USA, and the fantasies provided in Fantasyland do not include exotic dancers.

A theme throughout these chapters has portrayed play as a continuing contest between older and younger, a tug-of-war between generations. Seen that way, Disneyland and Walt Disney World have been, in a sense, a clear victory for children. Girls and boys have carried their elders onto their own turf. But as for what was played on that terrain—the content, style, and nature of the amusements—that was firmly under control of parents and big business, sanitized versions of widely approved lessons from older generations.

The new amusement parks were mirrors of other changes in American life. The impressive attendance figures were in one way misleading. The number of customers in 1989—more than 250 million persons—was very close to the total population of the United States. But that did not mean that sometime during the year every American child and parent passed several pleasant hours screaming on some exciting ride or marveling at some fanciful mechanical creation. To play in the new theme parks, people needed much more money than they had for the old-style amusement parks. Most were accessible mainly by automobile and airline. A vacationing family typically spent hundreds of dollars on transportation and housing before paying the considerable admission price (by 1990 more than thirty dollars per person at Walt Disney World, not including what would be laid out for food and souvenirs).

Playing in these technological wonderlands, in other words, has become affordable only for middle-class Americans, including adolescents, who have acquired substantial spending money and buying power. Many of them visit theme parks two or more times a year. Other young Americans, those without the financial resources to get there and get in, never set foot in these places. This economic division, as usual, is also partly an ethnic and racial one. Every study of the customers who flood through the gates at these theme parks emphasizes that the crowds are far more white and much less black and brown than the population in the cities around them.

Coney Island and the other early parks were playlands open to virtually the full range of the public who could hop a trolley and buy a cheap ticket to pass through the gates. Along the boardwalks and midways was a mix reflecting the diversity of urban America. The new parks were just the opposite. In how we play, as in where we live and work and in so much else, America has sorted itself out, separating and isolating its people according to how much they earn and often by their ethnic heritage.

## AT WORK

The first decade or so after World War II was in one way a turning point in the working lives of American youth. If we could somehow calculate the number of hours and amount of energy children and teenagers spent holding down jobs and working around the home, that figure would probably be lower than ever before or since during the years 1945–55. Things had changed dramatically since early in the century, when nearly one out of five children between ten and fifteen was "officially" employed, and many more were laboring in ways that didn't show up in the census. Girls and boys plowed, made boots and bottles, gathered and sold junk, tended mules in mines, and harvested hay. By the 1950s, younger children had come to make up only a tiny portion of the work force, and older ones were moving away from jobs that teenagers had handled for generations. Boys and girls worked at home; but, even there, the hours spent at housekeeping, yard care and babysitting were relatively less. In terms of the nation's working life, young America seemed to be close to irrelevant.

With hindsight, it is evident that those years marked the beginnings of another change. Young children remained out of the work force, but older children were not so much abandoning working life as switching occupations. As discussed in chapter 3, teenagers were leaving the "old workplace" and entering the "new"; and, as the years passed, they crowded in ever larger numbers into these new occupations.

The "old workplace," where young women and especially men historically had found jobs, mostly involved factory work, skilled crafts, and farm labor. By 1940, mechanization and child labor laws had combined to virtually eliminate young people from skilled jobs and drastically reduce their numbers in factory labor. There were still large numbers of working teens on the farms, but these figures plummeted from nearly half of employed teenagers in 1940, to about 10 percent in 1960 and 5 percent in 1970.

Young workers were heading into two new categories of jobs: service and retail work. Service workers were not producing goods but essentially doing things for others: pumping gas in a "service station," cooking in a "fast food" restaurant, or cleaning rooms in a motel, for instance. Retail work involved some type of sales, from standing behind a counter at a department store to taking a customer's money at a drive-up window of a hamburger franchise. The numbers of teenagers in these areas surged especially after the late 1950s:

### Percentage of Workers, 16–17 Years Old

|      | Old Workplace | New Workplace |
|------|---------------|---------------|
| 1940 | 60            | 12            |
| 1950 | 47            | 26            |
| 1960 | 36            | 30            |
| 1970 | 22            | 39            |
| 1980 | 12            | 58[13]        |

As shown in the above chart, the figures for teenage workers in older and newer categories of labor almost exactly reversed themselves over the forty-year period 1940–1980. Just after 1960, the portion of teens who found their jobs in the new workplace caught up with that in the old. Then it streaked ahead.

This was part of a larger change in our economy. As the United States moved into what some historians call the "post-industrial" era, and as mechanized agriculture continued to send families from the farms to the cities, workers of all ages were switching over to new kinds of employment. Men and women of thirty and fifty were also moving out of factories and into service and retail work. Still, the shift was much more dramatic among teenagers. More important, the young people entering the new workplace were actually crowding mainly into two kinds of jobs. A survey in 1980 among high school seniors who held jobs found that just about half of them worked as store clerks and food-service employees.

Here, then, has been the trend: More teenagers have been finding jobs, and they have been leaving the diversity of older employments, on farms and in factories and mechanics shops, to work at a few sorts of tasks, mostly as check-out clerks and helpers in restaurants. Many of these young people are also working long hours. A study in 1990 revealed, first, that at any time during the school year, somewhere between half and two-thirds of all high school juniors hold part-time jobs. More than half of all employed seniors (and nearly a fourth of employed sophomores) work more than twenty hours per week.

This trend is interesting enough in itself, but behind it are other changes that show what has been happening in American families and in the U.S. economy. Early in the century, children worked partly to make money for themselves, but mainly because their parents depended on them. Over the next few decades, those who stopped working for pay did so partly because of new laws and changing technology and attitudes; but one of the main reasons, once again, had to do with economic necessity. Their families no longer required their labor or their income. Instead of working, older children stayed in school. As has been discussed in the sections on education in chapters 2 and 3, ever more teenagers were attending high schools. Furthermore, teenagers who remained in school rarely worked except at summer jobs. In 1940, less than 5 percent of seventeen-year-old students held any kind of a job. First middle-class families and, in the prosperous years after World War II, working-class and farming families could afford to keep their sons and daughters in school and off the job market until they were nearly out of their teens.

But the situation was changing again. America's "service" economy quickly expanded, opening up millions of jobs in restaurants, especially the cheaper and quicker sort, and in similar businesses. This work required little training and could be done efficiently by people working in short shifts. It was perfectly suited for inexperienced teenagers who were able to work a few hours a day after school. Millions of young people, especially

In the "new workplace" of American youth, teenagers often work twenty or more hours a week providing a huge portion of the labor in such service industries as "fast food" restaurants. *Courtesy of Burger King Corporation.*

those aged fifteen to eighteen, began pouring in to fill the demands of this rapidly growing job market.

These new young workers were not laboring to help their families get by, as had been the case in an earlier day. In fact, children of the poorest families have become the *least* likely to be employed, for reasons that will be discussed shortly. A survey in 1980 showed that the lowest rates of teenage employment were among families making less than $7,000 a year; the highest were in those making more than $25,000. Instead of handing much of their pay over to their parents, young workers have come to use their wages to buy what they want for themselves: clothes, music, cosmetics, jewelry, entertainment, and the other familiar items of the youthful consumer market.

The aftermath of World War II saw the rise of what has been called "luxury youth employment." The money made by working teenagers has fueled the hungry consumerism of recent decades. It has stimulated and supported many of the developments and products noted in this chapter and the one preceding, from rock and roll and video games to new foods and fashions. Among young customers, as with their elders, the line between necessities and extras has become increasingly fuzzy as teen part-time workers have found themselves with considerable money to spend on what draws their fancy.

This new pattern of youthful employment naturally has raised some troubling questions. For one thing, these working youngsters have continued to go to school. Is there time, some have asked, both to work and learn, especially when a student is flipping hamburgers twenty-five hours or so every week? Working can encourage some useful and admirable traits, many argue, such as self-discipline, self-confidence, punctuality, and getting along with varied personalities. Other investigators, however, admonish that too much part-time work invades the hours needed for an adequate education. Students who work more than fifteen or twenty hours a week, they have found, make poorer grades, live under greater psychological stress, and are more likely to suffer from alcohol and drug abuse than those who work only a few hours a week.

Moreover, the "new" workplace has lost some important advantages of the "old." Before the great change in where and how young people worked, a young man of fifteen or sixteen usually worked closely with adults. He was typically learning a trade, perhaps in a machine shop, or on a fishing boat, or on a farm, with a grown man nearby to show him what to do and how to do it. In that situation, young people learned more than just how to perform a particular job. They also learned about what it meant to be an adult, about spending hours a day in contact with people, usually outside the family, of different ages and personalities. In fact, the specific job the young man was learning was often the one he planned to pursue throughout his working life. Learning the ropes as a toolmaker, he usually planned on supporting a wife and children as a master of that trade. He hoped to work his way up to foreman of a factory where he started as a young teen.

In the "old" workplace, then, first jobs were rehearsals for the lives that teenagers would be living in a few years. Whatever the difficulties and dangers, this kind of work provided a kind of bridge between childhood and young adulthood.

But not so in the "new" workplace. In the kitchen of a franchise restaurant, adolescent boys and girls work almost exclusively with others their own age. Some critics consider this a problem. Their jobs, like their schools, separate them from adults and give them no experience or lessons in getting along with people of another generation. The work they do—frying frozen potatoes, assembling sandwiches, making change at a cash register, sweeping and mopping floors—generally is not what they plan to pursue as a career, either. There is no practical, long-term training to build into an adult working life.

Young people in the "new" workplace, then, usually are marking time, making money to spend for themselves, and gaining little specific experience they can put to good use in the years ahead. The problems and threats of these jobs, some critics say, may not be as dramatic and immediately dangerous as those of some old jobs, but they are problems nonetheless. As will be discussed later in this chapter, some new laws have taken these worries into consideration.

The working lives of these young people near the end of the 20th century were in some ways a culmination of changes in evidence at the century's start. On city streets in 1900, girls and boys had worked for nickels and dimes for their favorite pleasures and vices. Now young America was flexing its economic muscles, earning hundreds of millions of dollars a year to spend on extensions of these amusements. True, the youngest worked hardly at all, at least in the public marketplace, and the oldest earned their money in very different ways. But there were echoes from the past, too, with some of the same questions and concerns being raised: If some work is good for children, how much of it is bad for them, and does working in the wrong ways threaten both the children themselves and the society they will grow up to lead?

Not all young Americans, however, took part in the "new" workplace. The story of working children has always been full of contradictions and paradoxes, and the situation at the end of the century was no different. As more teenagers were taking jobs every year in "luxury employment," a minority was finding it increasingly difficult to find any work at all. And these job-seekers, unlike the others, needed to work, not to pay for entertainment and new fashions, but to buy the basics of life.

In the early 1960s, a series of studies and government reports told the nation of a growing crisis. During the 1962 school year, the President's Committee on Youth Employment found that the young people, ages sixteen to twenty-one, who were out of school and looking for work numbered between 600,000 and 800,000—as many people as lived in Boston or San Francisco. Those job-seekers were not spread evenly through the population. Most were from poorer families; African Americans predominated, and many lived in the inner cities. In one such area in a large city, 59 percent of males between sixteen and twenty-one, and 63 percent of those who had dropped out of high school, were unemployed. In another city, the figure was 70 percent.[14] But the problem was not confined to urban America. Some of the bleakest employment conditions, and some of the most grinding poverty, was in the countryside. As more farming was done by machines rather than by human labor, many displaced workers headed for the city. But others stayed behind, and these Americans, especially the younger ones with little work experience, found few opportunities for new careers. The situation was even worse in economically depressed pockets and more isolated areas. On the reservations of the Crow and Lakota Indians on the northern plains, the unemployment rate among young men crept upward toward 90 percent.

"I've been trying week after week to find a job," a young woman told an interviewer in the early 1960s. But she had no luck: "There seems to be a lot more people my age out of work than there are jobs." It was a lament that tens of thousands might have made. "I left school because I had to make some money," said an eighteen-year-old in St. Louis. He had left school to help his family, as his father had been out of work for two years. "When you keep looking for a job and can't find it," he added, "you start feeling you're being kept from getting the necessities of life." The same pattern could be found in every region. "This is a big city and I think I've been on every block where it is possible to look for a job," a seventeen-year-old from Boston reported: "Some places say there isn't a job open, some say you have to have a high school education, which I don't have; some say they want someone who's experienced. All I know is I need work and I haven't been able to find it."[15]

Such testimony, heard from San Diego to Miami and Philadelphia to Seattle, revealed a serious problem that deepened as the years passed. This youthful unemployment grew out of several changes, most of them described elsewhere in this chapter. In the evolving economy, the number of jobs was shrinking in those places where young people had found work for generations. Farming and factory work were the two most obvious examples. In the past, a son of sixteen or so might choose to leave high school in Duquesne, Pennsylvania, a Pittsburgh suburb, to work in one of the town's clamorous steel mills. "Dropping out" of high school in this case meant picking a course of employment that probably would lead to a secure and reasonably lucrative lifetime job. Teenage work fed directly to adult skilled labor that would provide the means of raising a family. The same might be said for an Ohio farmboy who chose to leave school early, ignore college, and stay on his family farm.

But after World War II, and especially from the 1960s on, those parts of the economy were withering while others boomed. With that, traditional routes from teenage work to adult careers were closed off. The jobs opening up, as already mentioned, were not the kind to channel young workers into lifelong careers. In fact, many young men and women who now were denied traditional opportunities could not find jobs even in the dead-end occupations of the "new" workplace. Those openings—in the service and retail industries, cooking in "fast food" restaurants and clerking in malls— were far more likely to be found in newly booming suburbs and on the city fringes, not in the poorer urban districts or in the countryside where jobs were drying up. The sons and daughters of America's economically blighted areas, then, were feeling a double blow: Jobs that had offered dependable paths into adult working lives were disappearing from the national economy, and most of the new jobs that were available for young people were cropping up in places beyond their reach.

Under those conditions, "dropping out" of high school took on a very different meaning. Earlier, leaving public education at seventeen or so could often be a reasonable option, a first step toward a good job. Now, "dropping out" more often meant limiting the chances of finding work in both the short and the long run. The better opportunities for employment among adults were in professional and white-collar careers, fairly technical work that typically demanded at least a high school degree and often some higher education. Even staying in school had its problems. Those parts of the country hit hardest by economic change and where employment opportunities were poorest were also the places where education was most likely to be severely underfunded. Schools in such areas were often the least equipped to prepare students for higher training, which was the key to the best jobs in the years ahead.

Several of the trends noted throughout this book were coming together to limit the economic prospects of the poorest young Americans. The transformations of rural America were shutting off possibilities traditionally offered to the young. Similarly, older industries had given way to businesses that held far fewer prospects for the urban poor. The continuing migration of middle-class families to the suburbs had taken with it many of the newer types of teenage jobs. Young people in impoverished neighborhoods and countryside were left with little besides dreams of work elsewhere, fuzzy fantasies of a better life, instead of practical preparation for pursuing such visions.

This situation naturally has raised concerns about the consequences of massive, and growing, youthful unemployment. Early in the 1950s, the Bureau of Labor Statistics was calling for "sympathetic and skillful help" for young people who were having an increasingly tough time finding work. Their arguments were basically the same as those used by reformers early in the century. Underprivileged girls and boys deserved our concern—they ought to be seen "as persons rather than problems," as the report put it— and by helping them, political leaders "will increase the over-all production of the Nation." Two educational authorities in the early 1960s, Robert Havighurst and Lindley Stiles, sounded an increasingly common warning: these "alienated" young job-seekers were a growing threat to the social order. They would do what they could "to achieve the symbols of man-hood" and find acceptance, respect among their friends, and money to buy what they wanted. Unable to work through the usual channels, they might turn hostile toward society and express their anger through "destroying property, burning school buildings, and attacking law-abiding people." Somehow, the threatened society had to find a way to widen their oppor-tunities and, if work was unavailable, to provide "the *moral equivalent of work*." The stakes were high, they argued: "Alienated youth might be con-sidered a national emergency equal to or worse than that of the 1930s."[16] These themes—that help must be given to underemployed youth both for ethical reasons and out of concern for the American economy and social order—have been heard over and over throughout the decades since then. Jobless, alienated adolescents are "social dynamite," as James Conant put it, dangerous elements who might still become productive citizens if given the chance.

Those fears have proved real enough. As will be discussed in the legal section of this chapter, some of the highest crime rates in the nation are among some of the American young, particularly those living in places that have felt the worst effects of these economic changes. Havighurst and Stiles warned that young men who see little economic future "may turn to the delinquent gang for 'moral support' and for instruction in ways to get money," a prophecy that seemed remarkably accurate by the 1980s. One of those "ways to get money" has been especially troubling among under-employed adolescents: the sale of drugs. In a sense the expansion of the drug trade, with its disastrous side effects, might be seen as a survival of an old pattern among the working young. At the opening of the 20th cen-tury, as described in chapter 1, children and young people in the poorer regions of urban America were pressed into three types of labor: industries, "tenement work," such as making cigars and cheap clothing, and the "street trades," such as peddling candy and newspapers, gathering junk, or running errands. The first two types have virtually vanished, as have most kinds of street trades.

But one kind of sales has flourished on inner city streets: Drug dealing, or selling and delivering illegal narcotics, might be seen as an updated version of hawking goods on street corners of turn-of-the-century Chicago or Pittsburgh. Children in both cases were drawn to a vigorous market that paid them money they used for their own purposes. Then and now, there has usually been a pecking order among the street dealers, with younger initiates working through older ones having contacts among adults. The young street tradesmen ninety years ago were sometimes in league with criminals—and investigators found, in fact, messenger boys and others often sold and delivered drugs, such as cocaine and various opiates, to prostitutes. The youthful drug trade, in other words, might be pictured as the result of today's children of poverty pursuing one of their few remaining economic options. But, on the other hand, drug dealing is something quite new. As an economic enterprise, its costs, both to the peddlers and society, are enormous. The most extreme accusations against "street urchins" and messenger boys did not come close to describing the price of today's drug trade in terms of the other crimes it inspires, the violence it produces, and the deaths from the products themselves.

In the 1990s, as in 1900, the issues surrounding the work of young Americans, or the lack of it, ultimately were bound up with the other aspects of children's lives. The problems of unemployed adolescents cannot be separated from concerns over education, its goals and its support, just as the dilemmas of high school "dropouts" are connected to students' economic prospects. And all that is inseparable from issues of crime, the law, government policies, health, and the rest of the child's world, including the entertainments he or she chooses to buy with the money earned on the job, whatever it may be.

In the years since 1960, a great deal of the working world of children has changed, but some things have remained much the same. As is true of the "new" workplace and the problems of the youthful unemployed, these "old" continuities have raised troubling questions about young people, their place in society, and government's responsibilities toward them. Although there has been a dramatic decrease in jobs among young people on American farmlands, not all child labor on the farm came to an end. Boys and girls continued to work on thousands of family farms, especially in the summers and during the peak of the laboring seasons. In fields from California to New Jersey, but especially in the South and West, teams of children also worked with adults as hired gang labor in the cultivation and harvesting of potatoes, sugar beets, strawberries, grapes, apples, beans, and several other crops. Because much of this work took place at times other than when the census takers made their rounds—and because much went unreported because it was illegal—the extent of agricultural child labor has continued to be much greater than the official statistics seem to tell us.

These children obviously were working because their help still was useful, and even essential, to their parents. They could be seen most often in fields where machines had not yet come to dominate all the work. Cotton and many other products previously cultivated and picked by hand now were mostly harvested mechanically; however, many others, especially fruits and vegetables grown on huge stretches of western land, still relied heavily on the bending of human backs. Often adults and children did part of the labor, machines the rest. Parents on those farms often expected their daughters and sons to provide part of the necessary human effort, especially if they were operating on the financial edge, with little money to spare for hired labor. Farm children also earned vital income for their families by hiring out to others, planting and picking for neighbors or strangers, much as young people had done since early in the history of the nation.

Besides children working on or near their family farms, tens of thousands of others were part of one of the largest and oldest migrations in the history of the continent, ongoing since the late 16th century: the movement of Latin Americans back and forth across the border separating the United States and Mexico. In the 20th century that human movement has ebbed and flowed, but the general pattern has been one of increase, considerably so in the years since 1940. Like all such tidal flows of population, this one was produced by forces that both "pushed" and "pulled" people into movement. Many families in Mexico and countries to its south lost jobs and their places on the land because of economic changes and social disorder. Thus "pushed" into motion, they were also "pulled" toward the north by the hope of work.

Work was available, especially on farms, from California to New York and Michigan to Alabama, but most of all on the Pacific coast and in the Southwest. The U.S. government had tried to clamp down on that immigration during the depression years, but the war brought a sudden and desperate need for farm labor. The government reversed itself and encouraged farm workers, or *braceros,* to come north and harvest the food needed by soldiers and workers in war industries. The number of Latino workers recruited for agriculture rose from just over 4,000 in 1942 to 120,000 in 1945. Concurrently, thousands more streamed across the border illegally. In 1946, when 82,000 were admitted legally, more than 66,000 were caught entering the U.S. at the far western end of the international boundary.[17] Many thousands more certainly made it across undetected. The number of north-bound immigrants has risen and fallen since then; but, overall, there has been a huge increase in Spanish-speaking newcomers searching for work, particularly in recent years.

Many Latino immigrants came and worked as families, moving from job to job during the peak working seasons, fanning out over agrarian America wherever there was a need for cheap labor. When fathers and mothers went into the field, they typically took their children with them, at least the older ones. Help from boys and girls was necessary. Wages were pitifully low, less than $600 a year in 1946 according to one report; in 1960 the U.S. Secretary of Labor reported annual income of migrant workers averaging less than $900, "the lowest wages in the entire American economy." Children's hands were essential to help the family survive.

As always, it has been extremely difficult to determine how many children have been working in agriculture at any particular time. The American Friends Service Committee estimated in 1970 that at least 800,000 young people under sixteen were working farms as wage labor—that is, not as family helpers, but as paid labor—a number amounting to roughly one out of every four agricultural wage workers; and that was probably a low estimate.

A spot investigation of fewer than 2,000 farms in 1961 found more than 5,000 boys and girls working illegally, 1,314 of them migrants and 4,137 local residents. In some parts of the West, the portion of immigrants was much greater. For instance, in Oregon's Williamette Valley, a picturesque and fertile basin that had first drawn pioneers up the Oregon Trail in the 1840s, at least half of the farm workers in the 1970s were estimated to be migrants, and three out of four of the seasonal laborers were children. Most local children worked in the fields, as did virtually all the young immigrants. There, and in Washington state, an estimated 98–99 percent of migrant children over six years old worked picking strawberries, beans, and other crops.

Young Americans continued to work in such numbers partly because the laws allowed far greater latitude in such work than in most other areas. The main federal legislation governing child labor, the Fair Labor Standards Act of 1938, only outlawed agricultural labor by males and females under sixteen during the hours when schools are in session. After school during the academic year and throughout the summer months, young boys and girls can be hired to work at virtually any age and under virtually any conditions. Even the law's limited protections, furthermore, do not apply

While most farm families have abandoned agriculture since World War II, the children of migrant workers continue to work in the fields. Their work often is grueling and dangerous and their living conditions primitive and unhealthy. *Courtesy of The Denver Public Library, Western History Department.*

to children employed by their own families. Apart from these standards, there are no federal restrictions on the number of hours children can work. Those who work by "piece"—that is, in proportion to the weight of what is picked—are not guaranteed a minimum wage. State laws typically have given no additional protection. Michigan exempted all agriculture from child labor legislation; New Jersey permitted all youngsters twelve and older to work up to sixty hours a week, ten hours a day.

Even those lenient laws, however, have been widely violated. Enforcing the provisions has been extremely difficult, partly because agencies have had far too few investigators to cover a business that, by its nature, is spread over a huge area. In the nation's leading agricultural state, California, for instance, enforcement was up to the Division of Industrial Welfare, which, in 1970, had forty-four persons to oversee the state's 3,000,000 workers, 400,000 of them in agriculture.[18]

Besides understaffing, enforcement has been held back by attitudes that are as old as the American republic. "Six years is none too soon to start work on the farm," wrote an Indiana poultry producer, who also was shocked that anyone would wish to take away the privilege of agricultural labor, "the greatest thing in the world for children." This conviction, commonly expressed since colonial days, took on fresh power during the years since World War II, when so many poor urban youngsters seemed to be out of work and drifting into delinquency and crime. A woman in New Jersey would rather have seen country children at work and learning "the ethics of money than add[ing] our rural youth to the masses of aimless, drifting unemployed urban welfare recipients," and an official for the American Farm Bureau Federation testified before Congress that farm work by children was a "socially desirable" force that would combat juvenile delinquency. Charges of exploitation, he added, triggered "emotional reactions unrelated to reality."[19]

It was certainly true that many children working for their parents, doing chores and pitching in when the need was greatest, were learning self-discipline, commitment, and the value of hard work. In many other cases, however, agricultural labor was posing significant dangers to the young workers. In the first place, the mechanization that had freed so many girls and boys from farm work was hazardous to those young people still in the fields. Tractors, mechanical pickers and cultivators, hoppers and rolling bins for carrying the picked produce—all these could maim or kill children unlucky or careless enough to get in their way. Unlike in 1850, or 1910, or even 1950, a field of tomatoes or sugar beets had become a kind of rural factory, with perils similar to those of a textile mill or coal mine earlier in the century. Newspaper headlines told of what could happen:

Youth Loses Leg from Baler Accident in Montana
Farm Machine Mangles Boy Age 9 in California
Tractor Beheads 12-Year-Old Boy in Illinois

A study of nearly eight hundred deaths in tractor accidents in thirteen states revealed that one out of eight victims had been under fifteen years old; some had been as young as five. Details of farm accidents could be as gruesome as in any big city factory. A boy, twelve, had both arms torn off by a feed grinder. An Idaho girl the same age, picking potatoes during a "crop vacation" allowed by local schools, had her pony tail caught in a potato-digging machine. She was horribly mangled and killed.[20]

Other dangers are no less real, if not as obvious, as the wheels and the whirling blades of farm machinery. Scientific advances in agriculture have brought the increasing use of chemicals as fertilizers and insecticides. While these materials have made American farms much more successful, they have also threatened farmers of all ages in ways unknown in an earlier, less productive era. The same apple orchards and bean fields that are nourishing millions of Americans can be poisoning the adults and children who work in them.

As with the laws covering the ages and hours of child farm laborers, those governing hazards on the farm, from poisons or anything else, have often proved vague and difficult to enforce. In factories and other industries, the Fair Labor Standards Act requires the secretary of labor to verify that no threat or hazard exists before children under sixteen are allowed to work there. Farms, however, are exempted in that children under sixteen can legally work anywhere in agriculture so long as no investigation has found any danger there. Boys and girls, in other words, cannot work in a factory *until* it has been proved safe, but they can work on a farm *unless* it has been found to be unsafe. The result is that thousands of young laborers in the countryside continue to labor under threatening circumstances.

Some of those threats have been especially difficult to guard against. Work around chemicals supposedly is regulated by laws passed during the 1970s, but enforcement has proved complicated, and protection for children has been especially troublesome. Some pesticides—those causing death or serious injury on contact—are tightly regulated; but others are less closely controlled, even though they may pose grave dangers over time.

Children, moreover, are more at risk than adults. A growing girl or boy exposed to some field chemicals apparently are more likely to develop asthma, to have difficulty producing calcium for bone development, and to suffer reproductive disorders as adults.[21]

Besides the loss of life and limb to machines, and debilitation from exposure to toxic chemicals, farm work under the worst conditions can send children into adolescence and adulthood with physical problems that might plague them for the rest of their lives. A girl of eleven or thirteen who does "stoop" labor, picking berries or potatoes for eight or ten hours a day, can develop severe gynecological difficulties. A child of either sex is more susceptible than an adult to heat stroke and to long-range ailments arising from excessive exposure to harsh weather. Lingering ideals of agrarian life to the contrary, the farm today is among the most dangerous places a child can work. California officials have ranked agricultural labor as the third most hazardous industrial employment and the most dangerous of all jobs in exposure to toxic substances.

Those young farm workers who are employed in full workdays for weeks at a time naturally suffer educationally as well. A study of more than five thousand such boys and girls hired illegally discovered that when they *were* in school they were placed in grades below what was normal for their age. Nearly eight of ten fifteen-year-olds had slipped back at least a grade. The more years these young workers labored in the fields, the farther they fell behind. Finally, those who have studied these children, especially girls and boys in migrant families, emphasize the psychological costs that this part of young America often pays. Migrant children "not only live in poverty, go hungry, suffer from malnutrition, but in addition live incredibly uprooted lives," observed the eminent psychologist Robert Coles, who studied and lived with these families for several years. They "eventually become dazed, listless, numb to anything but immediate survival."[22]

Looking back over the century, everyone would agree that much had changed in the child's world of work. Although a growing number of teenagers are taking jobs today, young Americans generally work much less than in 1900; and the youngest play far, far less a part in our nation's economy. Young people also are working in different ways than they did at the opening of the century or even thirty or forty years ago. Those who do work have used their labor to help pay for an unprecedented independence and a tremendous influence on the marketplace.

For all the change, however, child labor remains a troubling and controversial part of American life. Many adolescents, according to some critics, are suffering in their education and social lives because they are working too much; and, ironically, these usually are middle-class young people who are not really in need of the income. Others, whose families truly need the extra wages a child might provide, are facing desperately high levels of unemployment. And, after decades of investigations, calls for action and legislation, some boys and girls continue to labor, often at long hours, in dangerous and debilitating workplaces, not in stuffy factories and dank mines but in the oldest and most traditional setting of all, the fields and orchards of the American countryside. As in 1900, many of these children are immigrants, and, just as was true at the century's birth, they often are threatened by machines and poisoned air. As we near a new turn of the century, work remains both a rewarding and hazardous part of life for young America.

## AT SCHOOL

On the face of it the final years of the century have seen the culmination of an educational trend underway before 1900. More and more American children, of all racial and ethnic backgrounds and from all economic levels, have crowded into our nation's classrooms. In 1990, more than 52 million Americans were attending public schools. The growth through the century has been remarkable, especially since World War II:

### Total U.S. School Enrollment

| | |
|------|------------|
| 1900 | 16,885,000 |
| 1910 | 19,372,000 |
| 1920 | 23,278,000 |
| 1930 | 28,329,000 |
| 1940 | 28,045,000 |
| 1950 | 28,492,000 |
| 1960 | 41,762,000 |
| 1970 | 51,319,000 |
| 1980 | 50,334,000 |
| 1990 | 52,062,000[23] |

As can be seen from the above figures, growth in enrollment has come in spurts. During the generation of the Great Depression and World War II, for reasons already discussed, enrollment changed little for nearly twenty years; thereafter it soared as the baby boomers invaded the classrooms. The figures leveled off once again, but at first glance the statistics for the most recent twenty years might seem puzzling. As the baby boom busted in the 1960s, the numbers of students should have declined with it.

That's what happened—for a while. The year 1965 was a milestone of sorts; there were fewer children entering kindergarten than graduating from high school. The trend swept upward through the educational system in the 1970s. Enrollment in the elementary grades shrank by more than six million in the 1970s, encouraging city and town officials to sell thousands of school buildings and to convert others to museums and housing for various public functions. Appropriate to the aging of the national populace, some were turned into senior citizen centers. Of more than seventy thousand elementary schools operating in 1967, over eight thousand were closed by 1975.

The adjustment was made even more difficult by the continuing movement of the nation's people. As usual, young families with school-age children have been most likely to pick up and go looking for better times, and educational facilities have had to respond as Americans have flowed into some areas and abandoned others. Regions of economic boom, especially the West and parts of the South, have felt a continuing need for new classrooms. Areas of decline suddenly have had much more space than they needed. A similar pattern unfolded within cities. As families that could escape the inner city did so, enrollments steadily sagged. It was not unusual for the lower grades to have only half the students of the upper ones. In some places this precipitous decline has continued until the present. Duquesne, Pennsylvania, just outside Pittsburgh, was arguably one of the most important towns in the country in the mid-1940s, the center of American steel production and the bulging bicep of the war effort. In those years thousands of children attended Duquesne's several schools and more than three hundred young men and women were graduated annually from its high schools. In the mid-1990s all classes for all grades were held in one building, and the graduating class of 1995 had six students.

Two other changes, however, have pulled against the overall decline in enrollment. First, the average young American is now spending more years in school. The percentage of children aged seven through thirteen in school during the core educational years (from first through eighth grades) has remained quite constant: in 1960, 99.5 percent were enrolled; in 1991, 99.6 percent. Instead, students have been starting school earlier and staying later:

Percentage of Persons Enrolled by Age

|        | 5–6 yrs | 7–13 yrs | 14–17 yrs | 18–19 yrs |
|--------|---------|----------|-----------|-----------|
| 1960   | 80.7    | 99.5     | 90.3      | 38.4      |
| 1970   | 89.5    | 99.2     | 94.1      | 47.7      |
| 1980   | 95.7    | 99.3     | 93.4      | 46.4      |
| 1990   | 96.5    | 99.6     | 95.8      | 57.2[24]  |

As was true between 1940 and 1960, a big jump in movement has come among the youngest, as kindergarten programs have expanded and more working mothers have put their toddlers in class as soon as possible. At the other end of public education, teenagers have been staying longer in high school and then heading for college. In 1940, less than half of the population over the age of twenty-five had been educated beyond the eighth grade, but that began changing dramatically over the next generation. Comparing the high school diplomas awarded each year to the number of Americans at the age of seventeen, the ratio was 50 diplomas per 100 seventeen-year-olds in 1940 and 75 per 100 in 1991. College and university enrollments grew apace during those same years. Changes were especially dramatic among black youth. The median number of years of school completed by black males age twenty-five and older, for instance, rose from about eight in 1960 to twelve in 1990.

The second change has been a renewed rise of the birth rate, the so-called "baby boomlet." As the number of births once again pushed upward in the mid-1970s, schools and teachers were once more asked to accommodate more children by the late 1980s. The population between the ages of five and seventeen in 1990 (45.3 million) was greater than in 1960 (44.2 million); and by the mid-1990s, that figure was pushing once again toward 50 million. So the combined impact of these two developments—a new surge in births and a tendency for students to spend more years in school— has kept enrollment high. More than ever, education today is a common, unifying fact of life for young America.

The slowdown in the student surge in the 1970s eased the pressure on schools and teachers. The student-to-teacher ratio, so alarmingly high in the 1950s, fell; and as more teachers were hired in special education, counseling, and other new areas of emphasis, the ratio continued to fall. In 1960 there were about twenty-seven pupils per teacher; by the end of the decade the ratio had dipped to twenty-three, and twenty years later, it had slipped to eighteen. But one figure has continued to rise: the amount of money spent on education:

Expenditures on Elementary and Secondary Education (In Constant 1990–
91 Dollars)

| | |
|---|---|
| 1970 | 153,000,000,000 |
| 1980 | 177,900,000,000 |
| 1990 | 242,000,000,000[25] |

Schooling their children remains one of the biggest bills paid by the American people.

These years of expansion and change have also been ones of great controversy in education. Debates have always roiled around the quality of schooling, with some critics praising educators and others complaining of misdirected efforts and poor results. During the past quarter century, however, some alarming evidence has given these old, continuing arguments a new urgency. The standard measure of the quality of public education has been the Scholastic Aptitude Test, or SAT. This exam, given to most students planning to enter college, measures reasoning ability and basic educational skills. Students are tested in two broad areas, verbal and mathematical; the lowest possible score for each part is 200; the highest, 800. For individuals, performance on the SAT has become the key to admittance into the most desired colleges or universities. For the nation as a whole, the average scores are usually cited as the basic benchmark of how well American youth is learning—and how well educators are doing their jobs.

National averages of the SAT held steady during the 1950s, then rose slightly in the early 1960s, peaking in 1963. The next year they began a relentless twenty-year decline:

SAT Score Averages among College-Bound Seniors

| | Verbal | Mathematical |
|---|---|---|
| 1963 | 478 | 502 |
| 1967 | 466 | 492 |
| 1970 | 460 | 488 |
| 1974 | 444 | 480 |
| 1977 | 429 | 470 |
| 1979 | 427 | 467[26] |

Predictably, plenty of explanations were offered. Theories ranged from effects of radioactive fallout from the testing of atomic weapons and chemical additives in processed foods to international communism and new obstetric techniques. One intriguing idea draws on the long-noted pattern of higher achievement on IQ and other tests among firstborn children. Supposedly, these young people are more aggressive learners and strive more for attention. (Among our first twenty-three astronauts, twenty-one were firstborn or only children. The same is true, according to a study in 1970, of 89 percent of exotic dancers.) So, as those first children passed out of high school and their younger siblings took their place, performances might be expected to slacken; sure enough, the SAT scores took their biggest dip just as the second and third children among the baby boomers were reaching their final years of high school.

Obviously, however, there were other reasons. In the early 1980s, a committee of twenty-one distinguished specialists, headed by Willard Wirtz, a former secretary of labor, found a variety of possible causes for declining scores. One, ironically, was the broadening of educational opportunity. The trend of young people staying in school longer was especially notable among those from families of lower economic means, students who traditionally have scored well below those from more affluent homes. It follows that as poorer students stayed longer in school, and more of them took exams in preparation for college, the average scores would drop. However, the greatest surge of poorer young people into the upper grades was slowing by around 1970, and the slippage of scores did not slow correspondingly. In fact, some of the sharpest declines came in the mid-1970s. The performance of students from all economic levels and all ethnic categories declined.

The continued downward trend reinvigorated the debate over educational curriculum. Many critics, echoing the complaints of the "essentialists" of the previous generation, charged that schools had moved too far away from the teaching of fundamentals. Criticism was directed especially at the reduction of required courses and the increase of electives, new courses that many warned were trivializing education—classes in science fiction, detective novels, and the history of movies, for instance. The educational experience, the argument went, was being watered down. In the early 1970s, enrollment in advanced English classes decreased sharply, and some traditional subjects, such as geography, were given short shrift in curriculums. Critics also took aim at the "new math," with its emphasis on concepts over fundamentals, and at approaches to history and social sciences that stressed social issues but, some said, sacrificed basic information and literary quality. Defenders of the changes, like the "progressives" before them, countered that the new curriculum was simply keeping pace with an evolving national life and offering education pertinent to the lives of young people. Elective classes encouraged students to relate educational fundamentals to the world they knew best, and thus fed their creativity and kept them excited about learning. Because the SAT did not measure what students were gaining in these new classes, they said, the results were misleading. Test scores were declining, in other words, because the test asked the wrong questions.

Some mastery of the basics is obviously necessary, however, and by some evidence many students were not getting what they needed. Surveys of geographical knowledge in the 1980s discovered that in many high schools a majority of seniors could not locate their home town on a map. Four out of ten college freshmen in New Jersey in the late 1970s could not consistently write grammatical sentences. A broad-ranging study in 1975 produced some startling and embarrassing conclusions about the public at large. Roughly one adult out of five was unable to address an envelope, calculate how to make change, or read a classified advertisement. In comparisons with students from other nations, Americans consistently scored well behind most European countries and other developed nations.

The debate over educational quality continues and probably will never go away. SAT scores leveled off in the late 1980s, and math scores in fact rose. Then, in the spring of 1995, the College Board, which administers the test, announced a revision of standards under which future scores would be adjusted upward to reflect the long-term decline. To use a familiar term in high schools and colleges, in other words, the SAT results would be "curved," so a student who would have made a 424 now would score a 500. The action once more inspired criticism of lowering expectations and looser standards.

Disagreements over the goals and strategies of education are virtually guaranteed. All can agree that public schooling—its purposes, content, and methods—is vital to the nation's well being. As long as that is so, no one should expect anything but vigorous discussion and often heated arguments about what goes on in the nation's classrooms.

Among the most controversial aspects of public education has been its connections to that pervasive influence in American life—television. Even in the 1950s, some teachers already were claiming that the most enthusiastic television viewers among their students were becoming more passive, asking fewer questions and giving fewer answers; and as early as 1954, a study in the affluent Chicago suburb of Evanston concluded that children in the lowest academic quarter of their class watched several more hours of programs daily than those in the upper quarter. Over the next decades, critics continued to charge that television was undermining education. As its most obvious effect, some said the "tube" diverted children's attention from their studies and took up time that otherwise would have gone to

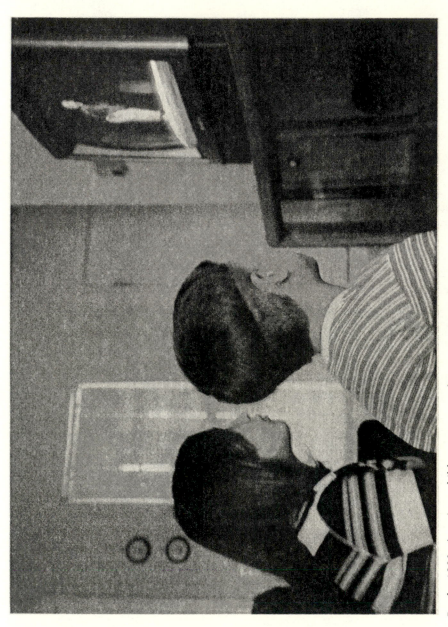

By the 1990s American children were spending an average of about twenty-four hours of every week, roughly one day out of seven, watching television. *Courtesy of the author.*

homework. Others claimed something more fundamental. Television was shaping youngsters' basic mental development in ways that were different from earlier generations.

Children's intelligence has always grown in part through mental stimulation from things and people around them. For hundreds of generations, human stimulus was mainly in the form of conversations with those nearby. For the past few hundred years, children also have expanded their minds by reading books. In both cases, children were required to interact with the source of the stimulus, responding to what was communicated to them. They took the symbols of words in books and used them to create their own unique mental images. Conversation and reading were both what the writer Marshall McLuhan called "hot" media: they demanded active engagement, even from someone sitting quietly with a book in his lap. Even radio was "hot," as it required listeners to imagine the details around the voices and sounds they were hearing. But television was different in that an entire reality was presented: sight and sound washed over an audience that sat and stared at the screen. Television is a "cool" medium in McLuhan's terms, as the viewer is passive. Critics warned that a child who watched television for thousands of hours during the crucial years of mental development emerged with a passive attitude toward learning. Such students grew up expecting teachers to keep them amused, much like their favorite shows, and they lacked the mental practice of learning through exchanges with others and with the world around them. Television, these critics charged, has stifled children's natural curiosity and has left them poorly prepared for genuine learning.

But after dozens of studies of television's effects on education and learning, the conclusions reached are complicated and contradictory. True, poor performance and excessive viewing are linked in some way. Low academic achievement is more common among children who watch more than about fifteen hours weekly; not surprisingly, performance is much worse among those who watch thirty-five or forty hours a week. The specific cause and effect, however, is uncertain. Would those students study more and be more engaged in the classroom if they had no television to watch, or are they just poor students, ones who have problems arising from other causes, who would spend those hours finding some way to pass their time, television or not, instead of doing homework? The same studies show that a modest amount of viewing, ten or so hours weekly, has little connection to low achievement. On the average, in fact, children who watch ten hours of television perform better than those who watch only five hours or so a week. Neither is there any conclusive evidence that watching a couple of shows a night has any effect, good or bad, on children's cognitive skills, creativity, or attention span.

There are strong indications, on the other hand, that television can be used constructively to educate young viewers. Programs can communicate lessons on health hazards and dietary matters, and some investigations have concluded that certain shows encourage "prosocial behavior" such as co-operation and tolerance of others. Television has promoted education more directly through programs specifically designed to sharpen skills taught in the classroom. Such programs first appeared in the 1960s on noncommercial, or "public," television, funded by private and corporate contributions and by government support. Early efforts, poorly produced and unimaginative, drew only small audiences. Children found them dull. Then, in 1969, public television served up a new show that would prove to be a spectacular success both in the size of its audience and, according to many educators, in its influence on young viewers.

"Sesame Street" was developed by Joan Ganz Cooney of the Children's Television Workshop, formed two years earlier with both private grants and support from the U.S. Department of Education. From the start, its guiding creative spirit was Jim Henson. Born in the Mississippi delta, son of an agronomist working for the U.S. Department of Agriculture, Henson grew up playing in the countryside around his father's research station. (A favorite pastime was watching and catching frogs; a playmate was named Kermit Scott. These two facts later would combine into a celebrated bit of American popular culture.) Henson became infatuated with puppetry in high school after his family moved to Maryland. Later, while a student at the University of Maryland in the early 1950s, he devised a new variation of ancient forms, a combination of a marionette and puppet—a "muppet," he called it. During this time, Henson was also becoming involved in television production. First working in local productions, he and his muppets gradually attracted wider attention, including an appearance on an early version of the "Tonight" show. "Sesame Street" brought together Henson's skills with those of his wife and collaborator, Jane Nebel Henson, another puppeteer, Frank Oz, and a creative staff that included the songwriter Jeff Moss, a veteran of the classic children's show, "Captain Kangaroo."

On "Sesame Street" muppets coexisted with human characters, including Susan, Gordon, Luis, Maria, David, and Mr. Hooper. Because the show initially was intended especially to reach preschool viewers in the inner cities, its setting was a city street. In time, more than two thousand muppet characters appeared, with a handful becoming genuine superstars. Among the most popular were the close pals Bert and Ernie, the towering Big Bird, the garbage-can-dweller Oscar the Grouch, and the Cookie Monster. Most famous of all were Miss Piggie and Kermit the Frog. The technique of the muppeteers was masterful. Henson and Oz manipulated the large, fuzzy characters directly with their hands and with rods colored to blend in with the background. The effect was astonishingly lifelike, but much more important was the individual personalities that Henson and Oz managed to convey in each of their creations. The muppets, as much as their human counterparts on the show, became actors. "Sesame Street" spread beyond the United States to be shown in eighty-four countries and adapted into thirteen other languages. Within the United States in the late 1980s, the show was watched in nearly 70 percent of all households with children under six.

The content of "Sesame Street" was pitched mainly to children from two to five years old. Its staff included not only producers and writers but also psychologists and educators, who worked together to integrate new research on early childhood learning into its programs. The programming interspersed films and cartoons with sketches featuring recurring characters, all of it designed to teach and reinforce basic reading and mathematical skills and to stimulate cognitive development. Henson and the others pursued these pedagogical goals through the slickest methods learned from advertising and cartoon animation, spiced with humor that tended sometimes toward the bizarre. Following up on the fact that young children pay at least as much attention to advertisements as to programs, each show was "sponsored" by a number or letter of the alphabet, complete with commercials touting the virtues of the number "6" or the letter "J." The general strategy was to teach children by catching their attention and keeping them entertained, much as Dr. Seuss had in his pioneering *The Cat in the Hat.*

And it worked, at least according to some measurements. Two years into "Sesame Street's" phenomenal popularity, studies showed that its young viewers consistently learned more than those who didn't watch. They also had larger vocabularies and more highly developed thinking skills. The production techniques apparently sharpened visual and spatial analytical abilities. And because television had spread through virtually all of national culture, from the wealthiest to the poorest homes, the educational potential of the programs, unlike learning in classrooms, cut across economic lines. Critics, however, wondered whether the sometimes frantic pace of the action shortened attention spans; and, more fundamentally, they questioned the long-term value of visual education that had no direct exchange, as with teachers in classrooms. Nonetheless, "Sesame Street" and another program that appeared shortly afterward, "The Electric Company," demonstrated that television could be a pervasive part of the education of younger children. Both shows also strove to teach social and ethical lessons—toleration of other ethnic groups, reconciliation of conflict, and dealing with life's difficulties.

Landmarks in the application of video technology to education, the muppets were yet another case of children's culture—in this case the popular culture of their learning—spreading outward into national life. Miss Piggie and Cookie Monster became almost as familiar to adults as to their children. Feature films produced by major studios, starting with *The Muppet Movie,* drew huge audiences. "Rubber Ducky," a song written by Jeff Moss for the television show and performed by Ernie, cracked the top ten list of the nation's most popular records. In 1976, Henson, Oz, and their creations moved into prime time with "The Muppet Show," a half-hour evening program with Kermit the Frog as master of ceremonies and a different celebrity guest host each week. After being turned down by a major network because of fears it would not appeal to enough adults, "The Muppet Show" eventually was watched each week by more than 235 million persons in a hundred countries, then became the most popular syndicated show in the history of television. Rights to the muppets have recently been bought by the Disney entertainment empire. Plans for expansion of Disneyland and Walt Disney World (see the section in this chapter on play) include new rides based on Oscar the Grouch, Big Bird, and others of the furry crew.

## HEALTH

The larger picture of the health of young America, from the early 20th century until the present, has been one of steady and impressive improvement. Throughout the century, and especially since World War II, killers that had taken children in their early years have been gradually tamed. Since the 1960s the number of deaths from measles, whooping cough, diphtheria, scarlet fever, and other previously terrifying childhood maladies has been so low that the census no longer calculates them. Others, notably pneumonia and influenza, remain significant threats but are far less dangerous than before. (Influenza and pneumonia accounted for 202 deaths per 100,000 persons in 1900; that figure had shrunk to 30 in 1970, and 13.4 in 1990.) As a result, the overall infant mortality rate has continued to fall. In 1970, about twenty infants per year died for every thousand live births; in 1990, only nine were lost.

Yet other patterns, much more disturbing, have also endured throughout the century. There has been a startling, even stunning, inflation in the costs of medical care. Total health expenditures rose from $12.6 billion in 1950 to $74.4 billion in 1970, then soared to $675 billion in 1990. Costs of hospital care grew during the same period from $3.8 billion, to $27.5 billion, to $258 billion. The zooming price of medicine has far outpaced that of virtually every other essential budget item. The price index of housing, for instance, rose about 400 percent between 1950 and 1990; during the same period, the per capita costs of hospital care rose 6,800 percent.

This steep ascent in the cost of health care has been difficult for American families and, obviously much harder for some than others. The many who cannot afford to pay for their own medical expenses and who have no medical insurance either do without or rely on some form of publicly funded medicine. Steep medical costs and their consequences raise once again another troubling theme in children's history in this century: the close connection between health and wealth.

As discussed in previous chapters, there have always been disparities in the health and medical care among American children, most obviously because of differences in the money that families have to determine what is needed and to pay for it. Near the end of the century, as was true at its start, the infant mortality rate is considerably higher for some, depending on a baby's race and the family's economic condition. The rate in 1990 for black children was about 18 per thousand live births, about twice the national average and roughly the same as for all American babies in 1970. Improvements for African-American infants, that is, lag about twenty years behind the nation at large. The rate among children in poverty, regardless of race, is far above the national average. Children whose parents earned less than $3,000 in 1967 were half again as likely to die before their first birthday compared to luckier ones born to parents with incomes of more than $10,000 a year (32.1 deaths per thousand compared to 19.9).[27]

Poor children under five today already are well behind others in height, weight, and other basic measures of physical development. They are more susceptible to various diseases, especially those closely associated with poor sanitation. An African-American newborn is more than three times as likely to die of meningitis as a white baby, for instance. Because of the large numbers of children in poverty, these conditions have left the United States, despite its boast of having the world's most productive economy, lagging well behind several other nations in the health of its children. In 1992, the

United States ranked twentieth in the world in infant mortality and seventeenth in the percentage of one-year-olds fully vaccinated against polio.

Medical help for the poor is usually administered through public hospitals and clinics. Those facilities often have a heavy workload and too few doctors and nurses. In the care of mothers-to-be, there has been a return to more reliance on midwives. That solution to limited medical care has been common in rural America since the beginning of the century, but now is increasingly seen in our largest cities. While these midwives must be certified according to standards of training, they lack the expertise of doctors, and consequently there is a greater risk of their not detecting problems during a mother's pregnancy, labor and delivery. An investigation by the *New York Times* in 1995 compared conditions of childbirth in the city's public and private hospitals. In private facilities, 5.5 percent of babies were delivered by midwives; in public ones, the rate was 21.6 percent, and in one hospital in the poverty-torn Bronx, it was 71.3 percent. During fetal distress, when a struggling baby was cut off from oxygen, caesarians (taking a baby surgically from the womb) were performed in 61.9 percent of the cases in private hospitals, but only 26.8 percent in public ones. The grim bottom line was that the risk of dying was about 40 percent greater for babies coming into the world in public hospitals.[28]

In other health matters, too, the odds continued to work against poor children. The incidences and mortality rates of most childhood diseases were greater. A less obvious, but more pervasive, threat came from how these children ate—or rather how they didn't. Investigations in the late 1960s, one by a U.S. Senate subcommittee and another by the Citizens' Board of Inquiry into Hunger and Malnutrition, found widespread hunger among children in many settings, from Columbia, South Carolina, and rural southern counties, to Appalachian mountain communities, to Indian reservations and migrant labor camps. Contrary to common impressions, the researchers discovered that most poor Americans were not receiving any food from federal relief programs. Malnutrition, rather than declining as incomes rose among most Americans, was, in fact, rising sharply.

After interviewing doctors, teachers, and governmental officials, the Citizens' Board came to a series of conclusions shocking to many during this postwar era of expanding national power and wealth. Substantial numbers of infants survived their first month only to die before the age of two from causes traced to hunger; protein deprivation was causing irreversible brain damage among some children under two, while between 30 and 70 percent of children in poverty suffered from nutritional anemia, stemming from too little protein. Teachers reported that many children often "come to school without breakfast, . . . too hungry to learn, and in such pain that they must be taken home or sent to the school nurse"; doctors told of case after case of premature deaths among children arising from malnutrition.

These findings were strikingly similar in content and tone to investigations shortly after the turn of the century. To be sure, the numbers were different; the frequency of malnourishment and near-starvation was less in the 1960s than in 1900 or 1910. But just as was true at the century's start, most Americans were largely ignorant of these conditions; and twenty-five years later, there was every indication that the situation was, if anything, getting worse. The incomes of the poorest families were slipping downward, and they were even less able to feed their young properly. The critics who called for help in feeding hungry young Americans used arguments that were much the same as those of six decades earlier. For moral reasons and for the good of the nation, something ought to be done, they said. Poor nutrition took a terrible toll in infant deaths, brain damage, retardation, slowed learning, alienation, and violence. There was an appalling ignorance about the extent and severity of the problem. The Citizens' Board in 1967 reported a "litany of hunger," quoting from those they met:

There are days without any food, four or five at a time, the parents may go hungry and the child may live on powdered milk . . .

You buy the cheapest meat you can, neck bones and that kind of stuff and have it a couple of times a month . . .

I am not able to buy [my children] milk or food or nothing day in and day out black eyed peas, grits, flour, maybe fatback, sometimes potatoes, beans . . .

And the children go to bed hungry. Sometimes they cry.[29]

As these young children grew a little older, they faced other dangers to their health, which also in some ways were associated with poverty and race. Among the many ironies in the story of the health of young Americans is this one: as medical discoveries have reduced the hazards from disease, new threats have taken their place, especially for teenagers and young adults. Most of these dangers are not of the old "natural" sort—not, that is, illnesses or environmental assaults. The threat to young people in recent years instead has come from one another and from their own behavior:

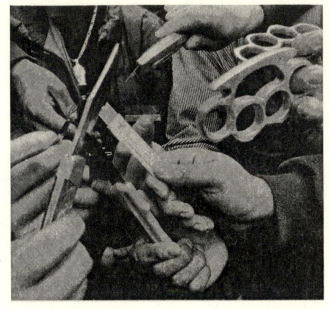

Students at a New York City high school show weapons they bring to classes every day. With the increase of violence among American youth, some schools have become armed camps. *Courtesy of Marilyn K. Yee/NYT Pictures.*

**Cause of Death (1991) of Persons 15–24 Years Old (Number of Deaths per 100,000 Persons)**

| | |
|---|---|
| TOTAL | 100.1 |
| Accidents | 42.0 |
| Auto | 32.0 |
| Homicide | 22.4 |
| Suicide | 13.1 |
| Cancer | 5.0 |
| Heart | 2.7 |
| HIV | 1.7 |
| Other | 13.2[30] |

As shown in the above chart, three causes of death dwarfed all others in 1990: accidents, homicide, and suicide, which together accounted for more than three-fourths of all fatalities in the age group of persons fifteen to twenty-four. Even among younger children, from five to fourteen years, accidents and homicides are currently responsible for half of all deaths.

Social and behavioral mortality has caught up with and surpassed "natural" death among the young. Cars, guns, and knives have replaced bacteria and viruses as the main threats to young America. From one point of view, these "social" deaths are testimony to our national affluence. The single most voracious killer among the young is that technological marvel that has shaped so much else in our lives in the 20th century—the automobile. Many children are killed in accidents for which adults are responsible, of course, but many more fatalities are the result of teenagers driving either their own cars or one kept in the family garage. Americans own half of all the autos in the world, and American youngsters have been especially enthusiastic in using them to search for excitement, sometimes with fatal results. Only a rich country could afford the many cars that have become the most common weapon in the death of its youth.

From another angle, these deaths are still more evidence of the costs of poverty. Violent fatalities are far more common among the poor, and the most disturbing recent trend has been a sharp turn upward in the incidence of violent assaults and murders, especially with firearms, among the poorest young. Not all deaths from gun wounds are from assaults, of course. The gun is the weapon of choice among young suicides: a child or teenager kills himself or herself every six hours in America. A large number of accidental fatalities are from gunshots, many from children playing with firearms kept around the house; and children have been caught in the path of gunfire. During the past several years the United States has become one of the most heavily armed societies in the world. Between 1985 and 1989 gun production grew by 42 percent, and in the mid-1990s another handgun was made every twenty seconds. With so many guns around, a large number of serious accidents and deaths are almost inevitable.

Nevertheless, many fatalities are the intentional murder of one person by another, in the overwhelming number of cases with a firearm. In this, the United States can claim undisputed leadership:

**Murders with Handguns, 1992**

| | |
|---|---|
| Britain | 33 |
| Sweden | 36 |
| Switzerland | 97 |
| Canada | 128 |
| Australia | 13 |
| Japan | 60 |
| United States | 13,220[31] |

A very large, and rapidly rising, number of those murders are being committed by teenagers and preteens, and, in by far the greatest number of cases, young people strike out not against adults but against one another. Fourteen children and teenagers are killed with guns daily. Among persons aged sixteen to nineteen, 91 out of a thousand were victims of a violent crime in 1991; among those between fifty and sixty-four years, only ten in a thousand were. Since 1988, teenaged boys have been more likely to die from gunshot wounds than from all natural causes combined.[32]

With African-American families much more likely to be poor, rates of violent assault and homicide are highest of all among black youth. A black child born today is nearly four times more likely than a white one to be murdered, and the most dangerous years are those of the middle and late teens. The most common weapons in this mayhem are firearms, especially handguns:

**Homicides by Firearm: 1991 (Males, Ages 15–19, per 100,000)**

| | |
|---|---|
| Whites | 11.8 |
| Blacks | 123.6[33] |

Children growing up in the poorest, most violent urban regions have come to live in something like a war zone. Individual stories illustrate the level of brutality and suggest its effects. By the time he was fifteen, a Milwaukee boy had seen family members and neighbors stabbed, beaten, pistol-whipped, overdosed on drugs, robbed, strangled, and struck with shovels. At nine, he saw his mother kill her boyfriend. At twelve, he was questioned in a shooting; at fourteen, arrested for carrying a handgun; a year later, he was charged with murdering a fellow gang member.[34]

One of the most rapidly growing businesses in such blighted areas is burial insurance for clients under twenty. Children no longer take survival for granted. When asked about his hopes, a ten-year-old boy in a Chicago housing project answered: "If I grow up, I'd like to be a bus driver."[35] Thinking of the future in terms of "if" instead of "when" seems a natural response in a chancy world where even the most basic assurances no longer apply. In parts of New York City, schoolteachers now urge their young students to cross streets in the middle of the block, not at the traffic lights: it is safer to dodge the speeding cars and trucks than to venture near the street corners, where most shoot-outs occur, usually during disputes over drugs.

The clear and disturbing connection between poverty and mortality among our children might be seen, on the one hand, as one of the most persistent themes in the American story. The grind of poverty contributed to the deaths of thousands of boys and girls in 1900; in the 1990s, one study estimated, about 10,000 children die annually from effects of poverty.[36] Many more, then and now, suffer higher rates of disease and lower levels of physical development and achievement because of insufficient diet and poor medical care. Even if we consider only deaths from such "natural" causes as disease, life expectancy among the impoverished newborn is significantly shorter than among those birthed into even modest affluence. And the dangers to the poorest of young America are much greater still if we include such "unnatural" deaths as murders and injuries from violent crimes. Poverty itself may not kill the young directly, but it aids and abets things that do. This has been true throughout this century of dazzling wealth.

But looking especially at the stunning rise of violent deaths among the youthful poor, we might also see such threats to life as one more instance of a prominent change that weaves throughout these chapters. This has been "the century of the child." Adults have made the young more and more the centers of their lives; public entertainment and fashion have been increasingly infiltrated by children's styles and wants; the economy has come to be influenced steadily more by the buying power and demands of our youth. And here too, in the violation of health and well being by assault and murder, young America is taking the lead.

Some of the most successful advances in the health care of young Americans have come in dental treatment. Until fairly recently dental care was not a major family concern. Parents moved into action only when problems arose that could not be ignored, such as an inflamed tooth causing severe pain. The answer usually was to remove the offending tooth. Middle-class families during the first few decades of this century were likely to visit the dentist for periodic checkups and the filling of at least the worst cavities. Beyond that, scant attention was given to trying to change the mouth's structure. Crooked, irregular, and protruding, or "buck," teeth were considered common facial features, and little was done to correct them. Tooth decay and the frequent loss of teeth, especially during and after middle age, was looked on as a natural part of life's cycle.

Even in the late 1950s, one survey showed, about half of all children under fifteen had never had a dental appointment, and, among poor families, the percentage was much higher.[37] But attitudes were changing, especially among families who could afford the costs of dentistry, partly because of scientific advances and partly because of larger trends in American society. The United States always has been a leader in dental medicine; the world's first dental school was Baltimore's College of Dental Surgery, founded in 1840. Throughout the 20th century, U.S. research has contributed to new methods and tools of dental medicine, such as rapid, water-cooled drills to reduce pain, improved methods of anesthesia, and lighter and more durable material for fillings and artificial teeth.

One of the great breakthroughs in dental care, especially among the young, grew from the observations of a Colorado dentist. When he opened a practice in Colorado Springs, he noticed, first, that many patients had brown, discolored teeth. Next he found that, despite the unsightly appearance, those teeth were remarkably free of cavities. Curious, he began to investigate and found that the city's water supply contained high amounts of the chemical fluoride. Scientists first were skeptical, but gradually they began to consider the possibility that fluoride reduced tooth decay. In 1944, a series of experiments were begun in a few communities. One part fluoride was added for every million parts of the public water supply. Some complained about this "forced medication," but the results were more successful than the most optimistic predictions. After ten years, the rate of dental decay among children was reduced by more than half. City after city began introducing fluoride to their water systems, and toothpaste manufacturers quickly jumped on the opportunity to boost sales by adding the chemical to their products. The result has been a dramatic decline in cavities and improvement in dental health, especially among the young. A study of nine-year-olds in the mid-1980s revealed that two-thirds of them had no cavities at all in their permanent teeth.

More was done to prevent problems that earlier were considered unavoidable facts of life for the young. Techniques were developed, for instance, for treating children's teeth with a solution to make them less porous, then applying a sealant to the surface to make them resistant to bacteria, thus further reducing the chance of decay. An entire field dedicated to treating dental problems of the young—pediatric dentistry (earlier called pedodontics)—has expanded considerably during the generations since World War II.

One result of this new medical technology has been the widespread appearance of one of the most familiar sights among American children and adolescents, teeth braces. Orthodontics has been among the most rapidly growing professions of the postwar years. Its main purpose is to correct "malocclusion," or irregular positioning of teeth, which can lead to loss of teeth, chronic pain, and even deformities of the jaws and face. Correcting these problems, of course, also improves the patient's appearance. To realign teeth and jaws, orthodontists typically install various "appliances," the most familiar being wire braces, which are worn for up to two or three years.

Braces and other orthodontic appliances have become an expected sight in middle schools and high schools. Millions of youngsters during the past forty years have gone through the initiation of kidding and jokes and being called "metal mouth." Along the way, that jibe has become less appropriate. Metal braces have been increasingly replaced by clear ceramics using adhesives and flexible wires developed initially as part of the government's space program. Braces are not universal among those who need them. Poorer adolescents continue to live with improperly aligned teeth and the problems that come with them. Treatment is far more common in middle-class families, who can afford the considerable expense. By the 1990s, the entire process of treatments and checkups cost, on the average, more than two thousand dollars. Nonetheless, well more than three million persons under the age of twenty were wearing braces in 1990. The total investment in their orthodontic work approached $7 billion, an amount nearly twice what was paid out to all physicians and dentists for all medical treatment in 1950.[38]

The phenomenon of expanding and improving dental care is partly an expression of increasingly sophisticated technology, steady improvement in mastering the body's imperfections, and the remarkable affluence of post-war America. Behind the glitter of millions of braces is the dedication of parents to spending resources, not just on their children's well being, but also on their appearance—literally the face they present to the world. They are determined to send their sons and daughters into the future looking as good as they can.

Yet even as medical treatment has become infinitely more effective, and even as it has been used to correct such relatively minor bodily defects as improper tooth alignment, a terrible new threat to life has arisen that so far has defeated efforts at destroying it. The threat is AIDS (Acquired Immunodeficiency Syndrome). Technically, this is not a disease but a breakdown of the body's defenses against diseases; its victims die usually from a wave of infections unchecked by their bodies' usual defensive responses. The body lets down its guards after it is invaded by the HIV virus (Human Immunodeficiency Virus). This virus is transmitted from one person to another through different human fluids, especially blood and semen. Once transmitted, the deadly HIV normally lives inside its new host for years, sometimes as long as a decade, before the body begins to lose its ability to fight off infections. Once this happens, the process of dying is slow, painful, and grotesque.

The great majority of AIDS victims have been adults. Especially during its first years in the United States, AIDS was confined almost entirely to homosexual men and to users of drugs, who received the virus through hypodermic needles previously used by infected persons. More recently, HIV has been passed increasingly between men and women during sexual intercourse. In these instances, children have not been threatened.

But, virtually from the first, infants and young people *were* falling ill and dying from AIDS. Children (and adults) acquired AIDS through transfusions of blood taken from others carrying the virus. Once this danger became known, authorities began taking precautions to test existing blood supplies and to screen new blood donors so new supplies would be uninfected. By that time, however, thousands of persons, children included, already had taken in the fatal blood. The very young could, and still can, be exposed to AIDS in a second way. Pregnant women share their blood supply with the babies growing inside them. A mother-to-be with AIDS therefore can pass on HIV to the infant she is carrying, although this will not necessarily happen. Infants infected *in utero* (inside their mothers) will have to fight the virus throughout their lives, which are tragically short.

As of 1995, an estimated ten to twenty thousand children under thirteen were "HIV-positive," meaning that they carried the virus that leads to AIDS. More than five thousand children had developed AIDS. As precautions against exposure through blood transfusions have been put into place, most new infections have come from pregnant women passing the virus on to their unborn children. This terrible legacy, however, occurs only about 30 percent of the time. In some cases, infants are infected while in their mothers' wombs; but in others, they are exposed only at the very end of pregnancy, in the final moments of birth. Increasingly, therefore, babies of HIV-positive mothers are delivered surgically by caesarian section. Even so, a toll still is taken among these youngest victims. In 1994, of about four million women who gave birth in the United States, seven thousand were HIV-positive; and about two thousand of their infants took the virus with them. Assuming a cure is not found very soon, all will die.

Treating children, especially the youngest ones, poses difficulties even greater than in the case of adults. Diagnosis is trickier. The standard test for HIV looks not for the virus itself, but for the antibodies produced in response to the virus. Most newborns carry with them their mothers' antibodies, even if they are free of the virus, so doctors often must wait up to fifteen months to be confident in their analysis. That poses a dilemma: If an infant is infected, doctors naturally want to begin treatment as soon as possible, but treating babies who are not sick also causes problems, because the powerful drugs used against HIV can have their own damaging effects. AIDS also progresses much more rapidly in infants than in adults, largely because their immune systems are still developing and are less able to resist assaults from infections and diseases. These youngest casualties and their doctors, then, face a maddening paradox. Premature, incorrect diagnosis can hurt a healthy baby; failure to diagnose early enough can shorten even more an infant's already brief life.

The strategy for treating children is basically the same as for adults. The virus causing AIDS invades human cells, changes their genetic structure, and causes the cells to produce more of the virus. Because the virus in effect becomes part of the body's basic functions, attacking it directly would likely do as much harm as good. So doctors instead work to suppress the effects of the virus through combinations of medications. The techniques are similar to those used to treat some varieties of cancer. Some advances have been made, but the results are mixed. The most effective drug in slowing the effects of AIDS among adults has been zidovudine (commonly called AZT). In 1990, this drug was approved for infected children, but five years later, a long-term study among patients from three months to eighteen years old found, to researchers' surprise, that AZT was ineffective in slowing AIDS among the young and, in fact, had several dangerous side effects. Other tactics are being tried, but wrestling with the virus in child patients thus far has proven even more frustrating than among their elders.

And even more than with most other fatal diseases, AIDS raises difficult social issues for the young and their parents. There are complicated and troubling questions involving the law and education, discussed elsewhere in this chapter. Because the mothers of most young patients are also suffering from AIDS, the plague by its nature has a devastating impact on families. By the end of the century, more than 125,000 children will lose their mothers to AIDS. As mothers grow ill, many infected children are left in the care of grandparents, who must face the doubly tragic burden of caring for first their children, then their children's children, watching each generation die in its turn. Many other young AIDS patients are put into foster homes. Those adults, too, are asked to carry an extra emotional and physical weight. "It's very hard," one woman, whose foster son had died at nine, told a reporter. "There were a group of children my child used to go to the clinic with, and they're all dead now except two. One after another they died."[39]

The terrifying nature of AIDS has also led to the ostracism and mistreatment of its victims, young and old. Every investigation has shown that the virus cannot be passed to another person by casual physical contact or through items touched by infected persons; yet the fear understandably runs deep, and children, "the loneliest victims," usually spend their shortened lives isolated and avoided by all but a few. Education of the public has had some results. Probably the most effective appeal for understanding came from Ryan White. At fourteen, White, a hemophiliac, contracted HIV from a transfusion of contaminated blood. Taunted and shunned by classmates in Kokomo, Indiana, he found greater tolerance when his family moved to another town. During the next few years, as he went through the usual treatments, White spoke before congressional committees and scores of audiences, making understated, but eloquent, pleas for greater funding for research, more education on the illness and its causes, and greater compassion for its victims. When he died in 1990 at eighteen, White was praised by President George Bush for "helping us understand the truth about AIDS." Mothers and fathers, however, continue to tell of children isolated and badly treated. As AIDS takes its toll, these parents hope, as one mother put it, that "more people will open their hearts to the people who have it—at least for the children."[40]

## CHILDREN AND THE LAW

Since the opening years of this century, civil authorities have struggled with the dilemmas of children and the law. Those dilemmas will remain with us, because they arise from a fundamental contradiction within our society and its values. We recognize, on the one hand, that young people deserve both the protections and the obligations of our laws. But we also believe that children are basically different from adults. They are more vulnerable; their characters and skills are still being shaped; they are not always fully responsible for their actions; they are properly subservient in many ways to the parents who bear responsibility for them. These beliefs, as discussed in earlier chapters, have been some of the bedrock assumptions of this "century of the child." So we recognize, on the other hand, that children cannot, and should not, stand before the law in all the same ways as their elders do.

Over the past nine decades, this dilemma has been acted out in various ways. The juvenile courts, for instance, were born when advocates like Benjamin B. Lindsay fought for a system in which children would be exempt from the legal demands and penalties expected of adults. A necessary result seemed to be that juvenile judges and other authorities were given great flexibility to respond to the particular circumstances of each girl or boy brought before them. But such a system, intended to allow courts to deal with children's problems compassionately and effectively, also gave officials powers much greater than in the rest of the judicial process. In the name of shielding them from the legal demands and penalties of adults, juvenile courts could also deny children the legal protections that adults enjoyed. As a result, young Americans sometimes were subjected to supervision, taken from their homes, and even incarcerated for behavior that would have been punished lightly or not at all among people past their twenty-first year.

This situation naturally raised troubling questions, but, remarkably, the U.S. Supreme Court heard no case from the juvenile court system until 1966. In *Kent* v. *U.S.,* involving a sixteen-year-old accused of robbery and rape, the Court required that hearings be held similar to those in the regular criminal system. The next year, the Court handed down a decision with far broader consequences. Gerald Gault, fifteen, had been accused of making obscene telephone calls. He was given a hearing, after which an Arizona juvenile court judge sent the young man to the state industrial school until he reached the age of twenty-one. After Gault's parents sued for his release and the state supreme court refused to grant it, the U.S. Supreme Court reviewed the case. The result, *In re Gault* (1967), imposed a new set of more stringent guidelines for due process in the juvenile court system. Gerald Gault had been given virtually none of the constitutional safeguards that adults could expect, the Court said, and he had been sentenced to several years' confinement for a crime punishable among adults by a small fine or brief imprisonment. This treatment was possible simply "because Gerald was 15 years of age instead of over 18." The Court concluded that juvenile courts must act by a much higher standard of due process.

That new standard generally has been applied in cases of children accused of criminal activities. Even before the Gault decision, some states had begun their own reforms. Following an investigation over several years, New York, in 1962, passed the Family Court Act, which insisted that children have legal representation in juvenile courts to insure that they understood the charges, the procedures, and the options open to them. Another response to these new procedural demands, however, has been simply to leave many young people entirely under the control of the system's bureaucracy. As many states have implemented new standards for children in the courts, they have also lumped many others under such headings as "persons in need of supervision," or PINS. These young people are mostly insulated from the courts and the guidelines governing them. How they are handled under the system remains largely at the discretion of case workers.

The above issues have raised questions about the treatment of "troubled children" whose behavior has been at odds with society's rules. Other questions have focused on a different concern, the need to protect innocent children and to define their rights within their own families. Like the other sets of questions, these have proved surprisingly complex and have produced no simple answers.

The issue of children's rights has been propelled powerfully forward by a growing alarm over child abuse. Mistreatment of young girls and boys is nothing new. Some historians, in fact, consider physical and emotional abuse one of the most pervasive themes in the lives of young people throughout the history of virtually all societies. Many memoirs of American childhood from the colonial period into our own time offer us ample evidence that some parents and other adults have exploited, beaten, sexually molested, and emotionally bullied young people throughout the nation's history. Concern has deepened during the past thirty or forty years partly because some evidence has suggested an increase in child abuse during that period. The most extreme measure of danger to the young, the homicide rate among children ages one to four, tripled between 1950 and 1975. Among the youngest Americans, murder is now a more common cause of death than any disease. By some estimates, as many as two million children are seriously abused annually. There have been many different opinions given for the apparent surge in such mistreatment, starting with simply the greater number of children during the baby boom and the later boomlet. Another frequently cited cause has been the emotional stress brought on by the deepening troubles of the poorest Americans and the rapid rise in single-parent families, especially those headed by women with the lowest incomes.

All authorities agree, however, that recent attention to child abuse has also arisen from a heightened awareness of an old problem. Shortly after World War II, some doctors began to pay more attention to some recurring patterns in the physical problems among children brought to them. One, for instance, was a frequent pairing of broken bones in the arms and legs with head injuries and bruising of the brain, apparently from blows. The implication, of course, was that the boys and girls were victims of beatings, not the falls and other accidents their parents claimed were the reasons behind the injuries. At a symposium in 1961, a pediatrician proposed the phrase "battered child syndrome," a term he and several colleagues defined the next year in the *Journal of the American Medical Association*.[41] Newly alerted to this combination of signs among their young patients, doctors began reporting higher and higher numbers of apparent batterings. A growing attention among specialists to abuse generated a wave of publicity that, in turn, led to a broadening public awareness and alarm. It was in this climate that government agencies reported the frightening rise in cases of mistreatment. What seemed to be an intensifying social problem, in other words, was partly a recognition of what had been there all along.

The widening concern over child abuse led to laws designed to give children greater protection. Eventually, for instance, every state passed laws requiring that doctors report apparent cases of abuse to authorities. Many states revised their legal definitions of child abuse and imposed harsher penalties. Almost everywhere, state agencies were allowed expanded authority in removing children from homes, at least temporarily, when there seemed to be significant evidence of severe mistreatment. A federal law, the Child Abuse Prevention and Treatment Act (1973), set standards for all state legislation, including a provision that states have the authority to take a child for at least three days out of a family setting that seems to be a direct threat to the child.

The alarm over child abuse and the laws that followed on the one hand have been an admirable attempt to protect the youngest, most helpless citizens against an old, terrible threat. But this development has brought with it some major complications. First, legislation about abuse began to breach the sturdy wall that, in the past, had separated the family from the powers of the state. That, in turn, raised troubling questions about fundamental rights within the family. Where do the rights of children stop and those of parents begin, and how do the interests of each family member fit with the others in the eyes of the courts? These questions, stemming from concern over protection of children, are among the most challenging in American law today.

The courts always have recognized that parents have both extensive responsibilities and rights. Mothers and fathers are expected to provide their children with food, shelter, medical care, education, and a safe and reasonably stable environment in which to grow up. The specific definitions of these duties naturally have been vague, usually expressed in phrases like "necessities of life" and "minimum standard of living." While expecting parents to live up to those responsibilities, courts have long granted them virtually full control over their sons and daughters. Fathers and mothers have been considered like "executives" with vast authority over their "business," the family; and their powers are challenged only if parents are proven "unfit" or a threat to the safety of their offsprings. In a case in 1904, *Rule* v. *Geddes,* the courts held that a teenage daughter had no right to a hearing challenging her parents' decision to send her to reform school because the law did not recognize any right she had to select her own course of life. This broad power of parents has usually been granted under the

Constitution's Ninth Amendment, which has been interpreted as upholding the "right of privacy" and the protection of the family from undue intrusion from government.

Under this wide umbrella of powers, parents have the right to control their children's environment, expect their help in family work, and make virtually all decisions affecting their lives. Any money earned by children belongs to their parents. Fathers and mothers are permitted broad latitude in punishing their children, including with spanking and other physical means. State and local authorities have traditionally been extremely reluctant to challenge these powers and others that long have been permitted by the courts.

The concern over child abuse was bound to raise questions about parental limits, however. When does corporal punishment move from reasonable discipline to dangerous mistreatment? When does neglect become abuse? Is verbal abuse, a poor diet, excessive demands for work, or a thin winter coat evidence of an "unfit" parent? The spreading awareness of the worst mistreatment, plus the more general social concern over children's well being, have combined to challenge, to some degree, parental powers.

One result has been the expansion of the field of children's rights within the legal profession. Prominent advocates, including Hillary Rodham Clinton, wife of President Bill Clinton, have called for greater judicial recognition of children's rights. A study in 1989 by the state bar association in Massachusetts had several specific recommendations, including the appointment of counsel for children in custody cases, specialists in children's rights among public defenders, and clearer guidelines for intervening in families and terminating parents' rights over their sons and daughters. A few critics would go much farther: "Child liberationists," like Richard Farson and John Holt, call for giving children most rights currently held by adults under our legal system. These would include, among others, the rights to vote, to hold property, to travel and live wherever the child wants, to make all educational decisions, and to receive fully equal treatment under the law.

As children's rights expand, however, they inevitably begin to bump into those of others who are closest to them, especially their parents. This complication has appeared most prominently when the courts, and even the children themselves, have challenged the right of men and women to continue their roles as parents. Taking a daughter or son away from her or his biological parent is, by its nature, a painful and traumatic undertaking. It likely brings great anguish to even unfit parents; failure to remove a child often perpetuates destructive neglect and abuse. It also raises troubling questions with no easy answers about the nature of the family and the rights of its members.

A dramatic illustration was the highly publicized case of "Gregory K." In 1992, this twelve-year-old Floridian sued his mother, asking the court to end her parental rights so he could be adopted by his current foster parents. His personal history certainly had been turbulent. After his parents separated, he spent much of his early years with his father, but when Gregory was nine, the child welfare system, citing neglect, placed him with his mother. She, however, left Gregory and his two brothers largely uncared for. Besides having a severe substance abuse problem, she was involved in relationships that social workers considered dangerous and destructive. The state placed Gregory in a series of foster homes; the last, headed by an attorney and his wife, had eight other children. Feeling secure and accepted here, Gregory, with the help of his foster father, sued his mother in attempt to make permanent his place in this family. In the fall of 1992, a Florida court agreed with Gregory, terminating his mother's claim to her son. Soon after, symbolic of his new life, Gregory changed his name to Shawn.

The public was fascinated by Gregory's case. Articles on it appeared in popular magazines and two made-for-television movies soon hit the airwaves. What set this case apart was not the common occurrence of a child being taken from his mother, but the fact that the child himself was taking the action of severing the connection. The popular view was that Gregory was "divorcing" his parents, assertively ending a bad relationship so he might establish one he preferred. This seemed to make the case a landmark in children's taking control over their own lives and enlisting the help of the law in doing so. Citing the woman whose refusal to move to the back of the bus was a pivotal moment in the early civil rights crusades, one journalist referred to Gregory as "the Rosa Parks of the children's rights movement."[42]

It wasn't long, however, before other questions were raised: Was Gregory truly acting on his own behalf, or was this rather a cause pushed by his foster father, whose legal specialization was children's law? Like all legal cases, this one cost the winners substantial time and money. How much of an opportunity, then, did the decision offer to children without the resources available to Gregory? How much attention would his case have gotten if he had not been so attractive and, in the words of one writer, "mediagenic?" It was noted, for instance, that his brother Jeremiah, a child suffering from Tourette's syndrome and living with foster parents of poorer circumstances, eventually was returned to his mother.

Most basic was the question of whether the rights of Gregory's mother had been adequately recognized. Rather than being judged entirely on whether she was so neglectful and unfit as to forfeit her son, some charged she was being condemned because Gregory's attorney claimed she lived an immoral life of sexual promiscuity, lesbianism, and drug abuse. Some critics felt that a short step from there could lead to removing children from parents with untraditional lifestyles. Sons and daughters might even sue to leave poorer mothers and fathers who could not support them as well as others might. "Neglect," in other words, was a relative term that might be turned against otherwise responsible parents who simply did not fit their children's or the courts' liking.

Children's rights tended to become tangled up in other ways with other familial interests. The heightened concern over abuse has coincided with a rising frequency of divorce, and as more couples have broken up, questions of child custody have become far more a part of daily life. Early in our history, children were almost always given to the father, under the prevailing presumption that the family's possessions were his, and, after all, a child was basically property. During the 19th century, that approach changed with the rise of the belief in women's naturally nurturing instincts. Children under seven typically were then awarded to mothers. By early in the 20th century, the "tender years doctrine" prevailed. Custody was granted to mothers unless strong evidence of their unfitness was presented. With divorce now common and great attention being paid to children's needs, that doctrine has given way to another: that the "best interests of the child" should decide which divorcing parent would get sons and daughters. Although mothers still are given custody in nine out of ten cases, a growing trend has been for courts to order "joint custody," an arrangement in which children usually move by an established timetable between their parents' households.

In this shifting of policy and grappling of interests among husbands, wives, and children, the young, as usual, have been especially vulnerable. They can become both the prize and the weapon in conflicts between parents and in the larger issues of women's and men's rights. Divorcing fathers charge that ex-wives seek revenge by denying them access to their children and by turning fathers solely into sources of financial support. Boys and girls, they say, have the right to the presence and attention of their fathers. Mothers, in turn, accuse ex-husbands of physical and emotional abuse of their youngsters and of using child support as a bribe for gaining greater access to their offspring. Children, these women say, have the right to be free from such pressures and mistreatment. Some critics argue that, in the pull and tug between former spouses, regardless of who is in the right or wrong, daughters and sons inevitably are the victims. Shuttling between households and even the most loving parents, children can lose the sense of security and continuity essential to their self-confidence and eventual maturity.

So it is that the rights of children inevitably conflict, on occasion, with those of mothers and fathers, men and women. The rights of the young are invoked by parents in their battles with each other, so that, paradoxically, boys and girls might be emotionally harmed in the name of their own interests. Even outside the family, at least in its legal definition, children are enmeshed in the assertion of new legal rights. Told by the U.S. Supreme Court that he could not have visitation rights with a child he fathered with a woman he never married, a California man founded an organization for others in his situation: Equality Nationwide for Unwed Fathers, or ENUF.[43]

The legal status of children, then, has become increasingly complex. The last thirty years have witnessed a greater awareness of the dangers to the young within the family and the need for their protection. Paralleling this has been an expanding definition of child rights. But with those changes— and in some ways because of them—girls and boys have become more vulnerable. In an irony fitting the contradictory story of children and the law, a new sensitivity to child rights has sometimes led to new types of exploitation unknown in an earlier, more legally repressive era.


The legal status of children continues to reflect our changing society and its difficulties. Like issues of child custody, the tragic epidemic of AIDS, discussed in this chapter's section on health, raises complicated questions about the boundaries among the rights of children, parents, and society at large. There are good reasons to test newborn infants for HIV, the virus that leads to AIDS. The sooner the virus is detected, the more quickly the child can be treated. Identifying ill infants, furthermore, allows doctors to measure and trace the course of a terrible and presently incurable scourge.

However, testing an infant can be viewed as violation of its mother's right to privacy. A newborn with HIV can have contracted it from only one source—its mother—and a doctor cannot test an infant, therefore, without also determining whether the mother has been infected. Specialists also note that many mothers who discover they and their babies are ill with this terrifying condition are emotionally crippled by depression and despair, so they fail to give their new sons and daughters the care they desperately need. Doctors, then, are caught in both a legal dilemma and a medical bind. If they try to protect an infant's best interests and its right to a quality of life, they intrude on the rights of its mother and risk undermining the very support they hope to give their young patients.

Besides dilemmas like these, new issues raised by unprecedented developments, our laws have continued to respond to new wrinkles in old problems familiar since the beginning of the century. In the area of child labor, for instance, a thirteen-year-old Wisconsin girl in 1974 applied for a job as a carrier for her local newspaper. She was told that the paper hired only news*boys,* not girls. Their reason was a state law, dating back to the progressive era, that forbade employment of females under eighteen in "street trades." As discussed in the first chapter, those laws were responses to fears that children working on the streets—peddling newspapers, running errands, selling candy—would be exposed to all sorts of vices and dangers, an alarm that was greater for young females than for males. But, in the 1970s, a law that excluded girls from such work raised issues of sexual bias. The young girl sued the paper on the grounds that its policy violated the section of the Civil Rights Act of 1964 forbidding employers to discriminate in their hiring on the basis of sex. The Wisconsin Supreme Court, however, turned down her plea and upheld the law. The law was within the state's power to protect the health and safety of the child, the judges ruled, especially given the increase in crime and the fact that girl carriers would be more likely to be assaulted than boys. The case raised one more irony in the history of children's law. To some, legislation passed with the honest intent of protecting young girls had come to be used instead to limit their opportunities.

Other changes in American life, on the other hand, have led to calls for greater regulation of working children, not less. In certain professional sports, such as tennis, increasingly younger players have entered the field. While they certainly have the talent, some critics wonder whether the pressures and demands of professional sports are appropriate for superb athletes who are barely out of childhood. It is one more case of exploitation and young people being pushed prematurely into adult work, they argue, this time, not ten-year-old boys and girls earning pitifully low wages in coal mines and textile factories, but gifted teenagers making millions while being emotionally battered. These questions were brought dramatically to the public's attention by the case of tennis star Jennifer Capriati. In 1990, at the age of thirteen—the same age the Wisconsin girl mentioned above was denied a paper route—Capriati entered the professional tennis tour. A year later, she became the youngest player ever to rank among the world's ten best female competitors, and she was earning more than six million dollars a year in product endorsements alone. Soon, however, her play began to decline and she became increasingly distant and depressed. Early in 1994, Capriati left the professional tour, and a few months later she and a few acquaintances were arrested at a Florida motel with several varieties of drugs, including marijuana, crack cocaine, and heroin. The problem, in the view of one of her former teachers, was how we use our younger athletes. Another authority recommended that players be banned from professional play until the age of eighteen (the age girls are allowed to deliver news-papers in Wisconsin). The present system is abusive, according to this com-mentator, and "there ought to be child-labor laws to prevent it."[44]

These questions, and many more, all are centered around the relationship between government and the child. What is the state's responsibility in protecting children? What minimum standards of care and support should young Americans expect, and how far should government go in insuring those standards? What form should that protection and support take? De-bates about programs developed in response to such questions still are among the most heated in public life.

Take, for instance, the issue of federally funded day care. The extensive programs under the Lanham Act during World War II, described in the previous chapter, were justified not so much on the needs of children and mothers but on the need for women's labor in the struggle against Germany and Japan. Once the war was over, mothers were expected to settle back into their homes and take care of children there. However, throughout the postwar years, millions of mothers stayed in or moved into the work force, even as young couples were producing millions of babies. One result was a continuing boom in private child care businesses. In the past, these had been called "nurseries," but especially from the 1960s, with a greater em-phasis on educational training of the toddlers in their charge, these insti-tutions have come to be called "preschools." By 1970, there were 1,150,000 three- and four-year-olds in preschools, a hefty increase of a quarter of a million during only the previous five years.

Preschool day care, however, is usually within the reach of only middle-class parents holding down reasonably well-paying jobs. A large and grow-ing part of the female work force was caught in a bind. These women, many of them single mothers, worked from necessity, not choice, and yet their low incomes could not cover the care needed for their preschoolers. In 1962, the Social Security Act was amended to provide federal funds for a wider range of programs for children, including subsidies for low-income families needing day care. That support has continued. In 1990, for instance, Congress authorized 2.5 billion dollars over three years to help pay for day care as well as before-school and after-school programs for boys and girls of working parents.

One of the best known federal programs to come out of the 1960s was related to this effort: Head Start, aimed at lower-income families, provided a one-year program designed to give three- to five-year-olds a firmer educational foundation for public education. Besides early instruction, it offered health examinations, advice for parents in seeking out other social services, and even limited help for adults looking for work. By 1993, more than 13 million children attended roughly 1,300 programs. Head Start has had its critics, although it is also among the most praised social efforts to emerge from a controversial decade of federal efforts toward alleviating educational and social problems. Most studies have shown that young graduates of Head Start show significant academic improvement, although some argue that these gains fade after a few years unless further help is given.

Much more extensive, and controversial, has been another government program—direct financial aid for children in poverty. As mentioned earlier, this support began with the Social Security Act of 1935, which established Aid to Dependent Children (ADC), later renamed Aid to Families with Dependent Children (AFDC). Originally payments were made to families headed by single mothers; without a male breadwinner, the reasoning went, these families could not take advantage of New Deal work relief programs such as the Works Progress Administration (WPA). Partly, the goal was to help keep children with at least one parent rather than putting impoverished girls and boys in foster homes. Later the law was amended to allow payments to families with a permanently disabled parent; and in states that agreed to such a policy, funds were also given to families with an unemployed parent. Federal money was channeled through the states. States were required to set up agencies to disburse the aid and to meet certain federal guidelines, but they were also allowed wide latitude in the standards they used to evaluate applicants and the amounts of funds they handed out.

The ADC program got off to a slow start. Only in the mid-1940s did all states accept the plan and set up the necessary machinery for it. In its first full year of operation, 1936, fewer than half a million families received support, and the number grew slowly over the next decade. After World War II, however, the figures began to soar. The growth followed the prodigious increase in American babies, for one thing, but it also mirrored other social and economic changes discussed in these chapters. The war and its aftermath drew millions of Americans from the countryside to the cities, and, over time, many families, especially African Americans in the inner cities, found themselves in difficult financial straits. By 1960, about six out of ten families receiving aid were in large cities, most of them in the inner cores. Ten years later, the percentage was even higher. By then African Americans, who constituted about 10 percent of the general population, made up more than 40 percent of AFDC families. The deepening urban poverty brought more and more persons onto the rolls of AFDC. More than 11 million persons were receiving funds in 1988, 7.3 million of them children.

Critics soon were questioning this rapidly expanding program. Near the end of the 1960s, President Richard Nixon called AFDC a "monster." Aside from complaints about zooming costs, some argued that the payments, originally designed to buttress families under stress and to encourage traditional values, in fact were undermining the family and encouraging immoral behavior. Because most aid went to households headed by female single parents, fathers had an incentive to walk away from wives and children. Payments increased with the number of children, so some charged that women were bearing more illegitimate babies to generate greater income. Defenders of the system answered that the men were leaving anyway, and that the minimal payments (which averaged about $180 a month in 1971) made any new babies a losing proposition.

Nevertheless, complaints were loud and angry. During the 1950s several states, mostly in the South, imposed "suitable home" restrictions. Under these new rules, money would go only to children with mothers whose behavior met certain standards. The Louisiana law held that if a mother was cohabiting with a man other than her husband, if she had borne a child out of wedlock since receiving payments, or if she engaged in "promiscuous conduct," all aid would stop. The results in Louisiana were dramatic. In one month, July 1960, the state ended payments to nearly six thousand families, and during that summer the number of children supported dropped from 102,962 to 72,250. The ax fell mostly on African Americans. While black children made up about 66 percent of children receiving help before the cuts, 95 percent of those taken from the rolls were black. In the wake of Louisiana's action, Congress passed new legislation eliminating such state guidelines. Both the costs and the extent of the programs have increased considerably. In 1995, about one child out of seven was receiving support through AFDC.

Criticism has continued and grown. In the more conservative political climate of the mid-1990s, there were renewed demands, this time not in state legislatures but in Congress, to end AFDC support to unwed mothers and to those who have not held jobs during the previous two or three years. Familiar complaints were voiced that the expense was too great and that the system encouraged promiscuity and undermined the family. Defenders pointed out that the majority of recipients got support only for a year or so, then went on to find employment. The typical AFDC household was not crawling with welfare-inspired toddlers; nearly three-fourths of the families had only one or two children.

Critics proposed new solutions that, in fact, were revivals of old ones. There was even renewed talk of public orphanages to provide more effective care for indigent boys and girls—the very system that was in place at the opening of the century. As they had for the past hundred years and more, people were debating and rethinking their government's responsibilities to young Americans. With the year 2000 just ahead, there was no sign that this debate would end.

# BIBLIOGRAPHICAL ESSAY

## General Works

The 1960s and the years since have been among the most turbulent and controversial in American history, and partly for that reason those decades have attracted plenty of attention from historians. There are several good and readable histories of the 1960s, including: David Farber, *The Age of Great Dreams: America in the 1960s* (New York: Hill and Wang, 1994); William L. O'Neill, *Coming Apart: An Informal History of America in the 1960s* (New York: Times Books, 1971); and Todd Gitlin, *The Sixties: Years of Hope, Days of Rage* (New York: Bantam Books, 1987). A history that concentrates on the "counterculture" of those years is Morris Dickstein's *Gates of Eden: American Culture in the Sixties* (New York: Basic Books, 1977). Another good source is Kim McQuaid's *The Anxious Years: America in the Vietnam-Watergate Era* (New York: Basic Books, 1989). For the decade that followed, often considered much less colorful than the tumultuous 1960s, Peter Carroll's *It Seemed Like Nothing Happened: The Tragedy and the Promise of America in the 1970s* (New York: Holt, Rinehard, and Winston, 1983) is richly anecdotal and filled with material on the daily lives of Americans.

The period from the late 1950s through the 1970s was controversial partly because of the many social and economic reforms attempted. On the civil rights movement, students looking among the many histories would do well to consider Taylor Branch's *Parting the Waters: America in the King Years, 1954–1963* (New York: Simon and Schuster, 1988) as well as Robert Weisbrot's *Freedom Bound: A History of America's Civil Rights Movement* (New York: Norton, 1990). On the Vietnam War, a good one-volume history is George C. Herring's *America's Longest War: The United States and Vietnam, 1950–1975* (New York: Wiley, 1986).

Among the most significant changes of the years from 1960 onward was the "women's liberation" movement and the growing influence of women in American politics and society. The best overview of these issues remains William H. Chafe's *The American Woman: Her Changing Social, Economic, and Political Roles, 1920– 1970* (New York: Oxford University Press); and *Women's America: Refocusing the Past,* edited by Linda Kerber (New York: Oxford University Press, 1982) offers a collection of insightful articles on the subject. On the immediate background to the years of this chapter, see Eugenia Kaledin's *Mothers and More: American Women in the 1950s* (Boston: Twayne Publishers, 1984); and for a useful resource, consult Judith C. Freeman's *Almanac of American Women in the 20th Century* (New York: Prentice Hall, 1987). The period of the previous chapter and this one are the setting for Rochelle Gatlin's *American Women since 1945* (Jackson: University of Missis- sippi Press, 1987).

Drugs and narcotics, another phenomenon associated with these years, have a long history in our society, although their use certainly has increased since 1960. For research on that history, see John Rublowsky's *The Stoned Age: A History of Drugs in America* (New York: G. P. Putnam's Sons, 1974) and *Drugs and American Society,* edited by Robert E. Long (New York: Wilson, 1986).

A basic resource for the previous chapters applies here as well, but only to a point. *Children and Youth in America: A Documentary History,* edited by Robert H. Bremner (Cambridge: Harvard University Press, 1974) in Volume III takes its excellent collection of materials on many aspects of children's history up to 1973. Another crucial work, Joseph M. Hawes and N. Ray Hiner's *American Childhood: A Research Guide and Historical Handbook* (Westport, Conn.: Greenwood Press, 1985), extends its coverage to the 1980s with an essay covering the years 1962 to 1983. In addition, there are three easily used sources that offer a valuable statistical survey of life in recent America: Bruce A. Chadwick and Tim B. Heaton, eds., *Statistical Handbook on the American Family* (Phoenix: Oryx Press, 1992), Dennis A. Gilbert, ed., *Compendium of American Public Opinion* (New York: Facts on File, 1988), and Kathleen D. Droste, *Gale Book of Averages* (Detroit: Gale Research Inc., 1994).

## At Home

Some of the books mentioned in earlier bibliographical essays apply here, too. Stephanie Coontz's *The Way We Never Were: American Families and the Nostalgia Trap* (New York: Basic Books, 1992) takes a hard and critical look at many recent criticisms and cries of alarm about changes in American families. What many see as new problems, she argues, in fact have been part of our society for generations, while other changes are much misunderstood or exaggerated. Of the surveys of the recent history of the family, two are particularly good: Steven Mintz and Susan Kellogg's *Domestic Revolutions: A Social History of American Life* (New York: Free Press, 1988) takes the topic into the 1980s, as does Elaine Tyler May's *Homeward Bound: American Families in the Cold War Era* (New York: Basic Books, 1988). Other useful sources include: Carl Degler, *At Odds: Women and the Family in America from the Revolution to the Present* (New York: Oxford University Press, 1980); Mary Jo Bane, *Here to Stay: American Families in the Twentieth Century* (New York: Basic Books, 1976); and Christopher Lasch, *Haven in a Heartless World: The Family Beseiged* (New York: Basic Books, 1977). Students also will find useful information on our social history during these years, including much pertaining to the family, in Landon Y. Jones's *Great Expectations: America and the Baby Boom Generation* (New York: Ballantine Books, 1980) and William Manchester's *The Glory and the Dream: A Narrative History of America, 1932–1972* (Boston: Little, Brown, 1974, and later editions).

Among those concerned about changes in families and family life, one of the most common fears is of children being forced to take on too much responsibility too soon, and, beyond that, a worry that childhood itself, as a distinctive and protected time of life, is threatened. One of the most influential statements of some of these concerns is Neil Postman's *The Disappearance of Childhood* (New York: Vintage Books, 1994). See also David Elkind's *The Hurried Child: Growing Up Too Fast Too Soon* (Reading, Mass.: Addison-Wesley, 1981) and Kenneth Keniston's *All Our Children: The American Family under Pressure* (New York: Harcourt Brace Jovanovich, 1977). Another worry has been the rapid rise in the number of families headed by a single parent, usually the mother. On this subject, see Robert Weiss's *Going It Alone: The Family Life and Social Situation of the Single Parent* (New York: Basic Books, 1979). Readers with access to files of the *New York Times* will find a helpful series of articles concerning single motherhood, under the running title "The Good Mother," published by that newspaper during October 1992.

On housing styles, especially in suburbia, consult a book mentioned earlier, Clifford Edward Clark, Jr.'s *The American Family Home, 1800–1960* (Chapel Hill: University of North Carolina Press, 1986), which has an excellent chapter on ranch-style homes; and for a much more critical commentary, see James Howard Kunstler's *The Geography of Nowhere: The Rise and Decline of America's Man-Made Landscape* (New York: Touchstone Books, 1993). For an illuminating and often amusing discussion of "drive-in" culture, consider Kunstler's book, just noted, and Kenneth T. Jackson's *Crabgrass Frontier: The Suburbanization of the United States* (New York: Oxford University Press, 1985). Directly connected to that subject are our eating customs, which increasingly have been observed in automobiles. On that, see Harvey Levenstein, *Paradox of Plenty: A Social History of Eating in Modern America* (New York: Oxford University Press, 1993); and on the most famous fast-food chain, see Maxwell Boas and Steve Chain's *Big Mac: The Unauthorized Story of McDonald's* (New York: New American Library, 1977) and John F. Love's *McDonald's: Behind the Arches* (New York: Bantam Books, 1986).

A landmark in the "discovery" of poverty in modern America is Michael Harrington's *The Other America: Poverty in the United States* (New York: Macmillan, 1962, and later editions), which contains material on poverty's effects on families. Specifically on the impoverished young is Alvin L. Schorr's *Poor Kids: A Report on Children in Poverty* (New York: Basic Books, 1966). The meaning of poverty for children, in their daily lives and, even more, in their emotional and psychological development, is the focus of a brilliant and moving series of studies by one of this country's leading authorities on child development, Robert Coles. Coles visited and lived with economically impoverished families in several settings—black families in the rural South, whites in Appalachia, Native Americans, Hispanic-Americans and others—and from that wrote five volumes under the general title *Children of Crisis* (Boston: Little, Brown and Company, 1967). They are essential reading for anyone interested in American childhood during the most recent thirty years. Coles also has given us three more general works on children's inner life: *The Moral Life of Children* (Boston: Atlantic Monthly Press, 1986), *The Political Life of Children* (Boston: Atlantic Monthly Press, 1986), and *The Spiritual Life of Children* (Boston: Houghton Mifflin, 1990).

## At Play

The two books mentioned in each of the other bibliographical essays on toys once more apply here; they are about the only sources of their kind, but they cover their ground well, in this case providing much detail and interesting background on various amusements and fads, from frisbees to Barbie dolls: Richard O'Brien's *The Story of American Toys: From Puritans to the Present* (New York: Abbeville Press, 1990) and Gil Asakawa and Leland Rucker's *The Toy Book* (New York: Alfred A. Knopf, 1992). Also helpful is Marvin Kaye, *The Story of Monopoly, Silly Putty, Bingo, Twister, Frisbee, Scrabble, etc.* (New York: Stein and Day, 1977). There has been surprisingly little written on what is arguably the most popular category of toy in the entire history of childhood—dolls. For a well-illustrated book on different types of dolls, there is Carl Fox's *The Doll* (New York: H. N. Abrams, 1973). And for both a history of the most successful doll in history and a revealing biography of the woman behind that phenomenon, see M. G. Lord's *Forever Barbie: The Unauthorized Biography of a Real Doll* (New York: Morrow and Company, 1994).

Amusement parks, on the other hand, have been the subject of some excellent histories. An invaluable source is Judith A. Adams's *The American Amusement Park Industry: A History of Technology and Thrills* (Boston: Twayne Publishers, 1991). This book considers amusement parks as business enterprises and includes plenty of good history of the industry at large and that of particular parks, up to

Disney World. The Disney empire, predictably, has proved especially popular among writers. John Finlay has an excellent chapter on the origins and significance of Disneyland, "The Happiest Place on Earth," in his *Magic Lands: Western Cityscapes and American Culture after 1940* (Berkeley: University of California Press, 1992. And Walt Disney World has had its own historian, who considers this greatest amusement park in history a reflection of much in American life: Stephen M. Fjellman, author of *Vinyl Leaves: Walt Disney World and America* (Boulder: Westview Press, 1992).

## At Work

A very useful starting place for research on young people in the workplace during the past thirty years is Ellen Greenberger and Laurence Steinberg's *When Teenagers Work: The Psychological and Social Costs of Adolescent Employment* (New York: Basic Books, 1986). This work surveys the major shifts in employment patterns among young people, especially the decline of the "old" marketplace and the rise of the "new," and raises some troubling questions about recent trends in the youthful work force. A larger and wider-ranging book, *Work, Youth and Unemployment*, by Melvin Herman and others (New York: Thomas Y. Crowell Company, 1968), brings together a selection of writings from many sources, grouping them into sections on the youthful labor market, education, family, juvenile delinquency, and proposed solutions to difficult problems.

As mentioned near the beginning of this bibliographical essay, Volume III of Robert H. Bremner's *Children and Youth in America* continues its documentary coverage through 1973; it offers an excellent selection of materials on the conditions and issues involved in working children and teenagers. Included are documents on changes in child labor laws and accounts of the working lives of those who work to help support their families. Rural and migrant children make up an especially large part of the latter group. Another important source, Ronald B. Taylor's *Sweatshops in the Sun: Child Labor on the Farm* (Boston: Beacon Press, 1973) also provides documents on the conditions of rural and migrant children. On migrant workers more generally, see Carey McWilliams's *Factories in the Field: The Story of Migratory Farm Labor in California* (Santa Barbara: Peregrine Publishers, Inc., 1971) and his *North from Mexico: The Spanish-Speaking People of the United States* (New York: Praeger, 1990), as well as William H. Friedland and Dorothy Nelkin's *Migrant: Agricultural Workers in America's Northeast* (New York: Holt, Rinehard and Winston, 1971).

There is limited published research on the work children do at home and its importance to their families. The best single source is *The Serious Business of Growing Up: A Study of Children's Lives Outside School,* by Elliot A. Medrich and others (Berkeley: University of California Press, 1982). This book considers not only how boys and girls work in and out of their households, but also how they spend their leisure time and even how they spend their money.

## At School

As has been true of reference materials for previous chapters, the best source on the history of education is Lawrence Cremin's *American Education: The Metropolitan Experience, 1876–1980* (New York: Harper and Row, 1988), which offers a wealth of information and intelligent analysis. A good popular survey of trends in schooling also can be found in Landon Jones's *Great Expectations,* cited above; and basic statistics on school enrollments and spending are easily available in *Historical Statistics of the United States: Colonial Times to 1970* (Washington, D.C.: Bureau of the Census, 1975), which has been mentioned several times in previous bibliographical essays. As had been true throughout the century, education inspired some of the most vigorous societal debates in recent times. A survey of some of these arguments, with strong opinions of its own, can be found in Diane Ravitch's *The Troubled Crusade: American Education, 1945–1980* (New York: Basic Books, 1983). Another useful discussion of educational issues can be found in Lawrence A. Cremin's *Popular Education and Its Discontents* (New York: Harper and Row, 1990). The most controversial issue in education has concerned race and attempts to desegregate American schools. Several good sources continue this story after the *Brown* decision of 1954 (see chapter 3), including: Reed Saratt, *The Ordeal of Segregation: The First Decade* (New York: Harper and Row, 1966); Benjamin Muse, *Ten Years of Prelude: The Story of Integration since the Supreme Court's 1954 Decision* (New York: Viking Press, 1964); and J. Harvie Wilkinson, III, *From Brown to Bakke: The Supreme Court and School Integration: 1954–1978* (New York: Oxford University Press, 1979). One of the most controversial books of recent years has revived the old arguments over whether some racial and ethnic groups are, in general, more intelligent than others, and if so, how educational policy should respond. Applauded by some, it has been criticized by others as repeating old errors in attempts to quantify intelligence: Richard J. Herrnstein and Charles Murray's *The Bell Curve: Intelligence and Class Structure in American Life* (New York: Free Press, 1994).

Another area of heated argument has been television and its effect (or lack of effect) on children, their learning, and their social skills. A good summary of the extensive research conducted thus far can be found in *Big World, Small Screen: The Role of Television in American Society,* by Althea C. Huston and others (Lincoln: University of Nebraska Press, 1992). Although its articles can be somewhat technical, this book is a very useful resource in untangling the complicated and confusing arguments surrounding this unavoidable part of children's lives. On the most popular and successful of children's educational television programs, see Gerald S. Lessar's *Children and Television: Lessons from Sesame Street* (New York: Random House, 1974) and Richard M. Polsky's *Getting to Sesame Street: Origins of the Children's Television Workshop* (New York: Praeger, 1974).

## Health

Public health, including that of children, remains one of the great unstudied areas of American history in the latter part of our century, as it is in earlier years. Students can pull out some basic figures from *Historical Statistics,* cited above, as well as the *Statistical Abstracts* published annually by the federal government. Among the best available sources, especially for documents, once again is Robert Bremner's *Children and Youth in America,* although it covers this period only up to 1973 and is strongest on government programs designed to deal with continuing problems in children's health. Remarkably little, too, has been published (at least in easily accessible form) on violence by and among the young. If available, a special report of a hearing before the House of Representatives's Select Committee on Children, Youth and Families (1989) will be very helpful: *Down These Mean Streets: Violence by and against America's Children,* which can be ordered from the Superintendent of Documents of the U.S. Congress. Other material can be found in periodical and newspaper articles (through their indexes). The *New York Times,* for instance, published a series of articles on "When Trouble Starts Young" in December 1994.

The national epidemic of Acquired Immunodeficiency Syndrome (AIDS) has produced a larger list of publications, some of them easily accessible to libraries. The standard work on the origins and early years of the disease in the United States is Randy Shilts, *And the Band Played On: Politics, People, and the AIDS Epidemic* (New York: St. Martin's Press, 1987). Another useful source is *The AIDS Epidemic,* edited by Kevin M. Cahill (New York: St. Martin's Press, 1983). Several books also are available on AIDS among women (and mothers), children, and adolescents: see Gena Corea, *The Invisible Epidemic: The Story of Women and AIDS* (New York: HarperCollins, 1992); David L. Kirp and Steven Epstein, *Learning by Heart: AIDS and Schoolchildren in America's Communities* (New Brunswick: Rutgers University Press, 1989); and Jeffrey M. Seibert and Roberta A. Olson, eds., *Children, Adolescents and AIDS* (Lincoln: University of Nebraska Press, 1989). There are also poignant personal stories by children and adolescents who contracted the disease, including *It Happened to Nancy,* edited by Beatrice Sparks, (New York: Avon Books, 1994) and *We Have AIDS,* edited by Elaine Landau (New York: F. Watts, 1990). Finally, Michael Thomas Ford has published *100 Questions and Answers about AIDS: A Guide for Young People* (New York: New Discovery Books, 1992), a very useful and informative book on the disease, its nature, prevention, and treatment, directed especially to students.

## Children and the Law

A brief but intelligent and well-informed summary of legal developments affecting children during the previous few decades once again can be found in Joseph M. Hawes's *The Children's Rights Movement: A History of Advocacy and Protection* (Boston: Twayne Publishers, 1991), which covers such issues as responses to child abuse, the new children's advocates, and changes in the juvenile courts. Several more detailed works on particular topics also are available. Child abuse, for instance, has been the subject of a wide range of writings. For a historical survey both of child abuse and the history of responses to it, for instance, students should consult Elizabeth H. Pleck's *Domestic Tyranny: The Making of Social Policy against Family Violence from Colonial Times to the Present* (New York: Oxford University Press, 1987) as well as David C. Gil's *Violence against Children: Physical Child Abuse in the United States* (Cambridge: Harvard University Press, 1970). The following books provide a sense of the range of other works: Ray E. Helfer, *The Battered Child* (Chicago: University of Chicago Press, 1987); Naomi F. Chase, *A Child Is Being Beaten: Violence against Children, An American Tragedy* (New York: McGraw-Hill, 1976); Murray A. Straus, *Beating the Devil Out of Them: Corporal Punishment in American Families* (New York: Maxwell Macmillan International, 1994); and Robert L. Geiser, *Hidden Victims: The Sexual Abuse of Children* (Boston: Beacon Press, 1979). Finally, there is a useful guide, written especially for teenagers, on child abuse, its causes and effects: Susan Mufson and Rachel Kranz's *Straight Talk about Child Abuse* (New York: Facts on File, 1991). For young people involved in abusive situations, it includes telephone hotlines and other means of getting help.

Ellen Ryerson's *The Best Laid Plans: America's Juvenile Court Experiment* (New York: Hill and Wang, 1978) has some material on recent developments in the courts, as does Peter S. Prescott's *The Child Savers: Juvenile Justice Observed* (New York: Simon and Schuster, 1982), specifically for the case of New York.

The debate surrounding foster care and adoption has been especially heated during the 1980s and 1990s. Two books in particular emphasize the need to cultivate emotional closeness, something very difficult within foster homes: Selma Fraiberg's *Every Child's Birthright: In Defense of Mothering* (New York: Basic Books, 1977) and Joseph Goldstein, Anna Freud, and Albert Solnit's *Beyond the Best Interests of the Child* (New York: Free Press, 1973).

On the broader issue of children's rights generally, interested readers can find a good introduction in Thomas A. Nazario's *In Defense of Children: Understanding the Rights, Needs and Interests of the Child* (New York: Charles Scribner's Sons, 1988). The issues raised here have inspired some who argue for a greatly expanded realm of legal protections and especially prerogatives for young people—the movement for "children's liberation." Two of the most outspoken advocates have stated their cases in books: John Holt in *Escape from Childhood* (New York: Ballantine Books, 1974) and Richard Farson in *Birthrights* (New York: Macmillan, 1974). For overviews on the liberation movement, students should consult *Children's Liberation*, edited by David Gottlieb (Englewood Cliffs, N.J.: Prentice-Hall, 1973) and *The Children's Rights Movement: Overcoming the Oppression of Young People*, edited by Beatrice and Ronald Gross (Garden City: Anchor Books, 1977).

## Personal Recollections

In addition to firsthand memoirs of growing up, there have been some books written by others on the lives of American children and the experiences of families. Two fine examples, telling the lives of families in two very different settings, have come from the period of this chapter: Donald Katz's *Home Fires: An Intimate Portrait of One Middle-Class Family in Postwar America* (New York: Harper-Collins, 1992) traces the lives of the various members of a suburban New York family from the early years of the baby boom to 1990. The children follow the course of many of their background, through the counterculture of the 1960s and into varied adults lives of their own. Set in the more recent past, Alex Kotlowitz's *There Are No Children Here: The Story of Two Boys Growing Up in the Other America* (New York: Doubleday, 1991) follows the lives of two brothers in the late 1980s living in a housing project on Chicago's West Side, one of the poorest and most violent areas of urban America. In many ways a horrifying account of life under the threat of gangs, drug wars, and domestic violence, it is also a moving tribute to these young boys and their mothers as they try to fashion a decent existence for themselves.

Among the memoirs of these years, one of the most interesting and moving is that of Tobias Wolff, *This Boy's Life* (New York: Perennial Library, 1990), his story of growing up with an abusive father, traveling cross-country with his mother, and living in a variety of unsettling situations before making his way through adolescence and then into war in Vietnam. The title is taken from Wolff's fantasies of an idealized youth inspired by his reading issues of *Boy's Life,* the publication of the Boy Scouts of America. Wolff went on to become a successful writer of fiction. An account of a woman who passed from a Bronx childhood into many aspects of the 1960s experimentation, from communes to drugs to varieties of eastern religions, is Meredith Maran's *What It's Like to Live Now* (New York: Bantam Books, 1995). From a very different background has come a moving tribute to modern rural life and the increasingly common death of the family farm: Ronald Jagar's *Eighty Acres: Elegy for a Family Farm* (Boston: Beacon Press, 1990). And for histories of families and evocation of life in two parts of the modern American West, see Terry Tempest Williams's *Refuge: An Unnatural History of Family and Place* (New York: Pantheon Books, 1991) and Mary Clearman Blew's *All but the Waltz: Essays on a Montana Family* (New York: Viking, 1991).

Among the most significant trends in immigration during the previous generation has been a surge from Asia, including groups, such as Vietnamese and Koreans, who had never before come to the United States in significant numbers. From the Asian community has come a body of reminiscent literature that has enriched the testimony from young America. For a selection, see Maxine Hong Kingston, *The Woman Warrior: Memoirs of a Girlhood among Ghosts* (New York: Knopf, 1977), Lydia Y. Minatoya, *Talking to High Monks in the Snow: An Asian American Odyssey* (New York: HarperCollins, 1992), and Le Ly Hayslip, *When Heaven and*

*Earth Changed Places: A Vietnamese Woman's Journey from War to Peace* (New York: Doubleday, 1989). The even larger immigration from Mexico, Latin America, and the Caribbean also has produced a considerable autobiographical literature. One of the most eloquent such memoirs is Richard Rodriguez's *Hunger of Memory: The Education of Richard Rodriguez* (New York: Bantam Books, 1982). It is controversial because of Rodriguez's opinion on bilingual education, but its greatest value is as an extraordinarily perceptive account of the emotional and perceptual complexities of growing up the child of Mexican immigrants in a middle-class white neighborhood in California. Another account from a Spanish-speaking group that has come to be one of the largest ethnic communities in cities of the Northeast is Esmeralda Santiago's *When I Was Puerto Rican* (Reading, Mass.: Addison-Wesley, 1993).

Finally, modern descendants of the original immigrants to what is today the United States—the Native Americans—have given today's student a wide range of memoirs about what it is like growing up American. Good examples include Mary Brave Bird's *Lakota Woman* (New York: HarperPerennial, 1991) and Janet Campbell Hale's *Bloodlines: Odyssey of a Native Daughter* (New York: Random House, 1993).

## NOTES

1. U.S. Bureau of the Census, *Statistical Abstract of the United States: 1994*, Washington, D.C., 1994, 10.

2. Landon Y. Jones, *Great Expectations: America and the Baby Boom Generation* (New York: Ballantine Books, 1980), 356.

3. Neil Postman, *The Disappearance of Childhood* (New York: Delacorte Press, 1982).

4. *Statistical Abstract of the United States: 1994*, 742.

5. Kathleen Droste, ed., *Gale Book of Averages* (Detroit: Gale Research Inc., 1994), 451.

6. Harvey Levenstein, *Paradox of Plenty: A Social History of Eating in Modern America* (New York: Oxford University Press, 1993), 229.

7. Ibid., 249.

8. *New York Times*, April 17, 1995.

9. *The World Almanac and Book of Facts* (New York: World Almanac, 1995), 383.

10. The government's definition of "poverty level" depends on the number of persons supported by a given income. It changes year-by-year to adjust to inflation. For 1992, for instance, a family of four was considered to be living below the poverty line if its total annual income fell below $14,335.

11. *New York Times*, September 17, 1992; December 1, 1994.

12. Judith A. Adams, *The Amusement Park Industry: A History of Technology and Thrills* (Boston: Twayne Publishers, 1991), 133.

13. Ellen Greenberger and Laurence Steinberg, *When Teenagers Work: The Psychological and Social Costs of Adolescent Employment* (New York: Basic Books, 1986), 61.

14. Robert H. Bremner, ed., *Children and Youth in America: A Documentary History,* Vol. III (Cambridge: Harvard University Press, 1974), 371–77.

15. Ibid., 377–79.

16. Ibid., 367–69.

17. Carey McWilliams, *North from Mexico: The Spanish-speaking People of the United States* (New York: Praeger, 1990), 239–40.

18. Bremner, *Children and Youth in America,* Vol. III, 409.

19. Ronald B. Taylor, *Sweatshops in the Sun: Child Labor on the Farm* (Boston: Beacon Press, 1973), 4–5; Bremner, *Children and Youth in America,* Vol. III, 399.

20. Taylor, *Sweatshops in the Sun,* 22–23; Bremner, *Children and Youth in America,* Vol. III, 395.

21. Arlene M. Hibschweiler, "The Toxic Workplace of the Child Farmworker," *Buffalo Law Review* 32 (1983): 343–372.

22. Taylor, *Sweatshops in the Sun,* 69.

23. *Historical Statistics of the United States: Colonial Times to 1970* (Washington, D.C.: Bureau of the Census, 1975), I, 368; *Statistical Abstract of the United States: 1994,* 151.

24. *Statistical Abstract of the United States: 1994,* 155.

25. Ibid., 151.

26. Jones, *Great Expectations,* 150–51.

27. Carl L. Erhardt and Joyce E. Berlin, *Mortality and Morbidity in the United States* (Cambridge: Harvard University Press, 1974), 194.

28. *New York Times,* March 5, 6, 1995.

29. Bremner, *Children and Youth in America,* Vol. III, 1335–40.

30. *Statistical Abstract of the United States: 1994,* 95.

31. *New York Times,* March 2, 1994.

32. Ibid., December 1, 1994.

33. *Statistical Abstract of the United States: 1994,* 101.

34. *New York Times,* December 12, 1994.

35. Alex Kotlowitz, *There Are No Children Here* (New York: Doubleday, 1991), x.

36. Statistics provided by Center for Study of Poverty, University of California, Berkeley.

37. Bremner, *Children and Youth in America,* Vol. III, 1294.

38. Estimate of 4.4 million persons with braces, 75% under twenty, with average cost of $2,000: from Carol Dilks, "The Return of the 'Metal Mouths,' " *Nation's Business,* March 1990: 76. Estimate of expenditures for physicians and dentists for 1950 ($3,530,000) from *Historical Statistics of the United States,* I, 318.

39. *New York Times,* November 21, 1994.

40. Cheryl Platzman Weinstock, "Children with AIDS," *FDA Consumer,* Oc-

tober 1990, 11. See also articles in *McCall's,* July 1989; *New York Times,* November 21, 1994, February 14, 1995, August 17, 1994; *U.S. News and World Report,* December 20, 1993.

41. Joseph M. Hawes, *The Children's Rights Movement: A History of Advocacy and Protection* (Boston: Twayne Publishers, 1991), 99–100.

42. Andrew L. Shapiro, "Children and the Court—The New Crusade," *The Nation,* September 27, 1993, p. 1.

43. Scott Coltrane and Neal Hickman, "The Rhetoric of Rights and Needs: Moral Discourse in the Reform of Child Custody and Child Support Laws," *Social Problems* 39:4 (November 1992): 405.

44. Mary Carillo quoted in "Losing Her Grip," *People Magazine,* May 30, 1994, 83.

# General Bibliography

No one has yet tried to tackle the intimidating job of writing a single, full account of children and childhood in American history. Neither has anyone taken on the smaller, but still huge, subject of the history of childhood in the 20th century. Much has been written on children and children's experiences, however. A good starting place for tracking down these many works is *American Childhood: A Research Guide and Historical Handbook,* edited by Joseph M. Hawes and N. Ray Hiner (Westport, Conn: Greenwood Press, 1985). This is a collection of essays on the history of American childhood from the 17th century into the 1980s. Its fourteen chapters are arranged both chronologically and topically, with essays on ethnicity and children's literature, for instance, as well as ones on childhood in the 18th century and the progressive period. Each chapter provides an interpretive look at its subject and a discussion of some of the most important literature; each concludes with an excellent bibliography.

Three very useful, broadly imagined books that bring together different perspectives on American childhood are: N. Ray Hiner and Joseph M. Hawes, eds., *Growing Up in America: Children in Historical Perspective* (Urbana: University of Illinois Press, 1985); Elliott West and Paula Petrik, eds., *Small Worlds: Children and Adolescents in America, 1850–1950* (Lawrence: University Press of Kansas, 1992); and Harvey J. Graff, ed.,

*Growing Up in America: Historical Experiences* (Detroit: Wayne State University Press, 1987). In studying children in this century, it naturally is useful to know something about the background leading to 1900. Some fine books on earlier periods of child-rearing, families, and children's and adolescents' lives include: John Demos, *Past, Present and Personal* (New York: Oxford University Press, 1986); Carl Degler, *At Odds: Women and the Family in America from the Revolution to the Present* (New York: Oxford University Press, 1980); Joseph Kett, *Rites of Passage: Adolescence in America, 1790 to the Present* (which keeps its emphasis prior to 1900, despite its title); and Harvey Graff, *Conflicting Paths: Growing Up in America* (Cambridge: Harvard University Press, 1995).

For students of any age, a superb collection of documents and other materials serves as an essential resource for investigating the history of children and young people in United States history. Useful for all periods and most topics covered in this book, it has been cited frequently in the text and all the chapter bibliographical essays. This collection of materials was gathered under the general editorship of Robert H. Bremner and supported in part by the American Public Health Association and the U.S. Department of Health, Education, and Welfare. Published under the general title *Children and Youth in America: A Documentary History* (Cambridge: Harvard University Press), this massive work is organized in three chronological divisions, each having two volumes. The first (published in 1970) covers the period from 1600 to 1865; the second (published in 1971) encompasses the years 1866 to 1932; the last (published in 1974) takes the history from 1933 to 1973. Included are a wide range of documents on subjects ranging from child health and labor, to attitudes toward children, to education, to institutions for dependent children. Besides Bremner's works, there are many collections of public and government documents that provide both basic information and important insights into American life, that of children included. One of the most useful and wide-ranging is *Historical Statistics of the United States: Colonial Times to 1970,* published in 1975 in two volumes by the U.S. Bureau of the Census. Its pages contain scores of statistical tables on population, the economy, social makeup and conditions, trade, agriculture, and many other areas.

# Index

Abbott, Shirley, 7–8
Abilene (KS), 86
Action Comics, 117
Addams, Jane, 23
Adler, Felix, 69
adolescence: and automobiles, 98;
   baby boomers in, 194; definition of,
   2; and health, 144; and polio, 229–
   31; and television, 193; and values,
   67; and vitamins, 144; and work,
   32, 38–39
adolescents: and adults, 64, 292; alienated, 296; and amusement parks,
   287–88; and birth control, 261; as
   consumers, 282, 288; and dental
   care, 323; and Dr. Spock, 237; and
   drugs, 296; and education, 303–4;
   guidance of, 2; as readers, 201; and
   responsibilities, 261; and school, 45–
   46; and sex, 261; and tuberculosis,
   62; and unemployment, 293–97,
   301, 304; and work, 40–41, 217,

292–93, 303–304. *See also* children;
   teenagers
adoption, 16, 174
adults: and adolescents, 64, 292; and
   AIDS, 323–26; and amusement
   parks, 287; attitudes of, 27, 88–89;
   and child rearing, 236; and children,
   1, 65, 67–68, 105, 110, 117, 287;
   as children, 134; and comics, 203;
   and control, 204; as criminals, 66–
   67; and discipline, 1; and drug dealing, 297; and farms, 34, 302; and
   games, 199; health of, 145; and
   HIV, 324–26; and movies, 23, 111,
   113; and music, 203, 206; and tenement work, 36; and toys, 27, 106–7,
   110, 278; values of, 67, 199, 203,
   275, 278; as viewed by children, 22–
   23; wages of, 40; wrongful death
   awards for, 156
*Adventures of an American Cowboy,
   The,* 23

**About the Author**

ELLIOTT WEST is Professor of History at the University of Arkansas in Fayetteville. He is the author of *Growing Up with the Country, Childhood on the Far-Western Frontier* (1989) and co-editor of *Small Worlds: Children and Adolescents in America 1850–1960* (1992).